KU

Foreign Investment Strategies in Restructuring Economies

Foreign Investment Strategies in Restructuring Economies

LEARNING FROM CORPORATE EXPERIENCES IN CHILE

JOHN M. KLINE

Quorum Books
Westport, Connecticut • London

Library of Congress Cataloging-in-Publication Data

Kline, John M.
  Foreign investment strategies in restructuring economies :
learning from corporate experiences in Chile / John M. Kline.
    p. cm.
  Includes bibliographical references and index.
  ISBN 0-89930-779-5
    1. Investments, Foreign—Chile. 2. Investments, Foreign—
Developing countries. 3. International business enterprises—
Chile. 4. International business enterprises—Developing
countries. I. Title.
  HG5342.K57 1992
  332.6'73'0983—dc20   92-12114

British Library Cataloguing in Publication Data is available.

Library of Congress Catalog Card Number: 92-12114
ISBN: 0-89930-779-5

First published in 1992

Quorum Books, 88 Post Road West, Westport, CT 06881
An imprint of Greenwood Publishing Group, Inc.

Printed in the United States of America

The paper used in this book complies with the
Permanent Paper Standard issued by the National
Information Standards Organization (Z39.48-1984).

10 9 8 7 6 5 4 3 2 1

For my family and friends in Chile

Contents

Acknowledgments

The author benefitted from the assistance of many individuals and programs during the research and writing of this book. A principal debt of gratitude is acknowledged to the numerous individuals who willingly shared their time and experience during the many hours of interviews. Most executives, private experts, and government officials told their stories with conviction backed by a willingness to answer sensitive questions, only occasionally asking that certain information be treated in a confidential manner. Their candor was at times surprising but always appreciated. Without this degree of cooperation and openness, the research would have been impossible.

A second category of acknowledgments is due to the various programs providing financial or other assistance that made the field research possible. The Walsh Fund of the School of Foreign Service at Georgetown University provided support in 1989 for initial background research and an exploratory trip to Chile to test a field research design. The Fulbright Commission awarded the author a grant under the American Republics Research Program, and Georgetown University approved a sabbatical that allowed the author to collect material and conduct interviews in Chile from December, 1989, through August, 1990.

While in Chile, the political science department at Universidad Católica and the Fulbright Commission office in Santiago generously provided office space and secretarial assistance. Individuals in other academic programs, and research institutions including particularly CIEPLAN, offered access to research materials and an opportunity to attend seminars and discuss relevant subjects. Officials in the Chilean government, foreign embassies, and international organizations also proved responsive to requests for interviews and access to documents. The author also wishes to acknowledge his work as a consultant to the Inter-American Development Bank (IDB) in conducting an investment climate study of Chile during late 1990 and early 1991. This project eventually led, in mid-

1991, to IDB's approval of Chile as the first recipient of an investment sector policy loan for $150 million under a new program associated with the Enterprise for the Americas Initiative. Although material developed for this internal study is not used directly in this book, the opportunity to work with IDB personnel and meet with Chilean officials during this period provided valuable insights and further understanding of key investment policy issues.

Finally, an expression of sincere gratitude is owed to the many colleagues and students, too numerous to mention individually, who offered constructive criticism, suggested improvements, assisted in research and editing chores, and provided support and encouragement over the long conception and birthing process for this publication. A special note of appreciation goes to immediate family members Rosita, Christina, and Cecilia who patiently endured the travails of long hours and grumpy moods while also sharing in the joys of strengthening extended family and friendship bonds during our time in Chile. Of course, the material contained in this book is the sole responsibility of the author, who alone bears the burden and blame for any deficiencies found in representations or conclusions expressed herein.

Introduction

Chile is a land of variety and contrasts. From the sun shining off glacial blue ice near the continent's southern tip to barren salt flats in the Atacama desert some three thousand miles north. From the pounding of Pacific surf on Viña del Mar's resort beaches to Portillo's ski slopes high in the Andes near the Argentine border just four hours away. From the teeming workday crowds of downtown Santiago, home to roughly one-third of the nation's population, to deserted stretches along the Carretera Austral where volcanos shadow the gravel roadbed and frequent waterfalls drape nearby slopes.

The population is relatively homogeneous among Latin American nations, but significant divisions still exist marked by differences in economic status, political outlook, and social standing. Shaken from a paternalistic, almost feudal, past by political and economic upheaval in the 1970s, the country has struggled to regain its societal footing and shape a national consensus on a common future. In this sense, over the last two decades Chile has confronted many of the challenges now facing other restructuring economies in Latin America, Eastern Europe, and elsewhere.

Most foreign press reports on Chile's political changes described a battle between communism and military dictatorship. Later came stories of an impending economic miracle based on free market capitalism. The reality, of course, was far more complicated but even more interesting. When one leaves headline characterizations behind, a complex web of discrete events and practical decisions emerges that shaped Chile's dramatic transformation over the past two decades.

This book offers an examination of one part of this multifaceted story, focusing on the foreign investment strategies pursued by multinational corporations (MNCs) and by the government of Chile. This topic incorporates political, social, economic, and business factors, placed within the historical context of investor relations with developing countries in general and Chile in particular. The study derives from a firm-level investigation of why and how foreign corporations invested in Chile. A cross-sectoral analysis examines the relative influence of various factors on corporate investment decisions, followed by a look at the actual business operations that followed.

Based on these results, the book evaluates how recent experience in Chile may relate to foreign investment strategies pursued by companies and countries alike under conditions of radical economic restructuring. Government policy determines the access and operational conditions for foreign investors in a host economy while corporate management decides whether to invest under those circumstances and how the investment translates into operational reality. Certain public policy lessons can be drawn from Chile's experience with foreign investors that may help inform other Latin American and East European nations that are confronting similar challenges in their drive for democratization, privatization, and sustained economic growth. Similarly, international business executives can draw insights from individual case studies of recent and longer-term investors in Chile regarding how to adapt corporate strategy to both the risks and the opportunities of investment in a restructuring economy.

LESSONS FROM CHILE

Chile presents several unique advantages for analyzing foreign investment strategies in developing countries that are undergoing economic and perhaps also political transformations. Historically the nation swung between restrictive and facilitative foreign investment policies, at times presaging developments in other countries. During the 1980s, Chile stood at the forefront of many economic transformation initiatives, including privatizations, trade liberalization, nontraditional export expansion, and debt-to-equity swaps. Private foreign investment played a critical role in these efforts, helping Chile achieve an economic growth record that is instructive for development programs in countries that face similar economic transitions. In addition to its historical importance and relevance for current policy issues, Chile also presents a research opportunity to gather firm-level data to complement industry analyses and aggregate evaluations of how foreign investment affects national economies.

Chile's historical prominence on foreign investment issues stems primarily from highly publicized events surrounding the 1970 election of President Salvador Allende and his subsequent overthrow in 1973 by a military coup. In earlier decades Chile followed prevailing economic development strategy, using import substitution policies to encourage manufacturing activity to supplement traditional natural resource industries. This approach incorporated a larger role for state enterprises, attempts at regional integration, and pressures on foreign investors to increase local ownership. President Allende's election shifted Chile more sharply to the left, initiating forced nationalizations and a rapid increase in the economy's public sector. The expropriations burned deeply into the minds of foreign investors. Executives removed Chile from lists of prospective investment sites while carefully analyzing the fate of the huge mining operations run by the Kennecott and Anaconda corporations for lessons on political risk assessment and risk management techniques.

A period of political repression followed President Allende's violent overthrow in a military coup. Economically, a new era dawned with a radical free market approach that was adjusted and refined following a disastrous financial collapse and recession in the early 1980s. A welcome mat for foreign investment attracted a few major new projects during this period, but in general foreign investors did not flock to Chile simply because a Marxist regime had been replaced by a rightist dictatorship, even one that adopted free market policies. Most foreign investment awaited the right blend of economic opportunity and political movement that began in the mid-1980s, setting the stage for a mature partnership between foreign investors and Chile.

Current policy deliberations on the role of foreign investment in national economic transitions can benefit from examining Chile's success in designing policy reforms that provided a conducive climate for increased and sustainable economic growth. Included in the winning policy combination were:

— an extensive privatization program that shifted investment and economic initiative to the private business sector while reducing public expenditures
— a dismantling of trade barriers as part of an internationalization strategy that led the General Agreement on Tariffs and Trade (GATT) to rank Chile among the most open economies in the world
— nondiscriminatory foreign investment laws that provided a stable foundation for long-term corporate planning
— the most extensive debt conversion program among countries saddled with heavy external debt, stimulating domestic economic activity and eventually returning Chile to voluntary international lending markets
— a democratization movement that culminated in the return of a freely elected government committed to maintaining stable economic growth policies while placing renewed emphasis on meeting social needs and observing internationally recognized human rights

Practical considerations also make Chile an ideal research subject for a study of individual corporate investment strategies under conditions of major economic and political restructuring. The country's size, industrial structure, and identifiable foreign investment community allow a cross-sectoral analysis based on enterprise-level interviews. The competitive climate is vigorous, but many individual corporations and investment projects represent major elements of a business sector, permitting coverage of a significant portion of business activity through individual company interviews. Most corporate management is also centrally located in Santiago, facilitating personal contacts.

Results of this research are best presented in the context of sectoral analyses and individual corporate situations. Despite the common tendency to generalize about foreign investment and corporate investors, strategic concerns vary considerably across industries and by the experience, interests, and capabilities of the individual firm. Among the most important strategic elements identified and examined in the following pages are:

— the levels of ownership associated with management control issues, including when joint ventures work best, even with few ideal local partners

— financing options and combinations, including the roles for owner equity, bank and supplier credits, forward sales, and creative arrangements involving international agencies and the development of local capital markets

— technology transfer and adaptation in specific products, business infrastructure services, and management expertise, including recognizing special corporate strengths along a value-added business chain

— foreign investor advantages in building nontraditional exports and using an import substitution strategy in a small economy with open import policies

— the relative importance of provisions in a country's foreign investment rules and regulations for different business investment strategies

— the relationship between an investor's global and local investment strategies, including a role for local innovation under conditions of decentralized management flexibility

The original research for this study comes primarily from interviews with managers of more than seventy foreign corporations operating in Chile. Complementary discussions with local business executives, other private experts, and public sector officials added supplemental information and materials while providing a cross-check to corroborate or challenge interview data. An explanation of the research methodology and a list of companies interviewed is included in the appendix.

ORGANIZATION

The opening chapter begins with an historical summary of foreign investment in Chile, outlining principal early periods as defined by changes in government policy and public attitudes toward foreign investment. This section discusses the sectoral concentration of investment, relations between foreign and local businesses, and major issues that shaped the role of foreign investment in the country during these early years. The Alessandri, Frei, and Allende administrations are compared regarding their specific policies and negotiations with foreign investors, terminating with the Allende government's overthrow. The following section on the Pinochet years reviews the introduction of radical free market reforms and the formulation of policies designed to attract foreign investment.

The second chapter examines in greater detail the most important policy decisions that determined Chile's foreign investment climate during the 1980s and the part international corporations would play in the country's economic restructuring process. The key decisions involved actions that internationalized the economy, provided stable rules covering foreign investment and debt-to-equity swaps, implemented a widespread privatization program, and led to the return of a democratic government that reaffirmed a basic role for foreign investors in the economy. Careful study of these steps yields conceptual and procedural lessons for other countries considering whether and how to improve their foreign investment climate. Chile's experience does not provide a model to be superimposed on nations with different underlying conditions, but its actions can provide valuable information regarding the formulation and implementation of a foreign investment strategy.

The next four chapters contain most of the primary research material, arranged in sectoral units covering minerals and energy, nontraditional exports, financial services, and general industry. The initial three units provide both an overview of the economic sector and selected case examples of individual foreign investments. Case examples highlight important decisional and operational factors associated with specific investment strategies. The descriptions aim to provide enough detailed information regarding the foreign enterprise and its investment project to show the relative importance of various elements and of the investment's impact on the host country. The general industry chapter is somewhat more limited in discussing sectoral conditions, concentrating instead on especially significant cases and their link to important policy issues, both historical and current. Each chapter ends with a summary discussion of foreign investor participation in that particular sector.

The penultimate chapter assesses key issues for foreign investment strategies in restructuring economies based upon recent experience in Chile. The issues are grouped into clusters that relate to the literature on foreign investment in developing countries and updated for the Chilean findings. Assessments are based on the cumulative and comparative material presented in the sectoral chapters, with illustrative references to specific case examples. The final chapter then discusses the outlook for foreign investment in Chile through the turn of the century. A brief section suggests some possible modifications to general concepts and theories about foreign investment in developing countries. Finally, summary conclusions are offered regarding the guidance that experiences in Chile might provide for countries facing similar economic and political transitions and for international corporations that seek to do business amid the uncertainty and the opportunities of a restructuring economy.

Although usually not considered in the same manner, both companies and countries design and follow foreign investment strategies. These public and private policies interact, responding to each other in a way that makes an understanding of one incomplete without a practical appreciation for the other. This book traces both types of strategies as they developed during the sometimes chaotic but ultimately creative process that led to the current mutually beneficial relationship between foreign investors and Chile.

Foreign Investment Strategies in Restructuring Economies

1

History: Chile and the MNCs

Foreign businesses have played a prominent but not predominant role in Chilean history as far back as the mid-nineteenth century. Their economic importance and relationship to public policy trace broad arcs, with the pendulum-like swings growing wider and more abrupt as foreign investment increased. Contemporary history for foreign investors in Chile begins with the depressed interwar years of the 1930s. The following half century divides into segments defined by changes in political and economic philosophy linked to turnovers in the Chilean presidency.

After an initial period of growth led by import substitution policies, the Chilean government opted in the mid-1950s for a decade of greater market openness. Six years of increasing state intervention followed, aiming to couple economic and social reforms with a "Chileanization" of key economic sectors. A Marxist regime began the 1970s with three years of radical state control and nationalizations, only to be replaced by the military junta's reversal swing to free market capitalism. The 1980s ushered in domestic and global recession, followed by economic readjustment and a return to democracy at the close of the decade.

Multinational corporations responded to this evolving political and economic environment, at times becoming caught up politically within it, most notably in copper mining. The much publicized pinnacle of MNC prominence came in the 1960s when two foreign MNCs dominated Chile's critical copper industry. As noted in the landmark study of *Copper in Chile*, "All of *Fortune*'s 500 largest U.S. corporations combined do not play nearly the role in the economy of the United States or pay more than a fraction of the percentage of U.S. taxes that Anaconda and Kennecott alone supplied in Chile."[1]

The history of MNCs in Chile cannot be equated with the legacy of these copper titans alone, however, nor explained by the general *dependencia* view of foreign investment that held sway during much of the 1960s and 1970s.[2] An analysis of MNC activities in Chile reveals a shifting panoply of interrelated domestic and international influences.   In any given time period, foreign investment and MNC operations depended on the prevailing combination of:

1. recognized domestic economic endowments
2. world economic conditions
3. evolving MNC organization, management, and operational modes
4. Chilean and home country legal and policy attitudes toward MNCs
5. the local political/business consensus regarding domestic socioeconomic policy, including the role of foreign investment

This chapter surveys major policy demarcations in the contemporary history of MNCs in Chile, examining the broad public policy context in which foreign investors operated and the policy initiatives or attitudes that determined the investment climate. Each section analyzes the relative importance of the factors listed above, tracing major changes that influenced the evolution of this relationship. Subsequent chapters offer greater detail on how these factors applied over the past decade, based on sectoral analyses and case studies of individual MNC activities. This historical overview is thus intended to provide general background information as a context within which current policies and actions can be evaluated.

THE EARLY YEARS

Soon after independence in 1810, Chile was introduced to foreign-owned corporations by the British trading companies that inspired the concept of multinational business, and the country's earliest experience with this phenomenon resembles that of many other nations. During the late 1800s, British investors developed important nitrate deposits, establishing Chile's place in international mining circles. Involvement in Chile's financial sector and railway system complemented the trading and mining interests, reflecting British business patterns worldwide. Until the 1920s, British firms controlled two-thirds of all foreign investment in South America.[3]

Chilean investors initially dominated the country's small copper mining industry, exploiting extremely rich ore veins. As these deposits played out at the end of the century, world copper companies were shifting to large-scale, low-grade ore mining. Foreign firms developed technology and management skills for these operations and possessed the capital necessary to sustain relatively high risk, long-term projects. Many Chilean owners chose to leave the field, opting for investments with either less risk or higher speculative profits.

The El Teniente copper mine was sold to U.S. investors in 1904. A decade later it passed to Kennecott Corporation, which by the 1930s turned it into the world's largest underground copper mine. Anaconda bought Chuquicamata in 1923, a decade after work had begun on the deposit, and developed it into the world's largest open-pit copper mine. These large-scale projects probably preempted the entry of other copper MNCs that concentrated on developing deposits in Zambia, Zaire, and elsewhere. Meanwhile, world demand was growing for copper for electrical and construction uses, causing Chile's young copper sector to eclipse the country's traditional nitrate industry. The First World War period marked a turning point for foreign investment in Chile. British investment had peaked and the balance of new activity shifted to North American firms.

The two U.S. copper MNCs that came to dominate Chile's economic landscape were principal members of a tightly organized, seven-firm oligopoly that by the mid-1900s controlled up to 70 percent of world copper supplies outside the communist bloc. Their initial relationship with Chile was amicable, as both parties benefitted substantially from development of the country's copper wealth. Chile first imposed a 6 percent income tax on these operations, increasing this to about 20 percent during the interwar period. By the early 1950s, additional excess profit taxes and other charges pushed the total tax burden on the companies above 70 percent. Still, reports show Kennecott could have earned over 40 percent and Anaconda at least 12 percent on their Chilean investments, even at tax levels as high as 60 percent.[4]

The foreign investment climate is not, of course, reducible to a simple division of business income. Multiple historical influences emerged in the early post–World War II years in the interplay between business and politics, domestic and foreign. Two key factors were the growing economic role of U.S. MNCs and the spreading anti-communist fervor of the U.S. government.

A leader of Chile's Radical party, Gabriel González Videla, was elected president in 1946. He received support from Chile's Communist party, which claimed three of nine ministry posts in the González administration. As Chile sought increased foreign investment and loans, labor unrest developed at the copper mines and some other industries. Chile's Liberal and Conservative parties seized the moment to criticize Communist participation in the government, warning it would doom efforts to attract foreign investment. As labor disruptions continued and foreign investors hesitated, the Liberal party abandoned the government's coalition, increasing pressure for a swing to the right.

In October 1947 President González announced the discovery of secret letters purported to show the Chilean Communist party as part of a worldwide conspiracy to deny critical supplies to the United States in case of war. He broke trading and diplomatic relationships with the Soviet Union, dismissed the three Communist ministers from his administration, and sought extraordinary powers to confront strikes. A "Law for the Defense of Democracy" was passed that outlawed the Communist party, removed communist voters from electoral rolls, and authorized the confinement of communist leaders in remote parts of the country. Subsequently, the U.S. government reported favorably on Chile's improved investment climate, Anaconda announced plans for the largest single investment to date in Chile (a $130 million sulfides facility at Chuquicamata), and foreign loans to Chile's government agencies quadrupled in two years.[5]

Chile's general industrialization pattern reflected the import substitution approach of many developing countries, shaped by the impact of the world wars and interwar depression. In the immediate postwar period, nascent domestic industries sought protection from foreign competition. The international trade studies of Raúl Prebisch, an economist at the Economic Commission for Latin America (ECLA) in Santiago, linked import substitution to development. He drew heavily on Chilean data for a model which argued that international trade mechanisms benefitted developed nations at the expense of developing countries. Under this thesis, Chile suffered from a deterioration in its terms of trade that resulted largely from exchanging copper exports for imports of manufactured goods.[6] Dominated by foreign investors, the copper industry was at the center of this controversy. Problems escalated further when new international events sparked a nationalistic reaction against foreign influence.

In managing its Korean War economy, the U.S. government unilaterally set the price of copper in mid-1950 at 24.5 cents per pound, roughly one-half the market price outside the United States. Since its copper sales were controlled by U.S. MNCs, the Chilean government was forced to negotiate for improved terms and obtained only slightly better conditions the following year. This sequence of events seemed to confirm classic *dependencia* notions that perceive collusion between foreign MNCs and home governments to exploit the resources and maintain the subservience of developing countries. Already concerned that the private copper oligopoly caused a deterioration in Chile's terms of trade, the government decided it could not tolerate such direct foreign government control over its international market fortunes. President González annulled the pricing agreement with Washington in May 1952 and established a state sales monopoly to market Chile's copper production.

Unfortunately for Chile, the experiment with a copper sales monopoly failed. The state agency lacked both the expertise and international positioning to compete with established oligopolistic trading patterns once the Korean War ended, even though the oligopoly was itself beginning to lose its power. Not only did the Chilean copper agency fail to market its exports successfully, reducing the country's foreign exchange earnings, but the foreign copper companies declined to invest further to improve their operations, and output was beginning to trail off.

A coincidence of interests reemerged between local and foreign business goals as both favored a more laissez-faire policy to restrain state intervention in the economy. Conservatives had been concerned when General Carlos Ibáñez was elected president in 1952, since his perceived leanings were toward labor, agrarian reform, and state enterprise concepts. The government's copper sales monopoly and the larger state role envisioned in development models championed by Prebisch and others increased local business worries.

President Ibáñez proved responsive to a business campaign that urged shifting Chile toward private sector leadership and market forces. The primary symbol of this policy was the *Nuevo Trato*, or New Treaty, embodied in mining legislation passed in 1955. The measures lowered tax rates, established favorable expensing and depreciation allowances, granted equipment importation rights, and returned pricing and marketing controls to the companies. Proponents believed these measures would act as automatic stimuli, unleashing profit-driven corporate desires to invest and expand production in Chile's improved investment climate. In fact, materialized foreign investment in Chile's copper industry did expand for several years, but not by as much as hoped, and by the beginning of the 1960s this liberal policy toward business was attacked as a failure. World market conditions and the operation of the copper oligopoly did not sustain the massive surge of new investment predicted by the *Nuevo Trato*'s simplistic free economic model assumptions.

The Ibáñez Administration is also important for the adoption in February 1954 of Chile's first statute (DFL 437) specifically addressing foreign investment. Prior to this time foreign investors concluded contracts with the state through individual negotiations that usually focused on issues of tax and tariff relief. Several earlier pieces of legislation dating back to 1942 dealt with foreign exchange rights for repatriation of capital and earnings, but this new law provided the first official recognition of foreign investors. The legislation contained authority for profit repatriation, general tax rate stability, and special tax exemptions for investments promoting industrial development, transportation, or activity in natural resource sectors including mining, agriculture, and forestry.[7]

A Conservative party leader, Jorge Alessandri, was elected president in 1958. His administration was closely aligned with local business interests, guaranteeing a continuation of policies favoring less state intervention and regulation. Liberalization measures even extended to international trade where quantitative restrictions were eliminated, tariffs lowered, and a unified, fixed foreign exchange rate adopted based on a devalued peso. These steps helped stabilize inflation and encourage economic growth while moving the country away from an inward-looking industrial development strategy. Many of these liberalizations were short-lived, however. Growing imports and increased government spending on public works and housing created a trade imbalance and an overvalued currency. Beginning in 1962, a balance of payments crisis led to devaluation of the peso and the resurrection of trade protectionism.

Despite these problems, a revised foreign investment statute, DFL 258, was

passed in 1960. This law widened the scope of possible investments for
foreigners to include fishing activities and conferred broader discretionary
authority on the president to approve or reject special tax exemptions for ten to
twenty years. Non-copper foreign investment responded to the more regularized
legal environment for foreign investors. Beginning in 1960, these investments
ranged between $150 and $200 million for six of the next seven years, several
times higher than previous levels. On the other hand, new copper investments
dropped off significantly, bringing criticism of the *Nuevo Trato*. From levels
exceeding $100 million in 1957–59, copper investments plummeted to just over
$40 million annually during the last five years of the Alessandri administration.[8]

Neither foreign nor domestic investment responded as well as expected to
the Alessandri administration's initial policies. Private national investment
actually declined in both relative and absolute terms during the president's
term.[9] As Alessandri's economic program faced growing difficulties, however,
the local political climate turned particularly hostile for foreign investors, with
the bitterest invectives launched against the important and highly visible copper
MNCs. The perceived failure of the *Nuevo Trato* alone does not sufficiently
explain this antagonism. Another impetus for changed political attitudes was the
announcement of the U.S. Alliance for Progress initiative by the new Kennedy
administration. Meaningful agrarian reform was a principal feature of this
program, and such a step threatened Chile's landed oligarchy, which was closely
affiliated with Alessandri's Conservative party.

Recognizing that an aggressive offense can often provide a good defense,
important conservative spokesmen blamed Chile's development problems on the
foreign copper companies rather than the landed aristocracy. The controversy
split an Alessandri administration that, nearing the end of its term, avoided
taking a definitive stand on the issue. An important bridge had been crossed,
however. The interests of the foreign copper companies had been permanently
separated from those of local conservatives, who never again defended the
copper MNCs and increasingly supported nationalization of their assets.[10]

In summary, then, a combination of factors shaped this early history of
Chile's relationship with foreign investors. British and American companies
predominated, accounting for up to 90 percent of foreign investment that was
concentrated in mining activities, primarily in copper during the twentieth
century. Foreign firms also invested in electrical utilities and the telephone
service, but despite the relative growth of some industrial investments MNCs did
not dominate the country's light manufacturing sector. Chile's natural
endowments explain much of this pattern, since only its mineral resources were
well recognized at the time and the country's small consumer market held
limited attraction for foreign exporters, much less investors.

World economic conditions greatly affected Chile's development, most
notably via cyclical swings in the copper market but also through the impact
wars and economic depression had on fostering import substitution policies. The

international private copper oligopoly also influenced Chile's options, restricting the country's ability to improve its penetration of the copper industry and even limiting the impact of policy inducements designed to attract more copper investment.

Chile's early legal framework was deficient, but it improved toward the end of the period. Official policies proved unstable as the country's leaders tried different approaches to foreign investors during these years, changing even within the same presidential term. The role of local rather than foreign businesses appears most decisive, despite the occasional imposition of foreign (mainly U.S.) government-related priorities on Chile. Established local leaders successfully influenced several Chilean administrations to shift toward more favorable pro-business policies when important traditional interests were threatened. While foreign and domestic business interests often coincided, especially in the limitation of state intervention in the economy, when they diverged, local interests usually won out.

CHILEANIZATION AND EXPROPRIATIONS

A new era dawned on Chile's relationship with foreign investors with the election of Christian Democratic President Eduardo Frei in 1964. Frei had received 21 percent of the vote in the 1958 election, trailing both Socialist candidate Salvador Allende (29 percent) and the victorious Jorge Alessandri (32 percent). With Alessandri's decline in popularity, rightist and centrist groups feared the possible election of marxist Allende, so the Conservative and Liberal parties both finally backed Frei's Christian Democratic candidacy, giving him a rare absolute majority of the vote. The Christian Democratic party also gained a majority in the House, but not independent control of the Senate, in subsequent congressional elections.

The Frei program advocated a mixed economy with the government playing a more activist role. The administration adopted Chile's first crawling peg exchange rate system, reduced some import controls, and introduced 100 percent indexation policies for both taxes and wage adjustments. Toward the end of the Frei period, wages rose higher than anticipated and foreign borrowing increased to supplement inadequate national savings, but most general economic indicators remained favorable, aided significantly by an all-time high in world copper prices.

With regard to foreign investment, President Frei came into office on a moderate platform of Chileanization through negotiation. This program envisioned obtaining some form of Chilean participation (eventually 51 percent) in ownership of the large copper mines along with definite commitments to expanded production. Improved earnings from these increased operations would help fund other social and economic objectives, including agrarian reform. The copper MNCs, relieved not to face Allende's more radical nationalization proposals, were still distressed at the increasingly solid local political front arrayed against them.

The two primary foreign copper companies pursued divergent strategies in response to the new pressures. Essentially, Anaconda resisted Chileanization proposals while moving on its own to increase investment and expand operations in order to demonstrate its significant contributions to the host country. Kennecott, on the other hand, openly cooperated with the Frei initiative. Moving early to advance its own proposals, Kennecott negotiated a Chileanization package that significantly expanded its returns from a more highly profitable operation (albeit now minority-owned) without risking any additional corporate capital. The Kennecott strategy, later analyzed as a model case for project finance techniques to manage political risk, enabled the firm to emerge relatively successfully from eventual nationalization actions, in contrast to Anaconda's disastrous expropriation experience.[11]

The initial years of the Frei administration were marked by an acrimonious legislative debate over constitutional changes that linked authority for the Chileanization program with agrarian reform proposals. Conservatives argued that foreign companies were seeking inviolable guarantees for their investments while the property rights of local Chilean landholders could be subject to discretionary government takeovers at unfair compensation. Only with great difficulty did the Christian Democrats, under attack from both the left and right, finally succeed in passing authority for both programs in 1967.

The Chileanization approach did result in expanded investment, output, and a new pricing policy that yielded increased foreign exchange dividends for the Chilean treasury. New foreign investment in copper leapt upward, rising from $62 million in 1965 to $117 million, $213 million, and $507 million in 1966–68, respectively.[12] In 1969, criticism of corresponding corporate profits from the industry's successful expansion led the government to impose a surtax that purportedly violated the twenty-year guarantees recently granted by the Chilean Congress. Political pressures also convinced President Frei again to demand negotiations with Anaconda, which had continued to invest on its own while resisting the Chileanization proposals. This time the company reversed position. Rather than risk being drawn into a series of progressively tougher renegotiations, Anaconda asked to be expropriated fully, with compensation, and an agreement to that effect was announced in June 1969.

While the copper companies bore the brunt of the attacks against foreign corporations, the penetration of foreign investors into other industrial sectors also caused some concern. By the mid-1960s, foreign investors reportedly controlled over one-sixth of Chile's manufacturing sector, with concentrations ranging as high as 42 percent in electrical machinery, 49 percent in rubber, and 57 percent of the tobacco industry. These factors led the Frei administration to pursue a selective approach toward foreign investment. A pragmatic program

of controls and industrial encouragement attempted to channel new investment
into those sectors where the government believed it would be the most useful.[13]

Mining remained the dominant interest for foreign investors, even outside
the copper industry, in terms of newly invested capital. The minerals sector
accounted for 60 percent of total non-copper foreign investment from 1954,
when the first formal foreign investment law was adopted, through the end of
the Frei administration in 1970. General industry claimed over 38 percent of
the remaining investment. In stark contrast with developments that would occur
in the 1980s, less than 1.5 percent of foreign investment went into forestry,
agriculture, services, or other business sectors. Cumulative U.S. investment by
1970 reflected these sectoral distributions, with one important variation. One-
quarter of U.S. investment was in Chile's public utilities (primarily the
telephone company and electric utilities); general manufacturing represented 9
percent, commerce and tourism 6 percent, and general mining (including copper)
60 percent.[14]

The most significant policy impact on foreign investment decisions beside
the Frei government's copper industry actions came from regional negotiations
toward formation of an Andean Common Market. The Treaty of Montevideo
in 1960 had envisioned broad regional integration through establishment of the
Latin American Free Trade Association (LAFTA). Practical progress was
cumbersome and the benefits uneven, however, as the largest nations (Mexico,
Argentina, and especially Brazil) dominated the arrangement. Smaller members
began discussing a distinctive regional arrangement that would better serve their
needs. This concept was contained in the Declaration of Bogotá in August 1966
and endorsed the following year at a meeting of American presidents at Punta
del Este.

Five countries (Bolivia, Chile, Colombia, Ecuador, and Perú) signed the
Agreement of Cartagena in May 1969, formally initiating the Andean Common
Market (AnCom) or Andean Pact. Venezuela participated in early discussions
but did not officially join the group until February 1973. The organization
legally operated as a subregional entity under LAFTA's auspices. The pact's
multiple aims included eliminating barriers to regional trade; erecting a common
external tariff, beginning with initial agreement on a common minimum tariff
level; and establishing sectoral programs for industrial development that could
divide manufacturing operations among member countries in order to gain
economies of scale. The critical element for most MNCs, however, was the
pact's provisions on treatment of foreign direct investment, largely contained in
Decision 24, ratified on June 30, 1971.[15]

If enacted into national law (since it was not directly enforceable), the pact's
provisions limited new foreign investors to minority (no more than 49 percent)
ownership and required a "fade out" reduction of existing foreign ownership to
this maximum level if firms were to be eligible for the pact's integration
benefits. Limitations were placed on profit and capital remittances, and other

provisions sought to reduce the countries' dependence on foreign technology by restricting or prohibiting royalty payments while seeking to stimulate regional technological development.

Implementation of the pact's guidelines was uneven. Some nations failed to enact the tariff reduction schedule while Chile used the pact's safeguard clauses to limit its participation in trade arrangements after October 1972. Chile was the most aggressive country in implementing the pact's foreign investment provisions, however. While these actions occurred during the Allende administration, the impact on foreign investment in Chile was evident even prior to the pact's formal adoption by the Frei government.[16]

Materialized non-copper foreign investment dropped from $197 million in 1966 to $46 million in 1967 and $24 million in 1968, before recovering slightly to $59 million and $65 million in the next two years. These figures reflect the foreign investors' caution as discussions progressed first on the pact and then on the specific Decision 24 provisions regarding foreign direct investment. In contrast, authorized non-copper foreign investment figures climbed, jumping to a record $549 million in 1968, followed by yearly approvals of $155 million and $283 million in 1969 and 1970.[17] Authorizations, of course, positioned foreign investors to participate in the emerging regional integration scheme without actually committing them to materialized capital expenditures before it was fully clear how pact benefits and restrictions would balance out.

The Frei administration thus ended with a varied record in terms of its relationship with foreign investors. The Chileanization policy proved quite successful in relation to the copper industry, achieving a combination of increased investment, output, taxes, and local ownership. Kennecott fell into line, albeit more on its own terms than may have been initially appreciated by the Chilean negotiators. Anaconda had also now agreed to compensated expropriation. Despite these gains, the political invective aimed at the copper MNCs continued to escalate, with critics on both the left and right citing corporate abuses and calling for outright nationalization. Outside the copper sector, other prospective foreign investments were put on "hold" as corporations tried to assess the Andean Pact's impact on the one hand, while keeping an increasingly concerned eye focused on the upcoming 1970 elections where marxist Salvador Allende was again making a strong bid for power.

This time, the leftist candidate was successful. While his opponents split their vote between the Christian Democratic and Conservative party candidates, Allende held together a "Unidad Popular" coalition that combined socialists, communists, radicals, and the MAPU (a largely Christian Democrat splinter group), winning office with a narrow plurality (under 37 percent of the vote). Although President Allende lacked a parliamentary majority, his government moved ahead rapidly with an ambitious program to restructure the economy. The size and role of the state increased radically through both an expansion of government spending, which significantly increased fiscal deficits, and a nationalization campaign that captured most large private assets, transferring them to the public sector.

Foreign copper companies were the first target of the Allende program. Although promises of nationalizations were featured in all the major candidates' campaign speeches, this plan called for the complete takeover of Kennecott, Anaconda, and Cerro, a third U.S. firm that had begun developing a new Andina mine. The copper nationalization required legislation equivalent to a constitutional amendment, necessitating a two-thirds majority of the opposition-controlled Congress. So great was the national consensus on this issue, however, that the legislation passed unanimously in July 1971. While compensation could be paid over a thirty-year period, the government calculated that both Anaconda and Kennecott had received excess profits since the mid-1950s *Nuevo Trato* deal and thus owed back taxes that more than offset the compensation due them for their expropriated property.

The three firms had very different experiences in protesting the nationalizations. The government agreed to pay Cerro approximately book value for the Andina facility and the company helped complete the mine so that operations could begin. Kennecott used its unconditional Chilean government guarantees to take legal action to seize state property (copper exports and national airline planes) outside Chile. The U.S. government faced losses through Eximbank and OPIC coverage of Kennecott investments. Other creditor governments also expressed concern regarding fulfillment of long-term copper delivery contracts to customers in their countries. The resultant international financial and legal pressures finally forced President Allende to agree to pay Kennecott at least the guaranteed sale amount, effectively negating the company's bid to invoke foreign government assistance. Anaconda lacked any effective leverage; its protests went essentially unheeded, leading to a huge loss for the firm and the firing of its entire top management.[18]

An equally infamous case in Chile's historical experience with MNCs arose at this same time between the Allende government and International Telephone and Telegraph Company (ITT). In 1930, ITT had gained a fifty-year concession for the Chilean Telephone Company. A regulated monopoly, the firm continually won rate increases despite growing complaints that ITT was repatriating too much profit rather than investing to expand and improve the country's telephone service. In line with its Chileanization program, the Frei administration negotiated a buyout of ITT's operation in 1967, but could not fund the takeover. In May 1971 the Allende administration opened negotiations, but the two sides disagreed over appropriate compensation levels, with Chile offering about $50 million and ITT demanding three times that amount. The dispute turned acrimonious, involving labor union activity and the public media. Regulators denied a rate hike requested to offset wage increases and in October 1971 a government *interventor* assumed control of the company, effectively nationalizing the facilities and prompting an ITT appeal to the U.S. government for assistance.[19]

This case's notoriety comes not from the nationalization, but rather from charges of earlier corporate misconduct. Prior to the 1970 election, ITT attempted to enlist other investors as well as the U.S. government (including the CIA) in efforts to prevent an Allende victory. Revelation of these activities by U.S. columnist Jack Anderson outraged public opinion in Chile and elsewhere, leading to ITT's condemnation by President Allende and an extensive series of investigative hearings before the U.S. Senate Foreign Relations Committee.[20]

In the aftermath of President Allende's overthrow by a military coup, the ITT incident came to symbolize the darkest fears of developing countries that foreign MNCs might conspire with home governments to compromise a host nation's political sovereignty. Chile's military government finally settled with ITT, agreeing to $125 million in compensation. In an ironic and yet positive end to the episode, the parties forged a promising new relationship by agreeing to contribute $25 million apiece to establish a nonprofit technology transfer agency, Fundación Chile, whose successful contributions to national development are detailed in a later chapter.

Anaconda, Kennecott, and ITT thus headed the list of notable foreign expropriations and represented most of the value of uncompensated takeovers by the Allende administration, estimated at around $800 million. Other nationalized companies including General Motors, RCA, Armco Steel, Ralston Purina, and Bank of America were promised compensation at a total estimated book value of approximately $70 million. Nearly fifty other U.S. subsidiaries, valued at roughly $50 million, were not taken over during the regime's tenure.[21]

The Allende nationalization program was by no means directed only at foreign investors, although actions against this group usually attracted the greatest domestic public support. In reality, the administration sought authority to nationalize all large enterprises, potentially reaching 40 percent of the country's productive capacity and covering about one-third of private sector jobs. By the end of 1971, the government had taken control of more than eighty enterprises, including most important minerals operations; sixteen commercial banks that represented over 90 percent of outstanding credit; and key companies in business sectors including metallurgy, cement, textiles, fisheries, and wholesale marketing.[22]

As the nationalization campaign continued and spread into domestic industries, political support for the administration's actions dropped significantly. Worker groups disrupted operations and seized numerous factories, leading to government intervention under a rather obscure 1932 law that allowed a temporary takeover to assure the continued supply of vital products. Subsequent court orders to return operations to private owners, both domestic and foreign, were often ignored. The Allende administration thus attained control through nationalization and intervention of over 500 enterprises by mid-1973. Over 80 percent of these takeovers had not been approved by the Congress, which accused the administration of violating legal guarantees and procedures.[23]

During his first year, Allende's economic program reduced unemployment and inflation, increased real wages and economic growth, and improved income distribution. Unfortunately, these gains were achieved at the expense of fiscal responsibility as public sector deficits increased while the country's international reserves decreased. The costs of this upheaval set in the following year as growth stagnated and inflation jumped to 260 percent. In 1973, economic growth dropped by over 4 percent and the government resorted to extensive price controls on some 3,000 goods and services to combat a growing black market and inflation that reached as high as 600 percent. Quantitative and tariff controls were used along with multiple exchange rates to control foreign trade.[24]

Social discord accompanied the mounting economic chaos. Land seizures upset production in the countryside; frequent demonstrations shut down factories and commerce in the cities; a truck owners' strike crippled essential transportation needs; and paramilitary groups were formed to defend each side's vital interests. On September 11, 1973 a military coup d'état violently ended Chile's marxist experiment, resulting in the death of President Allende. This period in Chilean history thus ends at a peak of animosity between foreign investors and the state, symbolic of the growing confrontation in the 1970s between MNCs and developing countries. For Chile, however, an abrupt swing back to the other policy extreme was about to begin.

THE PINOCHET PERIOD

The military takeover of September 1973 altered the Chilean economy nearly as radically as it changed the nation's political life. The highly statist approach sponsored by the Allende government gave way to a fierce brand of free market capitalism promoted by a group of young Chilean economists trained in the views of Milton Friedman at the University of Chicago. Army General Augusto Pinochet quickly emerged from the military junta to assume the nation's presidency, ruling Chile until a return to democracy was completed in March 1990. The Pinochet years are roughly divisible into three distinctive economic periods, covering initial recovery and rapid economic growth (1974–81), financial collapse and readjustment (1982–84), and renewed expansion in a sounder economic environment (1985–90).

The initial period began with a brutal campaign of arrests, torture and killing aimed at eliminating marxist groups, particularly clandestine paramilitary elements. A state of emergency gave the military government broad powers that it used to the fullest, sometimes exceeding even these bounds and carrying out documented human rights abuses during what the junta viewed as a civil war situation.[25] Political opposition was negligible as conservative and centrist parties, which had attempted to obstruct the Allende program, supported the coup while leftist groups were silenced and driven underground. Officially, political activity was banned, with leftist parties outlawed and others declared "in recess"; the Congress was dissolved and strict media censorship was imposed.

This repression came amid the legacy of economic chaos inherited from Allende's final year when inflation ran wild, international reserves disappeared, and production essentially shut down as business became both a weapon and a victim in the country's all-consuming political battle. The turnabout in official economic philosophy was swift and radical once the military had seized power. The embrace of free market standards led to a reduced state role in the economy, including deregulation of many business activities, a progressive dismantling of the state enterprise network built up under previous regimes, and an opening of Chile's economy to international market forces.

With advice from an economic cadre anchored by nearly a dozen "Chicago boys," the Pinochet government administered shock treatment to the Chilean economy. Price controls were lifted and interest rates freed. Import barriers came down with the removal of most non-tariff restrictions and a reduction in tariff rates from as high as 750 percent to a maximum 35 percent in 1977, followed by a flat 10 percent rate by the end of the decade. The government returned many state enterprises to the private sector and enforced budgetary constraints on those that remained public. Government employment was cut by one-third and expenditures reduced by one-quarter as fiscal deficits were eliminated. A major tax reform initiated a 20 percent value-added tax while labor law changes banned unions and abolished wage policies, leading to a sharp decline in real wages.

Severe economic and social costs resulted from this drastic economic reform during the military regime's first few years. Poorer classes in particular paid harsh penalties for the combined effects of price deregulation, an end to subsidization programs, real wage declines, and unemployment close to 30 percent. Industrial production dropped and overall GDP fell while inflation remained stubbornly high, partly due to an effective one-quarter devaluation of the peso. Adding to these difficulties, world copper prices tumbled while OPEC-inspired price hikes sent the country's oil import bill soaring.

Recovery commenced in 1976 and continued into a boom period at the end of the decade, with inflation dropping while economic growth averaged approximately 7 percent. Unfortunately, the seeds of a subsequent bust were being sown by poor regulatory decisions made either to serve political objectives or to enforce an extreme free market philosophy.[26] Initial devaluations had reduced imports and stimulated export activity, but now a policy of progressive peso overvaluation was adopted to help fight inflation.

A decision in June 1979 to maintain a fixed exchange rate proved particularly disastrous in hindsight. Other damaging factors were the deregulation of foreign capital flows, easy access to recycled petrodollars from international banks, and inadequate regulation of domestic financial institutions. As a result, Chile's external debt nearly tripled between 1979 and 1982, essentially due to private sector borrowing. Interlocked dealings between large industrial groups and major commercial banks led to a build-up in poor quality loans. A domestic consumption spree drew in waves of nonproductive imports while the exchange rate choked fledgling export industries and a backward-looking full indexation of wages further undermined the nation's competitiveness.

Foreign direct investment played only a limited role during this period, but a series of policy actions helped set the stage for its subsequent growth. First, the government returned many nationalized properties to their former owners, both domestic and foreign. During this privatization campaign, a key decision was to retain Chilean state ownership of the large copper mines, meaning that the previously dominant MNCs would not be returning. The government did agree to pay compensation totaling almost $300 million for the expropriated mines. Overall, Chile's estimated stock of foreign debt from prior nationalization actions peaked in 1974 at over one-half billion dollars, placing a heavy burden on the economy for nearly a decade just to service the compensation agreements.[27] Nevertheless, some mutually acceptable settlement of the nationalization/compensation controversies was a necessary if not a sufficient condition for the resumption of new foreign investment flows to Chile.

Of course, not all foreign investors had left Chile. As will be seen in later chapters, some manufacturers and retailers used the loosening of financial and trade restrictions to restart operations that had been held in a maintenance status, or to reposition their businesses cautiously for the promised economic recovery. The military government openly courted other foreign investors, inviting firms both to restore and expand previous industrial facilities as well as to consider new undertakings. A liberal foreign investment law, Decree Law 600 (D.L. 600), to be examined in the next chapter, was adopted in 1974 as the centerpiece of this effort. While this move did not provoke an immediate upsurge in foreign investment, it did permit the government to initiate targeted negotiations with a few potential investors, resulting in further legal modifications and eventually several important cases that demonstrated the success of new foreign investments.

In an associated development, Chile's new eagerness to attract foreign investment put the country at odds with restrictions in the Andean Pact's Decision 24. The military government's initial pronouncements reaffirmed support for Latin American integration, but the junta's economic program as implemented by the "Chicago boys" team became clearly incompatible with the investment regulations and some of the trade arrangements called for by the pact. These conditions led to Chile's withdrawal from the Andean Pact in October 1976. The pact as a whole faced increasing difficulties as development models based on import substitution objectives lost credibility and attention shifted in the early 1980s to outward-looking export promotion strategies.[28]

The combined result of Chile's improved policy climate for foreign investment and its reinvigorated domestic economy eventually drew renewed attention from foreign investors. Materialized direct investment, which had languished under $100 million annually during the military government's first few years, jumped to $340 million in 1978, followed by comparable investment inflows over the next four years until the financial crisis took its toll. Authorized new foreign investments rose in parallel fashion from $800 million in 1977 to $1.8 billion in 1978. Authorizations exceeded $2 billion in two of the next three years, although only $200 million was authorized in 1980 during a controversial debate and plebiscite on a new national constitution. Foreign banks slowly reentered the economy, growing from two to four in 1977–79, before expanding rapidly in the liberalized regulatory climate when foreign credit fueled private sector growth.[29]

Chile's economic house of cards collapsed in 1982–83, its weaknesses exposed by the global economic crisis and subsequent recession. Real GDP dropped by 14 percent and open unemployment shot upward. The domestic financial system, crippled by its past unregulated lending practices, forced several interlocked financial and industrial groups into bankruptcy, leading to the break-up of some traditional family networks that had long dominated the local business community. On the international front, Chile joined other Latin American countries facing massive external debt payments at sharply higher interest rates.[30]

The financial collapse caused the Pinochet government to intervene, taking control of most major banks and many corporate enterprises in order to restructure the private sector's external debt. This intervention temporarily reversed the regime's privatization campaign and embarrassingly gave it nearly as much direct control over business operations as the Allende government had possessed. The fixed exchange rate gave way to a large devaluation, import duties rose to 35 percent, and public employment programs provided minimum income jobs for over 10 percent of the labor force. Negotiations with international financial institutions brought a rescheduling of the foreign debt and an agreement with the International Monetary Fund for an economic adjustment program.

The economic crisis strengthened increasingly vocal political opposition to the Pinochet government. Discontent spilled onto the streets with demonstrators banging empty cooking pots in actions reminiscent of protests during the Allende period. The government was forced to change its team of ideological economic hard-liners as it shifted to a more pragmatic approach. The future policy direction was set in 1985 when the new finance minister Hernán Büchi assumed control and the nation began its climb toward economic recovery. Having weathered the worst of the recession, the government began a measured return to a tempered version of "Chicago school" free market economics.

Authorized and materialized foreign direct investment had dropped steadily from the beginning of the recession until 1985 when a turnaround was sparked by improving economic performance and public policy innovations. Nonfinancial MNCs suffered under the balance of trade and payments restrictions brought on by the financial crisis, but in general were less affected than domestic corporations. As discussed in later chapters, a number of international firms looked beyond the impact of the global economic downturn and sought out good opportunities amid the local business failures, repositioning themselves for long-term market expansion.[31]

Foreign banks were also in a better position than domestic institutions, but their heavy Latin American exposure led most to retrench immediately. Although Chile adopted a responsible debt management program from the financial community's perspective, the banks were preoccupied with responding to larger debt overhangs in Mexico, Brazil, and Argentina. Few foreign banks differentiated their policy actions toward Chile until the country initiated a debt-to-equity swap program in 1985.

The Chilean economic adjustment program included several important innovations and restructuring decisions, examined in some detail in the next chapter, that stimulated new foreign investor interest while reinvigorating the domestic economy. A key retained policy, however, was the government's continued support for a philosophy of limited direct state involvement in the economy. A statist perspective did not reemerge from the experience with direct intervention in several collapsing private financial groups. The government maintained fiscal discipline, took steps to return intervened firms to the private sector, and resumed privatization of other state enterprises.

The Pinochet period began coming to an end in 1988 when a plebiscite was held under the 1980 constitution to approve or reject the military junta's nominee (Pinochet himself) for an eight-year term as president. Although demonstrable opposition to the regime had declined as the economy improved, political groups on the center and left gradually coalesced to campaign for a "no" vote, which would force free elections within a year. Some conservative groups supported the junta's warning that disapproval would mean a return to the political and economic chaos of the early 1970s, but the "no" position won over 54 percent of the vote with 96 percent of the registered electorate casting ballots. This result set in motion a return to democracy with free presidential and congressional elections in December 1989. Christian Democrat Patricio Aylwin, the candidate of a multi-party center-left coalition, defeated Finance Minister Hernán Büchi and Conservative party candidate Francisco Errázuriz in the election. President Aylwin took control of the government on March 11, 1990 while General Pinochet returned to his post as head of the army.

Many countries had kept Chile's military government at arm's length during the junta's tenure in power. Several socialist European nations maintained an exceedingly cool relationship, and state-related corporations looked for investment possibilities in other, more rapidly democratizing nations rather than in Chile. The United States government did not actively discourage U.S. companies from exploring investments in Chile, but largely under congressional pressure, several obstacles were placed in their path. The general attitude of Washington officials was that the Pinochet government was pursuing correct economic policy, but should move more quickly toward democratic political reforms.

The litmus test of U.S.–Chilean relations was the so-called Kennedy amendment, a legislative provision originally passed in early 1976 to restrict cooperation with Chile's military. The amendment became inextricably linked to a car-bomb attack on the streets of Washington, D.C., during the morning rush hour on September 21, 1976. The explosion killed well-known Chilean dissident Orlando Letelier, a former ambassador to the United States and defense minister in the Allende government. A young U.S. woman who worked with Letelier was also killed and her husband injured. The attack was linked to Chile's secret intelligence service. The junta's refusal to cooperate fully in the investigation or to extradite two accused officers caused an outcry that focused greater attention on the many charges of human rights violations.

Further economic restrictions came in 1988, with Chile's suspension from insurance coverage by the Overseas Private Investment Corporation (OPIC) and trade benefits from the Generalized System of Preferences (GSP). This action arose primarily at the urging of the AFL-CIO, the largest U.S. labor organization, to protest Chile's continued denial of internationally recognized worker rights. After the democratic transition in the spring of 1990, Chile asked to be reincorporated in the GSP program and both Chilean labor unions and the AFL-CIO supported the petition. In late 1990, OPIC coverage was restored and shortly thereafter Chile regained GSP status for over 350 products, signifying around $100 million annually in export benefits. In December 1990 President George Bush also certified that Chile was respecting international human rights standards, a required condition for lifting the Kennedy amendment sanctions. By that time the Aylwin government had initiated a commission investigation of past human rights abuses while offering improved cooperation in resolving the Letelier case.[32]

The period of democratic transition could have caused major concern among foreign investors. Early campaign rhetoric from some opposition parties strongly criticized the Pinochet government's treatment of foreign investors, particularly for privatization sales using debt swap financing. Foreign investor interest and activity remained strong and steady, however, and economic policy statements from the opposition coalition gradually began to emphasize stability and the maintenance of an open regime toward both international trade and investment. In the end, domestic businesses appeared more hesitant than foreign firms about undertaking new investments both preceding and immediately following the governmental transition.

NOTES

1. Theodore H. Moran, *Multinational Corporations and the Politics of Dependence: Copper in Chile* (Princeton, N.J.: Princeton University Press, 1974), 7. This classic work provides substantial historical information that is drawn upon throughout the chapter.

2. For a presentation of the *dependencia* theory, see Osvaldo Sunkel, "Big Business and 'Dependencia': A Latin American View," *Foreign Affairs*, April 1972.

3. "Historia de la inversión foránea en Chile," *Estrategia*, May 15, 1990.

4. Moran, *Copper in Chile*, 22, 24, 30; and Eric N. Baklanoff, *Expropriation of U.S. Investments in Cuba, Mexico, and Chile*, Praeger Special Studies in International Economics and Development (New York: Praeger Publishers, 1975), 69.

5. Moran, *Copper in Chile*, 175–78. Similar repressive actions followed the 1973 military coup overthrowing the communist-backed government of Salvador Allende, including the use of internal exile, purges of the electoral rolls and a ban on the Communist party. For another discussion of the González administration, see James R. Whelan, *Out of the Ashes: Life, Death and Transfiguration of Democracy in Chile, 1833–1988* (Washington, D.C.: Regnery Gateway, 1989).

6. See Raúl Prebisch, *The Economic Development of Latin America and Its Principal Problems*, Economic Commission for Latin America (Lake Success, N.Y.: United Nations, Department of Economic Affairs, 1950) and "Commercial Policy in the Underdeveloped Countries," *American Economic Review* 49 (May 1959), cited in Moran, *Copper in Chile*, 66–67. The validity of this thesis's application to Chile is challenged by Moran in pages 82–84.

7. Ricardo Zabala H., *Inversión Extranjera Directa en Chile: 1954–1986*, Documento de Trabajo No. 90 (Santiago: Centro de Estudios Públicos, October 1987), 7–8; and Merwin L. Bohan and Morton Pomeranz, *Investment in Chile: Basic Information for United States Businessmen*, prepared for U.S. Department of Commerce (Washington, D.C.: GPO, 1960), 9–10.

8. Zabala, 37.

9. Barbara Stallings, *Class Conflict and Economic Development in Chile, 1958–1973* (Stanford, Calif.: Stanford University Press, 1978), 86.

10. Moran, *Copper in Chile*, 131.

11. Theodore H. Moran, "Transnational Strategies of Protection and Defense by MNCs," *International Organization*, Spring 1973. Kennecott's "Chileanization" left it with 49 percent of a company reassessed at four times its prior book value, producing 64 percent more output after expansion, with revenue taxed at almost one-half the previous rate and a ten-year agreement for Kennecott to manage the new operation. This lucrative arrangement required no new Kennecott risk capital, since the company's contribution to expansion came from the government's payment for its majority share of

the mine plus a U.S. Eximbank loan, both guaranteed by the Chilean government.

12. Zabala, *Inversión Extranjera*, 37.

13. Thomas S. Mabon, "An Analysis of the Industrial Sector: The Chilean Case, 1964–1971," Master's thesis (Georgetown University, September 1973), 81–82; and Aylette Villemain, "Public Policy and Private Investment in Chile: The Life and Hard Times of the Corporación de Fomento de la Producción (CORFO) 1939–1980," Master's thesis (Georgetown University, May 1983), 28.

14. Baklanoff, *Expropriation of U.S. Investments*, 110–11.

15. The Council of the Americas, *The Andean Pact: Definition, Design and Analysis* (New York: The Council of the Americas, 1973), sec. 2: 4–5, 56, sec. 3: 8–10.

16. Esteban Tomic Errázuriz, *El retiro de Chile del Pacto Andino*, Apuntes CIEPLAN No. 58 (Santiago: Corporación de Investigaciones Económicas para Latinoamérica, November 1985). This work portrays President Frei as the initial instigator of discussions for a pact, but suggests Chile's political interests were as strong as its economic motivations, especially in seeking increased harmony with its neighbors over border disputes.

17. Zabala, *Inversión Extranjera*, 19.

18. Moran, *Copper in Chile*, 148–51.

19. William A. Stoever, "Renegotiations: The Cutting Edge of Relations Between MNCs and LDCs," *Columbia Journal of World Business* (Spring 1979), 8–9.

20. Senate Committee on Foreign Relations, Subcommittee on Multinational Corporations, *Multinational Corporations and United States Foreign Policy*, Hearings, 93 Cong. (1973), Part 1; and Select Committee to Study Governmental Operations with Respect to Intelligence Activities, U. S. Senate, *Covert Action in Chile 1963–1973*, Staff Report, 94 Cong., 1 Sess. (1975). For two contrasting views on these events, see Gregory F. Treverton, *Case Study in Ethics and International Affairs: Covert Intervention in Chile, 1970–1973*, no. 3 (New York: Carnegie Council on International Affairs, 1990); and Whelan, *Out of the Ashes*, Appendix I.

21. Baklanoff, *Expropriation of U.S. Investments*, 110–11. Some uncertainty still exists regarding the number of U.S. MNCs affected and their asset value. See also the information provided by Whelan, (*Out of the Ashes*, 329–32), drawn largely from Congressional testimony and published articles in the 1971–73 period.

22. Villemain, "Public Policy and Private Investment," 42; and The World Bank, *Chile: An Economy in Transition* (Washington, D.C.: Latin America and the Caribbean Regional Office of the World Bank, 1979), iii.

23. Baklanoff, *Expropriation of U.S. Investments*, 116–7; Arturo Valenzuela, "Political Constraints to the Establishment of Socialism in Chile," in *Chile: Politics and Society* 7, 17–18; and Maurice Zeitlin and Richard E. Ratcliff, "The Concentration of National and Foreign Capital in Chile," in *Chile: Politics and Society*, 298ff. For a broader political and social analysis of the Allende period see Arturo Valenzuela, *The Breakdown of Democratic Regimes: Chile* (Baltimore: The Johns Hopkins University Press, 1976).

24. "1970–1973: El fracaso del populismo," *Estrategia*, September 9, 1990.

25. Following the transition to democracy in 1990, the Aylwin government appointed a Comisión Verdad y Reconciliación to investigate and gather testimony on human rights abuses during the years following the military coup. The commission's 2,000-page report, presented to President Aylwin in February 1991, documented widespread abuses. The military disputed allegations regarding their responsibility and pointed to continuing terrorist attacks in a near civil war atmosphere following the coup. Evidence from the commission on specific illegal actions was turned over to Chilean judicial authorities for appropriate follow-up.

26. Alejandro Foxley, later finance minister under President Aylwin, describes the military government's economic policy as evolving from initial technical adjustments to stabilize the economy to an ideologically based reform of the entire society after 1979. He describes "seven modernizations" carried out in labor policy, social security, education, health, regional decentralization, agriculture, and justice that constitute "the core of the radical conservative program in Chile." Alejandro Foxley, *Latin American Experiments in Neoconservative Economics* (Berkeley: University of California Press, 1983), ch. 4.

27. Zabala, *Inversión Extranjera*, 26–33.

28. Karen Remmer, *Military Rule in Latin America* (Boston: Unwin Hyman, 1989), 158; Eugenio Lahera, *Quince años de la Decisión 24. Evaluación y Perspectivas*, CIEPLAN, notas técnicas no. 82 (Santiago: Corporación de Investigaciones Económicas para Latinoamérica, June 1986), 25; and Tomic, *El retiro de Chile*, 7–8, 10–13. Tomic also critically views Chile's decision to withdraw from the pact as a choice to associate with MNCs and world markets rather than with Latin American neighbors (pages 14–15, 23–24).

29. Zabala, *Inversión Extranjera*, 19; The Economist Intelligence Unit, *Chile: Country Profile 1989–1990* (London: The Economist Intelligence Unit Limited, 1989), 6; and The Institute of International Finance, Inc., *Financial Sector Reform: Its Role in Growth and Development* (Washington, D.C.: The Institute of International Finance, Inc., February 1990), 104.

30. The Economist Intelligence Unit, *Chile*, 10ff; and The Institute for International Finance, Inc., *Financial Sector Reform*, 92ff.

31. Remmer, *Military Rule*, 169; and Patricio Rozas and Gustavo Marín, *1988: El "Mapa de la Extrema Riqueza" 10 Años Después* (Santiago: Ediciones Chile América, 1989). The latter authors characterize MNC actions during this period as taking advantage of Chile's economic crisis to replace or forge alliances with previously dominant local capitalists.

32. A special investigating judge of the Chilean Supreme Court reopened an inquiry into the Letelier case and on September 23, 1991 ordered the detention of the two accused officers who also faced lawsuits brought in civilian courts under laws passed by the new democratic government. "Chile Holds 2 Figures in Letelier Case," *Washington Post*, September 24, 1991. Additional background on the Letelier case is provided in Whelan, *Out of the Ashes*, 735–42.

2

Key Restructuring
Decisions of the 1980s

Five key policy decisions mentioned in the previous chapter warrant additional separate analysis because of their importance in restructuring Chile's economy and defining its relationship with foreign investors during the 1980s. These steps include the internationalization of the Chilean economy, implementation of the foreign investment statute (D.L. 600), adoption of a debt conversion mechanism (Chapter XIX), privatization of state enterprises, and the decade-ending return to democracy. While past experiences shaped many actions and attitudes toward foreign investment, the various historical strands converge in these relatively few interrelated decisions. The joint elaboration of these restructuring policies laid the foundation for the country's more mature partnership with foreign investors.

INTERNATIONALIZATION OF THE ECONOMY

Chile's decision to open its economy to international market forces is a critical element of its restructuring strategy that affected both the nature and number of foreign investment operations. The policy foreshadowed the subsequent shift in global development strategies from import substitution policies linked with subsidized state enterprises to export promotion policies stressing nontraditional products and greater reliance on the private sector. Breaking ranks with its neighbors, Chile consciously tied its economic fortunes to the market economies of major industrialized nations, particularly the United States, during the early- to mid-1980s. Chile's open market policies are also notable for their breadth of application, covering virtually all sectors, imports as well as exports, with minimal distortions from government protection or promotion programs.

Withdrawal from the Andean Pact best symbolized Chile's choice of an international open market strategy. The pact required strong government direction of the economy in line with agreed rules and sectoral market divisions. State enterprises played key roles as instruments of government policy and as direct participants in the economic process. Regulations narrowly defined the involvement of foreign enterprises, seeking primarily technological benefits with minimal compensation or sacrifice of local control. Since the pact represented the most advanced regional integration scheme, its abandonment by Chile appeared to some critics as a choice of global integration and MNC relationships over both nation and region.[1]

The internationalization strategy settled into a productive pattern following the recession of the early 1980s. Prior to that time, the use of foreign exchange policy to fight domestic inflation and the unregulated flow of speculative capital into the country fueled a consumer import boom while strangling new exporters. During the following years, macroeconomic trade, investment, and financial policies all worked together to support an open market reallocation of resources. Chile's trade performance under the new set of policies is particularly impressive. The country doubled its export sales over the 1980s from $4 billion to over $8 billion. In the process, exports increased in relation to gross domestic product from under one-quarter to almost one-third. Imports declined by nearly an equivalent ratio as import substitution occurred due to greater domestic efficiencies rather than protectionist trade barriers. Import composition also shifted to incorporate more purchases of productive capital goods rather than consumer items.

Recent export growth has drawn heavily from nontraditional product sales as Chile's diversification strategy has begun to pay dividends. While copper production increased by 38 percent between 1980 and 1988, fish, forestry, and fruit production grew by 200–300 percent. Non-copper sales accounted for all the country's export growth in 1990 as copper exports dipped 5 percent while non-copper income increased 11 percent. This result continued the long-term decline in copper's total export share from 80 percent in the early 1970s to roughly 45 percent in 1990. During the same two decades, Chile more than tripled its number of exported products while doubling the number of recipient countries. Overall, Chile's healthy trade surplus sustains its development policies while enhancing its international economic stature.

This international orientation and a new confidence in the Chilean business community reflects the development of a broad consensus as to the benefits of an international open market strategy. The democratically elected government which took office in 1990 endorsed the core elements of the former regime's trade and investment policies, pledging their continuation. The first issue of the new government's publication on foreign investment featured highlights from a speech by Minister of the Economy Carlos Ominami, a prior critic of some international market strategies. He now reassured businesspeople that an economic policy-making consensus recognized market forces as the most efficient way to allocate resources and that, for Chile, "the Free Trade Policy cannot be put in doubt."[2] Finance Minister Alejandro Foxley reinforced these views in an interview, stating "we are maintaining policies intent on keeping the Chilean economy as a very open economy, with low unitary tariffs, a strong private sector and no barriers to foreign investment."[3]

The restructuring decision and subsequent formation of a consensus on an international open market strategy were important ingredients in Chile's economic success throughout the 1980s and a fundamental component of its evolving relationship with foreign investors. The country's market economy, including its openness to international economic forces, sets the competitive context within which most businesses must operate. This environment allows foreign investors to be flexible and innovative, potentially generating far greater benefits to the domestic economy than those provided under inward-oriented development strategies.

Foreign corporations can survive and even thrive in protected host economies, adjusting to and often seeking to perpetuate market advantages gained by the exclusion of potential competition. In such cases, these investors generally offer little continuing advantage to the nation once initial gains are realized from the original investment. The investor has little incentive to enhance its operation beyond steps taken in response to governmental demands or threats since the basic terms of profitability are set by artificial barriers rather than the MNC's abilities to combine its various resources in response to a competitive system of market-directed rewards.

Chile is among the upper-income developing countries with the worst prospects for deriving benefits from MNCs through an inward-looking development strategy. The country's internal market is too small to attract foreign investment of significant size and scale solely on the prospect for import-substitution sales. Higher import barriers would almost inevitably mean an inefficient allocation of domestic resources and higher consumer costs, absent some form of market enlarging strategy. The Andean Pact was one such approach to expand market size, but its efforts to erect external trade and investment restrictions in order to achieve internal trade and investment liberalization floundered on both economic and political shoals. Chile's decision to opt out of the pact and essentially redirect its energies toward penetrating developed country markets gave the nation a broader and richer target for exports to complement its limited domestic market.

The requirements of international market competition created new opportunities and enhanced the role of foreign investors. Chile had only a few sectorally concentrated large firms with extensive international experience. MNCs possess the scale, resources, access, and adaptability to help reorient the economy to overseas markets. An outward-looking policy provides a better basis for taking advantage of an MNC's full storehouse of values than a strategy focused on domestic market exploitation.

Of course, international open market policies also increased Chile's vulnerability to global forces, including the impact of foreign business practices. This fact, together with the requirements of national political sovereignty, dictated the adoption of public regulations to govern the actions of foreign investors. These rules sought to encourage productive resource flows while avoiding or cushioning possible socioeconomic costs to the nation. In general, Chile established a broad, facilitative framework that introduced few distortions at the microeconomic level, opting for nondiscriminatory rules rather than bureaucratic mechanisms with wide administrative discretion. The centerpiece law for this foreign investment policy was D.L. 600.

FOREIGN INVESTMENT RULES (D.L. 600)

Chile passed its key foreign investment statute (D.L. 600) in 1974, the year following the military coup. The law established one of the most liberal investment regimes in developing countries at that time, guaranteeing generally open and nondiscriminatory treatment for foreign investors in terms of both entry conditions and subsequent treatment of business operations. A delayed response by foreign investors to the law's passage reflected their caution at Chile's initially uncertain political and economic environment as well as the unproven nature of the legal guarantees. Nevertheless, the law's application was progressively elaborated through negotiations and developed into a stable foundation for Chile's restructured investment climate.

The foreign investment policy is grounded in a philosophy based on free access to markets and sectors, nondiscriminatory national treatment (that is, the same treatment accorded to domestic firms), and minimum government interference. In line with the country's international open market strategy, foreign investors are restricted in only a few areas of the economy, including uranium mining, television stations, coastal shipping, certain public utilities, and national security industries. Reforms during the early 1980s, many carried out in conjunction with privatization actions, opened most other activities to domestic or foreign private investors, including telephone and telecommunications, many mining ventures, and financial activities encompassing even the nation's pension system.

A prospective foreign investor in Chile must supply general information about the anticipated project in an application to the Foreign Investment Committee established under the 1974 law. Investments over $5 million and those involving foreign governments or certain public service projects require approval of the full committee. Permanent committee members include the minister of economy (chairman) and the ministers of finance, planning, and foreign affairs, with participation from other ministries as relevant to a given project. The committee's executive secretary, with the chairman's approval, can authorize foreign investments under $5 million. In concept, this application process could act as a discretionary screening mechanism, but in practice it has proven pro forma, responding primarily to foreign exchange regulations and pre-contractual information needs.

Once the application is approved, an investment contract is drawn up using a standard model that establishes a public deed between the investor and the state of Chile. This method provides the strongest guarantees for the investor since the contract terms cannot be altered by subsequent legislative changes in foreign investment rules. The contract contains standard guarantees applying to all investors and can include additional grants of privilege, particularly for larger-scale and export-oriented projects.[4]

The law recognizes foreign investment in several forms, including freely convertible foreign exchange, new or used tangible goods, technology that can be capitalized, loans tied to an investment project, and profit capitalization from earlier investments if the profits are eligible for repatriation. For most projects, the actual investment must occur within three years after approval, but mining ventures may take up to eight years. These terms can be extended by the committee to eight and twelve years, respectively, for especially large and complex projects. This approved investment period accounts for both the lag time and the statistical discrepancies between authorized and materialized investment figures.

The fact that the law imposes no time or level of ownership limitations on foreign investors constitutes a distinct shift from the Andean Pact's Decision 24 regulations. Possible regulation of access to internal (local) credit is the only permissible exception to nondiscriminatory national treatment for foreign investors. After-tax profits can be remitted without limit at any time and capital obtained from the sale or liquidation of the business may be repatriated after three years from the date of the actual investment (although in January 1992 the government proposed lowering this restriction to one year). The contract guarantees investors access to the official foreign exchange market for such remittances. Some regulatory supervision is stipulated regarding foreign loan conditions, royalty and service fees, and foreign exchange requirements for imports.

Foreign investors can obtain a guaranteed fixed income tax rate for a ten-year term from the enterprise's start-up date, choosing either a 49.5 percent overall rate or a 40 percent rate with variable surtaxes for excessive profit remittances. (The January 1992 government proposal mentioned above would also reduce the 49.5 percent rate to 42 percent.) This fixed rate guarantee appeared to provide valuable security, particularly for large mining ventures, in light of Chile's history of taxation at rates up to 60 percent during the 1950s and 1960s. The law also gives the firm a one-time option to shift from the fixed rate to the prevailing national rate. In practice, most companies covered by the tax guarantee system have opted out of the fixed rate as soon as their operations became profitable. The prevailing effective rate has been as much as 12–13 percent lower than the guaranteed rate and taxation policy remained relatively stable into the early 1990s.

In cases of foreign investments over $50 million, the law permits additional guarantees if agreed to in the contract. The contractual period, including the fixed tax rate guarantee, can be extended up to twenty years. Export regulations as well as depreciation and other tax treatment rules may also be written into the contract. Offshore accounts can be authorized for income earned from export sales, with the proceeds used to pay for approved expenses such as supplies, technical assistance, principal and interest repayments on loans, and profits. The availability of this mechanism further reduces the risks associated with making financial transfers out of the country, helping to reassure foreign lenders and suppliers as well as the investing enterprise about repayment timing and conditions.

The relative importance of these D.L. 600 provisions to foreign investors has varied depending on the size, sector, and nature of a specific project. In general, the measure contains four key elements that, in combination, provide a potentially attractive, facilitative framework for new investment. The central element is the national treatment principle as applied to both entry and operating conditions.   This standard offers a broad scope for possible investment opportunities while promoting the concept of fairness and equality before the law. A second important factor for investors is stability and security, which D.L. 600 guarantees by offering a contract with the state of Chile for a period ranging from ten to twenty years, including the option of a fixed tax rate. Standards of operational effectiveness and reasonableness are offered by the repatriation rules, permitting immediate profit remittance while restricting capital outflows for only three years (or one year if the proposed reduction is adopted), with guaranteed access to foreign exchange to make these promises effective. Finally, the statute permits adaptation to special conditions, recognizing inherent differences between large and small-scale investments, mining and other business ventures, and export-oriented operations.

As mentioned earlier, passage of the foreign investment statute in 1974 did not spark an immediate rush to Chile despite the law's relatively liberal provisions. Against the backdrop of the turbulent Allende years and the military junta's repression, many potential investors preferred to wait for demonstration cases of successful negotiations for investment contracts under the statute and substantial evidence over time that the stated guarantees would prove effective. Several negotiations with early investors were particularly important to test the law's applicability and identify practical modifications which might be needed.

The first major D.L. 600 contract was not signed until 1977, following nearly two years of discussions between the government and St. Joe Minerals Corporation. This investment, described in the next chapter, was made to develop the important El Indio gold mine. Negotiations on several other large projects helped lay the groundwork for an influx of more diverse investments during the economic "boom" that preceded the recession of the early 1980s. Subsequently, the law was modified late in 1985 and 1987 as Chile entered a sustained phase of growth boosted by a major increase in foreign direct investment in both traditional and nontraditional business sectors. At the same time, Chile adopted a complementary measure that established a debt conversion mechanism.

DEBT-TO-EQUITY SWAPS (CHAPTER XIX)

Chile established Latin America's first sustained and arguably most successful debt conversion program in 1985. Chapter XIX of the Central Bank's Foreign Exchange Regulations provided the primary channel for foreign investors to convert Chile's external debt instruments into local equity investments. Related provisions allow other types of debt conversion, including Chapter XVIII and its annexes which are used by local enterprises, mainly banks, to repurchase debt. While relevant to Chile's overall debt reduction strategy, these other channels do not hold the significance of Chapter XIX in shaping the country's relations with foreign investors.

The innovative debt swap program responded to the development of a private international secondary market for Latin American debt following the region's financial crisis. Chilean debt could be purchased at deep discounts, beginning as low as thirty cents to the dollar but normally trading at about two-thirds of the debt instrument's face value. Under Chapter XIX provisions, a prospective foreign investor could apply to the Central Bank, supplying detailed information on the nature and purpose of the desired investment and the foreign debt obligations that were to be used.

When granted authorization, the investor then redeemed the debt at the Central Bank for Chilean pesos at a rate closer to the instrument's face value, thereby getting an effective up-front cash incentive. The government redeemed the debt at less than its face value, thereby retiring external debt early at a discount. Over the first several year's of Chile's program, total discounts averaged between 30–40 percent, with the government claiming one-third of the discount. The investor's average incentive or subsidy amounted to approximately one-quarter of par value or over two-thirds of the dollar investment.[5] More than $3.5 billion of foreign debt was converted to equity investments through Chapter XIX from 1985 to 1990, accounting for approximately one-third of Chile's external debt reduction. At an approximate 77 percent conversion rate of face value for this entire period, these debt-to-equity swaps represented over $2.7 billion of foreign direct investment in Chile over the period, or roughly 46 percent of the total, with the other 54 percent invested through D.L. 600.[6]

The Chapter XIX authorization process is lengthier and less pro forma than a D.L. 600 application. To qualify for conversion, debt must be restructurable foreign currency obligations of over one year, generally payable to commercial banks. A screening process attempts to eliminate "round-tripping," a scheme by which funds flow out of Chile and then return through debt swap channels to claim the conversion program's incentive. Another screening objective is to promote "additionality," thereby using the debt swap incentive to encourage investments that would not otherwise occur rather than effectively granting bonuses to investments that would occur anyway. The approval process also places restrictions on eligible sectors and business purposes to channel investments toward priority areas that have changed over time as Chile's convertible debt stock has decreased.

In addition to the approval process, Chapter XIX conversions differ from D.L. 600 investments in several significant ways. First, the agreement is reached with the Central Bank, a state agency, rather than with the Foreign Investment Committee acting on behalf of the state of Chile. Foreign investors believe the latter approach provides a stronger legal contract for a project than the former. The Central Bank guarantees access to the official foreign exchange market for capital and profit remittances, but ten years must elapse before repatriation of capital. Profits cannot be remitted until the fifth year of the investment, when up to one-quarter of earnings accumulated over the first four years can be remitted annually.

As a path-breaking endeavor, Chile's debt swap program had few examples from other countries to draw on. The general regulatory outline was filled in through case-by-case application as the government and foreign investors attempted to find matching interests. The first Chapter XIX transaction occurred in June 1985 with an initial investment of $10 million by Pathfinder Securities. Negotiations leading up to this transaction helped define the initial Chapter XIX regulations, just as subsequent deals elaborated their scope and application.

Significant differences exist between the economic sectors favored by Chapter XIX versus D.L. 600 investments. Minerals represented 47 percent and services 28 percent of all materialized D.L. 600 investments through 1990, compared to 12.7 percent and 10.5 percent, respectively, of Chapter XIX conversions. By contrast, manufacturing industries (35 percent) and export-oriented investments in forestry, agriculture, and fishing (23.8 percent) claimed the largest shares of Chapter XIX investments.[7] These differences reflect both variations in investor objectives and their comparative evaluations of the investment channels. Mining firms in particular perceived greater security for their long-term development projects in D.L. 600 contracts with the state.

Opposition to Chapter XIX investments arose from three interrelated objections. First, critics charged that swapping debt for equity adds little to the national economy if it does not bring "fresh" money to the country. The government's redemption of debt instruments above market value drew criticism as an unnecessary bonus to companies which intended to invest anyway (lack of "additionality"). The discount received by Chapter XIX foreign investors also appeared to give them an advantage over local investors. This perception became especially controversial when foreign MNCs won bids over local companies for control of state enterprises that were being privatized.

In general, these criticisms undervalue important benefits of debt conversion programs, particularly as administered in Chile, while exaggerating potential problems. On the positive side, debt swaps enabled Chile to reduce its foreign debt overhang, saving interest payments and paving the way to regaining eligibility for international private commercial lending in 1990. The government split gains from the discounted debt with the foreign investor, claiming an increasing proportion of the discount as Chile's program proved successful and its stock of restructurable debt decreased.

The focus on who gains from the debt swap also tends to overlook who loses in the transaction. When the debt instrument was first issued, Chile presumably benefitted from the use of "fresh" loan money. The creditor in that initial transaction suffered most of the loss from discounts given on the secondary market after the debt crisis erupted. In many cases, foreign banks investing through Chapter XIX used their own debt claims, meaning that their gain from the swap was in reality only a reduction of their loss.

Chile also benefitted from the increased investment activity stimulated by the Chapter XIX program. This conclusion, based on cumulative evidence from sectoral case studies described in later chapters, runs parallel to findings from research conducted by the World Bank's International Finance Corporation (IFC) on debt-equity swap programs in Chile, Brazil, Argentina, and Mexico. That study termed Chile's debt conversion program "a significant part" of the nation's positive investment climate which led firms without pre-existing business ties to look for investment opportunities in the country.[8]

Buy-outs using Chapter XIX funds attracted more criticism than new investment projects, especially if the buy-outs involved foreign banks that did not bring obviously new technology, marketing, or other such operational contributions to improve the business. Most banks lacked practical experience in industrial projects, acting as "silent partners" in a management role confined largely to financial oversight functions. However, this simplistic view overlooks the banks' catalytic role and undervalues the distinctive improvements introduced in many buy-out situations.

In Chile, "silent partner" foreign banks often utilized relationships established with MNCs in other countries to bring a "managing partner" to Chile. Because of this transaction, the IFC study reports, "the debtor country gets a new company and/or an injection of management talent, and often additional exports."[9] The study also found that, "In our sample it was quite common to find buy-outs or financial restructurings followed rather quickly by improvements or additions to productive capacity, including sometimes the opening of new kinds of production. This suggests that countries that do not permit swaps for buy-outs or financial restructuring may be losing the advantages of these follow-on benefits."[10] The present research on individual cases of Chapter XIX investments involving both buy-outs and new project situations supports this conclusion.

The IFC study also found significant but logical differences between bank and other MNC investments that used debt conversion. Banks view swaps as a way to diversify or liquidate poorly performing debt portfolios in countries where they are already over-extended. Since they would not normally invest further in that country, "virtually every investment made by banks would not have happened without a swap program." By contrast, the study reports that approximately one-half of investments by non-bank MNCs using debt swaps would have occurred anyway. Swap mechanisms appear especially useful in encouraging export-oriented manufacturing projects where competitive cost factors are particularly important, a conclusion consistent with the concentration of Chile's Chapter XIX investments in these sectors.[11]

Chile recorded the highest "additionality" rating in the IFC study at 64 percent. That figure is probably too low since the research, which took place in 1987, suggested that a program's additionality increases over time.[12] Early debt swaps may draw heavily from projects already on corporate drawing boards because most investments require a year or more of planning. Over time, a debt conversion program will stimulate more new investment planning. Chile's program continued to grow through the end of the decade and its additionality criteria were also progressively tightened.

From one perspective, Chile's Chapter XIX program was a victim of its own success. The country's restructurable debt eligible for conversion declined from roughly $14.5 billion at the program's outset to around $5 billion by the end of 1990. In the process the secondary market value of Chilean debt rose to around eighty cents on the dollar, a higher rate than for any other major debtor country. This rise wiped out most of the implicit investment subsidy available from the difference between the debt's secondary market value and the Central Bank's redemption value. Many debt holders also decided to simply hold the debt as an asset as Chile improved its standing in international financial markets. The result was a dramatic decline in Chapter XIX investment from a record $1.3 billion in 1989 to $412 million in 1990, with only around $20 million in new approvals during 1991.

The Central Bank had modified the Chapter XIX program in mid-1990, aiming to channel the remaining debt conversion funds to priority investment areas. In general, bank approval was reserved for investments over $5 million in new export or import substitution ventures, communications, tourism, energy, or environmental protection projects. Many financial sector investments were excluded, including insurance, pension management, investment funds, and leasing operations. Proposed debt swaps involving investments in existing activities or property were allowed only if the financing was essential for the project's development and represented a reasonable portion of the total resources obtained.[13]

In early 1991 another set of reforms was considered to bring certain Chapter XIX restrictions on profit or capital repatriation closer to the D.L. 600 standards. One issue, raised initially by the desire of a New Zealand investor (Carter Holt Harvey) to sell its stake in a major Chilean energy and forestry company, concerned Chapter XIX capital repatriation restrictions if a foreign investor sold its local assets to a domestic investor. A response was to allow faster repatriation if the foreign investor made a compensatory payment that would supposedly offset the investment subsidy gained through the debt swap transaction according to a schedule fixed by the Central Bank.

These debates over Chapter XIX modifications mark a winding down of debt conversion as a major element of Chile's foreign investment strategy. In addition to assessing the debt swap mechanism as an investment promotion device, three aspects of Chile's experience are noteworthy. First, debt conversion played an important although not dominant role in Chile's successful debt management campaign. Throughout the 1980s Chile cooperated with the IMF, World Bank, and private international creditor banks to reschedule and reprice its loans, obtaining new money to help it stay current on its debt service payments. The capstone achievement of this long effort was a September 1990 agreement to reschedule 1991–94 debt maturities with creditor banks. The favorable package included a rollover of $1.8 billion to 1995–2005, interest savings of around $190 million, and over $300 million in new money from bonds underwritten by a group of foreign banks, effectively returning Chile to the international financial markets. Chile's successful debt conversion program, linked to its other debt management policies, helped make the country a model for debt management strategies in the eyes of most international public and private lenders.[14]

A second factor in the Chapter XIX story relates to the efficiency and fairness of the program's administration. The approval process relies on greater discretionary authority than the D.L. 600 procedures. Chapter XIX applications require more time, information, and follow-up monitoring to insure the appropriate approval and implementation of proposed projects. Despite occasional complaints, the process generally operated in an expeditious fashion and few investors faulted the professionalism of Chile's bureaucracy. Nevertheless, as the program's norms and conditionality requirements tightened over time, procedures grew more cumbersome and oversight responsibilities of the Central Bank increased.

Two charges of major fraud under the Chapter XIX program surfaced in 1990, involving persons connected with projects supported by Spain's Banco Bilbao Vizcaya (BBV) and, in one case, the French Banque Worms. These cases drew fines amounting to over $10 million because approved debt swaps did not materialize into the proposed projects. Subsequent investigation revealed other instances of improper actions, a few involving apparently serious fraudulent activity, but most stemming from lesser transgressions of the increasingly complex rules. By August 1991 these problems were reported to encompass no more than fifteen of 357 Chapter XIX operations, representing only $200 million of the $3.5 billion channeled through this mechanism. Despite the several major infractions, these results were generally seen as both a validation of the government's ability to regulate the program and a reminder that over 95 percent of the agreements were implemented successfully.[15]

The final factor is the link between Chapter XIX investments and Chile's privatization program. To a certain extent, this relationship also raised fairness concerns. A few controversies about the sale price and procedures for privatization arose involving foreign investors who were using debt conversion funding. Political figures who objected generally to foreign ownership of former state enterprises were particularly incensed if a purchase involved financial incentives from a debt swap that was not available to domestic entities.

Privatization also played a key role, along with low real interest rates and the availability of domestic debt with reasonable maturity terms, in helping to restrain inflationary effects that can result from debt-to-equity swaps. The potential for greater domestic inflation from debt conversion is a danger facing most heavily indebted developing countries. By wedding the two programs together in a climate of sound macroeconomic policies during a critical time in the late 1980s, Chile avoided many monetary distortions that might have arisen. Privatization was more than just an adjunct to debt conversion, however; it was a key restructuring decision with broad implications for Chilean society.

PRIVATIZATION OF STATE ENTERPRISES

The privatization campaign in Chile was a corollary to the general free market philosophy pursued by the Pinochet government following the military coup in 1973. Privatization occurred in two stages, interrupted and indeed temporarily reversed by the recession in the early 1980s. The actions altered Chile's highly statist approach, decentralizing decision-making in the economy and opening a broad range of new investment opportunities for private investors, both domestic and foreign. Opposition to this change in course diminished as the economic situation improved. While few voices call for a renationalization of privatized activities, views still differ on whether the privatization process was well executed and, in particular, whether the state received adequate compensation for its assets.

The first stage of privatization which took place from 1974 to 1981 encompassed two major types of actions. First came the return to private ownership of virtually all domestic and foreign enterprises nationalized during the Allende regime (excepting most notably the Kennecott and Anaconda copper holdings that formed the core of state-owned CODELCO). This step simply reestablished the *status quo ante*, but was essential to regaining private investor confidence and encouraging entrepreneurial initiative. The second component involved the privatization of some other, longer-held government functions. The objective behind this action was both philosophical and practical. While widening the scope for private free market decisions, the government also addressed serious fiscal problems. State enterprises ran a $500 million deficit in 1973 and the government lacked the funds necessary to make investments needed to improve efficiency.

Chile's economic outlook improved as the country headed for the economic boom of the late 1970s. The state reduced its scope and role in the economy, privatizing some activities while imposing tighter financial discipline on enterprises remaining under its control. Overall fiscal expenditures were cut by one-quarter, helping the government turn a fiscal deficit into a surplus. This surplus enabled the Pinochet regime to undertake its most innovative and far-reaching privatization action in 1981 when a comprehensive reform of the social security system moved the country to a system of private pension funds. These rapidly growing funds have become the most important source of investment within the Chilean economy.

The 1982–83 financial crisis and recession halted the privatization process and sent it several paces backward. In January 1983 the government was forced to assume temporary control of most key domestic financial institutions as well as some corporate enterprises. Subsequent economic reforms allowed the government to resume the privatization process in 1985, with this second stage lasting until the Aylwin administration assumed power in early 1990. During the second stage of the privatization campaign, the Pinochet government returned intervened banks and companies to private control. Other traditional state enterprises were also sold to private sector investors through the nation's development corporation, la Corporación de Fomento de la Producción (CORFO). The state raised nearly $2 billion by selling thirty-three enterprises along with five banks and two pension fund management companies.[16]

Among the most important enterprises privatized by the Pinochet regime were the national telephone company (CTC), power generation firm (ENDESA), nitrate and iron producer (SOQUIMICH), and steel corporation (CAP). The best illustration of the privatization program may be CAP, which was fully nationalized in 1970 and privatized in stages from 1984 to 1987. While the steel firm was under state control, the government could not sustain adequate investment to improve the company's efficiency, particularly once the nation's lowered trade barriers subjected it to strong competition from Brazilian and other imports during a time of excess world capacity. CAP's losses reached $65 million a year in the early 1980s prior to the privatization decision.

Through privatization, CAP was able to embark on an investment program amounting to over $800 million, improving steel and mining activities while diversifying into areas precluded while under state control. Value-added production of iron pellets increased, overall competitiveness improved, new overseas markets boosted exports to over 80 percent of ore production, and an export-oriented forestry products subsidiary was established. From the government's perspective, an important element of the privatization action involved the promotion of "popular capitalism." Employees acquired approximately 37 percent of the privatized company, with nearly 5,000 employees holding an average of 11,000 shares. In 1989 those shares were worth $22,000, and their dividends amounted to nearly one-third of the employees' average salaries.[17] The Pinochet administration saw this mechanism as a way of increasing popular support both for specific privatization actions and for free market capitalism in general. CAP's president echoed the views of other managers in attributing some of the company's improved performance to increased worker involvement and productivity resulting from the employees' more concrete stake in the firm's success.

On the other hand, popular capitalism was a rather limited experiment whose longer-term impact is uncertain. Approximately 28,000 employees gained shares in privatized companies during the program's first four years as the total number of Chileans owning shares in companies increased about 40 percent to almost 600,000 people, or roughly 5 percent of the population.[18] The effect of privatized firms in broadening Chile's small stock market was certainly greater than the narrower impact from the addition of employee-shareholders. In fact, some officials speculate that many employees soon sold their shares for one-time gains, sacrificing periodic dividends and their role as partial owners, although through late 1991 no comprehensive study had yet tested this hypothesis.[19]

The sale of many state enterprises provoked harsh criticism from the political opposition. It was alleged that firms were sold too cheaply, in some cases benefitting supporters or members of the military government. Foreign companies participated more actively in the second stage of privatization bids, drawing on both the availability of Chapter XIX funding and their generally stronger post-recession financial position compared to many domestic enterprises. Protests of unfairness and general uneasiness over foreign ownership of traditional state facilities sparked some political attacks against foreign purchases. The controversy led a few firms, such as Citibank, to adopt policies against making Chapter XIX investments in privatized enterprises. Other foreign investors remained attracted to privatization sales, with or without the use of debt conversion funds.

General allegations regarding inadequate compensation for privatized assets became more specific when the head of CORFO under the Aylwin administration revealed results from a study that estimated a $2 billion loss from privatizations taking place under the Pinochet government from 1985 onward. Three-fourths of this total corresponded to the difference between the privatized enterprises' sale price and their book value as calculated by looking at acquisition costs and actualized values using tax agency rules. The remainder of the estimated loss arose from CORFO's assumption of some enterprises' debt.[20]

Since privatization sales generally occurred through a public bidding process, much of this dispute comes down to a difference between calculated book value and the enterprise's market value at the time of sale. When privatization sales occur during depressed economic times or when the enterprise is losing money or requires additional investments to improve efficiency, market value can appear low compared to book value. This perception is even more likely in retrospect, from the vantage point of better economic times and with the presumption that other interested bidders existed who were willing and able to pay a higher price. In addition, by focusing on comparing calculated prices for individual transactions, the debate sometimes overlooked broader economic and policy goals promoted by the privatization process as a whole, including stimulating new investor interest in Chile, relieving fiscal pressures on the state, and enhancing the role for private sector decision-making in the economy.

The controversy over whether Chile received adequate compensation for the sale of public assets is unlikely to be resolved to everyone's full satisfaction. The government announced that any case involving major improprieties would be sent to judicial authorities for investigation and appropriate action. Importantly, however, the Aylwin administration also reassured private investors, both domestic and foreign, that criticism of privatization actions carried out by the Pinochet regime would not lead to attempts to reverse the results through a renationalization of privatized firms.

The Aylwin government did halt new privatizations upon assuming power while it studied past actions and considered its own policy options. This process led to several initiatives, among them proposals to open unexploited resource deposits under CODELCO's control to joint venture development with private investors. CORFO also adopted measures to increase private participation in certain activities still under its control without necessarily fully privatizing the function. Among the areas approved for private investment were the freight portion of the national railway system and participation in certain state-controlled shipping and mineral resource enterprises.

DEMOCRATIZATION AND BUSINESS

Change and uncertainty surrounded Chile's return to democracy, complicating planning in the business community. Business did not play a leading role in the population's decision to move toward democratization, but its response to this movement promised to be a key factor in determining whether the new democratic government could sustain the military regime's economic growth record and enjoy the resultant political benefits. In the end, continued investment by foreign corporations, including new firms from countries with which Chile's democratization improved bilateral business prospects, provided an important boost for the Aylwin government and an even steadier source of major new productive investment than domestic enterprises.

Many domestic business leaders had grown uncomfortable with the military government's lengthy stay in power, but worried that a democratic replacement might bring political instability or economic socialism. The Pinochet government played up these fears in the campaign prior to the 1988 plebiscite, casting the "yes" or "no" vote for another eight years of Pinochet's rule as a decision between stability and growth versus a return to political and economic chaos. Victory for the "no" coalition prolonged the period of uncertainty as political parties then contended for support in subsequent national elections.

The Aylwin victory in December 1989 did not end the uncertainty. Speculation continued about whether the military, still headed by General Pinochet, would ultimately transfer power the following March. Assuming the transition took place, some observers wondered further whether democratic institutions that had lain dormant for sixteen years could successfully manage the difficult political and socioeconomic challenges they would confront without generating substantial social conflict and provoking a new military takeover.

During the national election, the domestic business community generally aligned itself with one of the two conservative candidates opposing Patricio Aylwin. Most businesspeople probably favored former finance minister Hernán Büchi, hoping that his technocratic skills would extend the half-decade of sustained economic growth, but his delayed candidacy and lack of political experience dimmed Büchi's election prospects. Foreign corporate executives also favored a continuation of the government's economic policies within a democratically elected framework but took no notable part in the electoral process.

Three factors worked to mitigate business worry about the democratic transition. First was recognition that the time was ripe for a reassertion of Chile's longstanding democratic tradition. The country had boasted one of Latin America's best records of unbroken democratic rule with the support of a highly professional but nonpolitical military. When a clear majority voted in 1988 for open and direct national elections, public sentiment for speedy democratization was undeniable. Any attempt by the military to sustain an undemocratic regime would itself have generated increasing social unrest and instability.

Developments in the resultant political campaign also helped reassure many in the business community, particularly the foreign corporations, as to the parameters for potential change should the political opposition gain power. The broad center-left coalition supporting the Aylwin candidacy formulated positions backing retention of the major pillars in Chile's economic policy. The primary thrust for change would be improving social welfare needs, especially in education, health, and housing, while retaining sound macroeconomic policy in a market economy open to international trade and investment.[21]

This general policy position was given practical impact by key economic policy advisers who acted to offset worrisome campaign statements made by some prominent spokesmen for coalition-member parties. While these latter figures expressed a preference for a larger government role in the economy and a review of recent foreign investments, the central economic policy advisers encouraged continued foreign investment and endorsed the maintenance of sound macroeconomic and fiscal policies.

An oft-repeated statement by Alejandro Foxley, widely expected to be President Aylwin's choice to head the critical finance ministry, was that the first year of an Aylwin administration should be viewed in retrospect as *más o menos* (more or less). This phrase came attached to assurances that the government would not repeat the mistakes of many populist governments whose stimulation of rapid economic growth and expansion of public programs rewarded supporters in the first year, only to produce growing problems the second and recession by the third year. The Aylwin economic team aimed for a steady growth policy after containing rising inflation in the first year, maintaining long-range investor confidence through sound and stable economic policies. (In fact, economic growth dipped to 2 percent the first year during the anti-inflationary adjustment program but recovered again to well over 5 percent in 1991.)

The primary concerns for business leaders, which appeared to worry local executives more than foreign managers, were the prospects for taxation and labor law changes. The coalition's promised improvements in social programs required some source of additional revenue and business taxes, which had recently been lowered, were the likely target. The eventual tax increase proved moderate, but it helped the government nearly double spending on health, housing, and education to around $1 billion a year.

Labor law reform was widely acknowledged as necessary, even within the business community. However, strong union support for the Aylwin coalition might mean large wage increases and significantly greater union power, diminishing business competitiveness, flexibility, and profits. Smaller firms and export-oriented businesses under the greatest competitive pressures were the most concerned with labor costs. Export firms also worried about labor disruptions affecting transportation schedules. Large national enterprises focused on the implications of greater union power and the possibility that expanded government programs would require increased public revenue.

More broadly, domestic firms appeared sensitive to the potential sociopolitical changes associated with the democratic transition and worried particularly that unions might engage in radical political activities reminiscent of earlier periods in Chilean history. Some companies hesitated to commit long-term investments for new projects until at least a year into the new administration, when both the labor and taxation issues had been settled and an economic adjustment program to contain inflation was proving successful.

Foreign firms, on the other hand, generally continued their long-range investment plans undeterred by the transition's potential for instability. As reported in a *Euromoney* special supplement on Chile:

> Remarkably, interest among foreign investors has mushroomed at a time of political transition from authoritarian military rule, which might be considered odious but stable, to democratic government, which tends to be raucous. That is partly because some foreign governments discouraged links with Chile under its military regime, and those barriers have now been removed. But it also indicates considerable foreign confidence in Chile's political and social stability.[22]

This belief of foreign investors in the strength and stability of Chile's fledgling democratic government was reinforced by the way the Aylwin administration managed its most serious and potentially dangerous political issues. Longstanding charges of human rights violations and the cases of "disappeared" persons under the military regime demanded the new government's immediate attention, but the army under General Pinochet watched closely from the sidelines, issuing ominous warnings against any actions that threatened the military's position. While not fully resolving the issue, President Aylwin's appointment of an investigative Commission for Truth and Reconciliation and their subsequent Rettig Report (named after the commission chairman) drew praise from nearly all parties. An editorial in the *Journal of the Chilean-American Chamber of Commerce* called the report "a tough document" whose publication was "a compliment to the civic maturity of the Chilean people and of their political leaders. . . . Views from all sides are being heard and freely discussed, proving once again the strength of Chile's democratic traditions. The image of Chile abroad has gained much from the way in which this delicate issue has been handled."[23]

Aylwin administration officials themselves expressed satisfaction and even admiration for the way foreign investors responded to the democratic transition. Fernán Ibáñez, executive secretary of the Foreign Investment Committee, reflected on the difficult and uncertain period when the democratic choices were still being made.

> Do you remember the Chilean atmosphere before the 1988 Referendum? Do you remember the atmosphere before the 1989 elections? Well, during those years the foreign investors, mainly American . . . were "voting with their money." While others were doubting, they decided to put their money in Chile and we feel that they deserve not only our respect, but also our admiration.

They believed that this was a feasible country in the long term, and that we had a number of advantages that we ourselves at that time did not see and which ensured long-term stability.[24]

Adjustment to democratic processes after sixteen years of military rule required good faith efforts by all parts of Chilean society, including its foreign business citizens. While not interfering in Chile's internal political processes, foreign investors acted in a responsible manner that reflected long-term confidence in Chilean society and its political and economic prospects. Although the story of Chile's transition to democracy is far from complete, results from the first full year were extremely encouraging as virtually all segments worked together to resolve differences amicably for the overall good of the nation. Stronger political differences surfaced the following year, but the system continued to function well. The people's historic choice for a peaceful return to democracy was a critical decision at the end of the 1980s that set the broad course for the nation's future as it moved toward the end of the twentieth century.

NOTES

1. Esteban Tomic Errázuriz, *El retiro de Chile del Pacto Andino*, Apuntes CIEPLAN no. 58 (Santiago: Corporación de Investigaciones Económicas para Latinoamérica, November 1985), 15, 23–24.

2. Foreign Investment Committee, *Chile: Foreign Investment Report: Informe sobre inversión extranjera*, no. 12 (Santiago: Comité de Inversiones Extranjeras (Chile), January–April 1990).

3. "Calm Hand on the Tiller," Interview, in "Chile: Building On Success," supplement, *Euromoney* (September 1990), 6.

4. Two useful reference sources on both D.L. 600 and Chapter XIX are Langton Clarke, *Investing in Chile*, 1990–1991 ed. (Santiago: Langton Clarke, a member firm of Coopers & Lybrand International, June 30, 1990); and Foreign Investment Committee, *Legal Framework: Chile*, 3d ed. (Santiago: Comité de Inversiones Extranjeras (Chile), July 1988). Current information and materials can be obtained from the executive secretariat of Chile's Foreign Investment Committee.

5. Joel Bergsman and Wayne Edisis, "Debt-Equity Swaps and Foreign Direct Investment in Latin America," International Finance Corporation Discussion Paper No. 2 (Washington, D.C.: The World Bank and International Finance Corporation, 1988), 21; and Felipe Larraín and Andrés Velasco, *Can Swaps Solve the Debt Crisis? Lessons from the Chilean Experience*, Princeton Studies in International Finance, no. 69 (Princeton, N.J.: International Finance Section, Department of Economics, Princeton University, November 1990), 23.

6. "¿Por qué cayó la inversión extranjera en el año 1990?" *El Mercurio*, March 18, 1991.

7. José Manuel Silva C., "El auge de la inversión extranjera," *El Mercurio*, March 3, 1991.

8. Bergsman, "Debt-Equity Swaps," 12.

9. Ibid., 17.

10. Ibid., vi.

11. Ibid.

12. Ibid., 11–12.

13. "Oficializada elegibilidad de inversiones vía Capítulo XIX," *El Mercurio*, July 17, 1990; and "Banco Central hizo cambios menores a los estatutos del Capítulo XIX," *La Epoca*, May 16, 1991.

14. United States Embassy Santiago, *Chile: Economic Trends Report*, State Department (United States Embassy Santiago: November 1990), 14.

15. "Juan Eduardo Herrera: 'Razones del ajuste ya fueron controladas'," *El Mercurio*, August 25, 1990; "Engaño a través del Capítulo XIX: Dos más dos son . . . fraude," *El Mercurio*, August 26, 1990; "Operaciones Capítulo XIX," *El Mercurio*, September 19, 1990; and "Los sobresaltos del Capítulo 19," *El Mercurio*, August 18, 1991.

16. "Stock Market Comes Alive," in "Chile: Building On Success," 26.

17. "Electing to Change," 10; and "The Stimulus of Privatisation," 37; in "Chile: into the 1990s," *Euromoney*, supplement (August 1989).

18. "Electing to Change," 10; "The Stimulus of Privatization," 37; and "Stock Market Comes Alive," 26.

19. Raquel Correa, "Rene Abeliuk, Ministro Vicepresidente de CORFO: Las privatizaciones en el 'Freezer'," *El Mercurio*, April 1, 1990.

20. "Dijo Ministro de CORFO: 'Informes de contraloría revelan altas pérdidas por las privatizaciones'," *El Mercurio*, September 22, 1990; and "Estiman pérdidas de US$ 2.050 millones por proceso de privatizaciones," *El Mercurio*, October 1, 1990.

21. *Chile's Economic Challenge 1990–1994*, Concertación por la democracia, prepared by the Economic Commission of the Concertación por la democracia for Patricio Aylwin's presidential campaign, 1989.

22. "Respectability Brings Investment," in "Chile: Building On Success," 20.

23. "After a Gloomy 1990, An Upbeat Mood For 1991," *Journal of the Chilean-American Chamber of Commerce* (April 1991), 5.

24. "Things Work Out Here," *Journal of the Chilean-American Chamber of Commerce* (September 1988), 17.

3

Minerals and Energy

Mineral resources are a traditional mainstay of the Chilean economy. The huge Andes mountains determine the country's unusual shape and difficult terrain, but they also promise a broad spectrum of mineral riches to be discovered and exploited. Foreign investors were first attracted by nitrates and later by abundant copper deposits, establishing a local presence to develop the resources into important export commodities. These mining activities were a central part of early and often heated debates about the role of multinational corporations in Chile. Mining and energy-related activities are also important to the recent maturation of relations between foreign investors and the Chilean government, particularly during the expansion of mineral investments in the mid- to late 1980s.

Copper dominates the mining sector and, to a degree, the Chilean psyche as well. Extraction and sale of the red metal have long provided the vast majority of Chile's foreign exchange earnings, ensuring that the country would feel the economic roller-coaster effects of cyclical price fluctuations in world commodity markets. Whereas oil resources constitute the prime national patrimony in some developing countries, the symbol of Chile's common wealth became associated with national control over La Gran Minería—the copper mining complex built by giant foreign companies but nationalized with broad public support some two decades ago.

THE LEGAL FRAMEWORK AND ECONOMIC ROLE

Nationalization of the cooper mines largely determined the character of relations between foreign corporations and the Chilean public during the early 1970s. The following decade saw progressive improvement in the mutually hostile perceptions dominating both sides of this relationship. In an effort to attract new investors, the military government adopted a series of specific mining codes aimed at providing additional guarantees of regulatory stability to supplement the basic foreign investment statute (D.L. 600).

The 1980 constitution guarantees private property rights, but clearly establishes state ownership of all mineral resources. The document nevertheless authorizes mining concessions through which private parties can explore and develop most mineral deposits. One type of concession is granted through organic law with rights and obligations enforceable in the courts. Administrative concessions can also be granted to develop resource areas reserved to the state, but these contracts may be terminated at any time by the government with corresponding indemnity payments.

The 1982 Mining Law, the basic organic law for the minerals sector, can only be changed by a 60 percent majority of the Chilean Congress, providing some degree of stability regarding its provisions. This law was brought into force when a Mining Code was issued in December of the following year. The code supplies systematic rules to govern concessionary rights relating to the discovery, development and operation of mines. Under the organic law, concessions are subject to the guarantees of judicial rather than more discretionary administrative proceedings.

These organic law concessions do not apply to certain resources reserved for the state, including all copper deposits that were under exploitation by the state-owned company when the 1980 constitution was adopted. Hydrocarbons, lithium, and minerals located in strategic areas, particularly along the nation's borders, are among the other reserved resources. The government may allow foreign companies to participate in some developments through administrative contracts; for example, through Special Petroleum Operating Contracts (SPOCs) authorized in 1985 for oil exploration in certain geographic regions.

The mining law and code were built on the solid foundation provided by the general D.L. 600 foreign investment statute. The most important provisions of that law as applied to natural resource investments are the legal standing of resulting agreements as contracts with the state, adherence to the national treatment principle, authorization of offshore accounts for major investments, profit and capital remittance guarantees with effective access to foreign exchange, and the option of long-term, fixed tax rates.

Initially Chapter XIX debt-to-equity swaps could not be used for mining investments, but the Central Bank authorized the first such transaction in 1987 and granted several subsequent requests for a variety of mining projects. Most mining firms chose not to use this financing approach, as some feared that its weaker legal status might somehow taint their major investments covered by the D.L. 600 guarantees and complicate repatriation timetables. The authorization of Chapter XIX swaps did prompt some foreign banks to take equity positions in a few mining ventures, however. Citibank and Chemical Bank were among the first approved for investments in gold mining projects.

These changes in Chile's legal framework combined with the country's recognized natural resource wealth, a recovery in world raw material prices, and the progressive demonstration effect of several successfully negotiated foreign-owned mining ventures to create a wave of renewed investor interest in Chile and a relative boom in minerals exploration and project developments after the mid-1980s.

A particularly wide gap exists between authorized and materialized investment figures in the minerals sector since time is required to prove the existence of substantial reserves and to develop the infrastructure and processing facilities needed to bring a major operation on line. Foreign investment in the mining sector authorized under D.L. 600 totaled $8.2 billion from the law's adoption in 1974 to March 1990 when the new democratic government took power, but only about $2.5 billion had been materialized by this date. Significantly, however, the actual commitment of materialized foreign investment funds continued apace, or even accelerated, through the democratic transition period, indicating substantial investor confidence in the stability of the country's legal guarantees and in the expressions of support from virtually all political parties for the basic investment framework. Shortly after taking office, Chile's new minister of mining estimated that foreign firms would invest some $4 billion in the country's mining sector over the next four years.[1]

Within the domestic economy, mining represents less than 10 percent of Gross Domestic Product (GDP) and it directly employs around 2 percent of the nation's labor force (about 100,000 workers). The sector's central role in Chile's economy stems from its critical importance to the country's foreign trade account and its direct connection with public revenue. Mining still provides over one-half of Chile's export income, although this proportion fell during the 1980s with the growth in nontraditional export areas.

Taxes on mining operations provide significant public revenue and the government also obtains income from state-owned CODELCO, which had accounted for about three-fourths of the country's copper output through the 1980s. Some 40 percent of CODELCO's export earnings go into the nation's treasury, while a constitutionally guaranteed 10 percent is automatically committed to the armed forces' budget. Including tax and other payments, CODELCO contributed as much as $12 billion to government revenues since its creation in 1976. Other state-owned enterprises in the natural resource area also pay into government coffers. In the late 1980s, combined annual contributions from CODELCO, Empresa Nacional de Minería (ENAMI) and Empresa Nacional del Petróleo (ENAP) totaled nearly one-fifth of government revenues.[2]

Copper exports have been particularly important in Chile's effort to meet its foreign debt commitments. The country benefitted from a combination of unusually high world copper prices and record national production levels during the late 1980s. A one cent change in the average annual price of Chile's copper exports can translate into a $30 million change in the nation's export receipts—upward or downward. As part of a structural adjustment loan from the World Bank, Chile established a Copper Stabilization Fund that is paid into during times of high world prices in order to provide a cushion for the country during expected cyclical downturns.

A significant shift is now well underway in Chile's mining sector. Dominated by state enterprises since the expropriation of foreign mining firms in 1971, the industry is experiencing a revival of private investment, especially from foreign corporations. Output from private mines is expanding rapidly, particularly as foreign investments in major new facilities begin to come on line, while growth in the state sector is stagnant or negative.

In 1989, mining sales abroad amounted to some $4.8 billion in a total Chilean export performance of $8.2 billion. Private sector mining contributed $1.8 billion of this total, roughly double the previous year's figure. Private mines are already the country's largest gold producers and are projected to become the top producers of silver and even copper by the mid-1990s. As output at CODELCO mines peaks and perhaps even falls due to declining ore grades and insufficient reinvestment programs, new and improved foreign-operated facilities are set to expand the nation's production. One new copper giant alone, La Escondida, will raise Chile's copper production by nearly 20 percent. By the early 1990s, Chile should increase its share of world copper production to at least 2.2 million tons per year, roughly matching the proportion of its one-quarter share of world copper reserves, and private mines will provide at least one-half of this copper output.[3]

COPPER

Chile's State Enterprise—CODELCO

Chile possesses the world's largest reserves of copper and has been the leading producer since the early 1980s, when it surpassed the United States in annual output. The dominant enterprise during the 1970s and 1980s was La Corporación Nacional del Cobre de Chile (CODELCO). This company, the largest in Chile, was created in 1976 by the Pinochet government to coordinate operations in mines that had been expropriated under the earlier Allende administration. Four properties formed CODELCO's divisions: El Teniente, Salvador, Andina, and Chuquicamata (including the Exotica mine), with the Tocopilla power plant in northern Chile added as a fifth operational unit.

CODELCO had been producing about three-quarters of Chile's copper output and providing substantial income to the state from its export sales, as mentioned earlier. Production was expanded rapidly through the 1980s to underwrite the government's economic program and generate foreign exchange to meet foreign debt servicing requirements. The enterprise now appears to be peaking in terms of its immediate potential. Its mines face a series of difficult problems that have built up over the past decade and whose resolution will require particularly uncomfortable trade-offs between political, social, and economic objectives.

During its drive to expand production, CODELCO made a number of technological improvements in its facilities but generally chose paths that maximized immediate output while minimizing current expenditures. Resulting production gains were often needed just to offset declining ore grades at established mine sites. Symbolic of the resulting problems is declining production at the Andina mine, where heavy new investment is needed to reach rich ore deposits located well below the rapidly depleting current production levels. Exploration is limited, usually confined to areas adjacent to existing facilities, such as the discovery of the Mansa Mina deposit near Chuquicamata which will help extend the useful life of CODELCO's activities in that region. Less than one-third of one percent of CODELCO's 1989 budget was devoted to exploration, and its general reinvestment levels are reportedly about one-third of industry standards. Top mining officials in the new Aylwin government charged that CODELCO essentially had not done any exploration for five or six years, but their own initial proposal for about $10 million in annual exploration expenditures was hardly sufficient to uncover significant new deposits.[4]

The difficult political choice for state-owned and operated enterprises, of course, is the trade-off between a decrease in current public revenue versus a potential income gain that may be realized at some point years in the future. This type of calculation is difficult enough when the planning decision involves the impact of indirect influences on investment, such as taxation policy. The dilemma is even more painful when the government has a direct connection to business operations and the choice appears to be between spending revenue on pressing social programs such as housing, education, and health care, or committing the same funds to a risky search for new ore bodies that may produce additional income sometime during the next decade.[5]

CODELCO owns almost one-third of the mineral resource land in Chile, but less than 4 percent is actually being mined. Although some deposits are under study for possible development, only partial geological survey information is available on most areas. Lacking the funds to study and certainly to develop these additional deposits, the Aylwin administration proposed in early 1991 a legislative change to allow CODELCO joint ventures with private sector firms. Debate on this measure was heated, with private sector spokespeople favoring authorization for full sales to private companies along with competitive bidding on joint venture projects. Labor union officials and some political representatives worried that changes would begin to "denationalize" CODELCO and change its operational structure. When finally passed the following year, the legislative changes permitted greater scope for CODELCO ventures in association with the private sector to provide additional financial resources, improve technology, and perhaps eventually expand Chile's reach into world markets and downstream value-added production.[6]

Beyond exploration questions, CODELCO requires massive reinvestment over the next decade just to address its most urgent modernization needs. El Teniente suffers from serious structural deficiencies that have closed some levels in its underground operations. Andina lacks processing facilities and is exhausting its storage space for waste tailings. Costs of production in CODELCO's divisions rose from forty-eight cents per pound in 1985 to nearly fifty-seven cents in 1990, lowering the company's competitive standing in the world and dropping two divisions out of the top-ten rankings of least-cost producers.[7]

Particularly difficult dilemmas confront the enterprise in the area of labor relations. Cost reductions achieved by private copper companies in Chile and elsewhere are creating strong pressure for changes in staffing levels and work rules, an exceedingly difficult task for state-run enterprises in any country. Some estimates suggest that CODELCO employs up to 3,000 too many workers for its current operations. Needed restructuring might reduce the workforce even more. About one-half of CODELCO's approximately 26,000 direct employees are engaged in support rather than production activities, well over the comparable ratio at competing private firms.[8]

Worker productivity in CODELCO facilities is rated at about one-third the levels achieved at mines in the United States and Canada, or by private firms in Chile. Worker absenteeism is high and accident rates run on average as much as four times higher than at comparable foreign-owned Chilean facilities. In CODELCO's largest mine at Chuquicamata, some 10,000 employees worked under a labor structure based on 3,500 job descriptions with little flexibility for worker reassignments among the categories.

One report on CODELCO's labor problems carried a story about a group of women at the El Teniente mine, "*las Tejedoras de Rancagua*," who were hired years ago to punch holes in computer cards. Their function became obsolete when the company switched to computers that did not use these cards, but the workers rejected reassignment and spent several years engaged in sewing.[9] A similar problem arose with drivers hired at the Chuquicamata mine. When the company switched to larger trucks with greater capacity, four drivers remained to operate each truck on every shift.

The military government did not rectify many such problems during its administration. The difficulties for a democratic regime in tackling these issues were highlighted during President Aylwin's first post-election trip to Chuquicamata. The unions strongly criticized his suggestion that the mine's employees held privileged positions in relation to other Chilean workers and might be called on to make some sacrifices. Collective labor negotiations the following year resulted in a strike that shut down the operation for a short time before a satisfactory but still costly compromise was reached.

Another problem at CODELCO facilities that is beginning to receive some attention is the serious environmental impact of its operations. Discharge or seepage from waste tailings at several mines causes water pollution problems. The Andina mine reportedly spills tailings into a river flowing through a fertile farming valley about twice a month, causing contamination warnings against irrigation until the leaks are fixed. ENAMI's state smelting and refining facilities reportedly exceed emissions standards on a regular basis, with the best performers recovering less than one-half of the sulfur produced while others release virtually everything into the air.[10]

As with CODELCO's other modernization challenges, making needed environmental changes will be a costly exercise. Some $240 million has already been spent as part of an environmental improvement plan to reduce the indices 10 percent by 1993 at the El Teniente mine alone. Another $250 million is slated for the coming years to reduce pollution associated with production at both El Teniente and Chuquicamata.[11] These expenditures, of course, mean a choice to reduce current government revenue without even the promise of compensating future productivity or income gains.

CODELCO has entered a new stage in its history where it has virtually exhausted the advantages gained from taking over operations at established mining sites and developing their most easily exploitable capacity. Now major expenditures are needed just to maintain current performance. The level of financial commitment and technological improvement required for a serious expansion of production appears to lie beyond a politically acceptable reach. Hence, despite CODELCO's recent dominance, the most dynamic changes in Chile's evolving copper industry come from foreign investors, whose major new projects will provide most of the impetus behind Chile's future competitiveness in world copper markets.

The Improvement Challenge—La Disputada

A striking parallel exists between many of the problems now facing CODELCO and the challenges confronted by Exxon during the last decade as it improved and expanded Minera Disputada de las Condes, a mining complex that was near bankruptcy when Exxon bought it in 1978. Exxon was looking for further overseas expansion at the time, and its Esso subsidiary had seventy-five years of experience in petroleum distribution and sales in Chile. The Exxon Coal and Minerals Group, which operates large coal mines in the United States and Colombia, owned rights to copper deposits in the United States and Australia but had no operational copper mines.

The acquisition got off to a rough start. Exxon paid state-owned ENAMI

$98 million in 1978 for most of Disputada and another $15 million in subsequent years to private parties for nearly all the remaining shares. Six months after the purchase, one of the mine's key plants at Los Bronces was destroyed by an avalanche, disrupting production and complicating improvement plans. In the face of low copper prices, Exxon committed $512 million during the next ten years to finance capital improvements. Since the operation continued to lose money until 1988, another $129 million was invested to pay wages and finance other cash needs that could not be met by Disputada's output. In brief, Disputada's long-term improvement program required a full decade and an investment of over $750 million before the complex showed its first profit.

One of Exxon's competitive advantages is its access to investment capital from its related multinational financing arms, so the company was able and willing to execute the project on its own. The D.L. 600 investment agreement negotiated to cover Disputada in 1978 restricted the firm's option to raise capital locally, so the investment was essentially all "fresh" money, generated without any use of Chapter XIX funding. This large capital commitment increased the company's risk exposure, making some parent company investors nervous. The firm also received criticism in shareholder meetings and elsewhere for investing so heavily in a country controlled by a military dictatorship. In short, the project was controversial without even turning a profit for a full decade.

Holding to its long-term plans, Exxon improved Disputada's efficiency and expanded its facilities, raising production from about 30,000 tons per year to over 112,000 tons by 1989, nearly a four-fold increase. These aggregate results reflect a series of specific improvements in technology, labor relations, and environmental controls. For example, a new crushing facility at Los Bronces is probably the world's largest ball mill and the mine tested what may be the largest truck as well.

Disputada provides jobs for 1,800 direct employees while nearly 5,000 workers are involved in contracted jobs, mostly on expansion projects. Management reached agreement with the union on new labor contracts including more flexible work rules, essentially buying its way out of certain practices it felt would limit labor efficiency in the expanded operations. Since Exxon took over, Disputada's safety record has improved from a lost-time injury index of 24 in 1978 to 3.6 in 1989, with its underground El Soldado mine setting a Chilean record of one million work hours without any lost-time injury.

Regarding environmental improvements, the Chagres smelter component of the Disputada complex has the best sulfur recovery system in Chile, and its 75 percent recovery rate is nearly twice as high as the nearest performer. The company also planted some 200,000 trees on an old tailings site near the El Soldado mine in a forestation effort that went beyond local legal requirements. Environmental issues also lie at the center of Disputada's second phase expansion plans for the 1990s. The mining complex is located in the Andes mountains high above Las Condes, a Santiago residential area whose citizens complained loudly that the company's operations jeopardized the community's water supply. Mainly at issue was management of waste tailings that had accumulated over years of operation, including a period when the mine was owned and operated by a large French mining company which left Chile during the Allende regime. The Los Bronces facility was nearing the point of exhausting its tailings storage area, bringing waste control requirements into conflict with the need to further expand the mine in order to cover its high fixed operational costs.

Even though cost recovery on its huge initial investment was just beginning with Disputada's first profitable year, Exxon negotiated a second D.L. 600 agreement in 1989 which authorized an additional $1.2 billion investment. Having received government approval, the company began a multifaceted second-stage improvement program designed to expand production and processing capability in an environmentally sound fashion. Some $400 million will be spent to triple capacity at the Los Bronces mine. A fifty-six kilometer pipeline is being built to slurry crushed ore from the mine's milling facility high in the Andes to a new plant located near the coast.

Waste tailings will now be stored at the new processing site where they cannot contaminate water flowing down the mountains for use in the city or on agricultural lands. A natural basin on corporate property will contain the tailings while excess water from the pipeline can be used for a forestation project, ensuring that no contaminants leave the site. The company will also spend an additional $50 million, utilizing the pipeline to remove seventy-six million tons of accumulated tailings from the Los Bronces mine and ending the current threat of contamination to Santiago's water supply. A special port facility at San Antonio is being constructed for $8 million to handle the copper exports, removing any risk of contamination to agricultural shipments that now leave from the town's existing port.

Finally, the company is planning an expansion of the Chagres smelter that could triple its capacity using a newer flash furnace technology. Estimated to cost over $170 million, this project would increase Chile's value-added processing capacity by upgrading an existing facility while also improving its environmental performance. Although Chagres already has the country's most efficient sulfur recovery system, the use of newer technology in an expanded facility would raise recovery rates from 75 percent to 95 percent, meaning an overall reduction in sulfur emissions despite a three-fold increase in processing capacity.

This still evolving case history shows the enormous challenge in addressing the combination of pressing needs that confront an enterprise seeking to improve and expand an existing copper mine in Chile. No local private company and probably few other foreign investors would have had the staying power to finance Disputada's growth, particularly when faced with a host of serious environmental problems and a full decade of losses.

CODELCO's challenge is similar, but its choices are more difficult. Exxon's strategies are drawn so that its executives can make selections among alternative investment opportunities based on potential long-range profit. CODELCO's government sponsor must make more ambiguous trade-offs between short- and long-term goals, selecting from among largely non-comparable alternatives involving economic and social welfare programs. How much worse CODELCO's task would be if it had inherited the Disputada facility in 1978, replete with its enormous funding requirements and serious environmental problems. The contrasting prospects between Disputada and the neighboring Andina mine discussed earlier highlight some of the contrasts in investment strategies.

The New Copper Giant—La Escondida

The unpleasant task of correcting old mistakes can be avoided if an investor develops a newly discovered ore deposit (assuming such a deposit can be found), but such fresh opportunities carry with them their own challenges. An example of this is presented by a new giant copper producer that is emerging to bolster Chile's leadership in world markets. The Escondida mining complex, located in the barren Atacama desert of northern Chile, will be the world's third largest copper producer. Open pit mining will expose over 660 million tons of minerals with an extremely high average 2.1 percent copper ore grade, making the mine a low cost producer for at least the next fifty years. Total reserves reaching over 1.8 billion tons could carry the venture well into the twenty-second century.

Foreign investors are developing this project from exploration, testing, and financing, to construction, production, and final export sales. The project's enormous size makes it atypical in certain respects, but its attendant importance and complexity provide good illustrations of a foreign investor's possible financial, technological, and managerial contributions to a host country. Initial controversy surrounding the project's financing scheme also points out the type of tensions that can develop when the operational requirements of an international business venture are pitted against local expectations regarding foreign investment benefits.

In 1979, Utah International and the minerals subsidiary of Getty Oil joined forces to apply new technologies in a systematic exploration program in Chile. This approach identified over thirty potential areas, but the discovery of La Escondida in 1981 led the firms to concentrate efforts on drilling and testing at that one site. By 1983, laboratory results confirmed the discovery's potential, but the world recession and the Latin American debt problem in particular made conventional loan financing impossible. Early project cost estimates ranged as high as $1.5 billion. In addition, important changes in the partnership occurred in 1984 when Broken Hill Proprietary (BHP) of Australia acquired Utah International and Getty Oil was purchased by Texaco.

When Texaco decided to withdraw from the Escondida venture, BHP bought its shares, but then sought other partners to spread the financial and political risks inherent in such a large-scale mining project located in a developing country. The new partners were Rio Tinto Zinc (RTZ) of the United Kingdom and a Japanese consortium led by Mitsubishi International. Share-holdings were split 60/30/10 among these three firms, although BHP later dropped to 57.5 percent when the World Bank's International Finance Corporation (IFC) joined with a 2.5 percent share.

The critical impediment to development of this ore body (which had lain undiscovered for some thirty-five million years) was adequate financing. At initiation the project was budgeted at $1.14 billion. The partners were willing to commit a large portion of the investment, eventually ending up with about a 43 percent direct equity stake, but up to $700 million in additional financing was still needed. After initial efforts to organize an international loan consortium proved futile, the sponsors decided to try a project finance operation with a somewhat unusual twist.

The major portion of the required financing was raised through advance sales contracts (up to twelve years) that committed over three-fourths of Escondida's future copper output to refineries in Japan (50 percent), Germany (20 percent), and Finland (7 percent). These long-term contracts were then used to obtain import financing from The Export-Import Bank of Japan ($350 million), the Kreditanstalt für Wiederaufbau of Germany ($140 million), and Kansallis-Osake-Pankki of Finland ($47 million).

Only the German institution had significant previous experience with project finance deals, and providing import rather than export financing was a particularly unusual twist for government agencies. However, support from domestic refineries and the technical endorsement represented by IFC participation in the project helped facilitate final approval. This credit package constituted the key financial element enabling the project to proceed. Remaining financing came from subsequent negotiation of medium-term sales contracts with refineries in Spain, Korea, and a smelter to be built in the United States.

Controversy surrounded the Escondida project early on. Some initial criticism appears to have been related to the political opposition's attacks against the Pinochet government's economic policies, including agreements negotiated under its foreign investment law. The sheer size of this new project also raised the nation's still-sensitive concern about foreign ownership of its copper resource patrimony. Two crucial objections, however, related to Escondida's use of project finance techniques.

A first concern stemmed from the use of project finance to manage the political risk associated with natural resource projects. Loans backed by foreign governments based on long-term sales contracts give those governments an interest in the maintenance of copper exports to their refineries in order to assure successful completion of the contract. This overseas stake in the smooth performance of a mine can lead to foreign government pressures against any host government actions that might disrupt the mining and copper delivery operations. Chile was quite familiar with this and other aspects of corporate political risk management from its experience with the pioneering maneuvers of Kennecott Copper in the early 1970s, as discussed in the earlier chapter on Chile's history.

Some critics of Escondida's project finance methods implied that the sponsoring companies were mortgaging the mine's future for political risk reasons rather than making a full-faith commitment to investment in the country. While some risk management advantages do accrue from this and other project management decisions (such as involving the IFC as a participant), the level of direct equity funding by the sponsors and the persuasiveness of other motivations for using the project finance approach eventually moderated this criticism.

The second and more potentially damaging charge against the Escondida project is linked to the general desire of developing nations to create more value-added operations within their country. This objective is especially pronounced in nations largely dependent on foreign investors to exploit non-renewable natural resources. For Chile, the smelting and refining processes—and beyond those, the manufacture of final copper-based products—are production stages that national authorities would like to see take place within the country. Escondida's long-term sales contracts with foreign refiners seemed to move in the opposite direction, keeping these value-added stages of development out of the nation's reach.

Two economic realities motivated the Escondida strategy. First and foremost was the need to raise significant external financing in a climate that argued against creating additional debt exposure in Latin America. Escondida used its future output to raise the money needed to bring the mine into production. Without the long-term sales commitments, foreign refiners would have had no interest in supporting financing for the Escondida mine. Financing was the critical element in initiating this new copper project, and output commitments to foreign refiners were the necessary component in putting the financing package together.

Economic considerations also argued against including a Chile-based processing complex in the Escondida project. Constructing such a new facility would have added about $600 million to project costs at a time when the billion-dollar mine itself could not be brought on line without the assistance of foreign refiners. In addition, while incremental expansion and technological improvements at existing facilities occurred, a general excess in world smelting capacity had existed for nearly two decades, putting a damper on most plans for building "greenfield" installations that would mean large new additions to current processing capacity.

Chile already has four refineries and six smelters, most in need of improvements. With a number of new copper mines scheduled to open by the mid-1990s, output may exceed Chile's domestic processing capability by enough to make construction of a new facility cost-effective. CODELCO and five foreign firms undertook a joint pre-feasibility study for a smelting and refining complex. Both BHP and RTZ were members of this group, suggesting that Escondida's principal owners were willing to explore the viability of proposals for a new Chile-based facility.

The Escondida firms were not among the sponsors of a full $900,000 feasibility study for the proposed complex announced in April 1991; however, neither were the other pre-feasibility study firms, including CODELCO, so it would be difficult to single out Escondida for criticism. ENAMI took over direction of the project with four private firms from Belgium, Canada, Brazil, and Chile. ENAMI hoped to develop a $450 million facility, with private investors providing at least 85 percent of the construction and operating costs. The full feasibility study is expected to determine whether the venture's projected return on capital and its relationship to world refining capacity are sufficient to justify such an investment.

Technologically, Escondida is a state-of-the-art complex. While no single stage is a revolutionary breakthrough, the combination of various technologies will allow other producers to "go to school" on the project. High technology communications and a 146 kilometer access road connect the isolated mine location with coastal cities. Located in a desert region where precipitation averages sixty millimeters annually, the site will meet its water needs by developing an underground water source that an United Nations project was unable to exploit successfully in the early 1970s. The plant itself was largely constructed in modules and then taken by truck up to the mine, where work camp living conditions are harsh.

The isolated location also led to a new approach in labor relations. Unhampered by established work-rule restrictions, the mine will use an unusual twelve-hour, four-days-on/four-days-off labor shift designed to increase productivity and improve worker satisfaction with their living conditions. This arrangement allows workers the option of spending essentially one-half of each month living with their families in Antofagasta (the closest large city), about 160 kilometers away. The company provides transportation to and from the mine and supports new housing projects in the city, making units available to workers on a subsidized basis. This latter benefit is an important contribution in a country where providing additional housing is a national priority.

An underground pipeline will use gravity to move copper concentrate in a slurry the 164 kilometers from the mine to a new port complex that the company is building to avoid congestion at existing facilities. Tests will determine whether a significant portion of the pipeline water can be treated sufficiently to be used for agricultural or other applications, with environmentally sensitive filtration and diffusion methods used to disperse the remaining water offshore. Since the polluting potential of a smelter is not present, the disposal of tailings in a nearby natural basin and dust control and worker protection at the mine site appear to be the only other major challenges facing this project. A policy of meeting the stricter of world or Chilean environmental standards has been followed for the entire Escondida development project. Expenditures for the project's environmental program are estimated to exceed $3 million.

Managerial expertise, the type of technological know-how necessary to bring the many parts of this mining complex together on line on time, is also an important component of the project. While expenditures and interest charges accrue throughout the construction phase, no offsetting income revenue can be earned if any one of the major parts (water, mine, concentrator plant, pipeline, port) is delayed or functions improperly. In this project, management brought the facility into operation in December 1990, seven months ahead of schedule.

As in most business ventures, time is money. Savings in financial charges range between $5.5 and $6 million for each month the project finishes ahead of schedule, added to a monthly savings of at least $2 million in overhead expenses. Equally or more important is the income side of the ledger, since early operations generate significant early revenue flows. Escondida will have a cost structure of about forty-five cents a ton and a daily output near two million tons per day at full production. Assuming a copper price of ninety-five cents (which is below the average price level for 1990), the project's earnings could reach $1 million a day, roughly matching the daily expenditure tabs during much of its construction phase.

With an early completion date, total project cost estimates dipped to $825 million. A large cost reduction resulted from the decision not to build a new power plant for use by both the mine and port facilities. The local electrical distributor, drawing upon the recent expansion of a coal-fired plant, offered sufficient power at competitive rates. This decision saved Escondida from building excess capacity into a new plant that could assure them sufficient future power, while simultaneously almost doubling customer usage of the local power network, helping to finance its recent expansion.

Other benefits flow from both the construction and production phases of Escondida's operations. Although some local firms have foreign corporate affiliations, Chilean contractors were awarded all but one specialty contract on a competitive bid basis. About 90 percent of the engineering work for Escondida was done in the country, and Chilean companies provided over one-half the fabricated items used in the project. In another tribute to local productivity, Escondida achieved the goal of becoming "the world's most efficient stripper" (measured in tons per unit of electric shovel capacity), removing 325,000 tons per day of overburden from the mine's copper deposit. Around 4,300 workers were involved during the peak of Escondida's construction efforts, and the complex will provide employment for about 1,000 permanent employees.

For its part, the Chilean government provided a sufficiently stable political and economic climate, even during a governmental transition which placed some early skeptics toward the project in positions of public authority. Escondida's foreign investment agreement includes the standard list of guarantees, the most important of which are probably the national treatment principle, the right to export, a twenty-year fixed taxation rate of 49.5 percent, and the use of an offshore account (managed by the Industrial Bank of Japan as trustee for the project's lenders) to pay authorized expenditures with the proceeds from export sales. Government support made the Escondida project feasible, and its foreign investors brought it to reality. The new copper giant will be active in Chile for many years to come.[12]

Chile's Broadening Base in Copper

Chile is poised to increase its copper production and broaden its base of copper producers in the early 1990s. In addition to the opening of Escondida and the expansion of Disputada, an array of other large and medium-size ventures will come on line with a mixture of foreign and local private ownership. These projects bring a wide variety of investors from different regions of the world, some introducing innovative techniques and all mobilizing the capital resources needed to turn Chile's copper resource potential into expanded output and exports.

Preparations for developing one of the newest and largest of these mines are being carried forward by Phelps Dodge, a U.S. company that has operated Compañía Minera Ojos del Salado in Chile since 1978. The firm's existing production from two small mines amounts to about 11,000 tons of fine copper annually, but it is about to develop what may be one of the country's four or five largest copper deposits, discovered at La Candelaria in 1987. Having already risked $18 million on exploration and feasibility studies at the site, the company estimates development costs for the first stage at around $500 million for a facility projected to yield approximately 100,000 tons per year. The firm expects to provide jobs directly for some 700 people after the mine comes on line, with indirect employment effects reaching about three times that figure. Some problems concerning legal rights to regions within the deposit area were resolved in mid-1991 and Sumitomo of Japan became a joint venture partner at 20 percent of the project.

Compañía Minera Mantos Blancos produces an equivalent level of copper after completing its latest round of improvements, which cost $25 million; the company had already invested nearly triple that amount in earlier expansion projects. Mantos Blancos is a complex that encompasses open pit and underground mines along with several different processing plants. Anglo-

American Corporation of South Africa, which opened its Chilean operations in 1980, is the majority owner of the company, holding over two-thirds of its shares.

The International Finance Corporation was an early participant in expansion of the Mantos Blancos mine and owned slightly over 15 percent of the firm. In June 1990 the IFC began a process of selling off its stake by offering shares equivalent to 1 percent of Mantos Blancos on Santiago's public stock market. The IFC was pursuing a two-fold goal. By selling its holdings in a successful project, the institution could reinvest its funds in other worthy undertakings. Rather than selling large block shares to a few major investors, however, the IFC sought to complete the sale in a way that also helped build shareholdings on Chile's small stock exchange. The IFC finished selling its shares in December 1990 for a total exceeding $30 million.[13]

Cominco of Canada outbid Anglo-American, a firm with whom it participates in several Chilean mining projects, when state-run ENAMI sold 90 percent of its rights to a copper deposit located high in the Andes at Quebrada Blanca. Superior Oil had invested some $35 million in exploring this deposit before abandoning it in the early 1980s in a dispute with ENAMI. Based on results from $8 million of new exploratory studies, Cominco raised its early output estimates and expects to produce up to 75,000 tons annually from the operation, projected to begin in 1994. Some of the mining process will be experimental since the facility will be the world's highest altitude heap leaching operation for copper, which may affect the bacteria used in a new heaping column procedure. The project will use a process patented by a local copper company, Sociedad Minera Pudahuel. Cominco's investment may involve around $300 million.

A new foreign investor in Chilean copper is Outokumpu, a multinational mining conglomerate majority-owned by the government of Finland. This firm invented "flash furnace" technology that can increase a facility's copper processing capacity. Utilized in over thirty-five countries, the process experienced some initial difficulties when first installed in Chile at CODELCO's Chuquicamata complex, but performance improved and it was chosen for use in Disputada's smelter expansion as well. Outokumpu Engineering has formed a small joint venture with a Chilean engineering firm to conduct local activities that might open the door for future exports of Chilean engineering services to Outokumpu's other foreign projects.

Outokumpu is the world's second leading copper manufacturing conglomerate. The company is vertically integrated but not well balanced among its various components. Possessing over 450,000 tons per year of copper manufacturing capacity, the firm's refining capability is 100,000 tons annually while its mines yield only 50,000 tons of copper each year. The corporation's large existing manufacturing capacity and its belief that fabrication should take place near major consumer markets limits its interest in Chile as a copper processing site. On the other hand, its interest in Chile's copper reserves is obvious.

Outokumpu's first foray into Chilean copper mining provided a lesson in political risk. The firm was to own 25 percent of a joint venture with Río Algom of Canada to acquire and develop the Cerro Colorado copper deposit. The project would cost $240 million and employ approximately 600 people to produce up to 60,000 tons of copper annually. In early 1986, shortly after initial financing arrangements appeared complete, the project was paralyzed by Outokumpu's decision to withdraw under pressure from Finnish labor and political groups. Student organizations and some political opponents of the Pinochet regime in Chile had urged sympathizers in Finland not to support the military government's economic policies, particularly regarding copper mining. They warned that Chile's mining laws would be among the first statutes revised by a successor democratic government. Politically controlled Outokumpu withdrew from the Cerro Colorado project and did not reactivate its direct investment plans in Chile until the country's transition to democracy.

The corporation's first major direct investment in Chile is taking place at the Zaldívar mine, located near La Escondida at a site whose ownership passed from Utah to Pudahuel before being acquired by Outokumpu for about $25 million. The use of Chapter XIX funding reduced the company's effective cost in this transaction, probably by several million dollars. Projections called for an investment of some $100 million (and perhaps much more if flotation facilities are added) for a facility that could yield about 40,000 tons of fine copper annually with a direct employment of some 600 people. The mine's output will all be exported to Outokumpu's own refineries located around the world, generating around $90 million in annual export sales.

A second copper project involving Outokumpu is Minera El Lince where the company holds 15 percent of a nearly $50 million project slated to produce about 20,000 tons per year. Another 25 percent is owned by a Chilean firm, Compañía Minera Carolina de Michilla (controlled by the local Luksic group) which operates a nearby copper mine. Chemical Bank supplied funding which gave it a 60 percent share in the project, with the reported expectation that the two mining partners will take over full control when the bank can profitably withdraw from the project under Chapter XIX regulations. A third copper project of roughly the same size is being undertaken by Outokumpu and local Minera Cardoen to exploit the Amolanas deposit. Overall, Outokumpu has announced plans to invest up to $500 million in various Chilean projects during the 1990s.[14]

Another interesting joint venture project that involves both Chapter XIX financing and a mixture of foreign and local investors is the Pelambres copper deposit. Held in an undeveloped state by local investors for many years, the site was bought in 1981 for about $25 million by Anaconda South America, the offspring of the company that had owned Chuquicamata before its expropriation.

The firm spent over $50 million studying the ore body before policy changes at its parent firm, Atlantic Richfield, led to a sale of the property for $10 million to the Luksic group.

The new Chilean owners turned to Midland Bank to help finance the deposit's development. As discussed in another chapter, this British bank had acquired a substantial amount of Chilean debt when it purchased Crocker National Bank in California. Chile's Central Bank approved the use of a Chapter XIX debt-to-equity swap to finance the project, with Midland expected to hold an 80 percent share while contributing over $50 million to develop Pelambres. In August, 1990 Lucky Goldstar of Korea announced that it would join the project, investing $30 million for a 40 percent share, equal to Midland's reduced participation. This investment is one of the largest by a Korean firm in Chile and adds a new marketing dimension to the project, with Lucky Goldstar planning to export about 80 percent of the mine's output to Korea where it operates refineries. Scheduled to come on line in 1992, this operation should employ at least 500 people and produce around 20,000 tons of copper concentrate annually.

An additional facet of this project and other ventures involving the Luksic group is the relationship between these mining interests and the group's ownership of Manufacturas de Cobre (MADECO), Chile's largest copper manufacturer. The firm plays a key role in discussions of how to increase local value-added content through the fabrication of copper-related products. In an interesting twist that shows the internationalization pressures on businesses, MADECO and CODELCO in 1987 entered into a joint venture (the Beijing–Santiago Copper Tube Company) with the Chinese government to become a major producer of tubing in that country. The plant began operations in 1989, but initial results proved disappointing and the Chilean partners reduced their combined ownership from 50 percent to 25 percent in May 1991.

Citibank (U.S.) is using Chapter XIX to convert some of its Chilean debt into a partnership with Shell (Dutch/U.K.) on a 40/60 basis to fund a $20 million project to develop the Las Luces copper deposit into a mine producing about 7,000 tons of copper per year. Shell also is involved in a partnership with Chevron (U.S.) and Falconbridge (Canada) in an equally split venture to develop the Collahuasi copper and silver deposit. This mine, originally a joint project between Falconbridge and Superior Oil, will require an expenditure of around $45 million to produce up to 35,000 tons of fine copper annually by 1992. Another deposit at Ivan y Zar is being developed by Rayrock Resources of Canada, with an expenditure of $25 million expected to yield some 13,000 tons per year.

Other mining operations will provide still more sources of copper production for Chile. Some gold mine operations, most notably the El Indio facility discussed in the next section, produce a substantial quantity of copper along with their precious metals. A number of small local copper producers have also been encouraged through the efforts of state-owned Empresa Nacional de Minería (ENAMI), which operates refineries in Chile whose process agreements cover the small miners' output and have offered price support programs during periods of low world copper prices. Foreign investment is clearly the driving force behind Chile's current copper expansion, however, and the variety of new investors is bringing a mix of strengths and skills that will help fortify Chile's leading position in world copper markets.

GOLD AND SILVER MINING

Chile was not among the Spanish conquistadors' primary early targets in their search for the New World's gold and silver, although evidence suggests limited diggings both before and during the first Spanish expeditions. A fledgling boom in the mining of precious metals, brought on by high prices during the 1930s, was snuffed out by World War II and the advent of fixed gold prices. Most significant Chilean gold mines eventually closed and no major new explorations were undertaken. Nevertheless, despite this lack of commitment to direct mining of gold and silver, Chile still produced substantial quantities of both metals, principally as by-products of the smelting processes at its huge copper mines.

Contemporary Chilean production of precious metals reflects the country's newly diversified mining structure. Copper mining still yields large quantities of both gold and silver. In addition, foreign investors have established two large gold mines that substantially increase the country's output, while both local and foreign companies are developing a number of medium-size mines that will also add to total output. Finally, state-run programs encourage numerous small mining and panning operations that contribute to national employment goals as well as production totals. Overall, major gold mines provide about two-thirds of Chile's output, while nearly one-quarter is a by-product of copper mining and the rest comes from small operations. Approximately 70 percent of the country's silver stems from copper-related enterprises with the remainder coming from both gold and silver mines.

In 1989, Chile ranked about eighth in world gold and silver production, but its position in both metals is expected to improve by the turn of the century. Gold production increased 27 percent in volume and 73 percent in export value between 1984 and 1989. The mineral resources are located primarily in the country's northern region and, to a lesser extent, in some southern zones. Economic development associated with expanded mining operations thus promotes Chile's regional development goals of decentralizing the economic activities now concentrated in the area around Santiago.

Foreign investment is playing a major role in the expansion of precious metal mining in Chile. Investors are backing their exploration and production expertise with the international fund-raising capabilities needed to underwrite new projects. In most cases, the direct involvement of foreign investors appears essential to the risky and enormously expensive business of turning potential mineral resources into productive mining operations.

The Pioneering Prospector—El Indio

A contemporary gold rush began in Chile in the late 1970s, sparked by confirmation of a rich ore deposit at the El Indio site located high in the country's north central Andes. This mine's development played an important role in stimulating gold exploration and production by proving the region's mineral potential and drawing in competing firms that feared getting locked out of a new supply source. Equally significant from the political and business standpoint was the demonstration effect El Indio provided through the successful negotiation of a foreign investment contract that set important precedents for new natural resource investments. On the level of project analysis, multiple changes in the mine's foreign ownership demonstrate how differential corporate strengths and operating philosophies can affect an investment over time.

The rise in gold prices around 1972 renewed interest in exploration efforts worldwide, but Chile's meager record as a gold producer and its serious political and economic turmoil left the country off most short lists of attractive exploration targets. By 1975, however, the management of St. Joe Minerals, a firm with prior experience in Chile, decided to send a geologist to assess possible gold prospects. He focused on a remote location where prospectors, "grubstaked" by entrepreneurs in the coastal town of La Serena, were hand-sorting ore from shallow diggings and carrying it down the rugged mountain by backpack and mules to the government's purchasing agency.

Despite the imposing challenges presented by the site's location, the geologist's initial assessment of the ore deposit led the company to begin serious exploration efforts, arranging to work with local families who held property rights in the region. Seventeen percent of El Indio still belongs to early family owners who live in La Serena. Simultaneous negotiations began with the government on a path-breaking foreign investment agreement under D.L. 600, leading to the signing of the first such contract in 1977, by which time the company had already invested approximately $6 million in exploration. Not until late 1978, after expenditures reached almost $10 million, did ore measurements clearly justify a major investment to develop the site.

The commitment of substantial risk capital for exploration purposes is one benefit provided by St. Joe Minerals that was unavailable from the deposit's local owners. In general, exploration costs must be borne by large mining concerns with the resources to self-finance their efforts, since banks and other traditional financial institutions are reluctant to loan money for projects which are not successfully past the exploration stage. The risk simply appears too great when an average of nine out of ten exploration prospects turn out unsatisfactory.

Word spread quickly that St. Joe was pursuing a promising discovery in Chile, attracting attention in the world's gold mining community. When the company successfully concluded negotiations on a precedent-setting foreign investment agreement, interest picked up further. The contract was made between the company and the government of Chile, giving it the strongest legal status and requiring mutual agreement for any significant changes. Initial conditions extended for a 30-year period, and the company was guaranteed national treatment and rights to overseas sales and foreign exchange.

International firms began sending teams to explore other Chilean sites and to reassess gold mines abandoned in earlier eras. This interest paid off with a rush of new gold discoveries in the 1980–82 period. By this time, St. Joe had invested over $200 million at El Indio in basic infrastructure (work camp, roads, power lines, etc.), mining equipment, and processing facilities. Only after this capital had been sunk could the company start production at the end of 1981 and begin recovering its investment.

St. Joe Minerals was a traditional mining company with expertise in exploration and new discoveries. In 1982 the firm was acquired by Fluor Corporation, a major international engineering firm which had done some of the early construction work at El Indio. Fluor's corporate expansion plans ran into trouble, however, when the oil market went flat a couple of years later. The firm grouped a number of its holdings together to form St. Joe Gold Corporation, which was put out for selected bids in 1987. The Bond Group from Australia came in with a preemptive bid of over $500 million. Adding some of its own properties, the corporation formed Bond International Gold (BIG).

BIG infused El Indio with a new dynamism that had been lacking after Fluor encountered financial pressures. As with their concurrent investment in Chile's telephone company, the Bond Group quickly initiated major investment and expansion plans, drawing on its financing expertise and bringing in some additional process technology. By the end of 1989, El Indio had opened new mines, installed plants and processing facilities, and more than doubled its capacity—treating 2,650 tons of regular ore per day along with an additional 1,000 tons of lower grade ore processed through a heap leaching method. This expansion raised total investment in the project to over $300 million.

The Bond Group ran into serious international financial pressures, however, and its two Chilean investments proved to be among its most easily marketable assets, leading to the sale of both. El Indio was purchased in 1989 by LAC Minerals of Canada, which spent $379 million to purchase the Bond Group's majority ownership of BIG along with some additional shares. These acquisitions gave LAC 65 percent equity control and in the process effectively doubled the size of its own operations. Although LAC had recently begun evaluating several smaller Chilean deposits of zinc, silver, and gold, it lacked significant overseas experience, operating sites only in Canada, the United States, and Uruguay.

The new owners put a temporary hold on parts of BIG's plans for El Indio until explorations proved the existence of sufficient additional reserves to justify further expansion. BIG's aggressiveness had outrun reserves at some of the company's other investment locations, leaving new processing facilities idle when the ore bodies played out. LAC soon embarked on continued project improvement, however, committing another $23 million to add processing facilities and expand capacity to 3,000 tons per day. In line with a traditional mining company's outlook, the firm also devotes $10 million annually to an accelerated exploration program to seek new reserves. Further expansion, especially at the nearby Tambo deposit site, could make El Indio one of the hemisphere's biggest gold producers.

This tale of ownership change reveals some of the distinctive characteristics and relative strengths and weaknesses of different foreign investors and their operational strategies. The traditional mining companies tended to operate with a relatively conservative long-term outlook, committing risk capital to finance explorations based on their internal expertise, but waiting to commit financing for processing facilities until the move was clearly justified by proven reserves. These firms generally prefer steady development, resisting the temptation to expand too rapidly in good times or contract too severely in bad times.

The Fluor Corporation provided engineering and construction expertise for expanding the mine's production facilities, but did not possess the internal mining experience to maintain a priority commitment to its new mining ventures when world oil conditions put a financial squeeze on the parent company's operations. The Bond Group injected a financial dynamism that may have been necessary to regain the project's forward momentum, but it did not possess the long-term outlook or operational mining expertise needed to assure stable development. LAC offers a mining firm's capabilities and perspective, but lacked the international experience which could have led it to be the initial pioneering prospector in post-Allende Chile.

In El Indio's case, the progression of owners appears to have been a rather fortunately timed series of matching project needs and corporate expertise. This result was produced through the mechanism of market forces rather than regulatory choices. In 1990, the El Indio complex of three underground and five open pit mines produced about one-third of Chile's gold output (approximately 200,000 ounces or roughly 6 tons) as well as an associated 1.5 million ounces of silver and 30,000 tons of copper. The enterprise annually exports ore valued between $120 million and $150 million. Over 1,500 workers are directly employed at the facilities, and service contracts provide additional indirect jobs. Among the mine's innovations are a flotation process that can attain 97 percent recovery on top grade ores and the use of a heap leaching process for gold recovery at high altitudes.

Two other El Indio processes also merit special mention as useful technological adaptations to local conditions. The development of a roasting process for Chile's high-arsenic content ores allows on-site removal of arsenic and antimony. Rather than facing a disposal problem with these undesirable elements, the company generates a saleable by-product, arsenic trioxide, that can be used as a wood preserver. In 1988, the firm produced about 8,000 metric tons, using the parent firm's overseas marketing connections to export most of it to the United States.

An automated filtering process reduces the water content of the mine's waste tailings, allowing direct recycling of most mill process waters and placement of the dry tailings in a tight valley location. This process saves about two-thirds of the initial construction costs for a traditional tailings dam while also avoiding possible environmental problems due to seepage or leakage. (Operating costs on the dry tailings process run about ten times higher than maintenance on a typical tailings dam, however.)

Foreign investors in the El Indio mine provided initial exploration capital as well as the subsequent financing and technological expertise needed to turn a few small diggings, operated with hand tools and pack mules, into a modern mining complex that produces roughly one-third of Chile's gold output. This leading position is being challenged as a result of the company's own success, however. El Indio's demonstration effect of both the country's mineral potential and the negotiation of a viable political-economic framework for natural resource contracts led to a wave of new investment projects that are about to enter into operation.

Chile's Golden Future—La Coipa

The major challenger to El Indio's preeminence among Chile's gold producers is the La Coipa complex, owned by Minera Mantos de Oro. This project is sometimes referred to as the Escondida of the gold sector due to the size and richness of its deposit. Production over the first couple years should exceed 6 tons of gold and 500 tons of silver annually. Feasibility studies project that the mine could produce approximately 65 tons of gold and 4,450 tons of silver over a twelve-year mine life. This output will help boost Chile's standing in world production of these precious metals.

La Coipa's history illustrates the organizational, financial, and technological contributions that foreign investors can make to a nation's development. However, the story also shows that not all foreign investors succeed. Years can pass with only halting steps toward project development before the right combination of circumstances and resources permits the full realization of a project's potential.

The first serious attempt to evaluate La Coipa's deposits was made at the end of the 1970s by the large multinational mining firm Consolidated Gold Fields PLC, based in the United Kingdom and South Africa. Despite its size and presumed power, and perhaps due to its reportedly aggressive tactics, the corporation could not reach an agreement with a number of local owners of the ore body. For nearly eight years the project's development was blocked by sometimes bitter legal disputes.

A young Brazilian entrepreneur who was the major shareholder of Canadian-based TVX Mining Corporation paid approximately $30 million to a Gold Field subsidiary for their rights to the deposit in 1987. He also managed to acquire the remaining rights from several local banks and a variety of small individual claimants, thereby consolidating all the various claims for a total of about $60 million. Although he had achieved unified control over the deposit, this entrepreneur had difficulty obtaining the additional financing needed to develop the project. Both La Coipa's contentious legal history and the Brazilian's lack of a proven track record on this type of major project reportedly worked against him with traditional financial institutions.

Financing finally came from Placer Dome of Canada, an important mining firm and one of the world's leading gold producers. Placer's own explorations in Chile since the mid-1970s had not yielded any successful projects. During the late 1980s, Placer's management was considering using some of its cash to become a type of mining bank, utilizing its internal expertise to evaluate projects that it would finance for a profit without assuming ownership or managerial control. The corporation ultimately discarded this approach, reverting to traditional mining activities, but in the meantime they agreed to provide a $40 million loan to TVX. The terms were extremely expensive, however, reportedly requiring repayment of $60 million plus additional interest within a year.

Even after this financial infusion, La Coipa's owner was unable to complete construction of a 1,000 ton-per-day processing plant before funding was exhausted, and it became clear that loan repayment conditions could not be met. To solve both problems, TVX and Placer formed Mantos de Oro to complete La Coipa's development, with Placer essentially converting the loan obligations into a 50 percent interest in the joint venture. Placer's overall position and a small additional stake in TVX itself placed it in effective managerial control of the project. Placer combined financing, technology, and managerial expertise with TVX's ownership of the deposit and initial development to bring the project to a production take-off point.

A small (1,000 metric tons) processing plant was established to train personnel, gain experience with the ore body, and provide some capital (about $30 million) from initial output to help fund further expansion. The second stage of development, which includes a plant with 15,000 metric tons capacity, will be financed primarily by an internationally syndicated bank loan of $250 million, raising total project investment to approximately $400 million.

The severity of the financial obstacles blocking La Coipa's development can be seen in the year-long negotiations required to arrange this second-stage funding, which was ultimately dependent on Placer's agreement to guarantee the loans directly. Chile's foreign debt situation precluded local enterprises from such financing options and even multinational corporations such as TVX lacked the leverage to put together a large enough package. Only direct managerial control by a major foreign investor experienced in the field and willing to mortgage parent company assets could generate the international financial backing necessary to develop La Coipa's untapped potential into Chile's largest gold and silver producer.

La Coipa's operations will reflect a range of technological and managerial innovations. The processing plant will be one of the largest in the world, with its output from La Coipa's open pit mines matching the production of many other facilities that use higher grade ore from underground mines. Its reverbatory furnace will capture another value-added stage in local gold production by turning out dore bars that can be delivered to nearly any refinery in the world. The fresh water requirement was reduced by 60 percent. A belt filter system will allow recapture and reuse of the facility's water while reducing the moisture content of conventional wet tailings by about one-half, leaving them more environmentally safe and easier to store. Placer follows the same worldwide environmental policies at La Coipa that it implements at its facilities elsewhere, often taking it beyond Chile's current requirements. The company's long-term expectation is that Chile will eventually adopt environmental legislation based on tighter world standards.

The experienced management of a company such as Placer is necessary to bring the many parts of this complex project on line on time, in order to begin generating production revenues to repay the large debt burden that would otherwise cause significant cost overruns. Improvements in labor conditions are also being implemented, including use of the two-shift, four-days-on/four-days-off system. Permanent employment is expected to reach 450 people. With company-provided transportation, this approach permits workers to live half of the time in towns such as Copiapó, away from the mine site where the temperature can drop to 25 degrees below zero at night. Housing and school assistance in the community, and roads, power lines, and living facilities at the mine site constitute some of the related physical infrastructure improvements associated with La Coipa's development.

Medium and Small Producers

Adverse conditions abound at the Choquelimpie gold mine in the northern Andes near Chile's border with Bolivia. Said to be the highest mine in the world, the venture uses heap leach methods to extract gold from low-grade ores, producing approximately 90,000 ounces in 1989, its first year of full operation. In contrast to El Indio and La Coipa, the area's proven reserves are small, perhaps enough for four to five years of operation. This limitation, coupled with the problems of pioneering high-altitude mining, gives rise to a strategy whereby investors hedge their commitment by keeping initial project expenditures to a minimum—a start-up cost of around $30 million added to the $8 million initial purchase price.

The venture, Minera Vilacollo, is jointly owned by the Dutch/U.K. Shell Group (42 percent), Canadian Westfield Minerals (35 percent), and U.S. Citibank (23 percent). Citibank set a precedent by gaining Central Bank approval to use Chile's Chapter XIX debt-to-equity swap mechanism to finance its share of the venture—the first time a bank had obtained permission to use its own debt for an investment in the country's mining sector. Vilacollo relies on subcontractors for functions such as earthmoving, directly employing fewer workers at the site than other firms. Labor conditions are a concern when working at this altitude, and negotiations have covered related health care and labor shift issues. Living quarters were built an hour's drive away at 3,500 meters above sea level, over 1,200 meters below the mine site.

The mine's crushing plant was designed to accommodate expansion and improvements if further reserves are located by the project's $2 million exploration program. Another unusual feature of the project is that mining takes place within a nature reserve, requiring exceptional care with elements such as the cyanide used in the heap leaching process. Shell is seeking exploration contracts from the government in other areas of the country and is counting on its performance in this venture to show that it is up to the environmental challenge.

Anglo-American (South Africa), Cominco (Canada), and Chemical Bank (U.S.) have combined to develop the Marte gold deposit, and the firms also conduct related explorations at nearby sites. Choosing a somewhat different route, Homestake (U.S.) is operating the El Hueso open pit mine under a ten-year lease from CODELCO, which had spent $20 million to develop the mine in mid-1987. Other substantial new investments have been made in medium-size gold ventures by foreign corporations including Chevron (U.S.), Dayton (Canada), Niugini (Australia), and Bridger (Canada) and Cluff (U.K.). Some deposits have changed owners several times during the past decade. As long as the Chilean economy remains open, this trend can be expected to continue as marketplace forces match the evolution of each project with the changing needs and capabilities of global enterprises.

A final aspect of Chile's precious metals industry arises from the National Gold Employment Plan, adopted during the recession of the early 1980s. This government program invested over $5 million between 1984 and 1987 to set up 160 panning operations, which employ more than 10,000 people and produce about 2,000 kilos of gold annually. The program's indirect stimulation of other small panning and mining operations is estimated to contribute at least an equal amount of additional gold production. This initiative is sponsored by state-run Empresa Nacional de Minería (ENAMI).

OTHER MINERAL RESOURCES

Chile is the world's largest producer and exporter of potassium nitrate and sodium nitrate and ranks among the top ten producers of molybdenum, rhenium, lithium, iodine, boron, and selenium. Among the other resources found in this mineral-rich country are iron, manganese, zinc, lead, calcium carbonate, sodium chloride, and sulfur. Foreign investors play no role in the production of some of these minerals. In other instances, privatization of state-owned enterprises introduced multiple foreign investors into certain businesses, along with employees and other local private shareholders, but did not change the essential national character or management of those corporations.

One publicly held company where this restructuring occurred is Compañía de Acero del Pacífico (CAP), the country's third-largest corporation whose two largest shareholder groups are its workers (30.5 percent) and an investment company reportedly controlled by the Swiss Schmidheiny group (just over 29 percent). A CAP subsidiary is the country's sole producer of iron ore and pellets; another subsidiary is responsible for over 90 percent of the nation's steel output, supplying virtually all domestic needs. A similar situation exists in Sociedad Química y Minera de Chile (SOQUIMICH), the world's largest producer of sodium nitrate, potash nitrate, and iodine. Nitrates, of course, were the key mineral resource that originally drew British multinational corporations into Chile's mining sector at the opening of the twentieth century.

An interesting dimension to these examples is that CAP and SOQUIMICH are among the Chilean enterprises most often cited as firms on the verge of becoming multinational corporations themselves. Both engage in major export activities and could expand their overseas marketing connections and benefit from broader experience in foreign production methods. These firms may even seek direct access to U.S. capital markets, following the pioneering move by Compañía de Teléfonos de Chile (CTC) to gain a listing on the New York Stock Exchange. SOQUIMICH signed a 1988 joint venture agreement with one of its investors, Israel Chemicals, aimed at establishing a new production facility in Chile. CAP is said to be exploring cooperative plans, including possible ventures outside the country with Mitsubishi of Japan, a long-time purchaser of its iron ore products who also became a 6.2 percent equity shareholder in the company.[15]

Two recent instances of direct foreign corporate investment in Chilean minerals can be found in the areas of lithium and calcium carbonate. The first case is important because it provides insights into the dynamics of strategic investment decisions within a major multinational corporation. The second example illustrates an investor's vertical growth strategy from mining and production to related construction activities, with an opening to international as well as domestic markets for the product.

A Change in Plans—The AMAX Story

AMAX had visited prospective minerals sites and operated a metals trading office in Chile during the 1960s, but the company was not a significant foreign investor. In an unusual move for the firm, which normally establishes overseas facilities only in connection with a specific project, an AMAX exploration office was opened in Chile in 1979 to evaluate opportunities presented by the country's new foreign investment and mining policies. Among the early prospects was a site in the northern Salar de Atacama desert that might yield lithium carbonate along with potassium chloride, potassium sulfate, and boric acid.

AMAX approached Chile's Corporación de Fomento de la Producción (CORFO) for direct negotiations on developing the site, but had to wait nearly four years for the project to be put out for public bids. After winning the right to pursue the project, the company had to negotiate for fifteen months to reach an agreement with CORFO, which was to become a 25 percent partner in the joint venture, named Compañía Minera Salar de Atacama (Minsal). A private Chilean firm, Molymet, also joined Minsal with a 11.25 percent share, leaving AMAX with 63.75 percent.

A three-year feasibility study begun in 1986 yielded very favorable results. The production process would involve pumping brine from wells into evaporation ponds, where the desert sun would produce a solution treated in processing plants to remove the various mineral products. The site proved to have desirable mineral concentrations several times higher than other global production locations as well as ideal solar radiation conditions. Estimates have shown that Minsal could be the lowest cost producer in the world.

The project was essentially designed for exports, although about one-fifth of the potassium output might be used to supply most of Chile's domestic needs. Minsal's lithium production would increase world supply by nearly 50 percent while making Chile the preeminent producer and exporter. This abrupt increase could deflate product prices since demand generally tracks world economic growth. The international market is dominated by two U.S. firms, Lithium Corporation of America (LITHCO) and Cyprus Foote Minerals, both of which produce at U.S. locations. Cyprus Foote, however, also has an operation in Chile, having established Sociedad Chilena del Litio (SCL) at another Atacama location prior to the Minsal project.

In fact, the Minsal negotiations followed the pattern set by the SCL venture.

After winning a public bid in 1975, SCL was established as a joint venture between majority owner Cyprus-Foote and CORFO. The government agency progressively sold its shares, ending its participation after SCL's government-authorized monopoly on lithium production in Chile expired in 1988. The termination of this sole producer agreement, which had perhaps been necessary to attract the foreign company into a risky Chilean investment in the mid-1970s, opened the door to the possibility of increased competition from the Minsal project.

Positive Minsal study results led the partners to initiate a decision timetable in 1989–90 regarding their continued participation in the project, the key elements of which were financial commitments to full development. A financing package of nearly $400 million was needed to underwrite the project, probably through a combination of foreign and local bank loans, supplier credits and equity investments. Outside creditors were unwilling to commit to the project until they knew the level of direct equity involvement by the partners. The main variable appeared to be CORFO, which had been exempt from initial spending until expenditures from the other two partners amounted to $12 million, a figure that was soon to be reached. A possible $80 million equity formula would set CORFO's proportional share of project financing at $20 million, a steep commitment for a new democratic government that was straining to find funding for a range of social programs.

In reality, an internal shift in AMAX's global business strategy placed a prior hold on final decisions. The parent company decided to refocus its financial and management resources, concentrating on proven core businesses involving aluminum, coal, oil and gas, and gold. The potash division that included Minsal was among the divisions slated to be sold or drastically cut back. Aluminum production was the key element in this revised strategy, since it generated about 80 percent of corporate income, and the company had just invested around $1.4 billion in two new Canadian aluminum facilities.

AMAX wanted to remove itself from the Minsal venture in a way that did not damage the fledgling project. The firm also wanted to maintain good relations with the Chilean government since it might continue to pursue other mining interests in the country, particularly in relation to gold mining. AMAX consulted with its partners and handled the announcement of its revised plans cautiously, emphasizing that changed corporate strategy rather than questions about the viability of the project were prompting its withdrawal.

Feelers were put out to selected companies, with media reports citing LITHCO, Cyprus Foote, U.S. Borax, BHP of Australia, and SOQUIMICH as potentially interested parties. LITHCO had lost to AMAX in initial bidding for the Minsal site and was negotiating with Bolivia to develop lithium reserves in that country. Cyprus Foote could add Minsal to its already expanding Chilean production, thereby becoming the clearly dominant producer in the industry. Possible SOQUIMICH interest in the project was said to arise primarily from the firm's possible use of potassium products included in the projected Minsal output.[16]

It is difficult to see how Chile can lose under most likely scenarios for Minsal's future development, although apprehension over concentrated market power would favor multiple domestic producers rather than a Cyprus Foote dominance. If Minsal's development is delayed too long, projects in Bolivia and Argentina may create further output adding to excess supply conditions, but Minsal's advantages should still make it the market's lowest cost producer. These conditions seem to indicate that a production shift could lower output at U.S. facilities in line with increases at lower-cost Chilean sites as long as competition is maintained and import restrictions are not imposed in consumer countries.

Despite its announced intention to sell its majority stake in Minsal, AMAX recommended to its Chilean partner in October 1991 that they proceed with the first $150 million development stage of the project, leading CORFO's general manager to express satisfaction with AMAX's actions which demonstrated continued confidence in both Minsal and in Chile's investment climate. While the full tale has yet to be told, the AMAX story thus appears to be that of a transitory investor who helped stimulate greater competition and prove the viability of a local project before deciding to move on through a responsible phase-out process under the dictates of its own global corporate strategy.[17]

From Mining to Production for Construction—Cemento Melón

Chile is a growing producer of calcium carbonate, the basic ingredient for cement. Cement is one of those commodities that is so common as to escape normal notice, yet so fundamental to a nation's growth that it spans industrial divisions from mining to manufacturing to construction services and is treated as a strategic industry in many countries. About two-thirds of Chile's calcium carbonate output goes into the production of cement, a field dominated by one local and two foreign firms. Most remaining calcium carbonate production is converted to lime for use as a leaching agent in mining or in agricultural fertilizers. A few large firms such as CODELCO operate their own calcium carbonate mines to supply internal needs, while some two dozen small producers also exist in the country's northern and central regions.

Cemento Melón was created in 1906 by Chilean entrepreneurs and began operations two years later. The company was nationalized by the Allende government and operated as a part of CORFO from 1971 to 1979. When the cement industry was reprivatized, a Chilean group took over some new facilities under the name Cemento Bío Bío; Cemento Polpaico was purchased by the Holderbank of Switzerland, which is associated with the Schmidheiny group; and Cemento Melón became part of Blue Circle Industries of Great Britain.

Blue Circle bid over $40 million for 82 percent of the enterprise in 1979, subsequently purchasing enough additional shares to own over 97 percent of the firm.

Blue Circle studied Cemento Melón's mix of old and new facilities and quickly adopted a $65 million expansion and modernization campaign that nearly doubled production capacity. Chile was at that time enjoying an economic boom during which construction activity grew at a frenetic pace. When the 1982 recession hit soon afterwards, cement production dropped nearly in half and the company's healthy profit returns dipped into the red. While trying to control overall expenditures, the company maintained its expansion commitment in the belief that overall growth would soon return.

One important expansion move begun in 1981 was the establishment of Premix, a ready-mix concrete company. Although a major world producer of cement, Blue Circle had failed to move into the ready-mix segment of the business in its home country (Great Britain), a forward integration step that became more difficult to accomplish as time went on. By 1988 Premix had gained a solid position with about one-third of the relevant Chilean market. Blue Circle also introduced new technological improvements in Cemento Melón's basic operations. For example, a half-million dollars was spent to install sonic nozzles in the gas conditioning tower (between the kiln and the electrostatic filter) as part of an operation that increased kiln efficiency by over one-quarter while also reducing dust problems.

Global cement production is overwhelmingly devoted to the domestic market and generally grows (or contracts) in line with GDP. This characteristic can yield steady if relatively unexciting growth over time, but aggregate figures are likely to mask cyclical swings in the construction industry that dictate a firm's short-term production and profitability levels. In order to enjoy the good times, cement producers must not cut back too severely during the hard times. For a vertically integrated firm such as Cemento Melón, this means maintaining adequate investment levels in operations ranging from minerals exploration and development at their mines to productivity improvements in the manufacture and delivery of cement to their customers. Like other mining companies, Cemento Melón operates on the basis of a twenty-year time horizon to introduce some stability into a fundamentally important but often volatile business sector.

The reality of cyclical downturns and slow overall growth were two of the factors that impelled Cemento Melón executives to consider diversification moves. Their resulting decisions show some of the decentralized flexibility within the Blue Circle organization which allowed development and approval of proposals for innovative local adaptations. In 1988, Cemento Melón acquired Emasil, a local company founded two decades earlier that was on the verge of bankruptcy. Emasil produced plywood, doors, windows, and other wood products used primarily in the construction industry. Nearly one-half the company's output was exported, mostly to Great Britain.

The Emasil acquisition capitalized on Chile's comparative advantage in forestry products and offered marketing complementarity since many construction companies buy both cement and wood products. The new firm's export sales also provided Cemento Melón with a partial hedge against both currency fluctuations and downturns in the Chilean construction industry. The company quickly followed the purchase price of $6 million with an equal financial commitment to expand and modernize Emasil's plants. A roughly similar vertical investment was made in forestry raw materials to supply the facilities. As output increases and quality improves, Blue Circle may prove useful in expanding Chile's small one percent share of Great Britain's wood construction market as well as in pursuing export diversification goals in the broader European Community market.

Blue Circle has generally reinvested at least 50 percent of the profits generated in Chile back into the country. The corporation's investment follows a consistent pattern, with an initial purchase followed quickly by investments in expansion and modernization programs. Diversification might be directed at acquiring complementary businesses like Emasil, whose recovery or growth require an infusion of capital, marketing, managerial, or other types of assistance, or at building new enterprises such as Premix.

Overall, Cemento Melón became an important part of Chile's cement industry by relying on a vertical integration strategy that begins with mine ownership and operation. The firm also used its multinational corporate ties to good advantage by introducing technological improvements and diversifying its operations, in the process adding an export dimension to the domestic market orientation of its original Chilean investment.

THE ENERGY SECTOR

Developments in Chile's energy sector are critically important to the nation's economic growth and to its international balance of payments position. Foreign investment plays only a limited role in this area, but several recent and proposed policy changes are designed to encourage more foreign involvement in selected activities. The government has fashioned rules that allow joint oil exploration ventures. Foreign capital is also involved in the development of natural gas resources and the expansion and operation of power generation facilities. Although some efforts are being made to increase domestic coal production, other potential energy resources such as geothermal, solar, and wind remain largely untapped.

Petroleum—Two Oil Sisters and Some Cousins

Esso (an Exxon subsidiary) was the first of the so-called seven sister multinational oil companies to establish a Chilean operation in 1913, followed six years later by Shell, whose initial enterprise was called the Anglo Mexican Petroleum Company. For many years the country's petroleum needs were limited, and the most promising local exploration area, identified by French geologists as early as 1892, was located in the far South's difficult climatic conditions.

Five years after the first successful oil well was drilled in 1945, the basic pattern for this economic sector was set when the government passed a law to create Empresa Nacional del Petróleo (ENAP), a state-owned and operated oil company. ENAP would manage the exploration, production, refining, and sale of energy products in Chile, with foreign companies limited to distribution and sales activities. A government-organized cartel arrangement reserved one-half of sales for a local firm, Compañía de Petróleos de Chile (COPEC), while Esso and Shell divided the remainder, obtaining 30 percent and 20 percent respectively.

This market division endured, even surviving nationalization threats during the Allende period when both Esso and Shell were reportedly targeted for takeovers. Chilean government inspectors were on the premises to monitor closely and learn about all of Esso's operations—steps that would facilitate a takeover attempt. The British and Dutch ambassadors intervened to help prevent a takeover of Shell's facilities. The Allende government decided not to force an early confrontation with these firms. Copper rather than oil was the symbol of Chilean nationalism, and both domestic economic difficulties and the chaos then reigning on world oil markets argued against causing any unnecessary disruptions in Chile's access to international oil supplies.

In the early 1970s a study confirmed significant offshore oil and natural gas reserves around the Straits of Magellan. Feeling pressure from spiraling world oil prices, the government fostered an exploration and development program that yielded results in 1978 when the first producing offshore wells were drilled. The effort was directed by ENAP, which had received some technical assistance from the multinational oil firms and had contracted with foreign companies for the sophisticated equipment needed to drill offshore in the Straits. ENAP's national production peaked in 1982 when it met over one-half of Chile's petroleum needs, but this figure has dropped steadily to less than one-fifth of consumption in 1990.

Declining national production impelled the government to revise its regulations governing the hydrocarbon sector. The nation's constitution guarantees that ownership of the resource will remain with the state, but the law now permits granting third parties the right to explore and produce through Special Petroleum Operating Contracts (SPOCs). By mid-1990, six of these risk contracts had been signed, setting up joint ventures between ENAP and foreign companies in regions not reserved exclusively for ENAP. Foreign firms have the benefit of bringing technological expertise for exploration in the country's northern region, since ENAP's experience is largely confined to the geological conditions found in the South. Joint ventures also help stretch the government's limited exploration budget, drawing in foreign companies to put up risk capital for the chancy work of seeking out new oil reserves.

Hunt Oil Company signed the first SPOC in 1988 for oil and gas exploration in the northern Salar de Atacama region. Negotiations were conducted with officials from Chile's Ministry of Mining and set the precedent for other SPOCs, including a second contract signed with Hunt early the next year for another area even farther north. Generally the contracts provide for a ten-year exploration period and 25 years for production. In practice, exploration seldom takes more than five–six years and is often staged in a way that provides for progressively serious commitments that begin with geological and seismic studies and move on to actual test drilling. Other negotiated terms include ENAP's right to use any resulting production domestically, a pricing structure pegged to a group of similar oil products, and guarantees regarding taxation, foreign exchange, and remittance of profits.

ENAP is a joint venture partner in all of the first six SPOCs, although its level of participation varies even within different stages of the same contract. For example, Hunt and ENAP were 65/35 percent partners on the first contract, but initially 80/20 percent on the second, with ENAP retaining the option to increase its share to 35 percent by the test drilling stage. Greater participation translates into a bigger share of any eventual production, of course, but it also signifies a larger initial financial commitment in ventures that cost around $10–12 million through the drilling of a test well. The risk associated with exploration was demonstrated all too clearly when the promising first Hunt/ENAP venture decided in July 1990 to abandon the deepest test well drilled in Chile after failing to find commercially exploitable evidence of hydrocarbons—after an expenditure of some $16 million on the project.

The SPOCs attracted primarily the cousins of the international oil industry. Hunt Oil is an exploration maverick, preferring to go into new areas first rather than following its competitors, in order to trade off more risk for the potentially greater rewards of a discovery. This approach made the company a good match for Chile's desire to test potential sites in the north. Hunt generally prefers to work alone and, while using ENAP services where it could, distinctly controlled the exploration operations. Other foreign companies signing early SPOCs for exploration sites in the north include Eurocan of Canada (two contracts), Maxus Energy (a U.S. firm, formerly Diamond Shamrock), and Pecten International (a subsidiary of Shell Oil in the United States). The Pecten venture was abandoned quite early, although the company had invested $1 million in seismic studies before ever signing the contract.

Interestingly, neither Esso nor Shell Chile elected to pursue the SPOC ventures. Both firms decided that oil prospects in the areas offered by ENAP for exploration did not justify the necessary expenditures. These firms are interested in more promising potential sites across the Andes in Argentina where, ironically, ENAP itself is participating in some exploration ventures. In fact, the Chilean state oil company is becoming a multinational corporation itself as it seeks to participate in prospective oil ventures located in several of its South American neighbors.

If not exploration, what function have the two multinational oil giants performed in Chile? The answer lies in the areas of imports, distribution and services, and diversified business interests in other economic sectors. Long precluded by law from petroleum activities other than importation and regulated sales, the firms nevertheless maintain a symbiotic relationship with ENAP with regard to pricing and sales policies. Unlike many other oil-producing countries, Chile chose not to subsidize local petroleum usage, instead pegging nationally refined oil sales to world prices plus transportation costs.

ENAP refines most of Chile's petroleum products from both domestic and foreign-source oil, but the multinational oil companies were free to import a greater share of their refined needs directly if ENAP pricing policies move its products too far out of line with world prices. This approach helps enforce a policy that realistically prices a commodity in which Chile has little national advantage, rather than encouraging greater usage through subsidized sales or burdening growth through higher-than-normal prices. (It is also doubtful that higher domestic prices would even stimulate greater development of local oil resources, given the relatively small domestic market and the country's limited prospects for oil resource endowments.) This system was superseded during the crisis introduced by Iraq's invasion of Kuwait, when Chile moved quickly to establish a Petroleum Stabilization Fund. This control continued to operate even after the crisis subsided through a price fund mechanism drawing on a $200 million loan from the Copper Stabilization Fund.

Esso and Shell play a more active role in the distribution and sale of petroleum products. The two firms still dominate this business activity along with COPEC, which itself established ties to other multinational corporations. In the late 1950s, COPEC entered into an association with Mobil that included producing and becoming the exclusive distributor in Chile for Mobil lubricants. The company sustained serious losses in the early 1980s, however. Ownership shifted between Chilean business groups, with the prevailing Angelini group aligning itself with a new foreign investor.

The joint venture investment company that purchased a majority share of COPEC was half-owned by the Carter Holt Harvey (CHH) group of New Zealand, giving CHH a roughly 30 percent share of COPEC. In 1987, CHH used both Chapter XIX and D.L. 600 mechanisms to provide COPEC with an infusion of over $200 million in foreign investment funds, enabling COPEC to pay off the debt load that had been burdening its business activities and embark on a sustainable expansion program. Ironically, CHH was far less interested in COPEC's petroleum business than in its forestry and fishing activities, where the New Zealand firm invested additional funds as will be discussed in the next chapter. Events in the forestry sector also led to discussions about the possible sale of the CHH stake in COPEC and a change in the parent company's ownership in 1991.

Although the three major oil companies still dominate the sale of petroleum products in Chile, their shares of the market are no longer determined by government regulation. Market deregulation was coupled with reinforced antitrust powers and enforcement authority. The government has conducted several investigations into charges of price collusion and restrictive business practices, usually involving the relationship between the oil companies and their many independent dealers, but found no irregularities. The changes reinvigorated activity in the sector. Five smaller firms joined in the fight for local market share, dividing nearly 13 percent of national sales among them. A major new entrant appeared in 1991 when Texaco announced its entry into the distribution market. The firm also was reportedly negotiating several SPOC exploration contracts with ENAP.[18]

The three major established companies acted to meet these challenges by expanding the number and quality of their distribution and service facilities. Both Esso and Shell maintain roughly equal proportions among company-owned, mixed, and independent dealer-owned stations. The advantage of franchised dealers is savings on the capital necessary to open new stations, but the companies believe it is also important to maintain direct customer contact to receive market feedback and test new products. Esso began to add a convenience store component to its service stations, and it invested about $10 million to upgrade and fully automate its distribution plants which run the length of the country. The firm also supplies aviation fuel to all the airports outside Santiago, maintaining high quality standards through frequent inspections and the use of technicians from outside Chile.

While expanding their petroleum marketing activities, Esso and Shell have used their long history and knowledge of Chile to identify other potential business opportunities in the country. Esso's experience helped convince Exxon to undertake its investment in Disputada, while Shell began a diversification campaign in 1980 that led it into multi-faceted investments in both mining and forestry.

Natural Gas—Risk and Commitment for Cape Horn Methanol

Chile's state-owned Empresa Nacional de Petróleo (ENAP) has been searching for ways to utilize the natural gas associated with the oil reserves it exploits around the Straits of Magellan. The company draws off natural gas with the oil it produces, burning off some but reinjecting most of it since the firm lacks the financing necessary to explore commercial developments. In 1981, ENAP put out for bid the opportunity to develop these natural gas reserves. This offer coincided with the increasing interest of Signal Corporation's chairman (who sat on Ford Motor Company's board of directors) in methanol. Produced from natural gas, methanol can serve as a clean fuel alternative for automobiles in addition to its normal chemical uses, primarily in the construction industry.

Thus began a seven-year struggle to match corporate and government interests against an evolving array of political, economic, and operational risks. Studied as a case example, the construction of a gigantic new methanol plant on the southern tip of Chile in the early to mid-1980s was an undertaking that should have failed most risk analyses across the board on political, economic, and operational grounds. A combination of unusual business and political commitment brought it to successful completion, however, and now the facility's $100 million in annual overseas sales have single-handedly taken Chile from a $70–$80 million net chemical importer to a positive export position in chemicals.

When ENAP's bid went out in 1981, political uncertainty was still high in Chile, particularly for a large natural resource investment. Energy investments were sensitive everywhere, and legal changes that would allow foreign companies to participate in Chilean oil exploration were still several years off. By contrast, risk analysts remembered clearly that only a decade had passed since the Allende government expropriated foreign-owned copper mines, seizing control over the country's most important natural resource. Although the subsequent military government arranged compensation for many nationalized facilities, it did not return the mines to private control.

The junta had campaigned aggressively to attract foreign investors, but few large new investments had taken place. Furthermore, several parts of its new foreign investment law would require potentially controversial modifications if a large methanol project was to be viable. Adding to the uncertainty, the ruling military regime was under attack internationally for human rights abuses and faced growing domestic opposition, particularly as an economic recession deepened.

Chile's economic troubles reflected the global recession of the early 1980s, creating uncertainty regarding any large new corporate investment. Latin America appeared particularly unattractive at the time due to the onset of the foreign debt crisis. While the magnitude of Chile's foreign debt did not compare with that of other, larger countries, its per capita burden and debt servicing ratio placed it in a comparable position regarding the denial of new foreign loans. Signal Corporation, which wanted only 51 percent control of a possible methanol project, could not find local partners willing and able to contribute up to one-half of the required equity capital.

Further economic doubts arose regarding the value of the plant's production since methanol prices were unstable, ranging between $80 and $250 per metric ton. In 1986, when nearly one-third of the capital had already been sunk in plant construction, methanol prices slumped to record lows, below what even the lowest cost producers could sustain. Some industry experts warned that in coming years producers might have to pay customers to take their product away. Future demand for methanol in automobile fuels also appeared more speculative as the energy crisis eased and old driving habits were resumed. This dismal economic outlook coincided with the project's need for a financial restructuring. Project managers had to seek easier terms from export creditors and even larger equity contributions from the project's partners.

Operational risks also plagued the project's outlook. The plant was to employ new technological applications, such as the world's largest furnace, created by putting two standard furnaces together for the first time and employing a unique catalyst-efficient spherical design. The remote location also required self-sufficient plant operations. Its only inputs are salt water from the ocean and natural gas supplied by a pipeline from ENAP. The plant uses natural gas by-products for its energy requirements and operates a desalination facility with environmentally sensitive water recycling and return capabilities, as well as other on-site facilities that enable it to operate without placing a burden on limited local public utilities. Assuring delivery to distant foreign customers was another risk faced by the project, leading to the purchase of two purpose-built vessels capable of delivering 90 percent of the plant's output according to the firm's own scheduling requirements.

Signal wanted a Chilean joint venture partner to provide local management expertise, but no established firms had experience or even much knowledge about methanol production. Further operational uncertainty was introduced when a huge U.S. merger fused Allied and Signal corporations, but some former Signal executives and part of the firm's business portfolio were later spun off to form The Henley Group. The Chilean methanol project was transferred through this corporate restructuring, coming to rest under the continuing control and commitment of some of its original promoters who now headed The Henley Group.

Only a firm and long-range commitment on the part of both business and government sponsors could have brought the Cape Horn Methanol project through these troubled times. Among the key factors responsible for its final success are:

—   ENAP's agreement to a twenty-year fixed-price contract for the natural gas. ENAP was guaranteed a base price, whether or not the gas was used, while the company agreed to a type of profit-sharing with ENAP in the event of possible increases in the world price of methanol.

- Chilean government agreement to modifications in the foreign investment law, subsequently applied to other large-scale projects as well, which permitted a twenty-year state-guaranteed contract allowing an offshore account subject to New York state law under which export earnings can be used to pay for certain approved expenditures such as repayment of loans, operating costs, and dividends. Related Chilean tax changes permitted local partners to invest in this entity outside Chile without having to pay double taxation on their dividend shares.
- Participation by the World Bank's International Finance Corporation, which finally took a 10 percent equity stake. Their participation lent a technical endorsement to the project and diffused some of its political risk.
- Participation by two local investors, principally the Compañía Manufacturera de Papeles y Cartones (CMPC), a leading Chilean forestry firm whose fiscally conservative management enabled it to escape the recession in better condition than many traditional Chilean business groups. While methanol lay outside its area of expertise, CMPC recognized the project's value to the country and contributed about 6 percent of the equity capital as well as helping to organize the project's management.
- Staffing by competent and internationally experienced Chilean managers and technicians. All the top management positions at Cape Horn Methanol were held by Chilean nationals, many of them previously trained in the Dow Chemical Company's worldwide operations. The availability of such experienced personnel is an important resource for the country and an indirect contribution of the activities of international corporations.
- A long-term commitment by Signal/Henley Group executives to the project. Financing was the necessary, if not entirely sufficient, condition for the project's viability, and this element was not available using the country's own resources. The corporation eventually put in far more equity capital and took a larger ownership position than it wanted, while still maintaining its belief in the control given to local management personnel.
- An international network of design, construction, and equipment suppliers that maintained interest in the project. Materials used in the plant came from eleven countries, with U.S. and German firms responsible for plant design and a Chilean workforce as large as 1,500 people during the peak construction phase. Participation by Japanese suppliers was especially crucial since they provided flexible credit financing to take the project through some particularly hard times.

The importance of these factors to Cape Horn Methanol's success are validated by the parallel failure of a nearby project to construct a $380 million ammonia-urea plant. This facility was to use the region's natural gas to develop fertilizer products that would be split roughly equally between domestic consumption and exports, potentially turning Chile from a $40-$50 million importer of fertilizers into an exporter of about the same magnitude.

Among the factors that led to the abandonment of this project were: (1) failure to agree on a fixed base price for natural gas sales; (2) lack of a major producer-sponsor with sufficient equity commitment; (3) job changes among the project's internal champions within Combustion Engineering, the primary constructor-sponsor; (4) bank concern regarding the project's debt burden due to its relatively high debt-to-equity ratio; and (5) uncertainty regarding government approval of Chapter XIX debt-equity conversions for use in the project.

By contrast, the Cape Horn Methanol project is a successful example of positive-sum negotiations between corporate sponsors and host government agencies under conditions of imposing uncertainty. The result can now be seen at the tip of South America in one of the world's largest methanol plants, whose output represents almost 5 percent of world capacity and about 12–15 percent of the methanol traded in international commerce. Including some production generated from its early completion, the plant actually recorded output at 103 percent capacity during its first year, compared to customary projections that run as low as 30 percent, given normal start-up difficulties for projects of this type.

Cape Horn Methanol's $300 million cost represents fresh money invested in the country (without the use of debt-to-equity conversions), about one-third equity investments from the project's sponsors and about two-thirds credits from equipment and construction contractors as well as participation by the International Finance Corporation. Export of the plant's production will bolster Chile's trade balance by around $100 million annually. National taxes will claim nearly one-half of the plant's profits. The state energy company will gain income from natural gas that otherwise would go unused, as well as sharing in the prospect for additional earnings if world methanol prices rise. The local economy, in a relatively isolated and underdeveloped region of the country, benefitted from expenditures and employment during the project's construction phase and will gain from continuing plant expenditures and the permanent employment of over 120 local workers.

In early 1991, the two Chilean partners in Cape Horn Methanol exercised an option to sell their shares, leaving The Henley Group with 90 percent ownership and the IFC with 10 percent. Subsequently, Fletcher Challenge of New Zealand, already a major investor in Chile's forestry sector, offered to buy Cape Horn Methanol for an attractive price that reportedly would leave The Henley Group with a good profit. Some time earlier Fletcher Challenge had bought a methanol facility in New Zealand and this purchase would make it the world's leading producer. Having brought the project to fruition, The Henley Group transferred Cape Horn Methanol to another foreign investor for whom the operations would be even more central to its expansion strategy.[19]

Natural gas was also at the center of discussions beginning in 1990 and 1991 regarding a proposal to construct a pipeline across the Andes that would carry Argentine natural gas to supply the Santiago area. Chile's major natural gas reserves are located too far south to permit cost-effective transport to the central region, but improved relations with Argentina and a serious air pollution problem in Santiago combined to spark discussions among public and private sector representatives from the two countries. The nature or extent of possible participation by multinational corporations in the development, transport, and distribution of these natural gas reserves is unclear, but since the project is itself multinational in character even the involvement of national firms will likely evolve into a distinctly multinational operation.

While legal and business partnership problems delayed the project, another similar cross-border arrangement was announced in mid-1991 between Chile and Bolivia. This effort, requiring an investment near one-half billion dollars, will use gas pipelines to transport Bolivian natural gas reserves to Chile's growing northern regions. Both of these projects could relieve the strain on hydroelectric facilities while reducing the financial and environmental costs of power generation from coal or oil resources.[20]

Power Generation and Alternative Energy Sources

Chile's electric power companies were a main target of the Pinochet government's privatization program in the mid-1980s. Goals of this program included developing worker shareholdings in their companies and making restitution to some property-holders who had suffered from earlier expropriation actions. Most of these enterprises became widely held by the public, with significant foreign investment in a few of them. Generally the foreign investor was a financial institution which utilized Chapter XIX debt conversion funding. Aside from general debate over such debt swaps, the key issues surrounding foreign involvement in these transactions concerned the investors' motivation, participation in management, and long-term intentions regarding the enterprise.

The most notable foreign investment in this sector was Bankers Trust's involvement with the privatization of Central Eléctrica de Pilmaiquén, which was initially purchased through an open bidding process. The bank worked to improve the power facility's financial standing before eventually taking it public, concurrently lowering its own participation. These actions were based on the bank's debt reduction strategy and linked to its growing involvement in development of local capital markets, as described in the Bankers Trust case included in the chapter on financial services.

Coal production is intimately linked to electrical power generation in Chile. Although the country mines some metallurgical coal, mainly for domestic consumption, the government encouraged expansion of the local coal industry primarily to help reduce the nation's dependence on imported oil. While all coal needs cannot yet be supplied domestically, growth has been achieved through a combination of improvements in state-run operations, privatization, and new foreign investment.

State-run Empresa Nacional del Carbón (ENACAR) is the traditional industry leader, representing about one-third of national production. Employing over 5,000 workers, the company has been engaged in a five-year, $40 million modernization program. A division of ENACAR was privatized in 1988 when a majority share of Carbonífera Schwager was sold to a combination of workers, pension funds, private companies, and the general public. Included among these investors are a number of foreign interests, with the Owens Group of New Zealand the largest initial foreign investor at less than 10 percent share ownership. With more than 2,000 workers, this company supplies somewhat under 20 percent of national output.

The newest major player in this market is Compañía de Carbones de Chile (COCAR), established in 1985 by COPEC and Northern Strip Mining of the United Kingdom. These two firms had formed a cooperative venture several years earlier to investigate possible coal projects, but their plans did not materialize until they won a public bid to develop a mine in northern Chile to supply coal for CODELCO's local power division. With a ten-year contract from CODELCO, the partners invested over $60 million to begin coal production in 1987. Output now rivals that of ENACAR, although the relatively low caloric value of the coal somewhat limits its attractiveness. Nevertheless, the company is undertaking a $9 million expansion program and has the International Finance Corporation as a 10 percent equity partner.

Other possible energy sources in Chile have not yet attracted commitments from major investors, foreign or domestic. Geothermal resources exist and some foreign firms have expressed a possible interest in their development, but the government was slow to formulate a specific enough legal basis for investment in this area to justify further concrete actions. One plan for a geothermal power station was abandoned in the early 1980s after only one bidder from Great Britain appeared in response to a proposal from CORFO, which also has some geothermal projects. In other alternative energy fields, scattered facility-specific projects exist that employ solar and wind energy resources, but these too lack sustained interest from major developers.

INVESTMENT STRATEGIES IN MINING AND ENERGY

Foreign investors do not dominate the Chilean mining and energy sectors the way Anaconda and Kennecott monopolized copper production prior to the 1970s, but they clearly provide the most dynamic motors of growth in Chile's drive to expand its presence in world mineral markets. Large-scale financing and updated production methods and technology are the key strategic factors enabling this wave of new foreign investors to turn dormant mineral deposits into increased export sales. Improvements in technological applications, employment opportunities, regional development, and environmental protection are among the related benefits flowing from this investment.

Financing is the most evident factor associated with foreign investment strategies in Chile's mining sector. Financing contains several component elements. First is the provision of risk capital for the up-front phase of exploration and feasibility studies. Internal corporate resources generally must cover these expenditures since few financial institutions will underwrite this type of activity. Projects that receive attention are the successful and profitable ones, but the public seldom hears about or quickly forgets the many more examples of explorations that turn up only insufficient ore bodies and yield no return on corporate investments. Superior Oil, Atlantic Richfield, Freeport Minerals, Chevron, Hunt Oil, and many other firms have absorbed substantial "dry hole" losses in the risky search for new reserves in Chile.

Foreign investors can also generate the magnitude of financing needed to develop commercially exploitable mineral deposits. This ability covers large-scale undertakings (Escondida, Disputada, El Indio, La Coipa) as well as the cumulative development of multiple medium-size ventures where foreign investors may join with local joint venture partners. Sometimes the foreign company finances a substantial portion of the venture through its own equity contributions or related corporate financing. Equally important are an investor's credibility and proven track record that enable it to mobilize international capital inaccessible to local entrepreneurs or even government agencies burdened with past debt. The IFC's participation in several ventures also proved valuable, both for the institution's direct financial involvement and the respect other potential investors have for the IFC's endorsement of a project's technical viability.

A related financing consideration is the ability of foreign firms to sustain an investment for the long-term development required in natural resource projects. Exxon's decade-long string of losses at Disputada, on top of its massive expenditures for mine expansion, is a perhaps extreme, but useful, illustration of this point. Many other projects underwent turnovers among ownership groups. This fact suggests that a potentially productive deposit is more likely to reach final development if it is continually open to the involvement of a broad community of international investors rather than dependent solely on local firms or even a small number of selected foreign investors.

Finally, Chapter XIX debt conversions played a useful, but not a major, role in the financing strategies for a number of minerals and energy sector projects. This mechanism helped draw into these ventures a variety of companies that lacked experience in Chile and may have stimulated development of a few more projects than would have otherwise been undertaken. In general, however, Chapter XIX regulations were seen as a less stable legal basis on which to risk substantial investment capital in this economic sector.

Mining law provisions and the guarantees of D.L. 600 agreements represent a more certain basis for resource investments, particularly when project scale enables the investors to negotiate access to offshore accounts to complement remittance, foreign exchange, and national treatment guarantees. Although the option of a long-term fixed taxation rate was viewed as an important sign of a stable investment climate, its operational significance appears negligible. As projects begin to show profits, most foreign companies opt out of the guarantee scheme. Chile's taxation policies were sufficiently stable that the prospect of higher current after-tax profits outweighed remaining concerns about future radical tax increases.[21]

Technology in these investments usually comes from innovative and updated applications rather than the introduction of radical new breakthroughs. Foreign investors stretched the limits of known technologies in their scale of operations and in untested geographic or climatic conditions. Improvements include the introduction of environmental controls that reduce impacts on air, water, and other surroundings beyond the levels achieved at most existing facilities in the country. Managerial skills are also being honed internationally and transferred rapidly to capable Chilean managers whose abilities are widely praised by foreign executives and whose prominence throughout top foreign-owned ventures stands as credible testimony to that praise.

In labor relations, foreign investors are introducing more flexible work structures and relationships in many mining ventures. Newer projects undoubtedly benefit from the clean slate upon which initial employment and work rules are being written, but even established facilities are negotiating with their unions to develop terms and conditions that create a competitive cost structure. In general, labor relations at foreign-owned facilities are good. Wages are usually at or above those at all but some state-run mines, and many conditions are superior in terms of worker safety and certain supplemental programs such as special housing support.

The mining sector's creation of direct permanent jobs will not yield impressive results for aggregate national employment because almost all large mining operations are heavily mechanized. These projects can make a substantial impact in local areas, however. In addition to creating new permanent jobs, construction employment during the development phase of a new facility brings in about three times as many workers, injecting substantial if temporary income into the surrounding economy. Since most mining projects are located in underdeveloped regions of the country, these ventures aid national goals of decentralizing economic activities, improving basic infrastructure in remote areas, and helping to achieve a better regional distribution of income.

The strategic role of marketing is more problematic, at least in copper production. Many new investors will channel output to their own foreign refineries or other overseas facilities tied into the project's development. This arrangement can provide certain benefits to the host country, particularly in the event of a market downturn due to oversupply conditions. The advantages are not so clear for a low-cost producer country such as Chile, however, especially when high prices prevail. Still, with a variety of foreign investors involved in new copper projects, the country and the companies may be able to maintain a combination of committed and open market exports, providing some overall balance in international marketing position.

International marketing channels are related to the issue of domestic value added, again most problematic in copper projects, but also a Chilean objective with respect to other minerals and natural gas development. Chile's immediate problem is that its small internal market and physical distance from major consumer countries act as disincentives to the domestic fabrication of many products for shipment elsewhere. Some additional refining processes may be accomplished locally when project scale and world market conditions justify new additions to capacity, as the Disputada and La Coipa cases demonstrate.

Four types of efforts are being made to increase the value of Chile's mineral resources. These attempts indicate the probable limits to a strategy of moving local activities farther down the value-added production chain in the face of international market forces. The first approach is simply to jawbone foreign investors into trying a next processing step in Chile, perhaps playing a catalyst role as did the ENAMI and CODELCO-led study of a possible new joint refinery project. While corporations with substantial investments in Chile may agree to evaluate local processing options within the framework of their global expansion plans, a shift away from existing investments in established foreign facilities is quite unlikely. Hence, success rests more on the prospects for global market growth than on current managerial discretion.

The second strategy is represented by the CODELCO/MADECO joint venture in China, as well as similar efforts in France and Germany. Here overseas investments are being made in semi-manufacturing or other fabrication stages involving copper-related products. Despite disappointing initial results from the China project, these ventures can draw through some Chilean copper exports while gaining production knowledge that may be transferable to domestic operations in Chile, if economic factors make such a step feasible. This approach mimics MNC strategies, with Chilean enterprises going abroad to gain the benefits of engaging in overseas operations. In 1990, only five firms were engaged in substantial copper-related manufacturing in Chile, consuming about 43,000 metric tons of copper in their products, the majority of which were exported.[22]

A third strategy seeks to translate Chile's leadership as a location for major mining ventures into a similarly strong position in the development and export of mining technology or related equipment. CODELCO took a modified converter process first used at the El Teniente mine in the 1970s and developed it into part of a technological package called the Teniente Process that is sold internationally. The El Teniente division was also exploring a possible joint venture project with a Canadian MNC in mid-1991, relating to the production of certain mining equipment in Chile.[23] Similar technological adaptations or even breakthroughs could arise from major new mining investments taking place in the country over the coming decade.

Finally, research is needed to find new or expanded uses for copper which would increase the overall value of the country's main natural resource. This objective is probably the least likely to result from private investment, but it could be extremely important to the country. The growth rate in world demand for copper is in long-term decline, dropping from 5 percent annually in the late 1800s to 3.5 percent through the mid-1900s, to 1.6 percent between 1970 and 1990. Aluminum, plastic, steel, and fiberoptics provide possible substitutes for copper in many areas. About 70 percent of copper use is now related to the conduct of electricity, and the red metal could suffer a further blow if emerging breakthroughs in superconductivity research prove commercially viable in a wide range of products.[24]

The concept of greater value added, of course, implies a current value from already existing activities. In addition to the financing, technology, and job benefits discussed above, foreign investment that expands mining output brings other immediate value to the host country. A positive balance-of-payments effect from new capital investment is followed by greater foreign exchange earnings from increased export sales and enhanced government revenue from the taxation of corporate income and other taxable business activities.

The balance of payments effect is time-dependent, with initial gains potentially reduced by later profit remittances, dependent on both reinvestment rates and the realization of an actual profit. Export gains are substantial since virtually all new production goes to satisfy foreign rather than domestic demand. Tax revenue is also time-sensitive, but ongoing operations are subject to certain tax levies, and even the guaranteed income tax rate option of 49.5 percent (or the proposed lower rate of 42 percent) would capture a major share of a foreign investor's locally generated profit before any is remitted to the parent corporation.

Another set of issues surrounds the question of ownership and control of mineral and energy investments. Chile's constitution makes it clear that the nation retains ultimate ownership of its mineral wealth, but foreign-owned and operated ventures clearly are playing an increasingly important role in developing those resources. In one respect, perceptions regarding the pervasiveness of foreign ownership may be somewhat less oppressive in Chile now than earlier in the nation's history. State-run enterprises are still a major force in mining and energy activities and foreign investors hail from many different countries, including smaller nations such as Finland and Korea. Additionally, foreign MNCs are not rushing to exploit every offered investment opportunity, such as in oil exploration or natural gas development. Still, all things being equal, national political tendencies favor local ownership over foreign, especially in the development of natural resources.

Of course, all things are not equal, and that is the reason Chile has moved to open its economy, including most minerals and energy projects, to participation by foreign enterprises. Most of the benefits enumerated above from foreign investment would not be realizable for Chile within the near term, based solely on local resources. The variety of ventures being pursued by Chile's state-run enterprises, including CODELCO, ENAMI, and ENAP, points up the reality of this observation. Some activities have been shifted to the private sector, some are pursued by public/private joint ventures, and a few are now the object of outreach efforts that extend these government-owned operations to the soil of other countries. For Chile, the trade-offs of foreign investment in this sector are put most starkly in terms of mineral wealth that would have remained a potential source of economic growth and income for the country rather than a developmental reality, if foreign investors had not become involved in the projects examined in this chapter.[25]

NOTES

Information in this chapter is drawn from interviews with corporate executives, government officials, and other knowledgeable experts in the field. The most comprehensive published materials used include the following: various materials supplied by the corporations; "Mining Survey 1990," *South Pacific Mail*, supplement, Santiago (June 1990); United States Embassy Santiago, *Industrial Outlook Report*, "Chile–Minerals," State Department, Economic Section of the Embassy of the United States in Santiago (March 1989); Foreign Investment Committee, *Mining–Chile*, 3rd ed., Santiago (July 1988); and selected articles in 1990–91, from two of the largest daily and weekly newspapers of Santiago: *El Mercurio* and *Estrategia*, respectively. Additional selected citations are provided in the text where necessary for specific references.

1. "Preven para próximos cuatro años: Inversión extranjera de 4 millones de dólares en minería," *El Mercurio*, February 26, 1990.

2. United States Embassy Santiago, *Industrial Outlook Report*, 5.

3. "Para el año 1994: Proyectan una mayor participación privada en minería del cobre," *El Mercurio*, November 30, 1990.

4. "Ministro de Minería Hamilton: 'Situación de Codelco es grave'," *El Mercurio*, July 31, 1990; "Informó subsecretario de minería: Codelco estudia invertir US$ 10 millones anuales en nuevas exploraciones," *El Mercurio*, July 28, 1990; Jorge Bande, "Codelco To Go For Productivity, Not Just Production," *South Pacific Mail*, 5–7; and Barbara Durr, "Chilean Copper Industry in the Melting Pot," *Financial Times*, November 1, 1989.

5. As CODELCO's president summarized this constraint on exploration: "El Fisco tiene otros roles, principalmente sociales, que son urgentes, y por lo tanto no puede distraer recursos vitales en financiar estas acciones que implican un alto riesgo." See "El metal rojo más allá de la guerra," *El Mercurio*, February 3, 1991.

6. "Tiene 31% de concesiones otorgadas: Codelco explota solo el 3,32% de sus pertenencias mineras," *El Mercurio*, March 15, 1991; and "Polémica sobre el cobre: Hamilton niega que asociarse sea 'desnacionalizar'," *El Mercurio*, March 14, 1992.

7. "Codelco: Negro el panorama," *El Mercurio*, June 16, 1991.

8. "Situación de Codelco es grave"; "Codelco: ¿Palos de ciego?", *El Mercurio*, July 1, 1990; and "Codelco Faces Production Crunch at Andina Mine," *South Pacific Mail*, 31.

9. "Codelco: ¿Palos de ciego?"; and "Codelco: Negro el panorama."

10. "Codelco Faces Production Crunch at Andina Mine."

11. "Contaminar, contaminar . . . ," *El Mercurio*, July 29, 1990; and "Para el período 1990–1995: Readecuan inversiones de Codelco," *El Mercurio*, August 8, 1990.

12. Just over a year after operations began, Escondida executives announced plans for a $200 million expansion by 1994 that could increase production nearly 25 percent. A key element in this expansion is the use of chemicals to leach concentrates from the ore, employing an improved process developed by BHP metallurgists.

13. "La corporación financiera: Inician remate en bolsa de minera 'Mantos Blancos'," *El Mercurio*, June 12, 1990; "En bolsa de comercio de Santiago: 0,9% de Mantos Blancos rematado en valor mínimo," *El Mercurio*, June 16, 1990; and "En US$ 32 millones venden 15,8% de Mantos Blancos," *El Mercurio*, December 27, 1990.

14. "Outokumpu invierte US$ 180 millones en Chile," *El Mercurio*, June 1, 1990; and "Outokumpu Takes Flier on Zaldívar Property," *South Pacific Mail*, 38.

15. "En el mercado secundario de acciones: US$ 233 millones buscan colocar en el exterior cinco empresas nacionales," *El Mercurio*, July 2, 1990; and "Al Bankers Trust: Israel Chemicals compró el 10,5% de Soquimich," *El Mercurio*, March 6, 1990.

16. "Proyecto minsal aún en compás de espera," *El Mercurio*, October 5, 1990; "Según informe de cesco: Amax gestiona vender su participación en Minsal," *El Mercurio*, September 1, 1990; and "Banco Rothschild negocia venta de participación de Amax en Minsal," *El Mercurio*, September 4, 1990.

17. "Proyecto de litio, potasio y boro: Tres interesados en el desarrollo de Minsal," *El Mercurio*, August 7, 1991; and "US$ 150 millones: Amax compromete inversión en primera etapa de Minsal," *El Mercurio*, October 1, 1991.

18. "Texaco iniciará distribución mayorista de combustibles," *El Mercurio*, September 7, 1991; "Enap negocia 4 nuevos contratos de exploración," *El Mercurio*, March 31, 1991; and "Combustibles: La sequía y la crisis," *El Mercurio*, November 7, 1990.

19. "Negocian venta de Cape Horn Methanol a Fletcher Challenge," *El Mercurio*, July 2, 1991.

20. "Anuncian la construcción de gasoducto entre Chile y Bolivia," *El Mercurio*, June 12, 1991; "Anunció Ministro Toha: Avances en plan integracionista con Bolivia," *El Mercurio*, June 26, 1991; and "Integración energética," *El Mercurio*, June 29, 1991.

21. United States Embassy Santiago, *Chile: Minerals Benchmark Report*, Department of State (United States Embassy Santiago: May 1990), 5–6.

22. Saul Alanoca, "Copper semimanufactures: untapped market opportunities, *International Trade Forum* (April–June 1991); and "Dijo Máximo Pacheco Matte: Codelco ampliará su base de negocios en el exterior," *El Mercurio*, September 30, 1991.

23. "Anunció Ministro Hamilton: Codelco e Inco estudian asociación para industria de maquinaria minera," *El Mercurio*, August 31, 1991.

24. "El metal rojo más allá de la guerra."

25. Hernán Guiloff, president of Chile's Sociedad Nacional de Minería, expressed this concept clearly at a seminar on foreign investment in Chile. See Hernán Guiloff I., Speech given at the Seminario Internacional: "Oportunidades de Inversión en Chile," Santiago, May 15 and 16, 1990, Photocopy.

4

Nontraditional Exports

A surge in nontraditional exports during the 1980s wrote a Chilean success story that promises to continue in the 1990s. Mineral output still represents the largest portion of Chile's foreign sales, but its export offerings grew and diversified in both products and destinations as the nation integrated its economy with the global marketplace. Together with minerals, Chile's three Fs—forestry, fishing, fruit (and other agricultural products)—give the nation a stronger and more stable export base. These natural resource-based sectors are further supplemented by increasing volume and diversity in other manufactured and service exports that range from blue jeans and plastic packaging to software and engineering services. Foreign investors are involved directly and indirectly in this development through financing, technology, marketing, distribution, and servicing. A flexible partnership often emerges with local and foreign enterprise strategies working hand-in-hand to formulate the complete package of materials, financing, and skills necessary to compete on world market cost, quality, and delivery standards.

Chile's export expansion and diversification campaign began in the 1970s and accelerated after surviving the recession of the early 1980s. In addition to maintaining a realistic and competitive exchange rate, the government undertook reforms to improve customs procedures, speed rebates of indirect taxes to exporters, and exempt capital goods imports from tariffs if they are used for producing exports. Promotional devices included tax incentives for small exporters, improvements to ports and related transportation networks, and the creation of an agency (ProChile) to disseminate information and facilitate contacts between Chilean exporters and foreign customers.

The policy succeeded as Chile's exports increased as a proportion of GDP from around 13 percent in 1970 to nearly one-third by 1990. Export earnings more than doubled from $3.9 billion in 1985 to $8.3 billion in 1990. Despite high prices, copper exports represented only 45.7 percent of the 1990 total, quite a drop from the 70 percent average during the 1960s or the 80 percent level registered in 1973. In 1971, Chile exported 412 products to 58 countries; by 1990, 1,343 products were sold to 112 countries. Between 1975 and 1990, the number of firms exporting from Chile increased from 400 to 4,000 enterprises.

The link between foreign investment and this growth in Chile's nontraditional exports is both flexible and diverse. Many investors favor large, export-oriented projects that are integrated directly with their worldwide operations. Joint venture investments combine particular MNC advantages with the skills and resources possessed by local partners in a strategic matching process that yields a variety of patterns and outcomes. Still other investors with a primarily local market orientation choose an experimental export strategy that contributes to national trade objectives while reducing the firm's foreign exchange exposure and fostering product diversification. Finally, some useful arrangements lack the characteristic of direct equity investment, with foreign companies serving mainly to market, distribute, or service the goods exported by Chilean enterprises. The following discussion surveys this broad array of strategies for investing in Chile's nontraditional export campaign.

FORESTRY

Forestry is the emerging giant of the Chilean economy. Based on the cultivation and development of a renewable natural resource, this sector is second only to mining in export potential and in its direct ties to both foreign investors and the world economy. The Chilean forestry sector grew over 20 percent on average from 1974 through the 1980s, surging ahead of former regional leader Brazil in exported products. Export sales topped $900 million in 1991, an exponential expansion from the $36 million registered in 1973, but short of the nearly $2 billion projected by the end of the century. This growth reflects a combination of increased domestic and foreign investment, encouraged by supportive government policies.

Chile's forestry potential lay undeveloped for decades. The country's native forests, which cover an area nearly as large as New York state, are generally unmanaged. The overmature trees are subject to center rot which destroys their commercial value except for wood chips used in pulping operations. Several forestry projects seek to exploit this native lumber and these efforts have raised environmental concerns. Most forestry expansion, however, is based on development of new radiata pine and, more recently, eucalyptus plantations. These projects combine Chile's natural climatic advantages with imported forestry management techniques and modern processing capabilities to build a nontraditional export industry.

Radiata pine is the key to Chile's forestry growth. This species matures after twenty-four years in Chile, at least six years sooner than in the other primary growing regions of New Zealand and Australia. Harder pine varieties grown in the United States and Canada require two and one-half times as long to reach maturity. In the past, Chilean pine wood suffered from a low quality reputation because poor forestry management practices left most of the wood knotted. Now, cutting and pruning techniques can yield knot-free wood and the accompanying tree trimmings may be used in several wood products, beginning as early as fifteen years after initial planting.

While the Chilean government has encouraged the forestry sector since the 1950s, a particularly important step was taken in 1974 with the adoption of Decree Law 701. This statute guaranteed private ownership rights of forests while providing subsidies covering up to 75 percent of the cost of new forestation activities. Additional bonuses are available for some types of forestry management activities while certain tax exemptions and rebates further lower the ultimate operational costs. This program stimulated plantings of over 1.2 million hectares, nearly all in radiata pine, during its first fifteen years at a public cost of about $70 million. Authorized to run until 1994, the program is now directed at encouraging forest management and reforestation activities in geographic regions beyond those where commercial operations have already been established.

The structure of the forestry industry reflects a progressive value-added chain. Beginning at the plantation stage, forestry products run first through logs, sawn wood, and boards before moving on to cellulose and paper and other finished wood products such as furniture. At the end of the 1980s, Chile's domestic market consumed about two-thirds of the country's production of paper and cardboard products and sawn wood, three-fourths of its boards, and only 40 percent of the wood pulp. By the end of the century, Chile's supply of wood suitable for sawing and pulping activities will quadruple as major new plantings begin to reach maturity. Some additional domestic growth is possible, for example in the housing sector, but export markets must absorb most of the country's new wood product offerings.

With the oncoming supply of lumber projected to far outstrip established processing capacity, Chile will require an investment of at least $3 billion through the turn of the century in order to exploit its forestry industry potential. Commitments for over one-half this amount had already been made by the beginning of the 1990s in proposed projects by local and foreign investors. These investments must fully materialize, and then be matched by an equal amount of new investor interest, if the sector's potential is to be realized.

Foreign investors play a crucial role in developing Chile's forestry sector by mobilizing capital, transferring and adapting technology, and diversifying export markets. The country's forestry projects also show the strategic functioning of mixed joint venture partnerships between local and foreign investors, and the promotion of new products and local value-added. Regional development and employment generation are important secondary benefits generated by the forestry projects. Infrastructure improvements and effective responses to environmental concerns are among the top issues that still must be addressed to allow this sector's full expansion in the future.

Competitors or Partners—Carter Holt Harvey's Choice

An important early foreign investor in Chile's forestry sector was Carter Holt Harvey Limited (CHH), a New Zealand natural resources enterprise concentrated in forestry, fishing and construction activities. The primary mechanism for CHH's investment is its 50/50 joint venture participation with the local Angelini group in an investment company, Inversiones y Desarrollo Los Andes S.A., that acquired majority ownership of Compañía de Petróleos de Chile (COPEC). As noted in the energy section of the previous chapter, COPEC is a leading Chilean natural resources conglomerate which was seriously weakened during the recession of the early 1980s. The initial CHH investment in 1987 of approximately $200 million allowed COPEC to lift its debt burden and undertake a major modernization and expansion campaign. CHH's ultimate interest in COPEC was not so much the firm's petroleum activities, but rather its substantial natural resource holdings in forestry and fishing. Drawing on its long experience with similar forests in New Zealand, CHH transferred technology and operational experience to the new venture while relying on its Chilean partner to provide local administrative and management expertise.

The CHH investment results from a strategic choice the firm made regarding whether to view the development of Chile's forestry sector as a competitor or as a partner. New Zealand and Australia are primary regions for growing radiata pine and CHH is firmly established as both a major producer and global marketer of the resulting wood products. Studies showed Chile's forestry potential based on its natural climatic advantages and the government's policies to encourage forestry development contrasted with some actions taken by New Zealand's government where land management and taxation changes were leading to a reduction in forest harvesting and new plantings. CHH was concerned about the prospect that new Chilean output could surge onto world markets in ways that would disrupt prevailing price patterns and did not want to be locked out of a friendly foreign production site. Seeing the rise of a potential new competitor across the Pacific, the company opted to become a partner in Chile's forestry development.

COPEC had entered the forestry sector in 1976 as part of its diversification activities, winning a public bid from Chile's development agency, CORFO, to acquire Industrias de Celulosa Arauco and Empresa Forestal Arauco. Three years later COPEC added Celulosa Constitución, allowing it to reorganize its holdings into one major production enterprise, Celulosa Arauco y Constitución, with affiliated forest plantation firms. This company was one of the two main Chilean forestry firms, the other being Compañía Manufacturera de Papeles y Cartones (CMPC), which is also the majority shareholder of related Industrias Forestales (INFORSA).

The capital infusion from CHH was instrumental to COPEC's overall economic recovery and essential for its forestry expansion projects. The initial $200 million investment occurred through both the Chapter XIX debt-to-equity and D.L. 600 mechanisms on about a three-to-one ratio. At the time, the use of debt swaps amounted to about a one-third discount on that portion of the investment. While the firm's basic interests likely would have led it to invest in Chilean forestry projects anyway, the use of Chapter XIX influenced the scale of the investment and the company's interest in follow-up improvement and expansion projects that have raised CHH's total stake to well over $300 million.

Two initial modernization projects aimed at raising the output of existing pulp plants. Production at the Arauco facility increased from 158,000 to 184,000 tons after completion of a $65 million investment project. Nearly the same amount was spent on technological improvements at the Constitución plant to improve product quality and environmental performance while boosting output from 232,000 to 265,000 tons per year. Concurrent efforts sought to expand the firm's forestry holdings to supply the plants. By adding new lands and undertaking planting campaigns, the enterprise in 1989 possessed over 330,000 hectares of forests with another 60,000 hectares suitable for forestation activities.

While improving existing facilities, the joint venture partners also moved to develop a major new processing plant. A second production line was approved at the Arauco site, dubbed Project Arauco II, slated to begin operations at the end of 1991 with a capacity of 350,000 tons per year. About 40 percent of the project's $600 million budget will be generated internally, with the remainder in loans from equipment suppliers and various financial institutions including the World Bank's International Financial Corporation (IFC). Over $10 million is allocated for an advanced environmental control system for water and gas emissions.

These three projects would expand Celulosa Arauco y Constitución's output of pulp from 390,000 to over 800,000 tons per year by 1992, effectively doubling production while simultaneously increasing the proportionate mix of higher-priced bleached cellulose. This output is slated for world markets, solidifying the firm's position as Chile's leading cellulose exporter. In 1989 the company accounted for nearly one-third of Chile's forestry exports, selling products worth more than $300 million in thirty-three countries, including some $220 million of cellulose. In 1989 the firm also signed an agreement with Sweden's Stora Kopparbergs Bergslag AB to explore another project that might include a cellulose plant with 450,000 to 550,000 tons per year capacity at a projected expenditure of $1.2 billion.[1]

These modernization and expansion projects are valuable contributions to the development of Chile's forestry industry. The emphasis on bleached cellulose means that Chilean output will command higher export prices along with its greater volume, but the country's small internal market limits business interest in locating there the next value-added production stage of paper manufacture. This step's requirements of large production scale and broad product range, together with existing capacity in or near the major consumer markets, appear to preclude significant corporate interest in Chile as a site for further processing of the cellulose output.

CHH and its Chilean partners have embarked on a different value-added forestry activity, however. Manufacturera de Fibropaneles Chile S.A. was conceived as a $30 million venture, one-half owned by CHH, that would produce 70,000 tons annually of medium-density fiberboard with nearly three-quarters of the output to be exported. Commissioned in October 1988, a facility located at Cholguan incorporates the latest technology in an energy center designed to provide all the plant's heating and drying requirements.

Although unrelated to the forestry sector, CHH also invested approximately $2 million in 1989 to acquire Fábrica Chilena de Envases, which produces flexible films and food packaging for the food processing industry. While not designed for export, this plastics business could benefit from the transfer of technology from related CHH operations in New Zealand. A modernization campaign during 1990 invested $1.3 million in improving the firm's equipment and procedures, promising spin-off benefits useful to the country's fruit and agricultural marketing sector.

In early 1991, CHH announced a decision by its board of directors to restructure or sell its business in Chile. This action resulted from a strategic purchase by CHH of the troubled Elders Resources of Australia. The transaction involving over $300 million would add close to one-half million tons of cellulose capacity and more than 400,000 tons of paper and cardboard capacity to CHH, also increasing its forestry holdings in New Zealand. Under pressure from its bankers to reduce the debt load incurred from this expansion, CHH needed the cash represented by its partial ownership of COPEC. While COPEC generated good profits, the gains were recorded on the books in Chilean pesos and Chapter XIX provisions prevented CHH from repatriating the profits quickly enough to meet its immediate financing needs.[2]

Ironically, this discussion of a possible sale occurred just as COPEC's major investments in forestry operations were about to expand production. A CHH departure from Chile would not result in immediate local changes, however. The Angelini group could exercise a first option to purchase CHH's shares and would retain operational direction of COPEC in any event. Additionally, a withdrawal would not likely tarnish Chile's attractiveness for foreign investors since CHH would realize a substantial gain on its investment, benefitting from a significant rise in the value of COPEC's shares.

A potentially serious complication did arise concerning Chapter XIX regulations. If CHH sold its shares to its partner (Angelini) or another Chilean investor rather than to a foreign firm, the capital repatriation restrictions would prevent the money's withdrawal from Chile. The government attempted to address this difficulty in the context of a modification to Chapter XIX that would permit earlier repatriation if an investor paid a compensation for the initial investment subsidy realized through the debt-to-equity swap discount. This rule adjustment reflects the country's programmatic shift from new debt conversion activity to the administration of past agreements.[3]

Toward the end of 1991, Brierly Investments became the major shareholder in CHH, thereby assuming control of its Chilean investments as well. This enterprise is a joint venture between a New Zealand investment group and International Paper (U.S.). The new owners announced reconsideration of the plans to leave Chile.[4] In terms of its foreign investment strategy, CHH must again choose between being a competitor or a partner in Chile's forestry development, but even if it leaves, a legacy of beneficial improvements already attained will remain behind.

Forging a Mixed Joint Venture—The Celpac Negotiations

Celulosa del Pacífico (initially abbreviated Celpac but now known as Pacífico) is a multi-sided venture with two major partners, Simpson Paper of the United States and Compañía Manufacturera de Papeles y Cartones (CMPC) of Chile. The project involves construction of a cellulose mill with a 315,000 ton per year capacity at a projected cost of over $580 million, much of which is supplied through a complex network of financial partners. The two key factors that determine the outline of this transaction are the need for technology transfer and creative financing, with product modification and market access also playing important roles.

As noted earlier, CMPC is the strongest local competitor to COPEC's merged Celulosa Arauco y Constitución enterprise. Controlled by the local Matte family, CMPC's stock is traded on the public exchange and the company is often mentioned among a handful of Chilean firms that could soon become transnational corporations and gain direct access to foreign capital markets. The company was battered by foreign competition and exchange rate problems during the early 1980s recession, but CMPC's conservative management philosophy helped it emerge with a relatively small debt load compared to many Chilean companies.

CMPC had made extensive use of the government's subsidized planting program begun in 1974 and by the mid-1980s, needed to expand its processing capability to handle the oncoming supply of wood. The firm already operated a cellulose plant at Laja that was similar in size to the projected Celpac facility and it was investing around $40 million to increase its capacity by another 30,000 tons annually. Nevertheless, in order to reach its expansion goals the company had to seek foreign partners to provide technological advancements and financing for a major new cellulose facility.

Technology was a key factor because CMPC did not want simply to rebuild a copy of its Laja facility. Chile's forestry industry had been a relatively closed community with regard to engineering personnel, and a foreign partnership could bring a cross-fertilization of ideas. An earlier technical assistance contract between CMPC and Crown Zellerbach had lapsed without producing great benefits, so the firm sought a foreign partner that was not a close potential competitor and that was willing to make a substantial commitment to the project.

Simpson Paper was a good match for CMPC's needs. Begun as a timber company, Simpson had built or acquired nearly a dozen pulp and paper mills in joint ventures with various firms. Almost all these facilities employ different technology, so Simpson engineers were familiar with a wide range of plant designs and operations, including the creative modification of existing facilities to improve their productive efficiency. Simpson is a private family-owned company whose short decision-making chain was compatible with CMPC's direction by the Matte family group. A Chilean national was a member of Simpson's board of directors, bringing the company an expert perspective on societal developments and business opportunities in Latin America.

Simpson was not experienced in overseas production. While it had acquired some tree-planting operations in Central America, Pacífico is Simpson's first industrial venture outside the United States. Long-range strategy dictated that the company consider diversifying its pulping operations, particularly since the firm is concentrated along the U.S. West Coast where proliferating environmental regulations promise increased restrictions on lumber operations. Chile appeared to be an ideal location for a forestry company looking to diversify its geographic base, and a joint venture opportunity with an experienced and compatible local firm would moderate the potential risk of a first overseas venture.

Two other secondary benefits arise from this partnership match. CMPC production is geared to long-fibre cellulose of the type derived from radiata pine, suitable for newsprint and common quality paper. Pacífico's initial production is tied to the supply of this wood from CMPC holdings, but the plant is designed so that it can also handle short-fibre cellulose needed for softer quality products such as tissue paper. Simpson is experienced with both types of cellulose and is helping to plant eucalyptus trees to provide short fibre raw materials. (This venture is taking place on land that does not qualify for government planting subsidies, but offers good tree growth potential.) Along with the Santa Fe project discussed later, Pacífico is thus broadening the base and range of Chile's forestry products.

The match between the partners' established marketing capabilities also offers potential complementary gains. Simpson entered the venture for strategic diversification reasons rather than to use its immediate output to supply established operations. Although the partners could purchase some output for internal use depending on market price and supply conditions, most of Pacífico's production will be exported with both firms assisting in its marketing. CMPC is better known in European markets, while Simpson is more established in the Far East. The Simpson reputation could be particularly useful among consumers unfamiliar with Chile and concerned about the reliability of supplies coming from a distant Latin American location.

The two-sided partnership broadened into a complex and multi-sided joint venture because of the need for creative financing, made possible by the use of the Chapter XIX mechanism. Traditional international financing was still inaccessible for projects in Chile and the partners wanted to avoid the hefty fees charged by investment banks by syndicating the loans themselves. Each partner committed $60 million in equity investment. Simpson utilized the Chapter XIX mechanism for its contribution, tempering the perceived risk of making its first major overseas investment. The World Bank's IFC arm provided $10 million in equity capital, which additionally proved helpful with prospective lenders as an endorsement of the project's technical merit.

In an unusual twist, the firms decided to use preferred stock as a part of the financing package and asked Bank of America, which already provided financial services to both firms, to take the lead in managing the lending arrangements. Bank of America arranged a package of $225 million from commercial banks, including itself, Manufacturers Hanover, Chemical, Midland, and Marine Midland. Security Pacific Bank was an early participant in the negotiations but withdrew before the final agreement, and a CMPC financial subsidiary joined the transaction to supply an additional $15 million in loans.

Following Central Bank approval, the banks' Chapter XIX funds were provided to Pacífico as loans on which the banks could draw interest. This element actually increased the amount of loans needed from the banks by $15–$20 million so that they could collect initial interest on the loaned funds. When the Pacífico plant becomes operational, the banks' loans will be converted to preferred shareholdings, eligible for dividend preferences over the two partner firms. The agreement ties dividends to a fixed formula to establish a base but also links it to the international price of pulp, allowing lenders to share in extra profit if it develops.

This potential profit-sharing arrangement was helpful in selling the financing package to the banks' international headquarters where the proposal competed against other potential investments. For example, the Pacífico loans would offer an estimated return that was less than the current return on far less risky U.S. Treasury bonds. The two partners can buy the stock back from the banks after ten years, a period that takes the banks past Chapter XIX restrictions on repatriated funds and avoids possible problems with U.S. regulations on bank investments in industrial enterprises.

Another $217 million was still needed to fund full project cost. Export credit agencies from Canada, Finland, and Germany filled this role, along with IFC loan money. These agencies' interest was based on prospective contracts for their nations' engineering firms and equipment suppliers. Pacífico's sponsors may have gained some additional bargaining leverage in negotiations on the terms and conditions of these loans due to the unusual structure of the project's investment. The combination of the partner's substantial equity contributions and the banks' preferred stock arrangement gives the project an unusually low debt-to-equity ratio, reducing its risk to the lenders. Perhaps as a result, these agencies agreed to a limit on the two sponsors' liability during the construction phase and no recourse during operations, conditions that then applied as well to the commercial bank partners.

The use of Chapter XIX debt-to-equity swaps was essential to the structure of this arrangement, one of the largest transactions approved by the Central Bank. The commercial banks involved all had significant outstanding debt exposure in Chile and, absent the opportunity to use Chapter XIX to diversify their debt portfolio, would have been no more interested in financing this project than other less exposed international banks. Since a less costly, smaller scale facility was not economically viable, this project probably would not have occurred without the Chapter XIX mechanism; or its initiation would at least have been delayed until Chile regained its access to traditional international financial markets.

Beginning operations early in 1992, the Pacífico facility will directly provide jobs for 340 individuals and provide indirect employment for 2,600 others. The project's $200 million in annual export sales will generate foreign exchange earnings, providing some internal balance to the expected eventual repatriation of Chapter XIX funds. The debt-to-equity swaps provided the foundation for a creative financing arrangement that combined with technology transfer benefits to generate expanded production, employment, and export earnings on global markets. Pacífico thus appears to be a project that would be viewed favorably even under the modified Chapter XIX objectives adopted by the new democratic government.

Turning Failure into Success—The Santa Fe Story

At the beginning of the 1980s, Industrias Forestales (INFORSA) was owned by the local Vial group which sought to expand into cellulose production. The company formed a 50–50 joint venture with a Spanish consortium headed by an entrepreneur who had built a number of pulp plants in Europe which were sold to other companies on a turnkey basis. The objective was to establish a company, Papeles Sudamérica, that would develop a long-fibre pulp plant at Nacimiento with a capacity of about 120,000 to 140,000 tons of pulp and paper per year, designed for the domestic rather than the export market.

Each partner contributed about $35 million and Banco de Exterior of Spain, where the Spanish investor was an important private shareholder, provided around $145 million in loans. The project's overall debt to equity ratio was relatively high, perhaps as much as 3.5 to 1. The Vial group's business interests were diversified and it was engaged in efforts to take over the Bank of Chile. Thus, both partners seemed more experienced and involved in the financial aspects of the forestry business than with its sustained operation and long-term development.

When the recession hit, this fledgling project could not be sustained by its sponsors and the enterprise went bankrupt in 1983 with the facility less than one-half completed. The project's bank receivers, led by Banco de Exterior, sold a related facility near Santiago that made corrugated cardboard for the fruit export industry to CMPC for about $36 million, but they were left holding the other Nacimiento location. The site sat idle for several years until 1989, when Forestal E Industrial Santa Fe agreed to purchase the partially completed facility for about $124 million.

The Santa Fe enterprise (named after a small town near Nacimiento) was a joint venture formed in 1988 between Shell (60 percent), Scott Paper (20 percent) and Citibank (20 percent). While these partners' goals and contributions differed enormously, together they produced a complementary match between project needs and potential results. The overall objective was to turn the incomplete plant site into a larger facility that would be the center of a forestry complex turning eucalyptus wood into short-fibre cellulose exports.

Feasibility studies showed that the original mill's design could be modified economically to expand it to a minimum world-scale output level of 220,000 to 240,000 tons per year while shifting to the production of short-fibre pulp. Despite the lapsed time, basic buildings were well constructed and much of the remaining equipment was usable or salable. Therefore, rather than razing the facility and beginning again, often the easiest and most economical process, the new owners were able to modify the existing design and complete the complex in a way that met their own production requirements.

Total project cost is estimated at $450 million. Nearly two-thirds of this amount is provided by the three partners, almost all drawn from Chapter XIX debt-to-equity conversion funds. The partners also agreed as part of the Central Bank's approval process to provide loans amounting to approximately 10 percent of project cost. Foreign supplier credits and local bank financing will cover the remainder.

Citibank is essentially just a financial investor in this project, one of several ventures where it has teamed up with Shell to diversify its debt portfolio through Chapter XIX investments, as discussed more fully in the chapter on financial services. The antecedents of this project thus trace back to 1983 when Citibank and Shell formed a 45/55 percent joint venture to acquire the Copihue forestry group, which includes an important sawmill complex.

After this first step in Shell's diversification strategy into Chile's forestry sector, the firm added several other plantation sites both to acquire standing timber and to begin a concerted forestation effort aimed particularly at short-fibre eucalyptus trees. While the Royal Dutch Shell Group operates other forestry projects in countries including New Zealand, South Africa, and Brazil, its activities in Chile have become its most important in this sector, headed by the developing Santa Fe project. Shell Chile also offered other foreign companies a potential joint venture partner with seventy years of local experience.

Scott Paper is one of the world's largest paper companies, with a particularly strong position in the production of soft tissues that require short-fibre cellulose. Scott had looked at the uncompleted plant at Nacimiento but was reluctant to pursue the project without a clear and sufficient supply of appropriate timber. Part of Shell's holdings included Forestal Colcura, which contained a mature eucalyptus plantation and Monte Aguila, an agricultural business that is additionally undertaking major new eucalyptus plantings. As part of the Santa Fe venture, the three corporate partners agreed to similar proportionate shareholdings in these two companies to provide the timber inputs for the Santa Fe plant.

For its part, Scott brought technology, operational expertise, and marketing arrangements along with its financial contributions. Shell lacked the experience in pulp production that Scott could provide and would gain knowledge from the partnership that might aid its expanding forestry interests. Scott gained access to a new supply of short-fibre cellulose from eucalyptus trees that mature in just eight to ten years in Chile's climatic conditions. Scott agreed to purchase a minimum of 50 percent of the plant's output up to a maximum of 80 percent at international prices. This marketing arrangement helps give the project some stability in a cyclical world pulp market. Nearly 95 percent of production will be exported, generating some $150 million in export value.

Up to 1,500 workers were employed in the construction stage of the Santa Fe plant, with about 350 permanent jobs created. The company consciously tried to limit hiring practices that might take skilled people away from other companies. Instead, Santa Fe interviewed educated individuals with little operational experience whom the company would train, using facilities outside the country if necessary. The plant would contribute to economic growth in the underdeveloped rural area surrounding it and the company undertook assistance programs such as special soft loans for housing. Sophisticated equipment valued at around $28 million is also being used to control the plant's local environmental impact.

The opening chapter of the Santa Fe story is testimony that a mixed joint venture between local and foreign investors is no guarantee of success. The full tale, however, shows how a correct match among joint venture partners can bring together the full package of resources needed for a successful business project, including the raw material inputs, processing technology, management skills, and international marketing channels. Beginning operations in April 1991, Santa Fe is helping Chile extend its forestry industry further into world markets, adding diversification into short-fibre cellulose.

Japanese and Other New Investors—Issues and Challenges

A growing number of international firms are investing in Chile's forestry sector, including several important projects involving Japanese corporations, among the first significant direct investments in Chile by firms from that country. Some of Japan's major trading companies have been active in Chile for several decades, but until recently neither these nor other Japanese corporations had major direct investments in significant production projects. Several projects involve the cutting of native forests, raising more sensitive environmental issues than those encountered in the cases discussed thus far.

Mitsubishi undertook the most extensive early direct investments, first in the fishing sector in 1978, followed by its participation in the Escondida copper project in 1985. Two years later the company invested over $10 million in Astillas Exportaciones (ASTEX), a fully owned facility located in the port city of Concepción. ASTEX produces up to 420,000 tons of wood chips annually, entirely for export to Japan. While the plant buys wood from many different parties, plans call for setting up a related plantation to grow primarily eucalyptus trees. Mitsubishi affiliates will invest over $33 million in a 10,000 hectare plantation near Concepción. While assuring a stable supply of wood for export to Japan, these plans also appear related to increased Chilean concerns about the use of native forests to feed wood chip plants.

C-Itoh is another Japanese trading company that entered Chile's forestry sector. The firm owns one-quarter of Forestal San José, a joint venture with First National Bank of Maryland (40 percent) and Chilean investors related to Compañía Chilena de Astillas (35 percent). Bank of Maryland utilized Chapter XIX for its portion of the funding, its first such venture in Chile, but C-Itoh opted for the procedurally faster and somewhat more secure D.L. 600 channel. The project, beginning operations in mid-1990, requires an investment of over $6 million as well as $3 million more in working capital.

The Forestal San José complex includes a mechanized sawmill that will employ 150 people to produce 40,000 cubic meters of wood annually; a wood chip plant capable of a 250,000 metric output with 120 permanent jobs; 10,000 hectares of plantation land to grow trees; and a new mechanized port facility capable of round-the-clock operations that load four cubic meters of wood chips per second, the fastest operation in Chile. The self-financed loading pier will avoid further burdening existing port facilities. Wood chips are light and do not require heavy port equipment, but they do need a particularly large storage area near the water to accumulate enough chips to fill a large vessel. Production is for export, primarily to Japan, and should yield $20–$30 million in annual sales. The company reportedly approached local universities and other experts for assistance in forestry management techniques in an effort to develop its own resources and avoid controversies about the use of native forests.

C-Itoh was also initially linked to a project by Daio Paper of Japan, which saw the trading company as an experienced local partner. Forestal Anchile, a joint venture 84 percent owned by Daio Paper, sought to acquire land for planting eucalyptus trees. Daio Paper considered investing more than $500 million over ten years to construct a cellulose plant, a newsprint plant, and a sawmill. Problems associated with management of the native forests and the absence of other sufficiently mature trees in the region caused some adjustments to this strategy. At the end of 1990, the company invested the first $57 million of a scaled back project to purchase forestry land in southern Chile.[5]

Sensitivity to the native forest issue stems from accusations made against Japanese forestry projects in Southeast Asia in areas such as Borneo, New Guinea, and the Philippines. Marubeni, another Japanese firm interested in wood chip investments in Chile's southern region, was awarded a cardboard chainsaw by a Japanese ecological group protesting the destruction of tropical forests. These concerns are not confined to the activities of Japanese investors, however. A Swiss-owned Richco enterprise expanded from exporting pine and eucalyptus logs and chips into a new operation that relied on native forests for its wood chip supply, sparking local protests.[6]

A particularly high-profile clash over the native forests occurred in mid-1990 when Compañía de Acero del Pacífico's (CAP's) Sociedad de Inversiones postponed Terranova, a major forestry project. Terranova's strategy involved the acquisition of 62,000 hectares of native forest, over one-half of which the firm proposed to maintain in its natural state while utilizing wood from the remainder and converting some areas into faster-growing species such as radiata pine or eucalyptus.

An initial investment stage of $50 million called for the construction of a plant that could produce 6.5 million cubic meters of wood chips annually for export primarily to Japan. Marubeni was associated with the project and would supply the export marketing channels. This first stage also required the construction of about 1,000 kilometers of roads and the modernization and expansion of port facilities at Corral to handle the export volume. Later project stages could involve a cellulose plant and other wood products. Uncertainty over regulations governing the exploitation and reforestation of native forests paralyzed Terranova's development, causing suspension of the project after an expenditure of around $9 million. Several hundred workers were laid off from a projected employee base of 1,000 people, which might have eventually meant up to 5,000 direct and indirect jobs for the region.[7]

In general, ecologists charge that the cutting of native forests and their reforestation with monoplantations of radiata pine or eucalyptus species would sterilize the soil, permit erosion from shallow-rooted trees, and deny endangered animals necessary habitats. Spokespeople for the forestry industry counter that forest areas were sometimes burned so the land could be used for subsistence farming or raising livestock. The native forests had little commercial value prior to the interest expressed by wood chip companies and many of the trees are subject to center rot which ruins the wood value.

Environmentalists often worry most about the practices of local companies that sell wood to large foreign-owned forestry firms. Smaller suppliers sometimes engage in harmful logging practices that strip and burn the land to allow easier and less expensive harvesting. Foreign investors interested in wood processing are thus sometimes urged to invest in the forests themselves. These enterprises are often more responsive to environmental pressures and can be regulated more effectively if they have an invested long-term stake in the management of local forest resources. With the application of proper management techniques, a thinning process can produce much of the wood needed for chip plants while a study of area soil and other conditions could determine whether harvested areas should be replanted in native trees or faster-growing varieties.

Environmental issues concerning exploitation of the native forests are complex, and Chile's new-found attraction for the forestry industry simply outpaced public policy and administrative decisions. Particularly with the election of a new democratic regime, the weighing of policy objectives and the formulation of implementing regulations require more time to establish clear guidelines for investors, local and foreign. Observers with differing perspectives on the problem generally can agree that Chile's Corporación Nacional Forestal (CONAF) needs more personnel and equipment for its national forestry service to increase patrols and control illegal practices. Beyond this point, debate in 1991 focused on a proposal to permit development only in some portion of native forest areas judged to be environmentally stable. From the standpoint of private investors, the absence of clear and stable rules is an important deterrent to further investment in this sector of the nation's burgeoning forestry industry.

Improving Wood Products—Pathfinder and Fletcher Challenge

Reports about the growth of Chile's forestry industry often focus on the two extremes—the success in attracting large capital investments needed for major cellulose facilities or the worry about possible environmental and other problems raised by the sector's rapid development. Other types of medium-size investments also occur as foreign firms explore Chile's potential for value-added wood products by improving and sometimes redirecting the operations of local enterprises. Two examples of this strategy are found in the investments of Inversiones Pathfinder and the Fletcher Challenge company.

Inversiones Pathfinder is associated with the Bin Mahfouz interests represented by the National Commercial Bank of Saudi Arabia. As mentioned in an earlier chapter, Pathfinder negotiated the first Chapter XIX transaction approved by the government of Chile. Mellon Bank (U.S.), Manufacturers Hanover (U.S.), and Bank of Scotland subsequently became minority investors in this enterprise with 18 percent, 10 percent, and 10 percent, respectively. The Pathfinder group's investment policy has been to seek good investment opportunities in firms with financial or management problems, particularly in sectors where Chile's natural advantages offer export promotion or import substitution potential, with the objective of assisting and/or restructuring the firm to improve its competitiveness.

After initial investments in fishing enterprises, Pathfinder acquired Maderas y Sintéticos S.A. (MASISA) in 1986. This firm had been established in 1960 with the help of German assistance and technology as Chile's first particle board factory. MASISA expanded production and locations in the mid-1960s and again in the early 1980s but became snarled in financial difficulties during the country's recessionary times. Over 1,200 employees staffed MASISA's various wood processing facilities. Sales were concentrated in the domestic market, and the company possessed the industry's widest distribution network with 300 dealers throughout the country.

Pathfinder linked up with Citibank in acquiring MASISA, with the bank contributing Chapter XIX money to help fund a modernization campaign in exchange for 25 percent ownership of the company. The new owners invested over $60 million over four years to more than double main plant capacity, bring in new technology, and introduce two new product lines by adding a plywood plant and the fabrication of some furniture parts, the latter designed primarily for export. Under final study was a plan for a $60 million medium-density fiberboard plant similar to the one constructed as part of the Carter Holt Harvey investments described earlier.

MASISA's forest holdings have been expanded from 60,000 to 70,000 hectares, about equally divided between native forests and pine or eucalyptus plantations. Nearly one-quarter of the firm's sales are now directed at the export market. Investments of the type Pathfinder is pursuing with MASISA can generate approximately three times as many additional export sales per invested dollar as more capital-intensive forestry projects such as the large cellulose plants. Quality and reliable marketing are key aspects of building a reputation for Chilean output in new wood product areas, however, and Pathfinder's international trading connections assist the firm in securing new export sales.

Fletcher Challenge presents a somewhat different example of flexible collaboration between domestic and foreign corporate investors to improve Chile's wood products industry and extend its international marketing reach. A New Zealand-based firm similar to CHH, Fletcher Challenge relies on forestry and wood products for about one-half its total business, with energy, primary products, and building and construction activities comprising other major divisions. The company had followed Chile's forestry growth for years, opening a one-person consulting office in Santiago in 1984 to monitor developments more closely.

Fletcher Challenge is more interested in processing than planting activities in Chile, but it did not see an appropriate opportunity until approached by CMPC, which wanted to sell a newsprint mill. In reality, CMPC was interested in acquiring a larger mill operated by INFORSA at the time, but the purchase would essentially give CMPC a monopoly position in the newsprint industry. This drew opposition from the government's anti-monopoly commission. CMPC might have sold the mill to Celulosa Arauco y Constitución but probably did not want to strengthen its traditional domestic competitor. On the other hand, Fletcher Challenge might have been interested in the INFORSA mill, but CMPC's local position seemed to give it an inside track on the purchase and the larger facility seemed a bit too big an investment for Fletcher Challenge's first venture into Chile.

Both sides found it convenient to structure the initial transaction as a joint venture with Fletcher Challenge retaining an option to leave its holdings at 51 percent. This approach allowed the firm to ease into its first Latin American investment while enabling CMPC to retain some participation in the mill in case the INFORSA purchase ran into unexpected trouble. A key element of the agreement was Fletcher Challenge's insistence that some forest land be included in the deal to give it a developed raw material base. CMPC reluctantly parted with 25,000 hectares, which has since been almost doubled to provide timber for the mill. The forests are mainly radiata pine and, based on experience with similar forests in New Zealand and concerned about environmental issues, the company has no interest in native forest holdings.

Fletcher Challenge obtained full 100 percent ownership in 1987, at a cost of $122 million, using a Chapter XIX debt-to-equity swap that brought an average discount of 35 percent on the debt paper and a redenomination rate of 90-95 percent by the Central Bank. The company's local subsidiary, Tasman Chile, operates the enterprise through two companies divided into forest and production activities—Forestal Bío Bío and Papeles Bío Bío. The company used $57 million of reinvested funds in addition to the purchase price to upgrade newsprint quality at the mill and expand output from 74,000 to over 100,000 tons per year.

Nearly 60 percent of the company's sales are exports, with most newsprint going to Latin American markets and some log exports to China, Korea, and

Turkey. In South America, only Chile, Argentina, and Brazil have major newsprint mills and Brazil is still generally a net importer of the product. The market can fluctuate, however, and Latin American consumption dropped by nearly one-third over the 1980s. Both CMPC and Fletcher Challenge therefore pursue expanded sales in other regions and have essentially complementary strengths with the former focusing more on Europe and the latter on Asia. A joint operation coordinates export sales to the Latin American market, with both firms seeking the best price for products exported from Chile.

Fletcher Challenge cites Chile's labor productivity, tree growth rates, adequate infrastructure, and stable forestry policies as attractive factors in their investment decisions. The firm's risk perception lessened after a few years' experience in the country as the nation made a successful transition to democracy while maintaining a relatively stable economy. Further possible investment in Chile's forestry sector will be linked to how well potential problem areas are managed, including the improvement of port infrastructure and the retention of cost competitiveness in labor and power usage, especially electricity rates. As mentioned in the previous chapter, Fletcher Challenge also purchased Cape Horn Methanol in 1991, thereby expanding and diversifying its investment interests in Chile.

An Unlikely Exporter—Kodak's Forestry Venture

In 1926 the Kodak company began operations in Chile, initially selling the photographic products generally associated with their name but soon expanding into graphics and medical supplies such as X-ray equipment. The firm acted primarily as an importer and wholesaler of these products, growing with the Chilean economy until the Allende government imposed strict import controls during the early 1970s. The company then had to reduce its size, allocating short supplies among its traditional customers.

When import controls were lifted under the Pinochet regime, the company hired and trained more people, bringing in new equipment such as mini-labs in the photographic area. Kodak eventually broadened its business portfolio to include fourteen different product lines, increasing employment from less than fifty to several hundred people. Two new areas led the firm into exporting from Chile. One undertaking results from a conscious corporate effort to become a nontraditional exporter; the other is an opportunistic outgrowth of diversified business support activities.

As a long-time investor in Chile, Kodak became sensitive to its role as an importer. Despite contributions in employment, technology, and tax payments, the company's business is subject to potential criticism as a net drain on the country's foreign exchange earnings. The Allende period showed the firm's vulnerability to political decisions regarding import controls and the company decided to complement its expanding Chilean activities with an export business that would help balance its trade account position.

Study revealed the forestry sector's promising export potential due to natural advantages in tree growth and relatively cheap labor for processing work. Chilean officials sought value-added activities beyond sawn wood and cellulose production. An incipient furniture export business had begun, growing from $398,000 to $18.4 million between 1983 and 1989. This activity was primarily in furniture parts, meaning that large mark-ups on completed furniture (following assembly and distribution to retailers) were gained outside the country. Kodak had no direct experience in lumber or wood products, but could offer marketing assistance for value-added products in the United States. The company proposed to manufacture finished furniture in Chile for shipment directly to retail establishments.

Kodak made two strategic contributions to this project. First, it surveyed retailers to learn their essential requirements for furniture purchases, which were high product quality and reliability of delivery under agreed conditions. Chile lacked an established track record as a furniture manufacturer and many U.S. retailers had doubts about the reliability of an untested supplier from the southern reaches of Latin America. Kodak overcame these misgivings, partly through placing the corporation's credibility behind the new product. This step was not taken lightly, since the product lies outside Kodak's normal portfolio and poor performance could affect the firm's overall reputation, which constitutes one of its important competitive assets.

The company's second strategic step was to pull together production expertise to make the furniture venture a success. It hired established design, sales and production personnel, already recognized among the furniture retailing community, for the Chilean operation. Determining that required expertise and technology was not already available within the country, Kodak brought in five top managers for the plant, acquired modern equipment in the United States and Europe, and arranged for the training of local personnel.

The furniture operation is structured as a 51 percent Kodak-owned joint venture named Los Andes S.A. Project start-up required around $5-6 million in local financing. The Chilean partner is a business group (Hurtado-Vicuña) that holds compatible views regarding product quality and long-term business perspectives. A notable member of the corporate board of directors is Hernán Büchi, former treasury minister and presidential candidate in the 1989 elections. The Kodak undertaking represents a type of value-added, nontraditional export project that he had urged during his influential tenure as head of the government's open market-oriented economic team.

The plant opened in mid-June 1990 with about 150 workers, a figure expected to more than double in two years. All production is directed at the export market. The first $3 million furniture order was shipped to New York stores at the beginning of 1991. Almost two dozen buyers expressed interest in the new products and the company anticipated that orders could reach nearly $30 million in annual exports. If realized, this figure would exceed Kodak's initial target of seeking a one-to-one relationship between export earnings and its import bill, which ranges around $20 million. Unfortunately, the deep U.S. recession retarded initial sales and disrupted distribution arrangements, causing delays and requiring additional management attention.

Kodak hopes this project, if successful, can help establish Chilean credibility in the U.S. furniture market and lead to an expansion of this industry in Chile. In the large U.S. market, a small number of major retailers could absorb the full production of several plants once supplier ties are established. In addition, related industries could be stimulated, such as in packaging and freight. Currently Kodak must import special packaging material to insure that the finished furniture arrives in good shape, ready for the retailer's showroom floor.

A smaller Kodak export venture, which takes place through intrafirm channels, grew out of its need for computer software for some of its products. The firm organized a local joint venture (ICI) with eight young computer specialists to supply software for Kodak products and provide follow-on work with its customers. The venture subsequently won a contract to provide software for Kodak's subsidiary in Argentina, beating out a U.S.-based company. This Chilean joint venture now aims to become the software supplier for all Kodak operations in the southern cone.

Kodak's strategic decision to become a nontraditional exporter from Chile depended on many factors, both external and internal. Chile has natural advantages in forestry and its open market regime allows imports of high technology equipment that can foster a growing software industry. Kodak's management structure is decentralized enough to permit its Chilean subsidiary room to innovate. The domestic market is too small to support local production in the company's traditional product line, but the firm's experience in Chile and its philosophy of good corporate citizenship led to the approval of plans for business operations, such as in computer software, that do not exist elsewhere in Latin America, and in furniture manufacturing, which does not exist anywhere else in Kodak's worldwide network.

Investor Actions and Outlook in Forestry

Forestry gives Chile an important complement to its traditional strength in minerals. While also based on natural resources, forestry is a renewable resource that may offer greater potential for value-added processing than mineral production. Foreign investors are attracted to Chile's combination of climatic advantages, cost competitiveness, and stable investment policies. The availability of debt conversion funding encouraged greater scale and diversity of forestry projects than would have developed without this financial tool. Chapter

XIX repatriation restrictions were generally acceptable for projects geared to the decades-long growing cycle of tree plantations.

The government's planting incentive did not play a similarly influential role in attracting foreign investors. This program was important in stimulating domestic forestry activity, however, which helped attract the attention of overseas forestry firms. A couple of Chilean companies strengthened their traditional presence in the local forestry industry through arrangements with foreign enterprises that contributed capital, technology, management techniques, or broader world market access. In early 1991, CMPC purchased 51 percent of an Argentine wood panel manufacturer for $11.5 million, announcing its own intention to be a technological and commercial leader in the region, and beyond.[8]

Case examples discussed in this section represent major developments in the forestry sector, but they do not capture all the emerging projects or related spin-off effects from this industry's rapid growth. For example, in mid-1990 the Swiss firm Cellulose Attisholz was authorized over $43 million in Chapter XIX funds for an anticipated cellulose project that is projected to cost $90 million. Union Camp Corporation (U.S.) formed a joint venture with the Spanish Lantero group, which itself has nearly eight years' experience in another Chilean joint venture. Nearly $25 million was invested in a plant to produce corrugated cartons, primarily for use by Chilean fruit producers. While sales are primarily domestic, most cartons will be used in agricultural exports, thereby merging the growth of two nontraditional export sectors in a complementary and reinforcing fashion.[9]

In another spin-off industrialization strategy, Chile's Tecnología Forestal (TECFOR) linked up with Austrian BBU to export a number of forestry tractors valued at $60,000. The two firms also agreed to arrangements for future production in Europe, using some Chilean components, while TECFOR is representing BBU's interests in an investment of several million dollars for a wood processing plant in Chile designed for housing construction products. In another exchange of production and technology, most forestry trailer trucks used in Chile are now manufactured locally, using New Zealand and Nordic technology.[10]

Capital-intensive cellulose facilities captured most of the attention regarding foreign investments in the forestry sector. These plants require a certain scale to be competitive on world markets and investors generally seek vertical integration to ownership of forest plantations sufficient to assure input supplies. Investors often bring management know-how, processing technology, and export market tie-ins along with the capital to finance the complex. The small Chilean market for most paper products appears to limit further value-added production except in cases such as packaging materials for fishing and fruit exports.

Value-added growth appears more promising for other forestry products, particularly furniture and certain construction materials. Chilean production could compete with output from foreign firms located in Asia and elsewhere that now use Chilean lumber or components to produce finished goods for sale in the United States. Initial capital investment barriers are not so high in these products. Foreign involvement can bring the technology and training necessary to assure quality control and marketing channels or expertise needed to overcome initial retailer resistance to an unknown supply source. Both these foreign investor advantages will presumably decrease over time as Chilean-based production becomes established and the country gains recognition as a reliable supplier of world quality wood products.

Parts of the forestry industry are labor intensive, particularly construction of necessary infrastructure along with seasonal planting and forest management functions. Value-added processing stages vary between capital-intensive cellulose plants and other woodworking operations that exhibit a wide range of mechanization. General industry growth has increased employment in all categories, but under current projections the proportion of forestry laborers involved in planting and harvesting will stabilize or decline while the component engaged in industrial processes should continue to expand. Expansion of the forestry industry aids regional development goals although projects have tended to congregate around Concepción, influenced partly by the proximity to established port facilities and the availability of harvestable forests.

Chile must address certain possible bottlenecks to further development in order to realize estimates that call for a doubling of current forestry investments by the turn of the century. Road and port infrastructure has sustained current growth but will require major improvements, with costs probably shared between the public and private sectors. In addition, a clear, sustainable, and enforceable policy regarding management of native forests must be developed to govern the exploitation of these resources. This policy should balance environmental and economic costs as well as the role of major corporate and artisanal forestry interests. These issues must be resolved in a way that assures investor confidence in policy stability in order to provide the strategic planning horizon required for major forestry investments.

FISHING

Fishing is the second of Chile's three major nontraditional export sectors that experienced impressive growth during the 1980s. A relatively small number of foreign investors played a significant role in the industry's expansion, in terms of both increased sales volume and diversification into new activities. The sector nevertheless encountered real constraints on further growth, imposed by the threat of depleting the nation's coastal fisheries. These limits to growth, combined with the industry's importance as a source of artisanal employment, created policy conflicts between large foreign corporate investors and small local fishing interests. The clash came to a head in 1990–91 when the new democratic government debated proposed changes to the nation's fishing law.

Chile's fishing industry encompasses several types of activities based on four different fishery resources. Traditionally dominant is the production of fish meal for animal feed and fish oil for industrial uses. Chile is the world's largest exporter of fish meal and ranks second to Japan in exporting fish oil. Sardines and jack mackerel are the main fish used for these purposes. Human consumption of these fish is limited except in surimi, a product sometimes used for imitation crablegs or as a sausage filler. These species are pelagic, or dark-fleshed fish generally caught from the ocean surface to a depth of approximately 100 meters. Usually concentrated up to one hundred miles off Chile's northern coast, the capture of pelagic fish extended southward over the 1980s to the region around Concepción. This fishery is highly subject to shifts in ocean currents, however, complicating both its tracking for capture and monitoring for resource conservation.

Demersal are white-fleshed fish (and crustaceans) found near the ocean floor and generally captured along the roughly ten-mile wide continental shelf. While this fishery extends nearly two-thirds of the way up the country's coast, most of the captures are made from Concepción southward to Cape Horn. Composed primarily of several types of hake, demersal fish are usually caught for human consumption. A third fishery is composed of benthonic or shellfish species that are found attached to the ocean floor. Packaged fresh, chilled, frozen, or canned, both demersal and benthonic products command a higher price than the pelagic species. Exports grew about 50 percent annually in the late 1980s, with Spain, the United States, and Japan as the leading importers.

Alongside the ocean fishing, a new aquaculture fishery has been installed in Chile, primarily in the inland marinas and numerous fjords located in the southern region. These enterprises include shellfish and algae, but most attention is focused on raising high-value fish that are not native to Chilean waters. Salmon aquaculture is the most successful, expanding over 200 percent annually from one metric ton in 1980 to over 4,000 metric tons in 1988. Output more than doubled again the next two years and could reach over 26,000 metric tons by 1994.

Foreign investors helped develop Chile's fishing industry into an important nontraditional export sector by introducing new technologies that expanded commercial fishing areas and led to higher value-added uses for the catch. In some cases substantial foreign financing was needed to utilize the advanced technologies; in other instances access to international marketing methods and distribution channels were the keys to promoting Chilean products.

Surveying Investors—CHH, Pathfinder, Nippon Suisan, and Others

Foreign involvement in Chile's fishing industry is reflected in the investment activities of Carter Holt Harvey (CHH), the New Zealand natural resources company introduced in earlier sections on forestry and energy. The firm's initial 1987 investment of $200 million gave it an equal partnership with the local Angelini group in the investment firm Inversiones y Desarrollo los Andes. The Angelini group already had significant interests in a number of Chile's principal fishing enterprises, with production facilities concentrated in fish meal and fish oil. CHH used its new partnership to invest in two fishing enterprises, bringing capital resources and processing technology to expand and improve the firms' operations.

The first fishing investment came indirectly through the partnership's majority control of Compañía de Petróleos de Chile (COPEC), giving CHH a 30 percent share of the company (one-half of the partnership's eventual 60 percent ownership). COPEC had expanded into fishing in 1980 when it acquired Pesquera Guanaye. Formed in 1962, this company operates about thirty vessels, primarily off the country's northern coast, to supply four processing plants. The firm is Chile's leading producer of fish meal and fish oil and its 1989 output represented close to five percent of world fish meal exports.

CHH involvement in Pesquera Guanaye sparked two major expansions in value-added processing. A second production line was installed in an existing plant at Tocopilla while a new $35 million fifth plant was built farther south at Coronel, allowing the company to extend and integrate its operations into that region. This expansion will give Guanaye the capability to process over 400 tons of raw material per hour in its plants. Both improvements introduced state-of-the-art equipment to produce prime grade fish meal whose higher protein content commands a better price. These changes will boost one-half of Pesquera Guanaye's southern production and one-fifth of its northern output into the prime grade category. The company also contracted for two more ships at a cost of $6.5 million to help supply the new plant.

In 1987 the enterprise entered demersal fishing by forming Pesquera Marazul, which operates as an affiliate of Pesquera Guanaye under COPEC's corporate umbrella. This operation is expanding in the central and southern regions with the purchase of new fishing vessels and a processing plant established at San Antonio. With products aimed at human consumption, this activity overlaps somewhat with CHH's acquisition of 46.9 percent of another firm, Pesquera Iquique, in conjunction with the same local partnership but outside the COPEC structure. The CHH contribution to this venture is exemplified by the San Rafael, a major new vessel whose deep-sea fishing capabilities and onboard processing capacity are suited to fisheries located in the southern waters.

Another foreign investor whose interests straddled a couple of Chilean fishing activities, along with forestry and agricultural enterprises, is Pathfinder. Controlled by the Bin Mahfouz group of Saudi Arabia, the company has three minority partners in Mellon Bank (18 percent), Manufacturers Hanover (10 percent), and Bank of Scotland (10 percent). Pathfinder's fishing investments began in 1986 when it purchased Pesquera Eicomar. The Dutch Rabobank joined Pathfinder as a partner in this venture. Using four of its own ships, Eicomar became Chile's largest exporter of fish sold for human consumption. Under Pathfinder's direction, the firm moved from only frozen fish sales into fresh and canned seafood as well, along with some fish meal production. Despite this initial success, Pathfinder decided in early 1991 to divest from this part of the fishing industry due to a serious decline in yields from traditional fisheries and a change in Chile's fishing law, as discussed later in this chapter.

The second and remaining part of Pathfinder's fishing activity comes from the development of Pesquera Eicosal, also in conjunction with Rabobank. Eicosal is developing salmon for export, with plans to expand from 1,500 tons in 1990 to 2,500 tons by 1993. This objective could yield as much as $12 million in annual export sales, principally to the United States and Japan. Rabobank's investment of about $4 million for a 31 percent share in Eicosal is providing working capital for the purchase of salmon eggs and fish meal for feeding, along with the necessary labor component. Chapter XIX funds were approved for Rabobank's contribution and also provide the basis for Pathfinder's various investments.

Exponential growth in salmon production offers clear testimony to Chile's development of nontraditional exports and their relationship with foreign businesses. Salmon is not native to Chile, so its central place in the nation's burgeoning aquaculture industry relied on its introduction from abroad, a continual supply of imported eggs, and the penetration of foreign markets for export sales. Foreign investors provided around 40 percent of the initial $200 million invested in salmon facilities. Companies from Japan, Norway, and Great Britain are playing an important role in developing Chile's salmon resources, along with other investors from New Zealand, the United States, and Canada. The United States and Japan provide the largest markets for Chile's fresh and frozen salmon whose export earnings rose from $19 million in 1988 to nearly $100 million in 1990.

British Petroleum Nutrition invested in Chile in 1988, initially in a joint venture (Trouw Suralim) that permitted doubling an existing facility's production of concentrated feed for fish and animals. Trouw International, a BP subsidiary, is a leading world producer of fish food. The company used Chapter XIX funding in 1990 to increase its stake in the enterprise and expand activities as a fully owned firm (Pesquera Mares Australes) involved in salmon cultivation. The new investment aimed to increase salmon production fourfold to 5,000 tons a year by 1995, with an export value of $30 million. Additionally, the firm dedicated some $250,000 and its laboratory facilities in Chile and the United States to investigate a sickness that had affected some of the salmon in Chile.[11]

Nippon Suisan combines salmon cultivation with deep sea fishing, including the use of factory boats. In 1988 the firm purchased Salmones Antártica from Fundación Chile, a specialized technology transfer institution discussed later in this chapter. Salmones Antártica is one of Chile's largest salmon producers and the first firm to use an open sea ranching program. Nippon Suisan, one of Japan's leading producers and marketers of seafood products, is also related to Empresa de Desarrollo Pesquero de Chile (EMDEPES), one of three major Japanese fishing enterprises in Chile.

Initial Japanese investments in Chile's fishing industry developed after EMDEPES had spent a couple years exploring fishing potential in the far southern waters. This firm, which is also related to Mitsui, invested an initial $7 million in 1978 using D.L. 600. Two other Japanese firms also made similarly oriented investments around the same time: Nichiro, which formed a company (Epenic) with Mitsubishi, and Taiyo. These enterprises operate factory fishing boats that can stay out from port roughly two months, with on-board processing of about 90 percent of the catch.

Japanese investors own about one-half of the dozen factory boats operating in Chilean waters, with Spanish and other largely foreign interests operating many of the long-line fishing vessels that work the offshore southern waters and coastal channels and fjords. As foreign investors, these firms can register for local concessions and fishing rights, sailing their ships under the Chilean flag. These vessels should be distinguished from other foreign factory boats that often operate in fishing grounds just outside the 200-mile territorial limits off Chile and Perú. Protests regarding these boats arise from charges that they stray inside territorial waters to fish and may use local ports to offload their catch, lowering local prices and straining transportation facilities without contributing directly to national welfare.

Several advantages accrue to Chile from these fleets, including their local purchases of supplies and contributions to national exports, but the gains are smaller than those from nationally based ships. Some of the larger foreign vessels that do operate under Chilean registry can reach farther offshore and operate in more hazardous waters than smaller local boats, thereby opening new fisheries to national exploitation. On the other hand, artisanal fishing interests complain that factory boats present unfair competition that can deplete their fishery resources in some areas. The larger boats are also less labor intensive, meaning a reduction in total employment to the extent that the fleets replace rather than complement the efforts of small local fishermen.

Debate Over a Revised Fishing Law

Chile's fishing industry fell victim to its own success at the beginning of the 1990s as strained resources threatened current and future production. Concern over the depletion of key fisheries led to a proposed revision of the country's basic fishing law to promote conservation and allocate the distribution of fishing rights. This proposal sparked vigorous debate that pitted several sectors of the fishing industry against each other. The government was forced to weigh the relative importance of national policies relating to resource conservation, artisanal employment, free competition, and national treatment for foreign investors. This last issue had precedent-setting implications, since revision of the fishing law brought the first significant claim from foreign investors that Chile was reneging on its legal guarantees of equal treatment.

Fishing law revisions were formulated in 1989, just as the industry exceeded all records for total catch, processing, and exportation. Pelagic fish dominated landings and the resulting production of fish meal and fish oil increased at least one-third over the year before. Higher-value fresh and frozen demersal fish generated over one-quarter of the sector's export earnings with a much smaller catch. In total, Chile's fishing exports amounted to $934 million in 1989, an increase of over 11 percent compared to the previous year.

The Pinochet government approved a revised fishing law in December 1989 just a few months before leaving office. Due to take effect on April 1, 1990, the law's implementation was postponed by the new democratic government to allow time for greater public debate on its controversial provisions. Several more postponements followed as the Chilean Congress considered revisions of the revision. Business fortunes shifted back and forth during these discussions, including the fate of early foreign investors in the fishing industry.[12] All parties to the issue agreed with the need to protect Chile's valuable fisheries. Many companies disagreed with the government and environmental groups, however, as to whether studies proved the existence of a threat to fishing resources serious enough to warrant the proposed restrictions. The main dispute revolved around which species were threatened, where to establish geographic control zones, how to use a quota system for a permissible catch, and which firms should be eligible for fishing rights.

Most companies objected to applying one control system to the entire fishing industry which covers diverse operations drawing on some 100 fish species in various stages of exploitation. Many firms in northern Chile have long-established fish meal and fish oil operations. Their catch comes from pelagic fish that migrate widely as temperature and currents shift feeding patterns, making them difficult to track and making it difficult to determine what control measures are needed. Since fish are not limited by national boundaries, Chile's companies also worried that conservation measures could simply increase Perú's harvest north of the border unless a bilateral agreement set common terms for both nations.

By contrast, southern demersal fish are easier to monitor and control, but the fishing industry there is newer and exploitation patterns are less well established. Traditional artisanal fishing interests sought to exclude more recent factory or other large vessels from the best fisheries. A related dispute erupted over giving priority to companies that used land-based processing facilities. All groups worried that a quota allocation system could mean an expanding statist role for government regulators. Workers' representatives opposed frequent shifts in fishing rights that would mean labor instability. Other groups supported free competitive access to check potential monopolistic abuses if traditional firms were granted indefinite rights to a limited supply. The debate proved most difficult for the new democratic government, pitting conservative opposition forces in the Senate against the Aylwin administration, with regional welfare concerns and constitutionality issues mixed in as well.

Business uncertainty created by the controversy plagued the industry just as its fortunes took a downturn. The sector experienced an overall decline of 10 percent in 1990, although export performance matched the previous year's earnings due to strong increases in high-value fresh and frozen fish exports. The capture of pelagic fish fell by more than a million tons, however, a decline of nearly one-quarter from the previous year, with the far northern region experiencing almost a 40 percent drop. A combination of overexploitation and shifting migratory patterns probably accounted for this result, which continued into early 1991. Problems in the northern fisheries represented a blow to firms that were expanding and improving their processing facilities to produce higher quality fish meal while also addressing environmental problems surrounding some plants. The Angelini group, which owned the broadest array of companies in the area, was particularly hard hit. The damage affected several ventures where CHH was an affiliated investor.

The main issues for most foreign investors were proposed revisions that would restrict foreign ownership in fishing firms to a minority share and reserve areas of southern fisheries for artisanal boats, effectively pushing larger foreign vessels into a smaller region of hazardous waters where few local boats could operate. Both proposals challenged the general national treatment principle regarding foreign investment and confronted early investors with a discriminatory change of rules that would lower the value of their established enterprises.

Proposals for restrictions in the southern zone played on the distinctions between foreign and domestic enterprises.[13] The objective was to reserve most of the region between 43 and 47 degrees latitude for artisanal fishing, severely restricting the activities of Chile-registered but largely foreign-owned deep-water trawling and long-line fishing fleets, many of them factory boats. The restrictions would cut some firms off from areas that had supplied over 40 percent of their catch while forcing them to contend with more hazardous waters below 47 degrees latitude that are sometimes closed by ice or other weather conditions.

The Spanish firm Pesca Chile entered Chile in 1983, investing close to $50 million to develop fishing activities largely in the region that would be closed to it under the proposed restrictions. The company announced in October 1990 that it would suspend plans to invest another $30 million due to uncertainty over the fishing law revision.[14] Japanese fishing companies also faced the uncertainty of potentially serious restrictions on their operations in the southern region.   Taiyo and Nichiro both sold their factory boats (three and one, respectively) in 1991 due to falling catches and uncertainty over the pending restrictions.

EMDEPES had already experienced the effects of earlier vacillations, purchasing land to begin development of an on-shore processing facility in 1981, when Chilean authorities moved toward a policy favoring such operations. The firm canceled this project to use more efficient on-board ship processing when the Pinochet administration decided against a preference scheme. New proposals would favor firms with processing facilities on land, a policy change that would disadvantage EMDEPES's established operations.

Proposals to restrict the southern fisheries raise one type of challenge to the national treatment principle. Advocates stress the importance of protecting the tradition of artisanal fishing whose social and cultural value to the nation reinforces the economic benefits of labor-intensive employment and local value-added activities in smaller coastal towns. Opponents point to the efficiency of larger fleet operations and their important role in the growth of Chile's fish export industry. This view stresses the contribution foreign firms made to developing the fishing industry in southern waters, arguing that it is unfair to change the rules now to discriminate against them.

Proposals to revise the fishing law's ownership provisions also challenge national treatment guarantees and business concern with stability in the rules of the game. The Pinochet administration's original revision called for majority Chilean ownership. Debate focused on a requirement that all fishing vessels must be 51 percent Chilean owned and the majority of a fishing company's directors, as well as both its president and manager, must also be Chilean citizens. Most nations restrict foreign ownership in various parts of their coastal shipping industries, so the objection to this provision was less to the general policy than to a fear of retroactive discrimination against already invested foreign firms.

A proposal to apply the restriction only against future foreign investment in the fishing industry, thereby grandfathering existing operations, received much support, although it was unclear how this exemption would treat possible expansions by those investors. During 1991 the Aylwin administration seemed to move away from this position, causing the foreign investor community to protest the proposed requirement as a violation of signed D.L. 600 guarantees that investors in the fishing industry would receive the same national treatment as local investors. Foreign firms did not view proposals to allow a transition period of several years as any real improvement, since both prevailing uncertainty over depletion of fishery resources and public knowledge of an enforced sale requirement would result in fire sale prices for their assets.

The CHH investment in Chile's fishing industry illustrates the travails for an investor presented by the fishing law's revision. The company would not have to alter its nearly 47 percent ownership of Pesquera Iquique, since its joint venture partner is Chilean, but the role of its executive as president of the firm could be affected. Pesquera Guanaye might require restructuring since that firm is owned by COPEC which in turn is effectively controlled by Los Andes Investment, a 50/50 joint venture between CHH and the Angelini group, although CHH thereby actually owns only around 30 percent of COPEC.[15]

These fishing investments are not the most important element of CHH's investment in Chile, but the firm took the lead in challenging the potential discrimination against foreign investors. This action stemmed primarily from its announced intention, discussed earlier in the book, to sell or restructure its Chilean investments. The fishing law's new restrictions could clearly diminish the value of its existing investment and restrict its options to sell its shares in the fishing enterprises to other foreign firms. CHH petitioned Chile's Foreign Investment Committee, as permitted under D.L. 600, to uphold that law's guarantees of national treatment as provided for under articles 9 and 10. When that body did not respond affirmatively, CHH petitioned the Chilean court system for redress, again as provided under D.L. 600.[16]

This dispute's potential significance clearly reached beyond the fishing sector. In an editorial titled "A Dark Cloud on the Horizon for Foreign Investment," the Chilean-American Chamber of Commerce's journal in May 1991 warned "This is a clear violation of the guarantees provided by D.L. 600 and will create considerable concern for foreign investors both in this and in other sectors. If fisheries investment must be majority Chilean, then why not mining, lumber, and agriculture?"[17]

In truth, there are valid reasons why the fishing industry might be treated somewhat differently than other sectors. The primary rationale derives from the high-priority need to protect fishery resources, which limits the growth potential for further exploitation of the covered species within designated areas of Chilean territorial waters. If resource limitations prevent a general increase in the fishing industry, then traditional social values and employment objectives in poorer coastal areas can justify political restrictions that preclude foreign interests from gaining a greater share of a static economic pie. Artisanal fishing still represents over 58 percent of the nearly 100,000 jobs in the fishing and related processing industry.

Two key qualifications modify this viewpoint, however. First, neither the conservation nor the social objectives justify applying discriminatory restrictions retroactively on foreign investors who had helped develop the sector economically under contractual national treatment guarantees. Second, the generalized restriction on foreign investment can limit growth potential in related fishing activities, including exploitation of new deep-water areas requiring large vessels and new technologies as well as further improvement in value-added processing and foreign marketing.

In mid-1991, Chile's Foreign Investment Committee agreed that provisions of the new fishing law which violated contractual national treatment guarantees should be changed. Restrictions may limit future foreign investors to minority ownership, but the limitations would not apply retroactively to existing investors. CHH expressed satisfaction with this solution and, while it does not address the geographic fishing restriction issue, most foreign investors felt the action upheld and reinforced Chile's commitment to its foreign investment guarantees.

The role of foreign investment in Chile's fishing industry is thus at a point of transition. During the 1980s, resources committed by foreign investors helped develop and draw attention to the sector, turning it into an almost too successful example of nontraditional export promotion. While financial resources were important, the application of better technology and marketing methods probably contributed the most to opening new fisheries, increasing catch volume, creating an aquaculture subindustry, improving the quality and value of processed output, and reaching foreign markets in Europe, Asia, and the United States. Resource limitations will place a cap on many activities for the foreseeable future, leaving the potential for divisive reallocation decisions among industry participants. On a brighter note, traditional fishing exports will remain important foreign exchange earners for Chile while aquaculture expansion in salmon and other species offer further growth possibilities for the sector over the 1990s.

AGRICULTURE

Fruits and other agricultural products provide the third major element in Chile's nontraditional export growth. Agriculture experienced tremendous turmoil through the 1970s and still faces periodic crises from natural disasters, financial difficulties, and overseas protectionism. Beginning in the mid-1980s, however, government policies aided a recovery in grains and other products that reduced or eliminated import dependence while sparking a surge of export promotion led by fresh fruit. Foreign corporations play an important role in export-oriented ventures, providing financing, technology, processing, and marketing expertise. These firms may also prove a key ally in meeting Chile's still formidable challenges to improve product quality, diversify markets, and fight foreign protectionism.

Agrarian reform measures in Chile during the 1960s turned into aggressive expropriations under the Allende regime when many large landholdings were forcibly broken up and redistributed. A partial restructuring occurred during the early Pinochet years when the government restored some properties, but this action essentially ended the country's efforts to impose land reform. Agriculture suffered further through the recession of 1982–83 from liberalized import policies and heavy indebtedness. New government policies aided subsequent recovery, expanding production of import substitution crops while encouraging export expansion for promising fruits and related products.[18]

The government encouraged domestic production of wheat, sugar beets, and edible oils by setting official margins with minimum import prices above the international market. This price band system reduces investment risk for expanded production by smoothing price fluctuations. Wheat and sugar beet output responded well to this policy, but oilseed production faced tough land competition from the first two crops' expansions. Contract purchasing, credit assistance, and irrigation projects also aided many farmers. In a few cases, such as milk production, protection against subsidized imports helped Chile recover to near self-sufficiency.

In general, foreign investors played little role in increased domestic production aimed at import substitution. Foreign trading interests were undoubtedly affected as agricultural equipment to some extent replaced foreign crop exports, but these changes did not stimulate significant investor interest. Some foreign firms did invest in food processing and distribution facilities, particularly dairy products, cereals and beverages, as discussed in a later chapter. For the most part, however, foreign investment strategies were more evident and useful in export-oriented segments of Chilean agriculture. Here, foreign investment and overseas business relationships helped develop a range of new export stars, led by off-season export of fresh Chilean fruit.

Fruit Exporters

Chile possesses significant natural advantages in agricultural production, particularly in terms of world exports. The country's impressive length encompasses a variety of climates, permitting cultivation of a broad selection of products at various times of the year. Its isolated environment, enforced by the high Andes to the east and the Pacific Ocean to the west, protect it from easy infestation by agricultural pests and diseases.

Geographic isolation imposes higher transportation costs to move products to major developed country markets, but this disadvantage is partially offset by the enormous benefit that comes from offering off-season production to northern hemisphere countries. Chile even holds a delivery-time edge in many agricultural products over major southern hemisphere competitors such as Argentina, South Africa, New Zealand, and Australia due to climatic and geographic conditions. In addition, labor costs in worker-intensive areas such as fruit production are one-quarter to one-third as much as in the latter two countries. Chile accounted for less than 10 percent of counter-seasonal fruit exports from southern to northern hemisphere countries in the 1974–79 period; by the end of the 1980s, Chilean exports represented more than one-half this total.

Acreage devoted to growing fruit essentially doubled over the 1980s, with grapes replacing apples as the most popular crop. Fresh fruit represented well over 80 percent of rising agricultural exports that reached nearly $1 billion by the beginning of the 1990s. Grape exports increased fivefold, claiming almost 5 percent of Chilean export receipts. Chile also exports pears, nectarines, plums, peaches, and an expanding quantity of kiwis. Export volume grew over the decade from 10 million to 100 million boxes of fruit annually, with some projections envisioning 150 million boxes by 1993. This enormous growth required the creation of an efficient and expensive support system to finance, harvest, store, transport, distribute, and sell the fruit in distant foreign markets. Several foreign investors developed strategic business plans that made important contributions to this sectoral development.

Dole's Standard Trading Company. Standard Trading Company is the Chilean subsidiary of Dole Fresh Fruit Company, the largest unit of Dole Food Company, which also covers the reorganized business of Castle & Cooke. This latter enterprise initiated operations in Latin America at the beginning of the century by cultivating bananas in Honduras as Standard Fruit Company, placing it in the infamous gunboat diplomacy era of U.S. relations with its southern neighbors. Its operations in bananas, pineapple, peaches, and other products took the company into many other Central and South American countries as well as the Philippines.

Standard Trading was established in Chile in 1981, beginning operations the following year with exports of nearly 2 million boxes. Dole invested nearly $75 million in this operation through the end of the decade, more than in any other location outside the United States during that time. Most of the investment came after the recession ended in 1984 and various government policy reforms were being instituted. The firm utilized Chapter XIX funding for $41 million of its investment, which constituted around one-quarter of authorized debt swaps for fruit export operations and nearly 12 percent of approved deals in the agricultural sector up to 1990. Chile's creation of the Chapter XIX mechanism helped draw attention to the country's growth potential as corporate headquarters reviewed the investment proposals of various business units competing for corporate funds. The resulting investment in construction of packing houses and cold storage facilities fueled a seven-year annual growth rate near 40 percent, propelling Standard Trading near the top ranking of Chile's fresh fruit exporters with around 12 percent of the national total or more than 13 million boxes.[19]

The large established producer base in Chile allowed Standard Trading to follow preferred company policy, adopted nearly two decades ago, of working with independent growers. The company can provide these growers with financial and technical assistance but demands top quality standards and enforces certain requirements such as restrictions on pesticide use. Nine plants operate throughout the growing regions to handle packing and refrigerated storage of the fresh fruits, including grapes, apples, pears, peaches, and kiwis as well as a smaller operation that handles raspberries and asparagus.

Although Standard Trading has not moved into direct growing activities, it did integrate vertically into the packing industry by establishing two new subsidiaries, Embalajes Standard and Cartones San Fernando, that produce wooden and cardboard packing materials, respectively. The majority of Chile's fruit exports are shipped in wooden crates manufactured locally, but cardboard containers may be gaining ground environmentally due to their easier disposal. Standard Trading also relies heavily on Dole's shipping fleet to transport its products, particularly during peak seasons, although the firm uses a liner service for off-season and some U.S. West Coast shipments.

Established marketing offices in the United States, Europe, and Japan give Dole's Standard Trading subsidiary an effective distribution reach beyond the capability of Chilean firms that generally sell to receivers in the final destination port. The company sells to professional buyers for wholesalers and supermarket chains, so consistent product quality and reliable delivery schedules are essential. Dole's international reach enables it to provide markets with a steady flow of supplies through the relevant product season. Its global connections also help Chile attain better market diversity as Standard Trading's exports flow less to the United States and more to Europe and the Middle East compared to overall Chilean averages.[20]

Multinational locations add to Dole's flexibility but also present the firm with difficult policy choices. In general, Standard Trading has chosen to support and work through Chile's Exporters' Association, including in disputes with the United States. The firm was hurt financially along with other local exporters when the U.S. Food and Drug Administration temporarily banned the sale of Chilean fruit in March 1989 during a controversial scare about possible cyanide poisoning. The company backed the Exporters' Association position seeking U.S. compensation for the serious financial injury suffered by Chile's fruit industry. The company can use its U.S. resources to help defend joint interests, as in this case, but in other instances it may become internally divided, such as regarding the application of U.S. marketing orders that can give U.S. products an advantage over Chilean fruit at certain times of the year. Overall, Dole's interest is best served, as is Chile's, by support for open international trade among all countries.

Standard Trading has not moved into the canned fruit business. Dole does little canning except for pineapples and some juice, and the parent firm has established juice suppliers elsewhere. Substandard fruit that does not meet export quality is separated during the packing process in the Standard Trading plants and usually sold for the growers who receive the proceeds. In the case of grapes, the growers separate the product by quality standards, selling the rejected fruit for the local market, juice, or raisins. Dole bid unsuccessfully in the United States to purchase the Del Monte company, which would have given it extensive canning interests. This is one instance where a Chilean subsidiary probably would have explored further investment opportunities had the parent's global strategy evolved differently.

From Three to Four of Five Large Traders. The top five companies (out of around one hundred export firms) account for approximately one-half of Chile's fresh fruit exports. Three of these firms were operated by foreign enterprises. Standard Trading competes with David del Curto, a locally owned company, for the honor of being the largest exporter of Chilean fruit. The U.T.C Company is controlled by London-based Saudi Arabian interests and Unifrutti Traders is owned by the Italian de Nadai family that operates out of Saudi Arabia. In 1990, a fifth large local exporter, Frupac, was sold to Chiquita Brands International, another of the world's largest fresh fruit distributors (formerly United Brands and United Fruit, also with historical roots in Central America).

One of Frupac's founders and its principal shareholder expressed mixed emotions over the sale, perhaps reflecting the views of other local observers. He lamented the loss of local control over another large exporter and professed a belief that Chileans could still organize and operate a dominant exporting firm in this field. While recognizing the foreign traders' positive effect on promoting fruit exports, he felt debt conversions gave these firms an unfair advantage over local investors. Frupac was under financial pressures, but its sale was voluntary; he even complimented foreign creditor banks for reacting more calmly than local ones to Frupac's crises. In the end, Frupac's old owners were satisfied the firm had done well and that Chiquita Brands would use its resources, distribution system, and large volume to take the firm to a new stage of development in the fruit industry.[21]

The other two large foreign-owned exporters, as well as several smaller ones, reflect Middle Eastern and especially Saudi Arabian interest in Chile's fresh fruit production, particularly apples. The more intriguing story may be Unifrutti's investment, which pertains to the de Nadai family from Italy. This group began operations during the 1930s in the Italian colony of Ethiopia where it prospered until being expropriated after the communist takeover in 1975. Left with only some import interests in Saudi Arabia, the group shifted its base of operations to that country with some Arab partners. The next decade the group expanded into the United States and, in 1983, into Chile.

Through an investment of some $70 million, Unifrutti's exports jumped from 800,000 boxes of fruit its first year to more than 10 million boxes by the end of the decade. The firm operates seven plants and has an agricultural affiliate, Uniagri, that owns several growing operations. The company can utilize some of the ten refrigerated vessels owned by an affiliated maritime group in Saudi Arabia to transport Unifrutti's exports. The firm's owner stresses product quality in achieving overseas sales and believes that brand name recognition and the global market information available to multinational trading companies will be key competitive advantages over the 1990s.[22]

Smaller Saudi Arabian investments also offer interesting tales of strategic entry and expansion of operations in Chile's agricultural sector. The Bin Mahfouz group, which controls the National Commercial Bank of Saudi Arabia, first invested in Chile in 1980 through a joint venture with the local Vial family group. BHC International, a trading company, went bankrupt with the rest of the Vial structure in the 1982–83 recession. The Bin Mahfouz group then used Pathfinder to negotiate Chile's first approval of a Chapter XIX debt conversion and made the first of five major investments, purchasing C & D (Comercio y Desarrollo) International, a fruit exporter. The firm gained an advantage in selling red apples in heavily managed Arab markets and exported grapes to the United States, Europe, and Japan.

Pathfinder linked up with Rabobank of Holland, an institution formed by agricultural cooperatives, as a partner to expand into the growing stage by forming C & D Agrofruta. Rabobank contributed additional capital through Chapter XIX and brought some knowledge for the growing operations where the objective was to introduce new varieties. The firm still buys products from other growers but operates its own vineyard and is pursuing the cultivation of new apple varieties. This venture follows Pathfinder's general pattern of trying to add joint venture partners that bring both financial resources and sectoral expertise to its projects in Chile's agriculture, fishing, and forestry sectors.

Despite its rapid growth and economic importance, the fresh fruit industry remains vulnerable to crippling disruptions on several fronts. Most growers' operations are highly leveraged and can face financial ruin from events largely beyond their control. As a group, growers require over $1 billion in credit annually to develop new land, purchase fertilizers, and pay temporary workers to pick the harvest. Around one-half this total goes to firms involved with export sales. Some 1,600 of the nation's roughly 8,000 fruit growers run large operations, but even these firms have difficulty finding enough collateral to secure sufficient commercial credit from the banking system (hence the intermediary financing role for some fruit export firms).

Individual fruit growers still bear most of the sales risk. Nearly three-fourths of the fruit is sold on consignment. Growers do not know until well after the sale what their income will be once various distributor costs are subtracted. Should fruit arrive during a mid-season supply "glut" or be judged lower quality merchandise, growers may not recover their costs and may face credit repayment problems. Some growers complain that export companies, particularly smaller firms, are slow to return sales income, essentially using the cash proceeds for a longer time than necessary. Large trading firms with quality control programs in Chile, trademark identification in the marketplace, and efficient transport and delivery systems can reduce some risks that face individual growers as long as sufficient competition exists among the trading enterprises.

Disruptions still occur and Chile suffered several unpredictable crises during the past several years. The most serious crisis broke in March 1989 with the grape cyanide scare and temporary restrictions on Chilean fruit sales in the United States and elsewhere.[23] Resulting damage to the Chilean fresh fruit industry was estimated at over $300 million, touching all segments of the industry but punishing particularly smaller growers and temporary workers. Denied access to their major export market, many growers dumped truckloads of grapes in city centers for free distribution before they spoiled. Prompt government action on an emergency credit program probably saved the industry from financial collapse but did not alleviate individual hardships. Foreign investors were hurt along with the rest of the industry but could draw on wider resources, as Standard Trading did by increasing its capital some $27 million to overcome the effects of the crisis.[24]

The following export season the industry was buffeted by an infestation of fruit flies apparently arriving with tourists or through shipments from neighboring Argentina. Transportation problems arose from a temporary closure of the Panama Canal that disrupted boat schedules. Prices plummeted when too many grapes, some of lower quality, reached the U.S. market during the prime season. Export volumes diminished in the 1990–91 season due to continued drought conditions in northern Chile, but growers and traders benefitted from higher prices, in part due to crop losses from harsh weather conditions in California. Exports to Europe increased by nearly one-third, contributing additional revenue while diversifying Chile's marketing base.

The fruit industry constitutes a major component of agriculture's emergence among Chile's nontraditional exports. An equally important social and political factor is its labor-intensive operations. Roughly one-quarter of a million workers depend directly on the fruit industry for employment, about one-half of them (mainly women) hired temporarily for periods of six to ten months. Related indirect industrial and service employment adds an equal number of jobs, meaning that roughly one-tenth of the nation's labor force depends on this sector's continued health and growth. Significantly, many jobs are located in rural areas, which helps improve living standards and stem migratory movement to the cities.

Seeking Added Value

Foreign investment strategies also aid Chile's search for increased value in its agricultural sector, tracing several paths that explore new crops, markets, and value-added processing. One approach seeks new products that may duplicate the enormous success of table grapes, drawing on the same climatic and off-season marketing advantages. Sales of berries and high-value vegetable crops such as asparagus are increasing but face obstacles due to potential transport problems. Highly perishable products may require air transport, raising total cost to the exporter. Low-volume, high-value products are also particularly susceptible to losses from mishandling during transport where damage to only a few crates can quickly turn potential profit into a loss.

Increasing market diversity helps guard against excessive vulnerability to disruptions in single market areas, such as occurred in the 1989 U.S. grape scare, as well as expanding the range of saleable products and their potential returns. On the high end of the scale lies the Japanese market where fruit exports increased after a five-year collaborative test for quality and phytosanitary standards. Product quality and presentational appearance are highly valued in Japan where expensive fruit are often bought singly to be given as a gift. International trading firms possess the experience and resources needed to help small exporters break into the Japanese market, overcoming implicit trade and internal distribution barriers. Other markets also offer potentially broader sales. Perfectly good fruit that may not meet exacting standards for sale in Japan, the United States, or Saudi Arabia may nevertheless earn good returns in many other countries.

Investment strategies also extend to value-added operations in the so-called agroindustry sector. Canned vegetables and fruits (mainly peaches and juices), bottled wine and dried fruits have established the most success. Although these operations exhibit increased value added, their profitability is not as clear as fresh fruit exports because Chile's comparative advantages are weaker. Hemispheric off-season growing patterns apply to fresh rather than preserved fruits and vegetables. In addition, much of the equipment needed for capital-intensive processed food operations must be imported. Nevertheless, Chile's growing agricultural production and the subsequent availability of products not meeting fresh export standards suggest a likely expansion of processed food operations.

Mega Marketing & Brokerage announced a new $1 million investment through Chapter XIX in mid-1990 to expand exports of dried fruits, especially raisins. A leading U.S. importer of such products, the firm had established a cooperative venture two years earlier with Santiago Trading, a local exporter with nearly a dozen years' experience in such exports. The new investment would allow the partners to increase their number of producers from ten to twenty and double exports to over $4 million annually. Approximately one-half the new funds would finance machinery imports needed to assure the standardized product quality required for international market success.[25]

Cargill also used Chapter XIX funds as well as D.L. 600 investments to expand the size and range of its operations in Chile. The company had acquired a metals-trading firm with a Chilean office, giving it a presence in the country dating from 1975, although it eventually left copper trading to concentrate on its core agricultural operations. Beginning in the mid-1980s with an investment of roughly one-half million dollars, Cargill developed four operating divisions that trade corn and wheat, import fertilizers, produce hybrid seeds for U.S. and European markets, and operate a plant for dehydrated fruits and apple juice, where it employs advanced technology involving genetic improvements. The firm may also explore other business opportunities in Chile that could utilize its large U.S. distribution system.

Cargill examined possible participation in a local value-added activity to develop an ammonia-urea project in southern Chile near the Cape Horn Methanol plant, but this project fell through, as discussed in the previous chapter. Chile's fertilizer needs do give the firm an important stake in imports for domestic market sales as well as the potential for agricultural exports. An additional interesting twist to Cargill's expansion in Chile relates to its relatively slow, staged development. The company seeks to avoid using large numbers of expatriate managers, so it geared expansion to the development of local personnel, at times using overseas training. Only one U.S. manager was employed in Cargill's Chilean operation in 1990, but several Chileans were already being promoted to Cargill units outside the country.

Empresas CCT (formerly Compañía Chilena de Tobacos) has a much longer history in Chile. It was founded in 1909 under Spanish ownership. The firm came under the control of a competitor, British American Tobacco (BAT), in the mid-1930s. BAT increased its shareholdings to around 70 percent by the mid-1980s, with the remainder still held by thousands of small local investors. The company figures in Chile's agroindustry sector not only because of its tobacco operations but also due to an expansion during the 1980s into food processing and exports.

Originally a plantation owner, CCT moved to contract buying at a fixed advance price from over 1,500 small Chilean tobacco growers whom the company assists with seeds, financial assistance, and updated technology for cultivating and drying tobacco leaves. In contrast to a local firm which operates under license to another foreign multinational, Empresas CCT uses Chilean tobacco and processes it locally. The company imports some tobacco to blend for flavoring and exports around 4,000 tons of Chile's tobacco crop with an important expansion projected for future. Filters and papers are also imported because the small size of the local market does not justify domestic production of these goods. The cigarettes themselves are not good candidates for export since most countries impose high tariffs on the product, although some exports are occurring.

The company faced difficult times under the Allende government's price control system that was coupled with imports of tobacco from East European nations such as Bulgaria. The industry was also one of the last to have price controls lifted under the Pinochet administration. Limited income precluded expansion plans until around 1980. While using some Chapter XIX funding, the company decided to rely primarily on D.L. 600 investments, first expanding its local marketing capabilities beginning in 1981.

In 1983, Empresas CCT and an Australian BAT affiliate (Amatil) began operating jointly a snack food company (Evercrisp) in Chile, a product area with established domestic consumption patterns where BAT had applicable experience elsewhere. Empresas CCT acquired Amatil's share of Evercrisp in 1985, the same year it purchased Consorcio Agroindustrial de Malloa, followed in 1988 by another agroindustrial firm, Conservas Deyco. These acquisitions gave CCT both facilities and name recognition in the local market, but their subsequent reorganization and expansion provided an export market capability that was the company's main diversification interest in Chile. The company also expanded the operations of Litografía Moderna, its subsidiary that manufactured packaging for cigarettes, to provide similar services for both Malloa and Evercrisp as well. By 1989, Empresas CCT had grown to an enterprise that employed over 2,100 permanent workers and up to 2,000 temporary jobs at the peak of the agrobusiness operating season.

Agroindustrial exports is a new business for BAT, which possesses similar interests only in Brazil and Malaysia. The initiative in Chile resulted from BAT's rather decentralized structure that gives local operations some flexibility to undertake "pioneer" operations for the enterprise. Central control is exercised primarily through financial requirements and on matters such as industrial safety standards. Thus, while CCT could draw on some BAT technical assistance, much of its agroindustrial export initiative, including its overseas marketing efforts, went beyond established areas of BAT experience.

Empresas CCT's domestic production and marketing covers several areas of fruit, juice, and vegetable processing, and its export operation concentrates in tomatoes, canned fruits, vegetables, sauces, and other finished products. The company contracts with around 250 local tomato growers each year for their production which is processed by a plant whose size was doubled at a cost of approximately $6 million. Malloa has a long-standing relationship with the Kagome company of Japan, which provides some technical assistance, to supply 4,000 tons of tomato paste annually. The firm also supplies other foreign companies on yearly contracts with tomato paste and products such as fruit juice to sell under their own brand labels. Empresas CCT initiated the export, mainly to Latin American countries, of its own labeled finished products such as sauces, marmalade, ketchup, canned fruits, and others. These steps enabled the firm to increase processed food exports to $20 million in 1991, covering some thirty countries.

Chilean wine production offers a predominantly local example of increased export sales, although foreign investors made important technology and marketing contributions that helped call attention to this product's potential. Wine exporters date back at least to 1910, when the Undurraga family began export operations. A Spanish investor, Miguel Torres, is credited with starting the latest export thrust in 1979 through his efforts to improve product quality and seek value-added returns. Chilean technicians were sent to France, the United States and elsewhere to study the latest technology and learn more about foreign consumer markets. In 1988, the French Rothschild group invested $3 million in a 50/50 joint venture that helped introduce the latest technology to the Los Vascos vineyard. Similar foreign investments provided additional financial and marketing resources to other Chilean vineyards including Concha y Toro and Errázuriz Panquehue. Chile became the third largest wine exporter to the important U.S. market, trailing only Italy and France. Total exports grew from under ten million liters annually in 1982–84 to over 40 million liters in 1990, with a further doubling projected in the next several years.[26]

In summary, foreign investment strategies in Chilean agriculture emphasize quality assurance and marketing assistance, with financial resources playing an important supporting role. The quality and marketing themes overlap because both are essential to gain access and establish a reputation for reliable delivery of high quality food products in world markets. Most multinational traders assist independent growers with financing and technical advice on quality control procedures. Many of these firms also helped build the expensive nation-wide infrastructure of packing plants, refrigerated trucks and warehouses, port facilities, and shipping vessels required to move Chile's fresh produce to distant export markets in a timely and cost-effective manner.

Foreign investment in agriculture exhibits a broad range of mixed-ownership and cooperative marketing ventures that extend from the field to grocery store shelves. Foreign direct investment is least in cultivation activities and greatest in processing and marketing. An export orientation predominates, with most foreign investors participating in joint export promotion efforts sponsored by Chilean agencies and private business associations. Mutual interests can develop from long-term contractual arrangements as well as direct equity investments; for example, the Port of Philadelphia handles most of Chile's fresh fruit exports, providing an important source of direct and indirect employment, accounting for up to one-third of stevedore hours at the port. These tie-ins create a common stake among enterprises that are in a position to represent import interests before regulatory and political bodies in the consuming markets. In addition, advantages lie in serving a globally integrated marketplace, making most foreign investors natural allies for agricultural exporting nations such as Chile that seek to remove entrenched trade barriers in many developed country markets.

DIVERSIFIED EXPORT PRODUCTS

Chile's nontraditional export success springs principally from its natural resource base in the three "Fs" of forestry, fishing, and fruit (as well as other agricultural products). Although the small domestic market inhibits production in other fields, the local business community, including some foreign affiliates, is proving surprisingly adept at developing other nontraditional exports within these constraints. These diversified sales fall into three general categories: spin-off products from the natural resource sectors; mainline manufacturing goods dependent on hard-won cost or marketing niches; and information-age products that utilize Chile's well-educated professionals and sophisticated communications network.

The first product category is typified by several examples cited earlier, including the export of forestry tractors and Kodak's elaboration of finished furniture exports. Engineering consultants from CODELCO's minerals operations are a services version of the same phenomenon. In a recent fishing industry example, two Chilean firms (Indo and Eperva) joined with a foreign company (Hetland Process) to adapt a Norwegian technological process for making prime quality fish meal to the species of fish found off Chile's coast. As the upgrading of Chilean plants slowed due to uncertainties over fishing law changes, the firms successfully marketed their innovation to several Peruvian facilities that draw from a similar fishery.[27]

More unexpected export gains arise from an array of manufactured products that seek out cost or marketing niches. Chile's textile industry fights low-priced foreign competition in many products, but its reinvestment strategy and technological improvements led to export success in other areas. Blue jeans top the list with more than $60 million in exports sales from 1987–90, principally in the United States. This initiative began in 1985, stimulated by a Gitano investment in Chile and the subsequent growth of local suppliers.[28] Athletic shoes (sneakers) shifted from an import to an export item during the late 1980s. Baby clothes made in Chile appear in some 300 stores in the United States. Continuing the theme of baby products, Chile's CMPC forestry firm used U.S. technology to produce disposable diapers, expanding in four years from an import substitution strategy to export sales in neighboring Uruguay and Paraguay.[29]

A Chilean firm exported flexible plastic packaging, primarily used to preserve and protect food products, to continental neighbors Bolivia, Uruguay, Ecuador, and Argentina; then it entered markets in the United States and Africa. Another national enterprise produces parts for civil and military aircraft under joint venture contracts with foreign aerospace firms. Chilean chewing gum, rope, and parts for cigarette lighters are other export items. Chilean wood is used to produce chop sticks, tongue depressors, and ice cream sticks for overseas sales. (Competition can be stiff, however. Chilean exports of some

70 million clothespins were knocked from the U.S market by cheaper Chinese versions.) One novel Chilean export schemes makes money by making money. Employing all local resources except nickel imported from Bolivia, Chile's national mint produces more than 160 million coins annually for countries such as Colombia, Argentina, Uruguay, Israel, and Spain.[30]

The third diversification category among nontraditional exports stems from global high-technology industries that can utilize Chile's educated human resources and its increasingly sophisticated communications infrastructure. The country reportedly has the largest installed capacity in Latin America for handling international computer traffic, tying its twenty-five largest cities directly into data bases in the United States, Europe, and Japan. Only Brazil among the continent's nations records more computer traffic volume with the United States. The expansion of Chile's university system and technical training centers as well as increased study abroad provides well-trained individuals who span many professional fields. Chile leads all South American nations in per capita rankings of individuals with post-graduate studies in the United States.[31]

Chile boasts the first Latin American company to produce and export products using genetic engineering. Bios Chile, which makes an antibody related to the treatment of growth hormones, signed contracts worth nearly $120,000 for export sales to the United States, Canada, and Belgium. Among other locally produced items offered for sale are a pregnancy test and a diagnostic agent for the disease chagas. New projects under development include a vaccine for hepatitis B and a growth hormone for salmon production.[32]

Success came even earlier for Chilean computational and software exports, which grew tenfold between 1980 and 1987, reaching $230 million. In the mid-1980s, Sociedad Nacional de Procesamiento de Datos (SONDA) overtook a Brazilian firm as South America's largest computational enterprise. SONDA was initially created to serve the computing needs of COPEC and remained a part of that company until its sale in 1991, to founder and general manager Andrés Navarro. SONDA's international competitive potential was recognized as early as 1984, when it established a 120-person office in Argentina to offer "on-line" services to the banking industry. In conjunction with a U.S. firm, the company competed for a similar banking contract in China, managing difficult translation problems in Chile. SONDA's software exports commenced in 1989; the following year its export earnings registered close to $6.5 million from sales to Indonesia, Venezuela, Colombia, Perú, Mexico, and Argentina. In 1991, SONDA created a joint marketing firm with Digital to promote sales throughout Latin America.[33]

One of Chile's early software exports to Mexico, Argentina, Venezuela, and Colombia was a package used on Ataris that covered educational courses and materials for school children. Another export product emerged from the University of Chile's need for an information retrieval system. An innovative software program called "Birds" was designed locally by a Unisys subsidiary with programming done at the university. The program was later marketed abroad, including a sale to the Beijing Library in China. Unisys also helped maintain and market a software program named "Proclínica," developed by the local Ettica company, as part of a software package sold to hospitals all over Latin America.[34]

Other exports arose from an undertaking between Unisys and Chile's Enersis electric utility company. After privatization, Enersis possessed excess computing capacity which it joined with Unisys's data services center to form a 51/49 percent-owned joint venture named Synapsis. The firm marketed a "SAM" software system for municipalities to Colombia and in 1990 sold seven U.S. counties "Xnear," a package useful principally to digitalize municipal plans and maps. Unisys also chose Chile as one of two South American locations for a regional software development center—a tribute to the country's engineers and its communications infrastructure. This center will be developing value-added, intra-company exports by conducting research for other regional Unisys affiliates.

The president of Chile's Committee of Software Exporters sees exports growing at nearly 20 percent annually. The chief of ProChile's services export group cites translation services as another promising field that can utilize the country's modern telecommunications system to link local translation specialists with customers around the world.[35]   In general, Chile's computer and telecommunications infrastructure, developed largely through recent foreign investments as discussed in the general industry chapter, provides a foundation for local service and information-based businesses by domestic as well as foreign investors.   Foreign investment helped nourish the growth of nontraditional exporting companies such as Synapsis and SONDA (now an MNC itself), while cooperative programs with national universities and other institutions expand the technical resources available to the Chilean economy.

Technology Transfer for National Development—Fundación Chile

Technology transfer lies at the heart of many national development strategies. Chile boasts a unique enterprise, Fundación Chile, which sponsors technology transfer to promote Chilean economic development, particularly in nontraditional export sectors.   Fundación Chile is a nonprofit enterprise established in 1976 through an agreement between the government of Chile and the ITT Corporation. History books record the acrimonious relations between ITT and the Chilean government in the early 1970s, reporting that ITT officials conspired against President Salvador Allende. The activities of Fundación Chile write a different and more harmonious chapter to that conflict.

The Chilean government and ITT disagreed over how to value the company's assets in order to set compensation terms for its expropriated property. Finally, an official of the military government proposed that both parties assign the amount in dispute ($50 million) to a new entity whose objective would be to stimulate Chilean economic development through technology transfer. Essentially each side would be contributing $25 million over a ten-year period, with ITT assuming initial management responsibilities. The organization concentrated on technological applications for Chile's natural resources, promoting nontraditional export potential before that idea became widely recognized as a national objective.[36]

Initially devoted to information dissemination through seminars and publications, Fundación Chile created the first in a series of "associated enterprises" in 1982. These companies tested technology transfers in agrobusiness, forestry, and marine resources. The technological applications required minor adaptations about half the time, substantial changes in about 15 percent of the cases, and a concentration on systematic integration into the business process in roughly one-third of the projects.[37] If these enterprises are successful their demonstration effect encourages other entrepreneurs to enter the field, and Fundación Chile can sell the pilot companies to finance a new generation of projects.

The first proof of this innovation-demonstration-sale cycle occurred in 1988, when Salmones Antártica was put up for public bid and purchased by a Japanese consortium, Nippon Suisan Kaisha, for $23 million. The project had begun in 1982 after Fundación experts determined that conditions in southern Chile could support a salmon farming industry. Over the next six years, Salmones Antártica became one of Chile's largest salmon producers, with aquaculture centers and open sea ranching programs that could yield 1,500 tons of salmon annually. The project helped encourage more than sixty new companies to enter the field, achieving over $50 million in annual sales by the time Salmones Antártica was sold. Two other enterprise projects, Salmones Huillinco and Finamar, were created in 1987 to produce and market Atlantic salmon fingerlings in pisciculture facilities and to produce and market smoked salmon, respectively. Finamar developed quickly, selling eighty tons of smoked salmon by 1990. The firm was sold the following year through an international bidding process to the local Chisal company, bringing $1.9 million for Fundación Chile.

Another successful example of the full enterprise cycle occurred in December 1989 with the sale of Fundación Chile's share in Procarne to its joint venture partner. Over a period of six years, this enterprise had established a business to process and market refrigerated beef using "boxed beef" technology. A fourth sale took place in 1990, involving Berries La Unión, which had been established to grow and export new varieties of berries. Other well established projects remaining under Fundación Chile's guidance seek to develop and produce small fruit, asparagus, and gourmet vegetables with export potential; cultivate oysters and other shellfish and fish varieties; and develop applications for industrial automation systems based on microprocessor technology. Newer proposals anticipate promoting the development and export of computer software and introducing new grape varieties in regions with unrealized potential for producing top quality wines. Fundación Chile also promoted a $3 million Technological Center of Wood Production to encourage higher value-added uses for quality wood products, including exported furniture and wood construction for housing.

Fundación Chile plays a significant role in promoting and certifying quality standards for exported products. Between 1985 and 1989, the institution annually checked and gave its quality approval seal to around 2 million boxes of fruit exports. This program assures the importer that products meet top quality standards and are processed and shipped so as to reach their destination in good condition. This certification program can sometimes lower an exporter's insurance rates, achieve better product prices, and help establish a good quality image for Chilean fruit products. Another Fundación initiative seeks more uses for "waste" fruits that do not meet export quality standards, such as a raisin plant for rejected grapes.

In 1985, Fundación Chile began to participate in projects outside the country. Technical assistance has been provided in Bolivia, El Salvador, Ecuador, Guatemala, Colombia, Argentina, and Egypt. This step might seem strange for an institution devoted to Chilean economic development, especially when some projects, such as work on an apple juice plant in Argentina, could be seen as creating competition for Chilean products. Following a strategy similar to other international businesses, Fundación officials expect to gain from seeing and working with technological applications in different countries, recognizing that the foreign institutions could probably obtain assistance elsewhere if Fundación declined to participate. These overseas activities are limited to no more than 10–15 percent of Fundación Chile's overall efforts, however, and they must pursue a full cost-recovery that is stricter than the standard employed for many domestic projects.

Fundación Chile is now self-sustaining, deriving over one-half its income from selling services and the remainder from its endowment income and the occasional sale of its associated enterprises. The institution had created a total of twenty-nine such enterprises between 1982 and 1990. The financial key to Fundación Chile's development was initial agreement on a $50 million founding contribution and the government's fulfillment of its funding commitment over the ten-year period, even during recessionary times in the early 1980s. The institution is now managed locally, with ITT retaining participation on the board of directors. The corporation's contribution in helping establish this unique enterprise will not directly benefit ITT's shareholders, but the cooperative relationship inherent in Fundación Chile provides a positive ending to the earlier conflict between the company and the country.

NONTRADITIONAL EXPORT STRATEGIES

A supportive and flexible alliance emerged between foreign investment strategies and Chile's goal of expanding nontraditional exports. In contrast with the mining sector, foreign investors exhibit a wider array of relationships with benefits falling more heavily on downstream portions of the production chain (from improved processing through marketing and service arrangements rather than in the initial exploration, financing, and construction of large projects). Forestry offers the closest similarities to mining in terms of some resource ownership and large-scale development strategies. In fishing and agriculture, foreign investors bring quality improvements and overseas marketing assistance. A range of intracompany and joint venture activities add further diversification through product spin-offs and experimental export programs.

A key challenge in developing a nontraditional export strategy is to establish and sustain production platforms, marketing channels, and consumer acceptance in several profitable foreign markets. This objective requires: volume production with quality controls at competitive world levels; transportation, marketing, and guarantee or servicing assurances to overseas sales locations; and sufficient financial resources to develop and maintain a full export package against the many vulnerabilities facing new products and suppliers. Chile's forestry, fishing, and agricultural industries did not possess sufficient range or depth prior to the 1980s to meet this challenge. Foreign investors played a key role in altering this situation.

Forestry benefitted from foreign management techniques, processing technologies, and overseas marketing channels. International firms could mobilize the long-term investment funds needed to build and sustain large projects over a lengthy growth and production cycle. Chile's Chapter XIX debt conversion program played an important role in putting together many of these major financing packages. Foreign investors opened new fishing areas, supported aquaculture experimentation, and developed profitable fresh and frozen fish export markets. Complementary improvements in processing technology benefitted the more established fish meal and fish oil products industry. Quality control, transportation, distribution, and stable financial resources were also key elements of successful investment strategies in Chile's agricultural export sector. Foreign investors are not so prominent in other, increasingly diverse export areas, although business arrangements involving some local subsidiaries are helping to introduce Chilean products into broader world markets.

Chile's government encouraged nontraditional export development through sound macroeconomic policies, an opening to international trade and investment flows, and the creation of small but effective export assistance programs headed by ProChile. The government also worked vigorously, both bilaterally and through multilateral institutions, to reduce foreign trade barriers that inhibited further export growth. Cooperative relationships evolved with an array of private business groups including the Chilean Exporters' Association and the Association of Export Manufacturers. Trade missions and fairs targeted new overseas markets such as Eastern Europe. The associations also worked to promote quality standards and certification programs to enhance the reputation of Chilean products while avoiding excessive government regulation. Chilean subsidiaries of foreign investors cooperated with local business association programs and supported international policies and mechanisms that expanded or reinforced open trade flows.

Foreign investment strategies based on promoting nontraditional exports from Chile exhibited two distinctive types of characteristics. The most obvious investment strategies involved large projects that were integrally tied into a firm's global network and oriented to export markets from their inception. A second, less-well-recognized strategy developed from local subsidiary initiatives within MNC organizational structures that encouraged or at least allowed local planning flexibility. These ventures generally involved spin-off products or consciously developed efforts to exploit local comparative advantages in fields that often broke new ground for the enterprise. In these cases, the investor employed advantages in financing, management, marketing, and corporate reputation to diversify both the firm's business and the country's export base.

The success of Chile's nontraditional export drive expands the range of potential relationships between local and foreign firms, including enhancing the opportunities and incentives for Chilean exporters to become foreign investors themselves. Depending on where a local firm's competitive advantages lie along a production chain from raw materials to final sales, the company may not require partnership with a locally invested enterprise. Other foreign companies may be able to provide the marketing, service, or other downstream support required for a successful export operation. Even long-term supply contracts with large foreign retailers could generate sufficient developmental business support while also providing a national ally against protectionist trade pressures. Eventually, a Chilean firm may decide to establish an overseas branch or subsidiary to expand its business operations, in effect becoming an MNC itself as SONDA has done in order to provide better data processing services to foreign customers. Indeed, from the further elaboration of forestry products to the provision of consulting engineering services, the future for Chile's nontraditional export sectors will become increasingly linked to a variety of international business relationships involving both local and foreign-controlled MNCs.

NOTES

Information in this section is drawn from interviews with corporate executives, government officials, and other knowledgeable experts in the field. The most comprehensive published materials used include the following: from the United States Embassy of Santiago—two in the series *Industrial Outlook Report*: "Chilean Forestry Sector: An Emerging Giant" (September 1989) and "Chilean Fisheries Sector: Growth: A Marketing Challenge for Maturing Fisheries" (November 1989), and a *Sectoral Outlook Report*: "Chilean Agriculture: Integrating into World Markets," prepared by Mark D. Roberts and Carlos F. Capurro (May 1990); from the Comité de Inversiones Extranjeras (Chile) in Santiago—three third edition sectoral investment guides: *Forestry: Chile* (July 1988), *Fishery: Chile* (July 1988), and *Agriculture: Chile* (July 1988); and selected articles from Chilean newspaper coverage in 1990–91, especially from *El Mercurio*. Additional selected citations are provided in the text where necessary for specific references.

1. Compañía de Petróleos de Chile S.A. (COPEC), "55a Memoria Anual 1989" (Santiago: COPEC, 1990), 16, 42–43.

2. "Copec, se vende o no se vende?" *El Mercurio*, February 24, 1991; and "Los sinsabores de Carter Holt," *El Mercurio*, April 28, 1991.

3. "Si se va del país: 'Carter Holt debería restituir diferencial de conversión de deuda'," *El Mercurio*, February 18, 1991; "Expresó Juan Eduardo Herrera: 'Cambios en Capítulo XIX deben ser válidos para el Security y Carter Holt'," *El Mercurio*, February 28, 1991; and "US$ 40 millones de compensación en caso Carter Holt," *El Mercurio*, April 17, 1991.

4. "Familia Carter Vendió Copec," *El Mercurio*, November 26, 1991; and "Carter Holt Reafirma Su Confianza en Chile," *El Mercurio*, November 28, 1991.

5. "Japoneses están impulsando un proyecto forestal por cerca de US$ 520 millones," *El Mercurio*, May 16, 1990; "Demostrado en diversos proyectos interés japonés en el sector forestal chileno," *El Mercurio*, June 13, 1990; "En Osorno: US$ 600 millones para un proyecto forestal," *El Mercurio*, October 6, 1990; and "En la X region: Reactivan plan chipero por 250 millones de dólares," *El Mercurio*, November 26, 1990.

6. Justine Maxudov, "Elephant Dance," *Journal of the Chilean-American Chamber of Commerce* (November 1989), 13.

7. "Inversión, en su primer etapa, es de US$ 50 millones de dólares," *El Mercurio*, July 29, 1990; "Clarificó la CAP: 'Terranova sólo está supendido temporalmente'," *El Mercurio*, August 10, 1990; "Socio japonés estudia su retiro del proyecto corral," *El Mercurio*, June 3, 1991.

8. "CMPC proyecta invertir US$ 100 millones en 1991," *El Mercurio*, March 11, 1991; and "Informó a Superintendencia de Valores y Seguros: Papelera concretó compra de 51% de empresa argentina," *El Mercurio*, March 29, 1991.

9. "Union Camp: US$ 25 millones invierte empresa norteamericana en planta de cajas de cartón," *El Mercurio*, July 5, 1990.

10. "Producidos por TECFOR: Exportarán tractores forestales a Austria," *El Mercurio*, April 2, 1990.

11. "Vía Capítulo 19: British Petroleum eleva inversión en empresa Chilena," *El Mercurio*, June 15, 1990.

12. "The Fishing Law—Is It Really A Monster?" *Journal of the Chilean-American Chamber of Commerce* (May 1990), 9.

13. See the commentary placed in newspapers by opposing business interests, for example: "El bien común y los intereses privados en la pesquería sur-austral," *El Mercurio*, insertion, September 23, 1990; and "La pesquería demersal sur austral: El desarrollo socio-económico y la preservación de los recursos," *El Mercurio*, insertion, September 23, 1990.

14. "Empresa española: Detenidas inversiones por US\$ 30 millones en el sector pesquero," *El Mercurio*, October 19, 1990.

15. "Los sinsabores de Carter Holt," *El Mercurio*, April 28, 1990.

16. "Comité de inversiones extranjeras envió informe al tribunal," *El Mercurio*, April 18, 1991; and "Según Anacleto Angelini: Legislación pesquera es como un zapato estrecho," *El Mercurio*, April 22, 1991.

17. "A Dark Cloud on the Horizon," *Journal of the Chilean-American Chamber of Commerce* (May 1991), 5.

18. One indication of agricultural depression was the drop in tractor imports (since there is no domestic production). Imports averaging 1,500 units annually during the late 1960s were cut nearly in half from 1974 to 1983, with imports in 1983 reduced to only ten tractors. Renewed demand topped 1,000 in 1985 and nearly 3,000 in 1986, sparked by governmental policy changes to stimulate agricultural recovery. See O. Muñoz and H. Ortega, *La agricultura y la política económica chilena (1974–86)*, separata no. 2, vol. 3:1 (Madrid: Ministerio de Agricultura Pesca y Alimentación, Instituto Nacional de Investigaciones Agrarias, June 1988), 23-24.

19. Jonathan Bass, "Inversión extranjera en la agroindustria chilena: La experiencia de Standard Trading Co. S.A.," Speech given at the Seminario Internacional: Oportunidades de Inversión en Chile, Santiago, May 15–16, 1990, Photocopy.

20. *1989 Annual Report: Castle & Cooke, Inc.* (Los Angeles: Castle & Cooke, Inc., 1990).

21. "Afirmó José Luis Ibáñez: 'Aún se puede formar la gran empresa chilena exportadora de fruta'," *El Mercurio*, October 22, 1991.

22. "De Arabia a los Andes," *El Mercurio*, December 9, 1990.

23. On March 13, 1989 the U.S. Food and Drug Administration (FDA) announced discovery of two Chilean grapes poisoned with cyanide and called for voluntary withdrawal of Chilean fruit products from sale. No other tainted fruit was found and charges flew on both sides, with U.S. commentators speculating on the work of terrorists in Chile while Chilean hypotheses ranged from a CIA plot to an FDA laboratory mistake. Early in 1991, fruit exporters and the Chilean government initiated U.S. judicial procedures to seek damages for losses suffered. Placing the controversy into legal channels calmed tensions somewhat, but the event generated widespread anti-American

sentiment for what Chileans saw as unfair and somewhat cavalier treatment by U.S. officials.

24. *Standard Trading Company S.A.: Informe Temporada 1988-1989* (Santiago: Standard Trading Company, S.A., 1990), 9.

25. "Mega Marketing & Brokerage: Inversión de US$ 1 millón hará empresa de EE.UU. en el rubro de fruta seca," *El Mercurio*, June 21, 1990.

26. "Nuestro embajador, el vino," *El Mercurio*, February 17, 1991; and "Vino Chileno, tercero en ventas en Estados Unidos," *El Mercurio*, December 13, 1991.

27. "Bienes de capital: Chile exporta maquinaria para industria pesquera," *El Mercurio*, September 20, 1990.

28. "A US$ 60 millones llegan exportaciones de jeans," *El Mercurio*, May 31, 1991.

29. Joaquín Lavín, *Chile Revolución Silenciosa* (Santiago: Zig-Zag, 1987), 35-36, 38; and "En Julio próximo: Venderán jeans chilenos en almacénes de Moscú," *El Mercurio*, March 28, 1991.

30. "Exportarán laminados a EE.UU. y Africa," *El Mercurio*, October 9, 1990; "Anunció Boisset: Enaer haría partes de aviones européos," *El Mercurio*, March 29, 1990; "US$ 200 millones exportó el sector manufacturero," *El Mercurio*, February 15, 1990; and "Embajadores insólitos," *El Mercurio*, Sunday Magazine, July 1, 1990.

30. Lavín, *Revolución Silenciosa*, 125, 77.

32. "Bios Chile I.G.S.A.: Chile inicia exportaciones de productos biotecnológicos," *El Mercurio*, March 12, 1991.

33. Lavín, *Revolución Silenciosa*, 27, 123-24; "En sus tres áreas de acción: A US$ 50 millones llegaron ventas de "Sonda" en 1990," *El Mercurio*, February 12, 1991; and "Sonda se asoció con Digital para vender a toda latinoamérica," *El Mercurio*, September 27, 1991.

34. Lavín, *Revolución Silenciosa*, 84, 124.

35. "Con el apoyo de prochile: Chilenos exportan servicios a América Latina Y Europa," *El Mercurio*, March 1, 1991.

36. Frank Meissner, *Technology Transfer in The Developing World: The Case of the Chile Foundation* (New York: Praeger Publishers, 1988), 10.

37. Ibid., 104.

5

Financial Services

The financial services sector of Chile's economy provides the lubricant that keeps the engine of growth and development running. Following a decade and a half of dramatic upheaval, this sector evolved an integrated mixture of foreign and domestic business elements in the mid-1980s. While overcoming a domestic financial collapse and external debt crisis, Chile managed to modernize its financial structure; generate increased domestic savings through a privatized pension system; attract an array of domestic and foreign institutional investors; fund new and expanded industrial projects; and create financial instruments to link the economy more closely with international markets. The result is arguably Latin America's most dynamic and sophisticated financial market. Despite its small size, Chile boasts many of the continent's most innovative financial programs and technologically advanced institutions.

Chile's financial sector swung between the extremes of forced nationalization and nearly unregulated private expansion during the 1970s. Foreign banks, driven from the country during the Allende years, reentered Chile cautiously, increasing their interest only as the economy boomed toward the end of the decade. The global debt crisis severely devalued foreign bank assets and changed the outlook in all of Latin America from business expansion to damage containment. In the meantime, many Chilean financial institutions were brought to their knees by a domestic recession that destroyed several interlocked business groups and forced a Central Bank takeover of the country's leading banks.

Strategic government decisions laid the foundation for the structure that would rise from this scene of financial devastation. Among the key elements for local institutions were the government's determination to reprivatize intervened banks as soon as possible through a recapitalization program; introduce greater regulatory supervision of financial institutions without discouraging gradual expansion and innovation; and maintain the integrity of the country's recently privatized pension system. With regard to foreign banks, Chile devised an external debt management strategy that combined the negotiation of restructured loan payments with the use of debt-to-equity swaps that worked in tandem with the continued privatization of state enterprises. Foreign banks received nondiscriminatory national treatment and were encouraged to introduce new technology and management techniques to improve efficiency in local capital markets.

Foreign investors play a complex and varied role in Chile's financial sector. Additionally, the character and strategy of the firms reflect the wide range of institutions involved, encompassing commercial and investment banks, insurance companies, brokerage houses, and related accounting and law firms, many displaying different degrees of local presence and commitment. Without attempting to provide a complete blueprint of these highly integrated activities, this chapter offers portraits of key banking and insurance investors, tracing their strategic decisions and operations as Chile's financial system evolved during the 1980s.

FOREIGN BANKS AND THE DEBT CRISIS

Foreign banks play a dual role in Chile's economy, negotiating as a group on debt management issues while pursuing diverse local operating strategies as individual institutions. The two roles are obviously interconnected. The massive debt exposure carried by many foreign banks, partly in Chile but more significantly in other Latin American nations, defines the parameters for their investment decisions. Within these borders of possible actions lies a broad field for applied decisions where each firm maps its own business path, combining local interests and options with its overall global strategy.

Chile's external debt problems did not present foreign banks with a crisis of the magnitude faced in Mexico, Brazil, or Argentina. However, in relation to the economy's size or its debt service ratio (the proportion of export earnings needed to meet loan repayments), Chile's problems were nearly as severe. In mid-1982, Chile's debt-service ratio stood at 116 percent, compared to 122 percent (Brazil), 129 percent (Mexico), and 179 percent (Argentina) for the three major debtor nations.[1]

Actions in Chile by government authorities and foreign banks leading up to the crisis reflect minor national variations within a general regional pattern. Various studies trace the broad causal forces that shaped the continent's problems and document the shared blame among public and private sector actors for the unsustainable run-up in short-term debt to foreign commercial banks.[2] Rather than duplicating these studies, this chapter focuses on the more highly differentiated follow-up to the debt crisis. During this period, Chilean authorities and their foreign creditors evolved a successful debt management program that returned the country to international voluntary lending markets by 1990. At the same time, while foreign banks negotiated jointly in debt reschedulings, this imposed commonality disguised very different local strategies for how individual institutions pursued their business and investment interests in Chile.

The Creditors' Committee and Manufacturers Hanover

Manufacturers Hanover, with one of the largest private debt exposures in Chile at approximately half a billion dollars, was chosen to head the international creditors' committee that negotiated debt rescheduling agreements. The committee, representing some 250 institutions, conducted discussions separate from but related to Chile's negotiations with the International Monetary Fund. From the beginning, Chile sought a cooperative restructuring package that enabled it to meet rescheduled loan payments while operating within IMF economic adjustment guidelines. The approach also involved several successful innovations, including a broad, sustained program of debt-to-equity swaps that stimulated foreign investor interest in the country; and a $300 million debt buy-back initiative funded through high copper export earnings.

Having regained economic growth under initial debt restructuring programs, Chile still faced the renewal of amortization payments totaling some $1.8 billion between 1991 and 1994. This burden threatened to extend or worsen an economic slowdown initiated by the new democratic government to contain rising inflation. Fortunately, Chile could draw on its record of responsible debt management actions to negotiate a new rescheduling agreement. The accord, approved after a short five-day session with the creditor committee headed by Manufacturers Hanover in late 1990, eased the pending repayment threat and marked Chile's return to the voluntary lending market.

The rescheduling package rolled over credits falling due to 1995 and later; saved Chile nearly $200 million in interest payments; created more flexible debt reduction conditions; and provided for some $320 million in new money through bank purchases of Chilean treasury bonds. Twenty banks from the United States, Japan, Germany, France, Spain, Switzerland, Holland, Great Britain, and Canada committed to purchase these Eurobonds in amounts ranging from $10 to $25 million. In complementary actions recognizing Chile's improved financial position, the IMF agreed that the country no longer needed the support of a conditional loan program and the U.S. Federal Reserve placed Chile in the category of a "non-restructuring country," signifying that bank loans to the country are considered recoverable and loan loss reserves are not required.[3]

Manufacturers Hanover actually had a small direct presence in the Chilean economy despite the magnitude of its debt exposure. The bank's experience consisted of a minor leasing company and correspondent banking relationships centered on the government finance market that collapsed in the debt crisis. With limited local operations, and confronted with even larger debt problems in other countries, Manufacturers Hanover staffed its chairmanship of Chile's creditors committee out of its New York headquarters, which managed the bank's overall response to the debt crisis. These circumstances largely determined the bank's goals and strategy which focused on maintaining the value of its Chilean debt.

In 1988, Manufacturers Hanover opened a branch office in Chile and contemplated developing an expanded, longer-term presence in the local market. Corporate banking and trade finance activities that utilize branch offices abroad appear the logical targets for increasing its finance sector business. The bank may also invest in some industrial and export projects, but its limited local experience and resources make assessments difficult, particularly for prospective investments large enough to impact significantly on the bank's debt portfolio. Manufacturers Hanover did team with several banks in using debt conversions to help finance the Celpac forestry project and joined in a proposed mutual fund with Citibank, Chemical Bank, and Security Pacific. In addition, Manufacturers Hanover purchased 10 percent of Inversiones Pathfinder in mid-1991, bringing its total direct investment in Chile to around $100 million.

Equally or more important, the bank's success in bolstering the value of Chile's debt makes its own use of debt conversions less necessary as well as more difficult. A healthy Chilean economy can continue to meet rescheduled loan payments, thereby cutting bank losses. The higher values for debt instruments reduce possible discount rates and shrink the scope for debt swap transactions. Manufacturers Hanover plays an important role as the lead bank for negotiating commercial debt restructuring agreements with Chile, but its influence in this respect is indirect compared to the impact exerted by other MNC banks with extensive local operations. While the bank retains a long-term interest in Chile, its direct involvement in the local market will likely remain limited relative to the size of its still outstanding exposure. Manufacturers Hanover's global merger with Chemical Bank in the latter part of 1991 will undoubtedly lead to some further restructuring of the two banks' Chilean operations.

The People's Banker and Industrial Investor—Citibank's Strategy

Citibank rivaled Manufacturers Hanover in exposure in Chile with nearly $490 million but chose a different local strategy based on its past experience, existing capabilities, and future business plans for the country and the region. The bank's time horizon stretched far backward and forward as it contemplated how Chile fit into its designs as a global institution. Local plans included an aggressive consumer banking operation, affiliated financial market companies, and a targeted debt conversion program designed to diversify and improve its portfolio within a policy framework responsive to national goals. This strategy promises to reinforce Citibank's position as one of the most prominent and influential foreign banks operating within the Chilean economy.

Citibank established a Chilean office in 1916, just two years after opening its Latin American operations in neighboring Argentina. The firm was nationalized by the Allende government in 1972, but returned in 1974 as part of a regional strategy that supports a presence in nearly two dozen Latin American countries. Periodic surveys of bank customers in Chile rank Citibank among the top six, and often first or second, among national banking institutions across a range of categories including size and importance, security and solvency, personalized attention, agility and innovation, future prospects, and probable bank of choice for customers switching accounts.[4]

The personalized attention category is particularly important to Citibank because it chose to develop an image as a "people's bank," building one of the larger networks of retail offices among MNC banks in the Santiago area. Technological improvements and a financial commitment to branch offices lie at the heart of Citibank's retail strategy. Indeed, the Chilean subsidiary developed a branch model that set a new standard for Citibank operations worldwide. Termed "citicenter," these models employ advanced technology that allows customers to obtain information and manage most of their banking needs directly, including transactions such as paperless deposits and inquiries regarding automobile or home loans and their terms of payment. The bank estimates that an office can achieve a 40 percent productivity increase in terms of customers served after installing the citicenter model.

Although it may not show up explicitly on the nation's trade ledger, this model became a new Chilean "export" in April 1990, when Citibank of Chile hosted the first of two seminars to demonstrate citicenter operations and to share their experience with Citibank executives from around the world. Bank representatives attended the sessions from countries such as Germany, Singapore, Hong Kong, Greece, Malaysia, India, Spain, South Korea, and Taiwan. By the following year citicenter models were operating in many of these countries and had also been installed in the United States, principally in the Chicago area. Chile's open market policies and relatively sophisticated technological infrastructure permitted Citibank to develop this advanced service model locally while the competitiveness of the nation's banking sector provided both a motivation and a realistic testing ground for the innovation.

Citibank also provides corporate banking, trade financing, and other related services that draw on its long experience and familiarity with Chile's business conditions. The bank gained significant additional knowledge of local industry during the late 1980s, when it employed debt-to-equity swaps to become a joint venture partner in projects located in key growth sectors. This action simultaneously diversified the bank's debt portfolio while enhancing its ability to offer debt conversion services to other potential investors.

Explicit internal criteria both restricted and guided Citibank's debt conversion strategy. Bank executives recognized early the political controversy surrounding the creation of Chile's Chapter XIX debt swap program. Perhaps remembering their nationalization experience in the 1970s, and certainly reflecting a commitment to substantial long-term involvement in the Chilean economy, the executives decided to avoid potentially sensitive privatizations and concentrate their investments in projects with clearly demonstrable benefits to the national economy.

In applied terms, this strategy meant that Citibank did not pursue a number of investment opportunities, including state enterprises being privatized by the Pinochet regime, public utilities or other industries heavily dependent on government regulation, and import-intensive businesses that placed further pressure on the country's foreign exchange earnings. On the positive side, Citibank targeted new undertakings or expansion projects that would make value-added contributions in developing Chile's competitive advantages, particularly those oriented to export markets. The potential for new employment, technologies, and markets were key factors assessed in potential investments. By using these criteria, Citibank sought to improve its portfolio and profitability while assuring that possible political or general public backlash over a debt conversion investment would not jeopardize its other significant local business interests.

Citibank wanted to convert up to $300 million and looked for suitable projects where it could invest a minimum of $5 million in combination with local or foreign corporations. The bank sought joint venture partners with good management capabilities and relevant project experience as well as a basic compatibility in business style, values, and objectives. Investments required Central Bank approval under the Chapter XIX regulations and a project's viability was also influenced by the available conversion rate as well as tax considerations and sector-specific legal restrictions. Citibank additionally had to conform to applicable U.S. regulations, including Regulation K of the Bank Holding Act that restricted investments in activities outside banking operations. The Federal Reserve modified these limitations to provide greater flexibility in heavily indebted countries but still regulated the amount, length of time, and investor role for U.S. banks in specific types of investments.

Citibank's initial investment decisions followed its self-appointed criteria well, producing minority shareholdings in export-related growth projects in the minerals and forestry sectors. Both mineral projects involved opening new mines with production geared entirely for export. Shell was Citibank's experienced production partner in both the Las Luces copper mine and the Choquelimpie gold project, with Westfield Minerals joining in the latter venture. Shell's extensive history in Chile, its commitment to long-term projects, and its prominent environmental concern made the company a particularly compatible partner for Citibank, which wanted to minimize risks that an industrial project might damage its general reputation and thereby hurt its core financial business.

Shell again acted as a key partner in two forestry projects, Copihue and Santa Fe, with Scott Paper adding its production and marketing experience in the latter venture. Pathfinder was the lead firm for the MASISA forestry project. Santa Fe's pulp facility followed the pattern of a new project designed for export production that would require some 1,000 permanent direct employees. The other two ventures would expand existing operations, enhancing the value-added processing of timber resources through a sawmill and particle board factories with output directed partly to exports. Citibank invested a total of $138 million in these five projects. Along with a $47 addition to its own capital, this brought the bank's total investment through debt conversions to $185 million by early 1990.

With Chile's successful transition to democracy, the Aylwin administration assumed direction of Chile's foreign investment policy and essentially reaffirmed the key elements of existing laws and regulations. During the electoral campaign, Citibank's investments appeared to meet the Aylwin coalition's statements regarding the types of benefits they expected foreign investments to generate. While the new government reviewed some past privatization actions and began a process to restrict Chapter XIX investments in certain business activities, the general risk from potential policy instability over foreign investments declined. Several Citibank investments following the governmental transition reflected modified decision criteria that responded to the changing political and economic conditions.

Citibank's $20 million investment in the Chilean fishing enterprise Coloso in mid-1990 largely followed the initial guidelines. Fishing was another key growth area for exports and Citibank's investment enabled Coloso to complete a modernization program begun in 1988, to raise the quality of its plants' fish meal production. In this case Citibank joined with an experienced local partner rather than a foreign firm. The investment also involved a business facing increased government regulation as Chile was in the process of revising its fishing law. Although potential restrictions on foreign majority-owned firms would not affect Citibank's minority shareholding, the law's revision would clearly lead to greater regulation of the industry, probably resulting in some type of allocated quota control over available fisheries. Given the country's economically troubled northern fishing industry, however, additional financial support from a new investor helped insure completion of plant modernization plans begun in more profitable times.

A smaller but similarly timed Citibank investment in Embotelladora Chile constituted more of an exception to the early pattern. This transaction of roughly $5.5 million gave Citibank a one-third share of the firm, making it a partner with American Express and the Ergas group which had founded the enterprise with an investment of around $7 million. American Express did not hold much Chilean debt and its bank activities focused on trade financing and establishing its credit card operations. The Embotelladora investment presented an attractive opportunity derived from the "cola wars." In line with its global strategy, Pepsi-Cola decided to reenter Chile to challenge Coca-Cola's established operations. Embotelladora Chile received an exclusive license to bottle and distribute Pepsi products. Citibank's additional capital support allowed the firm to continue its expansion program, opening new bottling plants and setting up distribution facilities throughout the country. While arguably creating new jobs, this case lacked some of the industrial production or export benefits of other Citibank investments.

Citibank's direct experience in conducting its own debt conversion investments helped it gain business managing the transaction process for other potential foreign investors interested in using the Chapter XIX mechanism. The bank conducted over $200 million in debt swap transactions for other companies, including some of its joint venture partners as well as enterprises such as Exxon, Renault, Unisys, Mennen, Paulaner, Pioneer Hybrid, and the Mormon Church. In addition to its industrial investments and direct banking activities, Citibank operated a number of Chilean financial affiliates that included trading, leasing, foreign exchange, stocks and bond agencies, credit card operations, and Financiera Atlas, the country's largest finance company.[5]

Citibank also positioned itself to participate in foreign investment funds that were gaining entry in Chile's capital markets. The company first received approval for two investment funds established through D.L. 600 at a level of $50 million each. When U.S. banking restrictions prevented listing the funds on the New York Stock Exchange, the bank delayed activating them while it explored ways to achieve alternative listings on secondary markets in other countries. As mentioned earlier, Citibank also gained approval for a joint Chapter XIX foreign investment fund that it would manage for Manufacturers Hanover, Chemical Bank, Security Pacific, and itself. This fund joined one approved for Chase Manhattan and two earlier funds established by Midland Bank as Chile's only foreign investment funds using debt swap arrangements. Both applications had been pending when the Aylwin administration altered Chapter XIX approval criteria to exclude any future debt conversions for this purpose. In practical terms, however, activation of the approved funds also depends on available debt conversion rates which have become less attractive in Chile. Only the Citibank-led fund was actually launched.

The changing economics of Chilean debt wrought other modifications in Citibank's investment strategy. As the value of debt instruments rose and discount rates fell, the option of simply holding the bank's remaining debt portfolio gained support. The bank's attention turned primarily to investigating the potential for a few large investments that would justify the nearly year-long management commitment required for a Chapter XIX transaction. With its concentration in export sectors, the bank also considered investment diversification, perhaps to import substitution businesses and other domestic growth sectors. Prospective investments faced a higher profitability hurdle than in the past due to reduced incentives for further debt conversion.

Citibank's strategy in Chile derives from a conscious combination of past experience, present needs, and future goals, with local decisions applied within the parent corporation's regional and global outlook. One important ingredient to determining Citibank's approach in Chile was the availability of a general manager with a previous assignment in the country who could thereby draw on prior experience in assessing current options. The self-restricting criteria precluded Citibank from involvement in many potential investments in existing and privatized businesses that promised more immediate profitability. On the other hand, Citibank's approach minimized risks from possible economic and particularly political changes that could undermine its broad involvement and long-range commitment to the economy. As economic and political conditions evolved, so did Citibank's applied decisions in pursuit of its general business objectives.

A Reluctant Investor's Reassessment—Bankers Trust

Bankers Trust offers a good contrast in strategies to the Citibank experience. The company lacked an operational history in Chile and initially perceived no future there either. Facing a local debt exposure of roughly one-quarter of a billion dollars, or about half the portfolio held by Citibank or Manufacturers Hanover, Bankers Trust sought ways within Chilean and U.S. regulations to cut its losses and move on. Under this strategy the bank became one of the earliest heavy users of Chapter XIX debt conversions and drew some of the harshest public criticism for investments in privatized ventures, including a controlling interest in the nation's largest pension fund management company. By the close of the decade, however, the evolution of Bankers Trust's experience in Chile had altered the firm's expectations and objectives, not only with regard to that country but also in terms of its relationship to potential new business opportunities in other parts of the world.

Bankers Trust maintained a representative office in Chile to manage its correspondent banking relationships during the build-up of its loan exposure, but essentially withdrew its staff after the debt crisis hit. The bank was not an operational force within the national banking sector. As the Pinochet government formulated its debt conversion program, a Bankers Trust executive traveled to Chile and, with the involvement of local consultants, set up I.M. Trust in 1985, an investment agency that evolved into their merchant bank operation. The executive encouraged the government to formulate debt swap regulations broadly, for example by including Central Bank debt under its coverage.

Bankers Trust viewed itself as a transitory investor. The task of its Chilean unit was to look for investments that could utilize the Chapter XIX mechanism as a way to get out. Becoming the first bank to swap its debt for equity in 1986, Bankers Trust purchased 40 percent of Provida, Chile's largest Administradora de Fondos de Pensiones (AFP), or pension fund management firm. Owned by the local Cruzat-Larraín group that broke apart during the recession, Provida was initially administered by a government commission and later sold under a government plan that offered 60 percent ownership to the general public, drawing some initial 8,000 shareholders and restricting Bankers Trust to a minority 40 percent share. The bank also acquired in the same transaction just over 90 percent of Consorcio Nacional de Seguros-Vida, Chile's largest life insurance company.

The acquisition of both the pension management and the insurance company stemmed from the connection between the two businesses. Each AFP awards a contract to an insurance firm to provide life and disability coverage for its subscribers (called "affiliates"). At retirement, or in the event of death or disability, the pensioner or his beneficiaries can opt for gradually declining monthly payments from the AFP or sell their account to an insurance firm for the somewhat greater security of a fixed real monthly annuity. For annuity reserves generated prior to 1988, every AFP retains some residual obligation to its subscribers if its insurer fails. Back in 1985, given the financial sector's recent collapse and the looser investment regulations on insurance companies compared to those applicable to AFPs, Bankers Trust concluded it had to control both Provida and Consorcio to protect itself from the credit risks involved. Bankers Trust invested a total of $46 million, including $3 million left as working capital in the special-purpose holding company set up to own its new acquisitions, BT Pacific.

Each AFP at the time worked with a related insurance firm. Although AFPs and insurance companies are administered separately, the contracts were profitable enough to raise concerns about collusion or sweetheart deals so Chile evolved a mandatory open bidding process. This process became highly competitive in 1990, with several related AFP/insurance contracts changing hands, including a couple won by Bankers Trust's Consorcio. The contract between Provida and Consorcio was renewed, but public controversy erupted when a minority Provida director protested that the contract should have been awarded to a new insurance firm affiliated with the Spanish Santander group that was unaffiliated with any existing AFP. This aggressive new entrant in the marketplace had bid unsuccessfully on several contracts.[6]

The insurance contract controversy is not really a foreign investment issue, since both local and foreign-controlled AFPs operated in a similar fashion. Moreover, the issue pales in comparison to earlier criticism of the bank's pension fund purchase. When added to the AFPs controlled by two U.S. insurance firms (discussed later), the Bankers Trust acquisition of Provida gave foreign MNCs a majority position in managing the nation's pension system. The core issue centered on a concern that MNCs would control not only the future retirement security of Chile's workers, but also the power to decide how to invest the country's most important source of domestic savings.

Foreign investors brought capital and managerial expertise to bolster the pension fund system. Both ingredients were needed to reassure individual investors that their future retirement was secure, especially when several local business groups behind the AFPs collapsed during the financial crisis that hit shortly after the system became operational in 1981. Bankers Trust's conversion of debt holdings to an equity control of Provida/Consorcio diminished the capital contribution in the eyes of some critics, however, because the foreign investment did not involve fresh money. Additionally, while the bank possessed internal expertise on the investment of funds, it lacked direct experience in pension administration or insurance, causing skepticism about its possible managerial contribution. Bankers Trust exacerbated this criticism by announcing shortly after it purchased the stake in Provida/Consorcio that its investments were for sale.

In somewhat broader terms, the pension fund involvement appeared to move counter to the bank's global corporate strategy that was shifting from commercial toward merchant or investment banking. Provida's unique role in the Chilean pension fund system required a far different outlook. Not only was Provida the largest AFP, with well over one-quarter of the system's subscribers, but it also operated the largest chain of branch offices with over seventy-five locations throughout the country. This make-up presented an important and particularly sensitive retailing challenge for Provida's operators because their more numerous offices outside the metropolitan Santiago area gave them a larger number of lower-salaried subscribers to service than other pension fund managers.

Although officially a minority owner, Bankers Trust effectively controlled Provida. Its management emphasis focused on improving investment portfolio decisions within the restrictions set by Chilean regulators; reducing administration costs and the fee charged to subscribers; and introducing more advanced technology, particularly in the storage and processing of data. For example, during 1989 Provida invested roughly one-half million dollars to increase its computational terminals by one-third and remote terminals by one-half, bringing nearly two-thirds of its widespread agencies on-line. Additionally, subscriber fees went down 10 percent, due mainly to lowered disability claims that reduced the cost of the Consorcio insurance coverage, thereby lowering the AFP's largest single expense item.[7]

Both improved service and lower fees were important because individual subscribers freely choose an AFP and can switch between firms at any point with several months notice. A firm's turnover can be large. In some months Provida processed nearly 7,000 people leaving, a roughly equivalent number switching in, and nearly as many first-time subscribers just entering the pension system. While expensive to administer, this freedom of choice was a foreign investor's best protection against criticism about foreign control of an AFP. Anyone who opposed investing in an MNC-controlled pension fund could choose to sign up with a locally owned AFP.

Freedom of choice for individual investors did not necessarily translate into assured political acceptance of foreign ownership in the pension fund system, however. As political tensions rose prior to the 1989 plebiscite, Bankers Trust hedged their risk somewhat and reduced their Chilean portfolio by selling 49.9 percent of B.T. Pacific, the holding company for its related Chilean investments, to Chemical Bank (20.3 percent), Bank of Tokyo (20.3 percent), and Marine Midland (9.3 percent). This transaction involved a Delaware-based corporate entity and took place outside Chile. Bankers Trust received payment in dollars for this offshore transfer that maintained all Chapter XIX obligations since the sale was to other foreign investors and did not involve the transfer of funds from Chilean operations.

In 1990, Bankers Trust completed the initial four-year waiting period and became one of the first banks to receive dividends under Chapter XIX regulations. The bank also entered a $31 million Chapter XIX transaction with its three recently acquired partners, in shares proportional to their holdings in B.T. Pacific, to form a new Chilean insurance company, Compañía de Pensiones (Compensa). This step reflected a decision to limit the further growth of Consorcio, which was already the country's largest life insurance company.

Another component of the Bankers Trust strategy was to exploit investment opportunities across a range of business sectors, essentially looking to perform merchant banking functions that could enhance profits until regulations permitted their repatriation or to develop the invested enterprises into attractive targets for other investors. This approach generally led to investments in existing rather than new undertakings; it included buying shareholdings in privatized enterprises and fit within the bank's overall withdrawal strategy. Consequently the actions also drew criticism that questioned the value-added benefits for the country of Chapter XIX debt swap transactions.

Among Bankers Trust's various shareholdings, two examples stand out as the most instructive cases for examining how the bank developed this component of its business strategy. The first case involved the purchase of Pilmaiquén, a hydroelectric company being privatized by the Pinochet government. The facility was nearly a half century old but was well maintained and could produce a good revenue flow. Involving the first such facility sold to private investors, the transaction drew more criticism than some later privatizations when all but one power generation enterprise shifted from public to private sector ownership. Critics cited the calculated replacement cost of Pilmaiquén in concluding that the sale price was too low. The Bankers Trust bid was several million dollars higher than any other investor was willing to offer for the facility at that time, however, and the sale was concluded.

Even more than with pension funds and insurance companies, Bankers Trust lacked knowledge of hydroelectric power generation, so it sought joint venture partners with such experience. The bank's underlying objective, however, related its purchase of Pilmaiquén to financial functions including investment banking and the pension fund system, where the bank was heavily engaged. The ultimate goal was to take the enterprise public, qualifying it as an investment for the pension fund system in early 1987.

This process began with refinancing the company through the public sale of long-term bonds. Several complications arose involving both Chilean and U.S. regulations, extending the time required to complete the transaction. One problem came from an interpretation that the bank had exceeded limitations under U.S. Regulation K, requiring the sale of nearly one-fifth of the enterprise. Because the investment was not a direct Chapter XIX debt swap transaction, but rather one made with dividend funds not yet eligible for repatriation, Bankers Trust could sell the shares under Chilean regulations to a local firm. This distinction also made possible the eventual public sale of the rest of the company's shares.

Another obstacle arose from the difficulty in obtaining a top rating from Chilean authorities for Pilmaiquén's bonds. The privatized firm, due to a legal reorganization engineered by I.M. Trust, became a new legal entity and therefore lacked a formal history regarding past financial performance. Three years of successful operating history were needed to achieve a rating sufficiently high to create a genuinely deep market for the bonds among the heavily regulated AFPs. Finally in 1989 the company went public and became one of the only new firms, aside from privatized enterprises taken public directly by the government, to qualify for AFP investments. Ironically, AFPs did not initially invest in the firm. Even Provida's directors decided to wait until at least two other AFPs invested, since Pilmaiquén, due to the Bankers Trust link, was considered a related enterprise. Nevertheless, Bankers Trust did succeed in taking the enterprise public and in the process sold down its ownership to under 20 percent.

The other informative case involved a Chapter XIX investment in Sociedad Química y Minera de Chile (SOQUIMICH), another government enterprise being privatized. Initially Bankers Trust's shares bought under the Chapter XIX mechanism amounted to only around 6 percent of the enterprise, plus a few related shares through Consorcio's investments. The bank wanted to arrange enough additional shares to form a package that might attract a future investor. A share level around 12.5 percent would enable an investor to elect a director for the corporation. Regulation K limits again restricted further direct purchases by the bank, so it turned to another type of merchant banking transaction with other financial investors to reach the desired share level, if Consorcio's holdings were included.

In January 1990 the bank sold the packaged shares to Israel Chemicals with an allied voting arrangement for Consorcio's shares. The transaction occurred outside Chile, again constituting a shift in ownership among foreign investors that maintained the capital repatriation restrictions of Chapter XIX but secured a dollar return on the sale of another of Bankers Trust's Chilean investments. Israel Chemicals was already a joint venture partner with SOQUIMICH in a project dealing with solar evaporation techniques and wanted to acquire an equity stake in the firm to further develop this relationship.

Despite the obvious self-interest in Bankers Trust's withdrawal strategy as exemplified in these last two cases, the approach yielded potentially important benefits for local companies and the Chilean economy that did not appear realistically attainable through other existing options. Bankers Trust used its expertise to restructure Pilmaiquén's finances and successfully placed the enterprise in a public stock market whose major deficiency is the paucity of quality listings. In the SOQUIMICH case, the bank also lacked sectoral expertise to contribute to the enterprise's operation, but it managed to fashion an investment package sufficiently attractive to draw in a firm that could bring technical experience to the operations.

The bank's role as a transitory investor turned it into a type of agent for the country, seeking out prospective investors who would bring relevant expertise and a longer-term commitment to an investment project. In this sense, the actions of a transitory Chapter XIX investor need not be judged as a zero-sum game in which the investor's gains are somehow the country's losses. Instead, both parties can benefit substantially, depending on the specific actions and outcomes of a particular case.

By 1990, Bankers Trust had reassessed and reoriented parts of its overall investment strategy in Chile. The bank will likely remain a transitory and facilitating investor in some projects, such as a modern shopping mall complex it helped finance with two local partners. Its central involvement with the pension fund system, however, changed dramatically. Bankers Trust announced its intention to maintain its AFP and insurance interests, the market value of which had accumulated to approximately $500 million. Furthermore the bank sought to replicate its success in other developing nations, drawing on its Chilean experience.

A corporate restructuring in early 1991, sent the Banker's Trust executive who had guided its Chilean operations to New York headquarters charged with the task of developing a new business function in pensions and insurance in developing countries. Chile would serve as a center of operations for South America. Delegations from Argentina, Colombia, Venezuela, Mexico, and even Poland had already visited seeking information and advice on possible pension fund conversions. The bank's Chilean experience was opening a potentially important new line of business for Bankers Trust in other areas around the world.[8]

During 1990, Santiago's subway cars and street signs carried a spirited advertising battle among the various AFPs for new subscribers. One omnipresent slogan read *"Provida es para siempre."* The companion text urged people to invest for the long term rather than playing games with their money by seeking to stay ahead of the ups and downs in investment earnings. The slogan plays cleverly on the essential security role of pension funds, but its attachment to Provida would have been ironic and probably counterproductive if Bankers Trust had not changed its public intention to sell off its controlling share in the enterprise. Very few things last forever, much less in a dynamic and competitive business world. As Bankers Trust's reassessed and reoriented its investment strategy, the bank changed its image from that of a very reluctant foreign investor to a long-term participant in the Chilean economy and an exporter of Chilean experience to other parts of the world.

THE EVOLVING FOREIGN PRESENCE IN CHILEAN BANKING

Chile's banking sector is still reorganizing itself after suffering the related blows of domestic financial collapse and the international debt crisis. Foreign banks comprise a significant but evolving part of this sector as individual institutions exit, enter, or refocus their market strategies in line with global objectives and local conditions. Foreign banks, which helped modernize Chilean banking practices, still possess advantages in serving multinational clients and supporting overseas trade. Domestic banks offer improved loan operations and technical services, drawing on updated management techniques and enhanced technological support. A further shakeout and reorientation of bank operations is likely among both domestic and foreign institutions as Chile moves away from strategies driven by debt management needs. Distinctions between foreign and domestic institutions may blur further in the process as the country continues its integration with the global economy and individual banks pursue alliances that improve their position in an increasingly competitive market.

An upsurge in foreign banking in Chile occurred during the 1978–81 period of rapid economic expansion. This activity was fueled by import growth and financial dealings associated with the misaligned currency as well as petrodollar recycling through foreign bank loans to developing country governments. Some foreign banks had just opened branch offices to supplement their correspondent banking relationships when the crisis hit. Priority concerns at these institutions switched almost overnight from lending and service expansion to crisis containment and debt management. Many domestic banks in Chile paid even higher penalties, suffering through a financial collapse that destroyed several family-owned corporate groups and resulted in a governmental takeover of key banking institutions.

The government recapitalized these banks, returning them to the private sector with the Central Bank retaining their bad loan portfolios. In this manner the Pinochet regime maintained its capitalistic free market approach, in effect saving the private domestic financial system, albeit under increased regulatory scrutiny. The situation presents a continuing problem for the Chilean government, however. The Central Bank still holds well over $3 billion in bad bank loans, representing nearly one-third of the underperforming assets it acquired from bailout and privatization actions that annually drain several hundred million dollars from Central Bank resources.

The government's intervention prevented a full market shakeout since weak domestic banks can continue to operate as long as the Central Bank holds their problem loans. On the other hand, the banks' commitment to repurchase their loan portfolios from future profits places a continuing burden on these institutions, laying prior claim to current and future proceeds and inhibiting the full funding of competitive service improvements. Two large domestic banks (Banco de Santiago and Banco de Chile) owe around two-thirds of the subordinated bank debt, an amount that exceeds their capital several times over.[9]

Foreign banks faced a similarly delayed shakeout period as the individual institutions struggled to define and refine their strategies for coping with a general debt crisis where the Chilean portfolio, while substantial for some, still constituted a second-level worry behind the major debtor nations. Only a few foreign banks chose to close their Chilean operations, but many other institutions narrowed their objectives to debt management goals that limited their local market involvement. Most foreign banks clearly wanted to reduce their exposure through a combination of debt sales and conversions, restricting local business expansion to fee-based service niches and swap-related forays into diversified corporate holdings or an improved capitalization of banking operations.

In terms of individual institutions, foreign banks outnumbered local banks by twenty-two to fourteen in 1990. These figures overstate their role in the local market, however, where foreign banks represented only around one-sixth of the system's loans and slightly more than one-fifth of deposits during the latter half of the 1980s. Over this same period, the foreign banks' share of local earnings dropped by nearly one-third to around 13 percent and their profitability amounted to roughly one-quarter the results obtained by local banks. Of course, some local banks gained from transactions converting their own debt and most profits were already committed under their agreements with the Central Bank.[10] Nevertheless, foreign investors were a significant but not a dominant market force in Chile's banking sector. As individual institutions, these banks continue to pursue diverse investment strategies as they seek to overcome past mistakes and improve future competitiveness, where Chilean operations constitute but one small part of a global financial picture.

Coping with Debt Portfolios—Diversity in Strategic Responses

Security Pacific was cited most often along with Bankers Trust as pursuing an aggressive exit strategy using debt-to-equity swaps. Despite an exposure of a couple hundred million dollars in Chile, the bank had operated through a small local office and lacked an experienced in-place management team to cope with its predicament. After closing its representative office, the bank might have simply sold off its debt, as it did in several other countries, had Chile not established the Chapter XIX program. Instead, Security Pacific hired a former head of the Central Bank and other experienced nationals and opened an office in 1986 to study debt conversion investment opportunities.

On the new officers' recommendations, Security Pacific began its debt conversion strategy the following year by purchasing 10 percent of Chilectra, gaining one of the last blocks of stock available from this electrical utility's privatization. Prior share offerings had been made to workers and pension funds. Although an important large investor, the bank did not possess the electrical industry expertise needed to seek a management role. Instead, the transaction was an opportunity for a financial investment in a mature, income-generating business. The bank paid above prevailing market value for its shares and was not deterred by criticism of the government's privatization campaign. Security Pacific's second 1987 purchase brought it control of Banco Urquijo, the Chilean subsidiary of Banco Hispanoamericano of Spain. Adopting the Security Pacific name, this bank extended the parent firm's reach into the local banking sector, particularly in trade finance and corporate banking.

Security Pacific was one of the first institutions to meet the profit remittance requirements of Chapter XIX. The bank also became involved in discussions of regulatory modifications on capital repatriation following an equity sale. The ten-year restriction on capital repatriation effectively discriminated against local businesses in the sale of a foreign investor's equity. Exchanges between foreign firms outside Chile provided the original investor with an immediate return while the new foreign equity holder maintained the debt conversion requirements. In 1991, Security Pacific received permission to sell part of its bank to local investors, associating itself with Sigdo Koppers in a joint venture that also encompassed leasing and other financial affiliates. Although diluting its ownership to a minority position, Security Pacific announced this action as a decision to maintain its presence in Chilean banking while gaining additional opportunities through its new partnership. This strategy was complicated a few months later, however, when Security Pacific announced its global merger with Bank of America, a step that will require further readjustments in the banks'

Chilean operations.[11]

Chicago Continental Bank opened its Chilean branch in 1981, just before the debt crisis struck, but it had already conducted commercial loan operations long enough with the country to accumulate an exposure of around $300 million. The bank pursued an essentially defensive debt management strategy, seeking to diversify its portfolio through Chapter XIX investments in established, profitable enterprises that provided an exit option of sale to another investor. Capitalizing their local banking operation permitted some profitable corporate banking activities while supplementing the benefits of a 50/50 partnership in a local stock brokerage firm in providing useful experience and information on local business conditions.

Chicago Continental invested almost exclusively in publicly listed, privatized corporations. The firm acquired around 20 percent of the Chilgener electrical generating company, 17 percent of the pharmaceutical firm Laboratorio Chile, nearly 20 percent of the sugar company IANSA, and 1.6 percent of the telephone company CTC, which made it that firm's seventh largest shareholder. Bank officials clarified their intention to act as a financial investor rather than seeking managerial control, anticipating an investment position of three to four years. Of course, this strategy still required taking an active interest in maintaining and improving the value of their assets. For example, the bank's local executive led a protest against management at a Chilgener shareholder meeting, claiming that a recent gas turbine purchase had resulted in a loss of some $4.4 million.[12]

Despite its strategy of acting as a financial investor in selected enterprises, Chicago Continental became embroiled in one of Chile's most complex and hotly disputed public management battles. The controversy centered around Industria Azucarera Nacional (IANSA), a firm holding a monopoly position in Chile's sugar industry. The government's price band tariff support system for sugar set the framework within which IANSA contracted to purchase sugar beets from local farmers, providing for most of Chile's domestic needs while importing additional supplies if necessary.

Chicago Continental bought over 18 percent of privatized IANSA in May 1988. The bank then assisted the French firm Sucden, a leader in the global sugar business, in a transaction to purchase a 13 percent share. Subsequently Sucden bought another 13.6 percent from the Chilean firm SOQUIMICH and sold 1.5 percent of these shares to Chicago Continental. Together, the two firms then held the largest stake in IANSA and they initiated a managerial change that placed Sucden in effective control of the enterprise. The action displaced the next largest shareholder group, Campos Chilenos, a firm operated by a tight management group that controlled many shares initially bought when the firm was privatized by workers and some producers from the sugar beet industry. This group then alleged the existence of a secret pact between Sucden and Chicago Continental that pledged joint voting to gain control of IANSA.

Legal suits and countersuits followed in an acrimonious struggle for control. Chicago Continental suffered from charges about a lack of transparency in its arrangements; Sucden faced conflict of interest allegations due to its global sugar interests and worries that it might dump excess sugar in Chile to the detriment of local farmers; and Campos Chilenos engendered suspicions that their control of IANSA could also bring conflict of interest problems resulting in higher than necessary prices paid for local sugar beet production. In mid-1991, Pathfinder became the major shareholder of Campos Chilenos. A subsequent agreement finally settled the controversy with Sucden and Chicago Continental reducing their shareholdings and Campos Chilenos under its new ownership group regained control of IANSA.[13]

Chicago Continental received Central Bank permission in late 1990, to sell some of its investments and it subsequently did sell its shares in Chilgener. The bank's assessment of local conditions nevertheless suggested a growing longer-term perspective on business in the country. Roughly one-half the bank's Latin American activity already occurred in Chile and executives expected to reinvest some of Chicago Continental's Chapter XIX investment profits in Chile even after the money could be remitted beginning in 1992. Further encouraged by successful negotiations on rescheduling Chile's debt payments, the bank perceived new business opportunities in secondary markets for Chilean financial paper. Another initiative was to open a capital markets firm to assist private firms that wish to be listed on public exchanges. Bank officials also reported exporting some of their experience from Chile's privatization actions to use in other Latin American countries now undergoing similar processes. Thus, while the bank's holdings in any individual enterprise could still reflect the view of a short-term financial investor, its general outlook evolved from defensive debt management and short-term exit to a longer-term search for good business opportunities in Chile and the application of its experience in other restructuring economies.[14]

Midland Bank became a Chilean investor through a side door by buying one-half of Crocker Bank of California in 1981, completing the takeover in 1985. Although Midland resold Crocker to Wells Fargo the following year, it retained the bank's significant Latin American debt portfolio. Almost overnight Midland became one of the largest non-U.S. bank creditors to Latin America with an exposure of around $6 billion, roughly 10 percent of which related to Chile. Although Midland had representatives in several large Latin American nations, the bank lacked experience in Chile. Crocker's representative office in Santiago had been unmanned for a couple years when Midland established its operations there in 1986.

Midland's initial defensive strategy sought ways to protect the value of its assets. Recognizing that its debt would not be repaid unless the economy was healthy, the bank sought Chapter XIX investments in a cross-section of industries as a way to both promote and benefit from Chile's economic growth.

Likely targets existed in the mining and nontraditional export sectors and two important Midland investments followed this path.   The bank provided essentially all of the working capital to develop the Pelambres copper deposit in a joint venture with the Chilean Luksic group, later selling one-half its 80 percent stake to Lucky Goldstar of Korea for $30 million.   Midland also participated in the innovative financial package for the Celpac forestry venture that envisioned turning performing loans into equity stakes once the project became operational.   Another Midland investment bought a 20 percent share of InverChile, a local brokerage house whose subsequent collapse is discussed later in this chapter.

Perhaps the most unique element of Midland's investment strategy emerged from nearly a year and a half of negotiations with government regulators.   The bank gained approval to use Chapter XIX debt conversions to establish two foreign investment funds, The Chile Investment Company and The International Investment Company of Chile, with capital of $30 million and $62 million, respectively.   Several other foreign banks and the World Bank's International Finance Corporation (IFC) joined these projects, adding further credibility to the concept of using foreign investment funds to develop Chile's capital markets. For Midland, this type of project came closer to using its core financial expertise than its industrial investments.   Two other banking groups received subsequent approval to establish similar funds, but government modifications then prohibited further use of Chapter XIX for this purpose.   Nevertheless, as the pioneer negotiator and implementer, Midland helped pave the way for foreign investment funds established under D.L. 600 provisions as well.

Although separate institutions, Midland and Marine Midland developed several common investment positions in managing their Chilean debt portfolios. Marine Midland opened a representative office in Chile in 1981, and confronted a couple hundred million dollars in debt exposure when the financial crisis erupted.   With few local resources, the bank essentially acted as a joiner, buying a part of investment packages formulated by other leading financial institutions. Hence Marine Midland joined the two Chapter XIX foreign investment funds initiated by Midland Bank and participated in the Celpac venture led by Bank of America, which also counted Midland among its investors.   As discussed earlier, Marine Midland joined with two other foreign banks to buy part of Bankers Trust's offshore holding company, giving it just over a 9 percent stake in affiliated pension and insurance companies, supplemented by a similar share in the new insurance firm (Compensa) subsequently launched jointly by the foreign partners.

Marine Midland's Chilean presence essentially ended in 1990, incorporated into the operations of The Hongkong and Shanghai Banking Corporation.   This entity had bought part of Marine Midland in 1980, completing the full purchase in December 1987.   Hongkong Bank established a Chilean office in 1982 but carried virtually no debt exposure except for the portfolio it inherited through the acquisition of Marine Midland. Partial ownership ties also link Hongkong Bank to Midland Bank, since the former owns nearly 15 percent of the latter. Hongkong Bank initiated a bid in 1992 to complete a full acquisition of Midland Bank, but during the late 1980s the two banks did not appear closely linked regarding their Chilean operations.

Entering Chile as the economic recession began, Hongkong Bank struggled to find its role in the local financial market. The bank lacked extensive experience in the region, operating only in Brazil and Chile. Its natural competitive advantage lay in economic transactions involving Asia, but corporate banking opportunities were limited and trading relationships with the region were dominated by primary commodities where the banking role is small. The greatest business potential may exist in encouraging investment in Chile by Asian firms, but this avenue has been slow to develop.

A potential competitor for Asian-related business exists in Bank of Tokyo, which established its Chilean branch in 1981, just before the recession. With several hundred million dollars in debt exposure, the bank followed a relatively low-profile role in joining projects such as the Bankers Trust-led investment group. Bank of Tokyo also conducts a profitable trade financing business and is active through the local Japan-Chile Chamber of Commerce in promoting Japanese investment in Chile. Specific knowledge of Chile is low in the Japanese business community, where executives tend to view potential Latin American investments through the filter of the region's debt problems. However, Japan now competes closely with the United States for the position as Chile's most important trading partner and offers a potential source for greater capital investment as well, both portfolio and direct. Bank of Tokyo signed a cooperation agreement with Chile's Foreign Investment Committee in August, 1991 to help facilitate information flow and promote direct investment opportunities in Chile to prospective Japanese investors.

Bank of America's experience in Chile is longer and more varied. Beginning operations in 1967, the bank left under pressure during the Allende years and then returned gradually, staffing up from a representative office to a full banking operation. Although the bank held several hundred million dollars in Chilean debt exposure when the financial crisis struck, it chose a restrained and somewhat cautious strategy, reflecting both a sensitivity to Latin American cyclical changes and the parent corporation's preoccupation with larger financial problems. Bank of America's innovative leadership in structuring the Celpac financing agreement was the central element of its investment activity, although even here the original initiative came mainly from the project's sponsors. The bank avoided politically risky investments and concentrated on trade financing and corporate banking activities where it possessed a solid foundation of experience and global customers. As mentioned earlier, the bank's merger with Security Pacific will undoubtedly lead to some restructuring of their Chilean operations and assets.

While less of a worldwide institution, Bank of Boston boasted an important regional presence in Latin America, particularly in Argentina and Brazil. Chilean operations dated from the economic growth period in 1979, but the bank avoided a large cross-border debt exposure and even phased out some early involvement with local family groups that later collapsed during the financial crisis. The bank essentially imposed performance hurdles on individual Latin American operations, closing a number of offices where operating results could not justify continued operations while retaining an active presence where business opportunities existed. Bank of Boston only engaged in a couple of debt conversion transactions to capitalize local banking operations and make a transitory purchase of corporate stock. Trade financing and other commercial banking operations constitute the bank's core business, although it possesses enough local offices to offer personal banking services as well, drawing mention in some customer surveys as one of the recognized top-level institutions.

Chase Manhattan also maintains enough offices and consumer banking services to gain some customer recognition, having similarly established Chilean operations in 1979. Heavily exposed in Latin America, Chase reduced its Chilean debt position somewhat through a series of corporate share purchases, including communications industry investments in ENTEL and CTC as well as a fishing venture in partnership with both local investors and Chinese interests. The bank received adverse local publicity when the government penalized it for a violation of banking regulations involving foreign exchange dealings. Bank executives described the case as a problem of interpretation regarding what was permitted. Chase reorganized and reoriented its Chilean financial operations several times, exploring the potential for a Chapter XIX foreign investment fund, dropping its leasing business, and emphasizing corporate finance as well as a limited expansion of personal banking operations.[15]

Life After Debt Trading—NMB and Socimer

Morgan Guaranty was one of the few MNC banks to pursue a full exit strategy after suffering losses during the 1982–83 recession. In leaving Chile, Morgan sold its license to NMB Bank of Holland, which opened its offices in 1989. NMB had entered South America in 1983, seeking to take advantage of business opportunities within the generally depressed economic conditions. The bank established a base in Uruguay, purchasing a local bank that possessed a Brazilian branch operation. NMB then set up a representative office in Argentina, subsequently buying Barclay Bank's local branch when that firm left the country under pressures induced by the Malvinas conflict with Great Britain.

Internationally NMB Bank engaged heavily in debt trading and conversion activities, in 1987 handling a turnover of some $3.4 billion through their asset trading operation.[16] This business brought NMB into contact with Chilean debt transactions and led to their interest in replacing Morgan Bank when the opportunity arose, particularly recognizing Chile's increasingly dynamic financial market relative to the rest of its South American neighbors. Holland's business relations with Chile had been somewhat restrained, partly due to the government's discomfort with the Pinochet military regime. For some years the government held a stake in NMB Bank and a high-level official sat on its board of directors, making a direct investment in Chile difficult until the democratization process became clear. The same year it began operations in Chile, NMB Bank merged with Holland's large retail Postbank system to form the NMB/Postbank Group.

In Chile, NMB continued its debt-related service transactions while looking to build its corporate banking and trade finance business. Unburdened by a heavy debt load, NMB possessed greater flexibility than many other banks in exploring potential corporate loan operations. NMB participated in the $110 million syndicated loan portion of the financial package for Celpac's forestry complex. In June 1988 the bank received public credit for extending the first voluntary bank loan to Chile since 1982, although the cited credit was essentially a project-oriented $10 million loan to the Enersis company for investment in improving electrical generation capacity. Several months later NMB authorized a $20 million commercial credit for the Chilean government, directed largely at funding foreign purchases for infrastructure and social sector projects. This action preceded the step taken by Chile's creditor bank committee to begin voluntary lending after the successful late-1990 negotiation of a debt rescheduling accord.[17]

NMB's entry into the Chilean market also tied its operations there to an innovative program launched jointly with the World Bank's International Finance Corporation (IFC). Approved initially for Chile, Uruguay, Malaysia, and Indonesia, the program used local NMB affiliates for project identification and analysis, with approved loans up to $7.5 million granted under the IFC's name with the IFC and NMB Bank sharing equally in the financing. This initiative uses the bank's on-site analysis capabilities to supplement IFC resources, permitting the partners to offer medium-term loans designed for new projects or expansions for small and medium-size businesses.[18]

Another financial enterprise drawn to Chile by debt trading and conversion activities that now must diversify its operations is the Socimer International Bank Group. This institution, founded in Geneva in 1975, engaged in Latin American trade financing operations including transactions for the Chilean market. The enterprise is part of the Transafrica Group, an old Spanish conglomerate originally founded in North Africa over 100 years ago. Horizontally rather than vertically integrated, Transafrica concentrates on trading activities that range across many business sectors. The trading of debt instruments led its affiliate Socimer Group to set up Chilean operations in 1985, although firm executives had earlier discussed possible debt conversion approaches with Chilean government officials during the formative stages of the Chapter XIX program.

Socimer became one of the early pioneers in managing Chilean debt swap transactions, complementing its international debt trading business and gaining experience for use in other national debt conversion schemes. The company actively sought out new foreign investors, often cooperating with foreign commercial banks under a fee-sharing arrangement to sponsor seminars in Europe or Asia on investment prospects in Chile. As the stock of Chilean convertible debt shrank and transaction margins decreased, Socimer sought to broaden its financial services business in Chile, promoting corporate finance, mergers and acquisitions, and economic and financial consulting functions along with its participation in Chile's first electronic stock exchange. The group possessed only a couple of small industrial investments in Chile, essentially connected to trading activities that involved a leather operation and a joint venture investment in a sawmill.

Changing Foreign Faces in Chilean Banking

The Santander financial group originated in Spain in 1857 to assist trade with the "new world." The major transformation in its Latin American operations came after the 1982 financial crisis when the bank shifted away from some Central American operations to concentrate on the Southern Cone countries of Chile, Brazil, Argentina, and Uruguay. The bank had opened a representative office in Chile just before the Allende nationalization campaign and was one of the first to follow Citibank in reestablishing banking operations in Chile in the late 1970s. Santander changed its operation from a representative office to a branch operation in 1978. Following its regional strategy shift, the bank purchased Banco Español–Chile in 1982, and undertook an investment campaign that made Chile the center for Santander's regional operations.[19]

During the decade Santander invested over $140 million in its Chilean operations. While the majority of these funds came under D.L. 600, the bank used Chapter XIX debt conversions for three projects. The first undertaking aimed at capitalizing its banking operations, in particular repurchasing the bad loan portfolio of Banco Español–Chile that was held by the Central Bank. Another project included the formation of an insurance company, mentioned previously, which was Santander's only insurance operation outside a joint venture business in Spain. The third deal and largest debt conversion amounted to an investment of some $27 million in privatized ENTEL, where the bank appeared to be a transitory investor in conjunction with ENTEL's purchase by Telefónica Nacional de España.

Santander built a broad financial services group in Chile that includes mutual funds, leasing, stock brokerage, factoring, and other affiliated activities to complement its banking and insurance business. The banking enterprise maintains a large network with over fifty offices and concentrates particularly on serving the credit needs of medium-size firms. Without a substantial investment position in the industrial sector, the bank poses little conflict of interest potential in analyzing customer loan applications and can draw on an overseas network to aid in foreign commercial activities.

Internationally the Santander group is associated with the Royal Bank of Scotland, which holds an equity stake in their commercial and investment banks, and with Nomura Securities of Japan, which has worked cooperatively to explore Japanese business interest in Chilean investments. Santander also bought a 13.5 percent share of First Fidelity Bank in the United States for $220 million, with an option to purchase an additional 10 percent. Another alliance developed in mid-1990, when the Kemper Investors Life Insurance Company (Kilico) made its first investment outside the United States, entering into a joint venture with Seguros de Vida Santander in Chile. With this venture serving as a testing ground, the two groups plan to explore areas of possible cooperation in other countries as well.

Santander brought capital, contacts, and aggressive competition to the Chilean financial community as it pursued its expansion strategy during the 1980s. The company itself benefitted from the ability to test its expertise and try new ventures such as the insurance operation in a dynamic Chilean environment. The country's small size but vigorous competition gave the enterprise good early feedback that will help inform its expansion plans elsewhere.

Another expanding foreign participant in the Chilean financial market is the Rothschild group. Rothschild helped manage bonds for Chilean projects placed on London's financial markets as early as the 1860s, but entered Chile through its favored joint venture approach only in 1979. That year the local Matte family group founded Banco Industrial y de Comercio Exterior (BICE) and at the same time teamed up in a 50/50 joint venture with Rothschild to form BICE Chileconsult, an investment banking services company. The two family groups had prior personal contacts and followed a similar, generally conservative business philosophy. The Matte group emerged from the early 1980s recession in relatively good financial condition and, in 1986, expanded its partnership with Rothschild to include the latter's participation in Banco BICE as well as initiatives in new financial areas.[20]

The partnership built a wide range of investment banking services to offer enterprises in Chile, including private equity placements, project finance, debt conversions, and stock exchange transactions. The groups received approval to create two D.L. 600 foreign investment funds—The Five Arrows Chile Fund Limited with a capital target of $150 million and CDFC Trust PLC F.I.C.E. with a $5 million limit. Rothschilds' established international standing was essential to launching new foreign investment funds on the European markets. Together the partners also possessed the size and stature to become involved in major project finance undertakings such as Escondida and Cape Horn Methanol, as well as a number of privatization actions including ENDESA, Banmédica, and Pehuenche. Banco BICE's standing with corporate customers in the forestry and mining sectors also gave the bank significant strength in trade financing activities.

Banco de Colombia en Chile gave way to a new domestic/foreign joint venture in early 1990, when ABN Tanner Bank opened its doors for business. This 50/50 partnership joins Algemene Bank of the Netherlands, which used Chapter XIX financing, with local investors led by the Villaseca family. Commercial banking and foreign commerce form the key targets for this operation. Executives announced plans to increase the number of local offices to provide better service, especially for small and medium-size exporters that could draw on the bank's overseas affiliates.[21]

Bank of Nova Scotia also used Chapter XIX funding to purchase a one-quarter share in Banco Sud Americano, in the process raising the locally controlled bank's capital by one third. Sud Americano already possessed over thirty local offices and the additional capital significantly strengthened its position in the Chilean market.[22] Centrobanco, the Chilean affiliate of Banco Central de España, is a similarly positioned player in the local market with plans to improve its network of over thirty local offices as well as perhaps to begin leasing and insurance activities.[23] Credit Lyonnais of France announced interest in forging an eventual association with a local banking group when it established a leasing company in Chile in July 1990, and already possesses a stake in an insurance venture.[24]

The story of Banco O'Higgins' evolution presents yet another perspective on the changing face and increasing integration of foreign and domestic elements in Chile's banking sector. This institution's roots trace back to 1888, when two brothers with interests in Chile's nitrate industry founded a bank in London to operate in Chile as Banco de Tarapaca y Londres. Early in the next century this entity became Banco Anglo Sud Americano, which was purchased by the Bank of London and South America in 1936.

Twenty years later local investors founded Banco O'Higgins. The Allende government nationalized both banks, passing the foreign bank's assets to the smaller national enterprise on August 30, 1971 after the foreign investors left the country. An agricultural cooperative (COPAGRO) bought the privatized bank in 1976, selling it to the Luksic group in 1982, which in turn sold Banco Español de Crédito (BANESTO) a 30 percent participation. Although this transaction brought some additional capitalization to Banco O'Higgins, the partnership did not flourish. The Luksic group bought out BANESTO's stake in 1989.[25]

Banco O'Higgins emphasized foreign trade as the key element of its financial business although it operates some forty offices and has invested in upgrading their technology. The bank was hurt by Chile's financial crisis in the early 1980s, when the Luksic/BANESTO partnership acquired it, but its bad loan portfolio was relatively small at roughly $120 million. In July 1990 Banco O'Higgins became the first private Chilean bank to complete, ahead of schedule, its reacquisition agreement with the Central Bank. Shortly thereafter the bank became one of only two private national banks to hold the top rating granted by a commission composed of the banking, securities, and pension funds authorities. In a further twist to an evolving internationalization theme, Banco O'Higgins also celebrated its economic well-being at the beginning of the new decade by moving to establish offices in Brazil, Argentina, and Venezuela, with plans to extend operations to Mexico as well.

FOREIGN INVESTORS AND THE INSURANCE BUSINESS

The insurance industry expanded dramatically in Chile during the 1980s, driven largely by deregulation, the introduction of new insurance products, and the linked growth of Chile's privatized pension system. A few foreign insurance firms opened or expanded operations during the early years of these reforms, but more investors bought into the system toward the end of the decade. Offered equal national treatment with local enterprises, several foreign firms attained key positions in the industry. Foreign insurers brought knowledge and experience with global rate systems and product innovations that broadened the offerings available to Chilean customers. In a relatively brief time, Chile developed a dynamic and modern insurance market. Showing remarkable growth, the insurance sector added breadth and depth to the pool of institutional investors who helped develop Chile's capital markets.

The history of Chile's local insurance industry traces to 1853, with the founding of the first national insurance company in Valparaíso, a predecessor of the current La Chilena Consolidada firm controlled by the Edwards family. A 1904 law authorized government inspection of insurance enterprises, but the sector's primary legal structure was set by a 1927 statute that established broad government regulatory and intervention powers. That law banned any new foreign investment in insurance and a tax on insurance contracts with firms outside Chile effectively discouraged the use of offshore enterprises. Another legal refinement further consolidated the government's powers in 1953, providing a state monopoly over insurance for the expanding number of public enterprises.[26]

This legal structure evolved into a static tariff or fixed-rate insurance system in which the government set rates to be charged for various types of permitted insurance policies. With little attention to minimal capital requirements for operating an insurance business, individual corporations often set up their own insurance firms. The number of insurance companies proliferated within this static and protected structure until nearly 140 firms existed to service a relatively small market. The Caja Reaseguradora, a mixed public/private reinsurance firm, was given monopoly authority to reinsure policies with foreign institutions and several consortia formed to spread the risk among national firms.

Under this system, insurance firms could achieve profitability with little effort as long as the government-determined rate structure remained adequate. Only during the Allende years was the sector threatened when the government minimized rate levels and studied whether and how to nationalize these service sector institutions. Disadvantages of the regulated system, evident even before the Allende period, stimulated discussion on possible reform measures. The fixed-rate structure provided little competition between firms and few incentives for product innovation. Entrenched business interests opposed significant changes, however, delaying reform measures for nearly a decade.

A revolutionary reform law received approval in 1980, opening the insurance industry to greater competition and international participation. While maintaining a supervisory body, the government freed rates on coverages and ended restrictions on reinsurance contracts. The public and mixed public/private monopolies handling state enterprise insurance and reinsurance contracts were restructured and eventually privatized. Competitive forces reduced the number of insurance firms from just over one hundred in 1979, to sixty-six in 1981, before stabilizing at around forty companies by 1985. Prices dropped significantly although total industry revenue did not fall proportionately after the recession years. Customers often used price savings to purchase new forms of insurance coverage that expanded as competitive offerings increased.

The parallel privatization of Chile's pension system added another dynamic growth element to the insurance industry. As mentioned earlier in this chapter, pension fund management firms collect premiums from their subscribers to purchase life and disability coverage for them, contracting with an insurance company to provide these services. When they retire, subscribers can also sell their pension account to an insurance firm for an annuity policy. These reforms stimulated increased business for the insurance sector and forged working relationships between pension fund administrators (AFPs) and insurance companies, with most AFPs sharing ownership links with their contracted insurers even though the firms were administered separately.

The previous discussion of Bankers Trust's involvement with Provida, Consorcio, and Compensa illustrates these tie-ins, albeit from the perspective of a banking institution investing in new fields of insurance and pension fund management. As noted, Bankers Trust and its later joint venture partners control the largest AFP and life insurance company in their respective sectors. The initiative provoked controversy in part because the bank used debt conversion funds and lacked relevant business experience. Additionally, the acquisition expanded foreign control in these sectors where two international insurance companies were also active participants.

Early Pension/Insurance Ventures—Aetna and AIG

Aetna entered Chile at the instigation of a local business group that sought a foreign joint venture partner for its new pension-related business. The Bank of Chile group formed the Santa María AFP. The bank possessed financial management experience but lacked insurance expertise which it realized would be needed to take advantage of the linked business opportunity available in the new pension fund system. The match appeared good. Aetna had general insurance expertise and over a century of experience with employee benefit programs related to pension funds. From Aetna's perspective, a minority partnership with an established Chilean group offered the company an opportunity for a low-risk learning experience in Latin America that might prove useful if Chile's experiment proved successful enough to be emulated by other countries.

The new partners closed their deal in early 1981, with Aetna investing roughly $11 million through D.L. 600 for a 20 percent share of Santa María and 40 percent of the related insurance company, Aetna Banchile. In addition to a life insurance firm to work with the pension fund, the partnership also activated a general insurance company with roots tracing as far back as 1899. When the financial crisis and recession battered Chile during 1982–83, Aetna increased its share of Santa María to 40 percent and then 44 percent. The partnership dissolved, however, when Bank of Chile fell apart in bankruptcy. The government intervened in Bank of Chile in 1983, requiring the sale of bank assets including its share of the AFP and insurance company.

Aetna bought the remainder of the insurance business and an additional 7 percent of Santa María, giving it a majority 51 percent stake in that firm. Aetna might have purchased an even larger share of the AFP under its original partnership arrangement, but the government wanted to make Santa María part of its "popular capitalism" program by selling shares widely to the general public, initially drawing over 6,000 shareholders. Aetna increased its investment in these enterprises by reinvesting approximately half their profits. The company also sold a one-quarter stake in its business in 1987, to the investment affiliate of Banco Hispanoamericano, Aetna's joint venture partner in Spain.

Aetna's firms are among the top few companies in market share for pension funds, life insurance, and general insurance. The company is not tied to the parent corporation for reinsurance services and seeks the best negotiable arrangement on international markets for the roughly two-thirds of its reinsurance needs placed outside Chile. Aetna also formed a mortgage company following a 1987 Chilean regulatory change that allowed insurance firms to compete with banks in offering home mortgages. Later in 1991, it launched a unit fund which invests in mortgages, leasebacks, and other forms of real estate investments. The company emphasizes training, including overseas assignments, and strives for innovative services for its customers such as being the first to offer plastic cards for checking an individual's account status on automatic teller machines.

The American International Group (AIG) entered Chile in 1980, forming two subsidiaries in the life insurance and the property and casualty insurance fields. This move responded to Chile's new insurance law that reopened the market to foreign insurance firms. Originally founded in Shanghai, China in 1910, AIG maintains a large international operation and was pursuing in Chile a strategy of further global expansion. As in Aetna's case, original investments occurred under D.L. 600 with later increases coming largely through reinvestments of profits. Unlike Aetna, AIG did not immediately engage in pension fund activities.

In 1986, AIG purchased at public auction AFP Unión, the product of a merger of two intervened pension funds (San Cristóbal and Alameda). These AFPs had been owned by two important local economic groups which failed in Chile's financial crisis. Probably due to the firms' poor financial condition, the government did not place the same limits on AIG's ownership share that it had on the Aetna and Bankers Trust acquisitions. AIG ended up owning nearly 90 percent of La Unión. This stake was later increased to full ownership in 1990, when AIG sought to establish complete control over its Chilean activities, partly in response to the collapse of a business where it had been a minority investor.

The collapse involved InverChile, a brokerage firm/investment bank that went under in 1990. Established in 1982 by local Chilean investors, the firm attracted a minority investment from the World Bank's International Finance Corporation (IFC) in line with its objective of developing and modernizing Chile's capital markets. Early successes in Chapter XIX transactions and the creation of a foreign investment fund encouraged AIG and Midland Bank to also take minority positions in InverChile. AIG owned around 16 percent of InverChile and later nearly 40 percent of an affiliated mutual fund company, while Midland Bank held a 20 percent share and the IFC owned 12 percent of InverChile.

Trouble arose from InverChile's excessive position in medium-term floating rate bonds issued by the government in connection with Chapter XIX debt swaps. Although a government obligation, these issues were a relatively new and untested instrument in the Chilean capital market. This problem was aggravated by InverChile's practice of using these bonds as collateral for repurchase agreements at a time when the market (i.e., the purchasers) lacked the ability to value properly the underlying security collateral. Although Chilean nationals held an aggregate majority share of InverChile and managed the enterprise, the firm's reputation became aligned with its foreign shareholders and the market came to look on InverChile's obligations as backed by those foreign investors.

InverChile's overextended position in these bonds exceeded prudential financial requirements and caused Chile's regulators to suspend the firm's operations, leaving mutual fund investors and creditor firms holding the repurchase agreements facing millions of dollars in potential losses. Several of InverChile's local shareholders reacted to the crisis in an unusual manner, offering to make good the potential losses through a pro-rata purchase of the illiquid securities. The foreign shareholders were invited to match this offer, and press accounts report government pressure on the three foreign investors to take some responsibility beyond their equity positions by contributing additional resources to help offset the losses incurred by other investors, particularly shareholders in the firm's mutual fund.[27]

The IFC refused to participate in a rescue package, arguing that its investor role only amounted to a type of venture capital contribution to help get the firm started. While absorbing its own direct loss, the IFC could not accept a broader liability that might set a precedent regarding its involvement in more than 1,000 similar projects in some 100 other countries.[28] AIG and Midland bought into the rescue plan, and eventually creditors and investors received over 93 percent of their original investments. AIG's local executive explained their decision by pointing to the nature of the company's business and its long-term stake in the Chilean economy:

> We have here businesses based on confidence. We are owners of an AFP and an insurance company, and the people in this country have bought our products because of their confidence in our group. After 10 years we have grown significantly and we act responsibly; therefore, we cannot permit an event such as InverChile to have a negative impact on our investments. I believe that we are victims in this affair, but we are going to fulfill our responsibilities. We have a large investment in Chile and a great interest in continuing our growth.[29]

With InverChile's collapse, AIG in Chile became predisposed against joint venture arrangements where management control rested outside the group. Subsequently, when AIG was offered the opportunity to acquire the remaining 10 percent of La Unión not held by the group, it quickly picked up the shares. AIG also developed several related activities with possible synergies to its core pension fund and insurance business. These undertakings include participation in a couple of foreign investment funds, a computer operation to manage data processing needs, a mortgage company that can produce investment packages for institutional investors under new government regulations, and a real estate firm whose business is symbolized by the huge new Torre Interamericana built in the heart of Santiago that houses the group's various operations.

AIG also assisted in the pioneer listing of the Chilean Telephone Company (CTC) on the New York Stock Exchange, providing certain liability coverage common under U.S. regulations but unusual for the Chilean market.

Additionally, AIG was one of the earliest firms in Chile to use career agents and mass marketing techniques for life insurance sales. The company has thus surged to the forefront of Chile's dynamic insurance market, committing new expertise and resources to improve the insurance products and services available to Chilean businesses and the general public.

Foreign Insurers New and Old

Assurances Generales de France (AGF) selected a similarly broad investment strategy in Chile's insurance industry but did not make its key move until 1990. Investing around $25 million, AGF acquired nearly full ownership of Consorcio General de Seguros while also purchasing 61 percent of both the general and life insurance subsidiaries of La Previsión and a 49 percent share of AFP Protección. Already in fifty countries, the company was expanding its global network, seeking to increase its proportion of international versus French-based business from around one-quarter to as much as 40 percent. Chilean insurance companies presented an opportunity to introduce new products to the market; the AFP investment was seen as a natural extension of these business interests because La Previsión Vida was the contractual insurer for La Protección.[30]

Cigna offers a good contrast with Aetna, AIG, and AGF in several respects. The firm's presence in Chile traces back to 1919, when the Home Insurance Company received a branch license and formed a local entity called "El Cóndor." Grandfathered under the law that prohibited further investments by foreign insurance companies, this operation became part of the Insurance Company of North America (INA) through a merger transaction. In 1982, INA merged with Connecticut General Corporation to form Cigna. Two years later Cigna acquired AFIA, an international insurance association with business in over 100 countries, including an affiliated company in Chile. With these pieces in place by 1985, Cigna began that year operating general insurance and life insurance companies in Chile under its own name.

In addition to its long history in Chile, the other marked difference is in the distribution of Cigna's insurance activities. Potential sales to MNC subsidiaries originally drew the company to Chile, but a large majority of its business now comes from indigenous customers. Virtually all the firm's sales are generated through insurance brokers and local agents. Fire and marine insurance were early mainstays of its business and health insurance provides a key area of recent expansion. Cigna's life insurance company operates with a smaller share of the market, lacking contractual ties to an AFP.

Important foreign insurance firms from Great Britain and Germany responded to Chile's insurance law changes in 1980, acquiring general insurance companies whose origins reach to early in the century. Two British companies,

Royal International Insurance Holdings and Commercial Union Assurance Company, acquired 64 percent and 32 percent, respectively, of La República, a firm founded in 1905. The German Allianz group bought essentially all the shares of another enterprise that had begun as Compañía de Seguros Sol de Chile in 1917, renaming it after the parent holding company. The Arab Bin Mahfouz group holds a minority one-quarter interest in El Roble and the newer El Raulí life insurance companies. The former, constituted by the Angelini group with participation from the Matte group in 1981, is contractually linked with AFP Summa which has similar investor participation.

Two more French firms made significant investments in the insurance sector at the end of the 1980s. The Chilean government wanted to privatize Instituto de Seguros del Estado, which had been the monopoly insurer for state enterprises. Breaking the company into two firms dividing general and life insurance coverage, the government sold the former as ISE Seguros Generales in 1989 to Les Mutuelles du Mans (73 percent) and Banco Credit Lyonnais (14.6 percent) for roughly $3.4 million. In 1990, L'Union des Assurances de Paris (UAP) acquired a controlling 51 percent interest in Continental Generales, a firm founded in 1937. UAP then created two new enterprises, Continental Vida and Crédito Continental, to extend its business into the credit insurance and life insurance fields as well.[31]

As mentioned earlier, Bankers Trust and its partners operate the largest life insurance company, Consorcio Nacional de Seguros, as well as the new firm Compensa. Santander life insurance company operates under the joint venture between Santander and Kemper. The Zurich Insurance Group purchased majority control of La Chilena Consolidada's life insurance business in 1991, aligning itself with the local Edwards group. Many other insurance companies remain under local ownership, including notably the extensive Cruz del Sur general insurance network of the Angelini group, and several other life insurance companies linked to locally controlled AFPs.

Related insurance services come from reinsurance agencies as well as agents and brokers. Two top MNC insurance brokers (who advise corporations on their insurance needs and contract for coverage) have operated in Chile for several decades, although their operations were restricted during the Allende years. Johnson & Higgins established a subsidiary in Chile in 1963, while Marsh & McLennan now operates with a local partner through a 40 percent-owned venture formally established in 1972. The British Sedgwick Group bought a one-half share of another insurance broker, Andueza y Compañía, in 1983. The partnership gave Sedgwick easier entry to the market through an established local firm while it in turn possessed experience with insurance rate analysis needed in Chile's newly deregulated market.

STRATEGIC INVESTMENTS IN FINANCIAL SERVICES

Despite tremendous upheaval in Chile's financial sector during the 1980s, or perhaps in part because of it, the country evolved the continent's most dynamic and innovative capital markets. Foreign investors played a key role in the revitalization and expansion of Chile's banking and insurance sectors, as well as its privatized pension system. Investments by foreign banks sparked strong criticism, especially when creditor institutions used debt-to-equity swaps to purchase significant shares in existing or privatized enterprises. Foreign investors also gained substantial market positions in many financial services, including the politically sensitive administration of several large pension funds. These firms help determine, under government regulations, how the largest segment of Chile's private savings is invested. Foreign financial institutions also provided a local competitive stimulus as well as an increasingly important link for Chile to global financial markets.

Banking sector activity provides a useful bridge between the past and the present. Many bank expansions occurred at the end of the 1970s as Chile enjoyed vigorous economic expansion and international commercial banks peddled petrodollar loans throughout the developing world. Foreign banks, along with governmental authorities, undoubtedly share some of the blame for the debt crisis that developed, and they also shared some of the resultant economic loss. The retrospective debate about relative burden-sharing goes beyond the scope of this study, but the attitudes and emotions surrounding it helped shape the political context for controversy over the banks' use of Chapter XIX debt conversions and their involvement in Chile's long but successful struggle to return to international voluntary lending markets.

One generalizable conclusion is that the debt swap program stimulated investment activity among heavily exposed creditor banks that would not otherwise have occurred. Although these investments are criticized for not bringing fresh money, the transactions initiated business activity in addition to whatever initial use occurred when the loan was first dispersed to Chilean debtor institutions. In many cases the banks promoted new or expanded projects that attracted other investment partners who brought additional experience, technology, and capital infusions. Even when banks served as temporary investors, selling to subsequent private firms or public shareholders, the business opportunities thereby stimulated may never have developed without the debt conversion activity. The fact that an investor came later does not mean the investor would have appeared sooner without the debt conversion activity. This conclusion is consistent with the slower economic recovery of most other debt-ridden countries where foreign creditor roles were essentially confined to recurrent negotiations on debt rescheduling.

In addition to pursuing a strategy of investment diversification, some banks expanded traditional or built new lines of business in financial services. Foreign institutions offered advanced credit analysis techniques, technological advancements, and more financial security—even with their debt problems—than most local institutions could provide. The banks' overseas offices and international expertise proved especially useful in Chile's drive to increase nontraditional exports, supplying trade financing and foreign market knowledge to assist exporters in expanding and diversifying overseas markets.

A second broad finding is that foreign banks did not act as a homogeneous cabal in their approach to the Chilean market. Responding to a combination of parent requirements and local opportunities, individual institutions pursued quite different strategies that yielded a wide variety of investment scenarios and experiments. Some ventures failed or led to unproductive management conflicts, but many other innovations succeeded, at times extending a bank's time horizon from a short-term exit strategy to the role of long-term investor in the Chilean economy. Market openness also attracted new bank investors, many unburdened by heavy debt loads, who brought fresh capital and even more competition to the financial system. The results enhanced customer services in Chile, producing some competitively tested innovations that are being transmitted through global bank networks to related institutions in other countries.

The insurance sector offers both reinforcing and supplemental conclusions to the banking sector survey. Insurance had stagnated for decades under a highly regulated tariff structure with only small representation from grandfathered foreign investors. The 1980 reform law opened the market to innovation and competition, including foreign insurers who appeared in two waves, coming both early and late in the decade. Foreign insurers brought experience in rate-setting and analysis as well as new products for introduction into Chile's deregulated insurance market. The firms also contributed new and reinvested capital, nearly all registered under D.L. 600 provisions, to help build and restructure the initially numerous but financially weak network of local firms.

Foreign investment in insurance, and in AFP activities, contributed significantly to stabilizing and retaining public confidence in the newly privatized pension system. Foreign investors revitalized weak and failed AFPs that had suffered from the broader collapse of local business groups. The deeper financial pockets of these foreign institutions added a sense of greater security to the new system while bringing enhanced management skills, particularly for the key institutional investor role that developed as the system grew into the country's most important source of private savings. Other benefits arising from the activities of foreign financial institutions include the creation of foreign investment funds, the encouragement of new public listings, support for American Depository Receipts (ADRs), and other similar transfers of knowledge, experience, and innovation.

The story is far from complete. Chile's capital markets need to be further strengthened and deepened by encouraging greater public shareholdings and developing better access to venture capital and longer-term loans for small and medium-size businesses. These steps would also broaden the distribution of economic benefits among the population compared to the historical control exercised by a relatively small number of tightly held family groups. Such changes may occur gradually as an indirect effect of the internationalization of Chile's financial sector.

Two other observations arise from the cases examined in this chapter. First, the highly professional role of Chilean regulatory authorities was evident throughout. Following the recession and through the Aylwin administration's early tenure, regulations were set with a keen sense of technical competence and socioeconomic requirements. Deregulation did not mean no regulation, and standards were enforced. A particularly difficult task, not described sufficiently in the case analysis, was the gradual loosening of restrictions on AFP investments that traded off the need to assure public confidence in the system's security with the diversification and higher returns attainable from riskier investment instruments.

The second observation relates to the actions of large, diversified foreign investors in Chile's economy. Critics often focus on the size of a foreign investment in a developing country, implying rather than substantiating a causal chain running from size through power to an implicit detrimental effect. By contrast, large investors in the financial services sector appeared to follow the most consciously designed strategy for investor responsibility, at least in part to ensure their long-term welcome within the host nation.

One illustration of this finding is Citibank's investment criteria that avoided potentially lucrative but controversial investments to concentrate on projects resulting in new or expanded employment and exports. A second example is the willingness of AIG to accept responsibilities beyond its legal obligations in the InverChile case in order to maintain the public confidence and trust in its reputation that are essential to its long-term business plans. An ironic contrast is the refusal of the IFC, an international public sector institution specifically charged with developmental goals, to undertake similar voluntary actions. The IFC based its position on arguably good precedential reasoning that nonetheless could have also been used by private foreign investors seeking to limit their obligations. This observation may not be easily generalized to all foreign investment, or even all large foreign investors, but it should give pause to those who are too easily swayed by implicit assumptions linking an MNC's size to detrimental effects rather than fact-specific analysis of its actions.

Finally, this chapter examined only the banking and insurance segments of a very broad financial services sector. Field research indicated, but could not fully cover, an analysis of other related business activities, some of which also involve important foreign investors. Probably most significant is the accounting profession, which is critical to the future development of Chile's capital markets. Legal and consulting services are also relevant to this sector as well as to other industrial activities. Although the picture must therefore remain incomplete, the sketches provided of banking and insurance companies offer several insights to the contrasting strategies employed by these foreign investors during the recovery and growth of Chile's financial services sector over the critical decade of the 1980s.

NOTES

Information in this chapter is drawn from interviews with corporate executives, government officials, other knowledgeable experts in the field, and selected articles from Chilean newspaper coverage of 1990–91, especially from *El Mercurio*. Additional selected citations are provided in the text where necessary for specific references.

1. Benjamin J. Cohen, "High Finance, High Politics," in *Uncertain Future: Commercial Banks and the Third World*, ed. Richard E. Feinberg and Valeriana Kallab, U.S. Third World Policy Perspectives, No. 2, Overseas Development Council (New Brunswick, NJ: Transaction Books, 1984), 112.

2. For example, in addition to *Uncertain Future: Commercial Banks and the Third World*, see Miles Kahler, ed., *The Politics of International Debt* (Ithaca: Cornell University Press, 1986); Richard E. Feinberg and Valeriana Kallab, eds., *Adjustment Crisis in the Third World*, U.S. Third World Policy Perspectives, No. 1, Overseas Development Council (New Brunswick, NJ: Transaction Books, 1984); and *Dealing with the Debt Crisis: World Bank Symposium*, ed. Ishrat Husain and Ishac Diwan, World Bank Publications, 1989.

3. "Por US$ 320 millones: Chile completó ayer subscripción de bonos," *El Mercurio*, January 12, 1991; and "Chile sale de 'Lista Negra' de bancos norteamericanos," *El Mercurio*, February 8, 1991.

4. "El pulso de la banca," *El Mercurio*, July 29, 1990; and "Póngale nota a la banca," *El Mercurio*, November 18, 1990.

5. "Branching Out: Citibank Tries Its Hand At Industrial Investing," *Latin Finance* (June 1989); and Edward M. Dreyfus, "Citicorp/Citibank: Inversiones en Chile vía conversión en deuda externa," Speech given at the seminar, "Oportunidades de Inversión en Chile," Santiago, May 15–16, 1990, Photocopy.

6. See local press accounts, especially for June 1990; and "Provida Sweetheart Contract Squabble Spills Into Print Media and Courts," *South Pacific Mail* (July 1990), 123.

7. *A.F.P. Provida S.A. Memoria Anual 1989*, Provida (1989), 10,12.

8. "Informó nuevo vicepresidente: Bankers Trust consolida su presencia en Chile," *El Mercurio*, January 17, 1991.

9. Embassy of the United States, Economic Section, *Chile—Economic Trends*, Prepared by Tom Kelly (Santiago, Chile, June 1991), 4,5,13; and "Los bancos: ¿Los buenos, los malos, los feos?" *El Mercurio*, September 8, 1991. The *El Mercurio* article

points out several difficult regulatory problems arising from the subordinated debt situation which is perpetuating banking distortions in a sector that needs restructuring and redirection to remain competitive in Chile's dynamic capital markets.

10. Francisco Martín López-Quesada, Speech given at the Seminario Internacional, "Oportunidades de Inversión en Chile," Santiago, May 15–16, 1990, Photocopy.

11. "La superintendencia de bancos: Aprueban joint venture entre Security Pacific y socios de Sigdo Koppers," *El Mercurio*, February 25, 1991; "El Security Pacific mantiene interés de permanecer en Chile," *El Mercurio*, March 8, 1991; and "Fusión de Bank America y Banco Security Pacific tendrá efectos en Chile," *El Mercurio*, August 14, 1991.

12. "'El Plan Brady no ha fracasado'," *El Mercurio*, February 18, 1990; and "Para este año: Chilgener aprobó plan de inversiones por 123,5 millones de dólares," *El Mercurio*, April 12, 1990.

13. See local press accounts from October to December 1990. Also see "Iansa: Al rojo vivo," *El Mercurio*, April 28, 1991; "Iansa: ¿En qué va la guerra?", *El Mercurio*, June 2, 1991; "De Sueden y Chicago a Pathfinder: US$ 40 millones involucra venta del 22% de Iansa," *El Mercurio*, July 9, 1991; "Pathfinder compró 16,4% de acciones de campos chilenos," *El Mercurio*, October 1, 1991; and "Humo Blanco en Iansa," *El Mercurio*, October 27, 1991.

14. "Nueva clasificación de bancos de EE. UU.: Reconocimiento al bajo riesgo que ofrece Chile," *El Mercurio*, February 9, 1991; "US$ 50 millones en nuevas inversiones evalúa banco Chicago Continental," *El Mercurio*, September 27, 1990; and "Chicago Continental Inicia Nueva Etapa de Negocios," *El Mercurio*, December 9, 1991.

15. "En la cumbre del Chase," *El Mercurio*, March 11, 1990; "Chase Manhattan Leasing se retiró del mercado," *El Mercurio*, November 26, 1990; "Presidente mundial de Chase: Arthur Ryan: 'En Chile cometimos errores'," *El Mercurio*, March 13, 1991; and "Respectability Brings Investment," *Euromoney*, supplement, "Chile: Building on Success" (September 1990), 21.

16. *Asset Trading and Debt Conversion*, NMB Bank (June 1988), 3.

17. "International Borrowing: Debt Conversion that Works," *Euromoney*, supplement, "Chile: Into the 1990s" (August 1989), 28–29.

18. *IFC-NMB Loans*, NMB Bank.

19. D. Emilio Botín, speech given at the Seminario Internacional, "Oportunidades de Inversión en Chile," Santiago, May 15–16, 1990, Photocopy; and Martín López-Quesada, speech at same seminar, same date.

20. "Rothschilds and BICE: Second to None," in "Chile: Into The 1990s," 38–39.

21. "En un plazo de dos años: Diez sucursales espera tener ABN Tanner Bank," *El Mercurio*, April 2, 1990; "ABN Tanner anuncia una fuerte incursión en banca de personas," September 10, 1990; and "Respectability Brings Investment," 21.

22. "Llegará a $23 mil millones: Elevarán en 33% capital del Banco Sud Americano," *El Mercurio*, September 13, 1990.

23. "$1.300 millones ganó centrobanco en 1er semestre," *El Mercurio*, July 20, 1990.

24. "En Chile: Empresa de leasing forma Continental Credit Lyonnais," *El Mercurio*, July 9, 1990.

25. Internal corporate summary of history of Banco O'Higgins, Photocopy, 2 pages; and "Moving Forward with Chile," in "Chile: Into the 1990s," 19.

26. "Síntesis histórica del seguro: De Babilonia a Valparaíso," and "Intervención estatal y libre competencia," *Estrategia*, Special edition, "Seguros y AFP," July 1990, 2.

27. "IFC, AIG, Midland Told to Pay for InverChile Loss," *South Pacific Mail* (July 1990), 121, 136; "Suspenden operación de filiales de InverChile S.A.," *El Mercurio*, June 20, 1990; and "Superintendente de valores: 'No había alternativa en situación de InverChile'," *El Mercurio*, June 21, 1990.

28. "CFI no concurre a proceso de rescate en InverChile," *El Mercurio*, July 12, 1990.

29. "Oliver Scholle, vicepresidente ejecutivo: Interamericana busca consolidar negocios de seguros y pensiones," *El Mercurio*, September 10, 1990. (translated from Spanish).

30. "AGF completó inversión de US$ 25 millones en Chile," *El Mercurio*, December 13, 1990.

31. For corporate profiles see *Estrategia*, Special edition, "Seguros y AFP," July 1990.

6

General Industry

A variety of manufacturing facilities populate Chile's general industrial sector. Many operations are associated with value-added processing of minerals, forestry, agriculture, or fishery resources discussed earlier. Most other industrial activities stem from a combination of providing business infrastructure goods and services and meeting domestic consumer needs. These operations are shaped by Chile's market size, which limits the scale of manufacturing activities directed at internal consumption, and its open import policy, which enforces competition and pricing discipline on local producers.

In earlier periods, market planning based on Andean Pact ambitions and other economic integration schemes led to the construction of some facilities that could not be sustained as these regional approaches came apart under political and economic differences. Similarly, national import substitution policies initially underwrote the operation of inefficient domestic plants that produced increasingly outmoded products, sustained behind high protective trade barriers. The domestic business community and population as a whole paid a high price for these policies, particularly during the country's abrupt shift to an internationally open market economy under the Pinochet government.

Foreign investors participated in various segments of general manufacturing industries before, during, and after these changes. Their presence and activities increased, however, as the economy moved to free market rules. Existing foreign investors faced difficult adjustment tasks, often finding themselves as vulnerable as local businesses when protective barriers were removed and new competitors emerged. Not all firms successfully made the transition, but a number of foreign investors modified their operations and explored new opportunities, at times striking off in strategic directions different from their parent corporation's main lines of business. Investors with decentralized management structures used local flexibility to find product niches that could sustain or expand their operations in the new market environment.

New investors also entered Chile, testing a mix of import and local processing strategies depending on product and competitive circumstances. Chilean policy set the broad framework for this competition and, in sectors such as automobiles and pharmaceuticals, influenced the business structure directly through legal formulations. This chapter traces foreign investment strategies across a number of general industrial sectors, covering transitions from the old to the new as well as examining cases of how an investor's global strategy and structure affect the options and choices of its Chilean subsidiary.

COMPUTERS AND TELECOMMUNICATIONS

Introducing Advanced Technologies—IBM, Unisys, NCR, and More

Chile boasts one of the most advanced technological infrastructures among developing countries, providing both a dynamic area of direct business expansion and an important complementary capacity for growth in other industrial sectors. The key elements in building Chile's high technology capability were combining an open import policy with flexible corporate planning and adjustment decisions in a highly competitive environment. This context contrasts sharply with Chile's import limitation and market protection strategy of the 1960s and early 1970s when firms had neither the motivation nor the ability to introduce the latest technological innovations to a minor Chilean market. The maturing relationship between Chile and its foreign investors is typified by the evolution from this earlier stage to the contemporary situation.

The core of a high technology sector rests with the computer business that supplies both hardware and essential software packages for applications in many different lines of business. The hardware field can be roughly categorized into three subfields of mainframe, minicomputers, and microcomputers or personal computers (PCs). Business structure and competitors differ among the three subfields, with a smaller number of firms engaged in the first two areas compared to the broad array of companies offering PCs and software applications. The three MNCs traditionally established in the Chilean market that offer products falling into the top level categories as well as lower applications are IBM, NCR, and Unisys (formerly Burroughs, prior to a merger with Sperry-Rand).

IBM and Unisys sold products in Chile in the early 1900s, with IBM establishing direct operations there in 1929, while Unisys continued working through a distributor (Grace) until opening its own offices in 1969. NCR set up a distributorship in the mid-1930s but upgraded the operation to a direct corporate office before the end of the decade. These offices conducted profitable but rather unexciting business, confined by import regulations and tied largely to expansion of the country's mining industry and government sector. When the Allende administration assumed power, extensive import restrictions virtually shut off the companies' supply of products and even many spare parts. With essentially nothing to sell, the firms scaled back operations and concentrated on maintaining customers' existing machines as well as possible, recognizing that replacement parts were sometimes unavailable.

The Pinochet government removed import restrictions and cut relevant tariffs from over 100 percent to the uniform 10 percent in a very short time. The open market policy aimed to draw in new equipment to overcome the technology gap created by past regulatory policies. This approach coincided with the remarkable technological progress occurring in the computer field as smaller machines with dramatically increased storage capacity and computing power were being produced at lower and lower cost. The policy also had the effect of increasing competition, allowing more firms to enter the Chilean marketplace without requiring a direct investor presence. Greater competition in turn drove all firms to upgrade their offerings by confronting them with the very real prospect of losing potential sales when older units had to compete with other firms' newest technological imports.

Computer companies investing directly in Chile hold potential advantages over computer importers in the area of customer service and responsiveness to opportunities for local adaptation and innovation. For example, Unisys formed the Synapsis joint venture with Enersis, resulting in an extension of data processing business and software adaptation and export through Unisys overseas network as described in the earlier chapter on nontraditional exports. IBM worked with Banco de Santiago to develop a computerized customer service system and formed cooperative ventures with Chilean universities to establish advanced educational networks that can link distant locations in Chile as well as connecting the universities with research and educational institutions in the United States. NCR entered a joint venture with Orden, a firm formed by a group of local engineers that had enjoyed some early success in exporting software and teamed up with SONDA, which needed additional financial support to expand operations. Locally invested MNCs can generally contribute more to, and derive more from these types of ventures than firms with a less substantial local presence, such as Digital, which is represented in Chile by SONDA and has formed a joint marketing firm to help promote export sales in Latin America.

Foreign investors in Chile's computer industry do not engage in local hardware production due to the country's small internal market. Brazil and Mexico are the only obvious Latin American sites with sufficient internal market size to justify some local production. Computer MNCs may develop certain associated activities in Chile, such as NCR's plant to manufacture continuous forms and Unisys's decision to create a software development center that serves the company's regional needs. The first example responds in part to Chile's advantages related to paper production. The second reflects both the high quality of locally trained technical personnel and the specific availability of Chapter XIX funding that helped swing the balance in favor of Chile during corporate consideration of competing regional locations for the center.

Technology transfer is the key element giving value to MNC computer operations in Chile. The transfer is both more efficient and effective under competitive market forces than in a directed or protected policy environment. Chile did not attempt to force companies to engage in inefficient local production of computer hardware; rather, its open import policy induced competitive pressures that assured the introduction of the latest equipment. The availability of advanced hardware was a necessary precondition for Chile to discover its potential competitiveness in software and data processing where local talent and product adaptations create additional value-added business opportunities.

Computer MNCs can provide useful complements to these operations through joint ventures and inter-affiliate export channels. An equally useful function arises, however, from demand creation and workplace applications of high technology equipment by other foreign investors. These local subsidiaries are familiar with the advanced hardware available in more developed markets and can demand comparable equipment in Chile under the country's open importation policies. Adapting this new capability to local market needs can bring dynamic progress to various business sectors, perhaps most evident in Chile's rapidly modernizing financial services. For example, Citibank could not have created its innovative citicenter operation to demonstrate as a model for branches in other countries if advanced computer capabilities were not available in Chile. In this sense, the computer sector stimulates and reinforces progress in other business sectors that use advanced hardware with local adaptations to create new competitive opportunities.

A related case of advanced technology products that tends to confirm conclusions reached regarding the impact of Chilean policy changes on computer MNCs is the experience of the Xerox corporation. The firm entered Chile just before the Allende government imposed such severe import restrictions that Xerox's business was initially limited to the rental of a small supply of older machines. A temporary break occurred when Chile was to host an international conference and the government wanted the best modern equipment available to service the foreign delegates. Xerox was authorized to import a half dozen new machines with an agreement that they could be retained in the country for business use following the conference.

The arrival of Chile's open market policies in the mid-1970s brought a business revival, leading to the importation of new machines to meet the competition and a shift toward final sales in addition to the rental business, again responding to competitive demands. The relative proportion of sales versus rentals tends to fluctuate somewhat, with rentals increasing in more difficult economic times. In general, the Chilean market pushes at the forefront of technological developments, with new product availability lagging behind introductions in the U.S. market by no more than six months. Global competitors for Xerox are active in the Chilean market although most work primarily through local distributors.

Xerox does not manufacture its equipment in Chile, again due to the limited internal market size, with production confined to Brazil and Mexico in the Latin American region. The firm did establish a plant to recondition machines, primarily rentals, and to check and prepare imports for sale to local customers. Total direct employment runs around 250 individuals, with perhaps two-thirds that number of indirect jobs coming from associated business activities. The advanced technology embedded in Xerox products is the more essential part of its activities, however, helping to integrate and improve business functions in many sectors of the economy.

The Telecommunications Link—Changing CTC's Foreign Connections

The telephone business began in Chile just four years after Alexander Graham Bell's famous invention when Compañía de Teléfonos de Edison was founded in Valparaíso in 1880. After experiencing several corporate transformations, this entity evolved into Compañía de Teléfonos de Chile (CTC) in 1927, when acquired by International Telephone and Telegraph (ITT). As discussed in the earlier historical summary, the Allende government intervened in the firm in 1971, assuming state control that was confirmed by a settlement between the subsequent military government and ITT that established compensation for the nationalized property. In 1986, the Pinochet regime announced its intention to privatize CTC, a task it completed two years later.[1]

The Bond Group of Australia won an international bidding process to gain a 45 percent ownership share in CTC. Bond beat out a strong bid by Telefónica of Spain, in large part because it offered to invest fresh capital through D.L 600 while the Telefónica bid relied more heavily on debt-to-equity swaps. Given the sensitivities surrounding a national telephone system and the history of ITT's past ownership of CTC, the sale sparked public controversy, including several court challenges as well as political criticism. Other shares in the company were sold to company employees, private pension funds, several foreign MNC banks, and numerous other investors, bringing the total number of shareholders as high as 35,000.

As described earlier in relation to the Bond Group's other large Chilean investment in the El Indio gold mine, this foreign investor's strength lay in financing rather than with any particular expertise in telephone operations. The new owner's principal task was to design and finance a development program that would meet backlogged demand and provide Chile with a modern communications infrastructure. The initial development program was ambitious, aiming at doubling Chile's telephone capacity by the end of 1992, matching in just five years the cumulative progress over the company's prior fifty-eight years.

While increasing the number of telephones, CTC sought to enhance their quality of service as well. Objectives called for full automation and over 71 percent digitalization of the network, aimed at incorporating voice, text, and image services in the same operation. The system would use extensive fiberoptic links between major cities and satellite connections to serve isolated rural areas. Related CTC value-added services available in many areas included cellular telephone systems, fax and data transmissions, and advanced supplementary services such as call-waiting, call-forwarding, and three-way calling. The five-year development plan envisioned an investment of $1.2 billion. CTC made dramatic progress over the next couple years if measured against historical standards but initially fell behind its ambitious schedule of targets. The number of lines installed jumped from just under 615,000 in 1987 to nearly 800,000 in 1989, while digitalization increased from 36 percent to over 51 percent. With further performance improvements during the next two years, CTC brought the number of lines installed to the originally planned level by December 1991.

CTC was a profitable operation, paying the Bond Group good dividends that, under D.L. 600 provisions, could be remitted without delays. The telephone company operated under a government-regulated tariff schedule whose rates for most services was determined by an economic model with a built-in real rate of return to the company of some 12 percent. If the firm performed more efficiently than predicted by the model, the resulting additional profit provided a further reward for improved operations. CTC's net profits jumped by 77 percent in just the first year of operation under its new owner.

Nevertheless, the company encountered an unexpected effect from the financial difficulties of the parent Bond Group's need to raise cash to meet creditor demands, as explained in the discussion of the El Indio case. As a result, the profitable and invigorated CTC operation offered a readily marketable asset, and the company was sold in April 1990 to Telefónica for approximately $392 million. The Bond Group may have gained as much $185 million from this transaction, but more immediately important to it was the cash infusion required to meet the parent firm's pressing financial needs.[2]

In contrast with the Bond Group, Telefónica is an experienced operating company with a long history in the industry. Somewhat ironically, Telefónica was founded by ITT in 1926 and nationalized by the Spanish government in 1945. The government retains close to a one-third share in the enterprise, foreign investors hold roughly one-quarter, and the remainder is spread among nearly a million small shareholders.[3] Although Telefónica faced challenges in upgrading its own services in Spain, the company perceived several potentially attractive investment opportunities in the privatization process spreading through

Latin America and welcomed this second chance to acquire the CTC property that had escaped it in the earlier bidding process. The sale was conducted outside Chile between two foreign investors and as such did not affect the foreign investment contract provisions regarding capital repatriation restrictions.

One of Telefónica's first actions was to revise and extend CTC's development program to reflect better several pragmatic constraints on expanding service, including difficulties in the management of outside contractors. As a result, the company adopted a somewhat slower paced expansion to a higher overall target, moving from the objective of 1.2 million lines in service by 1992 to a goal of 1.6 million by 1996. The revised plan for expenditures from 1988–92 anticipated a total cost of $1.4 billion, funded through a combination of operational revenue, supplier credits, and the placement of securities. Major equipment suppliers including Alcatel and NEC, together with commercial banking institutions, provided a significant portion of the financing. The most intriguing portion of the financial package, however, came from a step initiated by the Bond Group and carried to completion by Telefónica to arrange an historic share offering by CTC that resulted in its listing on the New York Stock Exchange.

On July 20, 1990 CTC became the first Latin American stock to be listed on the "Big Board" in New York and the first in over a quarter century on any American exchange. CTC became only the sixty-sixth foreign company on the exchange, representing the fifteenth country. The full package of 100 million shares occurred in two simultaneous offerings, one in the United States and Canada, and an international offering outside these areas. The mechanism used for the transaction was American Depository Shares (ADS), each representing seventeen shares of CTC stock. The initial public price for an ADS was set at just over $15, yielding an anticipated total of nearly $99 million, with the company receiving close to $92 million after deducting underwriting discounts and other expenses incurred in arranging the offering. CTC's stock price soared after its initial offering, reaching over $40 by mid-1991. This success led CTC to announce plans to issue up to $200 million in international bonds in 1992, marking another reentry step for Chile into international financial markets.[4]

This complex transaction required an enormous amount of preparation and cooperation among the parties involved, including the company, governmental authorities in both countries, and a number of MNC financial enterprises that assisted in the event. Chile's Central Bank established a mechanism through a foreign investment contract and the American Depository Receipts (ADR) Decree that granted foreign investors access to Chile's formal currency market to convert and remit proceeds from dividends or the sale of their shares. Bank of New York played a central role, acting as the depository for ADRs, which were the evidence of investors' ADS purchases.

Salomon Brothers performed a critical function as the main underwriter for the offering, covering over one-half the offered shares. The World Bank's

International Finance Corporation (IFC) also supported the transaction by agreeing to purchase as many as 300,000 ADS. Salomon Brothers already possessed valuable experience with Chile's financial community through its formation of the Chile Fund, one of the D.L. 600 foreign investment funds that trades on the New York market and is authorized to invest as much as $200 million in Chilean enterprises.

The significance of CTC's action reaches at least four different elements. For the country, the NYSE listing carries both symbolic and real importance. CTC's success sets a useful precedent that other major Chilean enterprises may use in seeking access to foreign financial markets. Among the firms mentioned that may use the ADR mechanism to raise money from abroad are CMPC, SOQUIMICH, CAP, ENDESA, and MADECO.[5] More specifically for CTC, the stock issue enabled Telefónica to comply with an agreement the Bond Group had made to reduce its shareholdings below 45 percent by 1992, in order to comply with a limit on ownership concentration and make the stock eligible for investments by pension funds.

Third, the transaction brings real financial benefits for CTC, contributing directly to financing its development program. In addition to the immediate cash infusion, CTC will derive follow-on benefits from lower financing rates on capital purchases and the potential for raising more funds on the major financial markets due to the firm's established presence and reputation as certified by its NYSE listing. Behind CTC's entry onto the Big Board lies a wealth of financial information and substantive analysis on the corporation that lay the groundwork for other funding proposals. Few corporations in developing nations prepare, much less publish, the detailed data required by the U.S. Securities and Exchange Commission (SEC). By successfully passing this major test of its commercial health and viability, CTC is better prepared to undergo subsequent analyses and can enter them backed by an important market endorsement.

The final important aspect of this event stems from its multiple multinational linkages. Chile's national telephone company moved rapidly from a plodding, underfinanced state enterprise to a dynamic private concern whose expansion is backed by substantial foreign capital. In several ways CTC is now itself a multinational firm with its managing owner headquartered in Spain and multiple shareholders, both direct and through foreign investment funds, scattered around the world. Several MNCs assisted in CTC's foreign fund-raising efforts and others are providing the equipment, technology, and related financing to carry forward the company's development plan. In association with Telefónica, CTC is even in position to bid and participate in agreements aimed at expanding and improving telephone services in neighboring countries.[6]

Beyond the basic national telephone service, foreign investors are integrally involved in the development of other telecommunications services in Chile. Telefónica bought a major 20 percent stake in Empresa Nacional de Telecomunicaciones (ENTEL) before its successful purchase of CTC. ENTEL is the major provider of national long distance and international transmission services. Telefónica appealed an initial ruling by Chile's antimonopoly authorities that required divestiture of its equity shares in one of the companies. On the other hand, CTC pursued legal reviews of its request to offer long distance services. The Chilean regulatory system covering the telecommunications sector, while less than a decade old, already appeared to require updating as the country entered the 1990s, in order to address the increasing competition and rapidly changing technologies.

Mobile phones based on cellular technology are another illustration of Chile's highly sophisticated capabilities and the role of foreign investment in their development. CTC holds a regulated concession for the Santiago and Valparaíso regions, competing with another concessionary firm, CIDCOM. This latter enterprise, one of the pioneers in mobile telephones in Chile, was founded in 1980, by a Chilean entrepreneur who linked up in a 50/50 joint venture with a U.S. firm to obtain the technology and financing needed to establish the service in the Chilean market. The enterprise nearly failed in the 1982–83 recession, due largely to the dollar's appreciation effect on the imported equipment.

The foreign partnership shifted to Pacific Telecom, through its Chilean subsidiary TU International, which increased its share in CIDCOM to 60 percent and then to full ownership, relying in part on Chapter XIX financing for its investment. As a carrier rather than an equipment supplier, Pacific Telecom was free to source the best equipment worldwide but could also acquire new technology through its foreign connections at less cost than an unassociated local enterprise. Subsequently Bell South purchased CIDCOM from Pacific Telecom in 1991. Motorola is another major player in the Chilean cellular telephone market, owning part of Telecom, a firm that along with VTR competes for cellular telephone customers in other regions of the country. VTR's largest shareholder is the local Luksic group (46.5 percent), but the venture also includes Italcable of Italy (35 percent) along with Chicago Continental Bank and Siemens.

Chile's success in developing a modern and efficient telecommunications system offers an essential building block for achieving progress in other industrial sectors. The country's small size and geographical isolation make a technologically advanced communications system imperative. This need applies to globally integrated MNCs, but it is equally valid for the development of local entrepreneurial efforts, allowing Chile's well-trained professionals to tap into information and research sources worldwide on a real-time basis.

Chile is at the forefront of communications technology in Latin America, and indeed surpasses the installed capabilities in some developed country areas because Chile's expansion utilizes the latest developments such as fiberoptic technology. Foreign investors bring financial resources and technological capabilities, which are not available locally, to this task. If conducted under an appropriate regulatory structure that balances the advantages of increased competition with the need for a fair return on large, up-front capital expenditures, the continuing expansion and modernization of Chile's telecommunications sector can offer important multiplier effects for economic growth and help ensure the nation's competitiveness in global markets.

AUTOMOTIVE PRODUCTS

Designing a Sectoral Policy in Autos—The GM Response

General Motors (GM) has conducted business in Chile for a half century, operating through local distributors and dealers until the late 1960s when the company invested equity to establish its own distribution center. Nearly a dozen automotive firms operated assembly plants in Chile at the time, far more than justified by the small market but a step essentially required by government policy in order to participate substantially in local sales. The multiple assemblers recovered their cost inefficiencies through high prices, safe behind protective import barriers. GM left Chile when the Allende government nationalized their facilities but returned to resume operations in 1974, following the changeover in governments.

The GM assembly plant was built in the northern port city of Arica, some one thousand miles from the main population centers of central Chile, as part of the government's regional development program. Using knocked-down kits imported from plants in other countries, roughly one-third from facilities in Brazil, the Arica plant assembled a variety of models over the years. In early 1990, the operation concentrated on two- and four-door light pick-up trucks with two engine sizes. Employing around 300 people, this plant produces nearly 9,000 vehicles a year.

Only one other assembly plant still exists in Chile, operated jointly by Peugeot and Renault as Franco Chilena. A related enterprise, Renault-Cormecánica, produces gear boxes. This latter firm exports around $15 million of its output annually to related enterprises, mainly in South America, although over $3 million in shipments were exported to France in 1990.[7]

Total automobile sales in Chile can vary widely. They peaked in 1981 at around 140,000 before dropping off to roughly 17,000 in the recession during 1983, and by the end of the decade sales had recovered to 50–60,000 units with a temporary jump surpassing 90,000 during the country's pre-election economic surge in 1989. Despite the fluctuations, automotive firms must rely on market projections to schedule supply orders through a pipeline that stretches nearly four months back to their main production locations. GM was the overall 1989 sales leader in Chile, with the Arica small truck plant holding roughly 10 percent of the market that year. With only a flat 15 percent tariff barrier to overcome (reduced to 11 percent in 1991), Chile's automobile market is extremely competitive, offering more than thirty different makes. Assembly plants could not successfully produce and sell old models in the face of this import competition.

Like many developing countries, Chile attempted to promote local value-added production in the automotive sector. Lacking sufficient internal market size, however, the country could not hope to build a substantial national industry through staged development plans as used in Brazil and Mexico. Instead, Chilean policy as formulated during the 1960s was limited to forcing companies into domestic assembly operations in order to participate in the local market. This approach proved costly in terms of ultimate consumer price and ran counter to the free market strategy adopted by the Pinochet government. A new policy formulation therefore emerged which used an incentive program to encourage rather than require local value-added content.

The incentive program grants the auto assemblers tax credits for both local content and exports. Originally the law required between 15 and 30 percent local content to qualify for credits up to 50 percent of the local content's value. The GM facility responded by increasing its local content value from under 5 percent to around 30 percent. In the automobile industry this level represents relatively "easy" production adjustments that can be achieved before technologically sophisticated or major scale components are involved.

The export incentive scheme offers an offset against import duties for the equivalent local value-added content of exported items. This program aimed mainly at using the assemblers' international experience and marketing channels to promote greater product or component exports. The Renault-Cormecánica exports benefitted from this approach, as did a product arrangement between GM and Goodyear, discussed below. GM considered promoting automobile bumper exports from Chile but could not find enough cost or quality advantages to break into the market as a new supply source. In another unsuccessful two-year effort, the company also explored the potential for exporting pressed wood covers for tires, but market shifts toward plastic products doomed this project.

GM initiated limited vehicle exports to Bolivia, a logical market for its Arica plant located near the border with Bolivia. This undertaking required cooperation with GM dealers managing sales in that region, but more importantly the plan encountered problems with the often acrimonious relationship between the neighboring countries that can make vehicles imported from Chile a distinct liability in sales promotion efforts. (In the integrated world of global automobile alliances, the best business solution for GM was to promote its light trucks from the assembly plant in Chile as Isuzu models when sold as Bolivian imports.) Nevertheless, total GM exports of parts and vehicles for 1990 amounted to a reported $12 million.[8]

Although Chile's policy had moved away from the disguised cost of earlier local content requirements, its automotive incentive program still drew domestic (and some GATT) criticism as too expensive and an unnecessary departure from the country's general free trade policy. Studies showed a $15.3 million expenditure under the program in 1989, translating into over $900 per vehicle for the two assemblers' combined output of just under 16,500 units. GM claimed that local assembly operations saved the country some $2,000 in foreign exchange per vehicle. A competing importer of Nissan products calculated costs differently, finding imports to be equivalent or cheaper in foreign exchange costs and arguing that the incentive program constituted a $9 million subsidy to GM to maintain its workforce of several hundred employees at the Arica plant.[9]

The competing statistics and views received public airing as the Aylwin administration considered revising the automotive sector's incentive program. Under a 1985 law, some incentives would decrease beginning in 1991, and the program would end in 1995–96. Importers and free market advocates argued that the incentives were cost inefficient and an unjustified departure from general open trade principles. The two companies and local suppliers related to the assembly plant operations argued for a revised extension of the program that would give them a stable planning horizon.

One proposal, endorsed in principle by GM, envisioned postponing incentive reductions if the companies met new investment or export goals. A GM executive suggested that the company might even be able to increase its exports to neighboring countries to 7,000 vehicles worth some $60 million annually if further progress occurred on regional economic integration plans and the Chilean law provided a viable basis for business expansion. Without a satisfactory extension of the law, however, the executive warned that Chile's automotive industry could disappear in 1992, driven out by cheaper import competition.[10] This policy debate thus raised the traditional issue of whether, how, and where to draw distinctions between inefficient protection for an industry and providing incentives to develop an industrial base that generates follow-on market expansion.

A revision of Chile's automotive sector statute in September 1991 concentrated incentives on export promotion, linking benefits directly to the increase or decline in automotive exports. General Motors was simultaneously initiating an expanded export promotion effort that reached 1,000 vehicles in the January–September period. Perú was the principal export market, benefitting from special adaptations made at the Arica plant to acclimate vehicles for the Peruvian region.[11]

Local operations offer the foreign investor some opportunity to benefit from adapting products to market tastes, such as GM's decision to outfit their light trucks with a wooden overlay for the truck bed to help resist denting and other hard-use wear. GM also worked closely with dealers to improve sales and service facilities and invested in local warehouses to assure an adequate and timely availability of replacement parts. Nevertheless, GM would be unlikely to invest in an assembly plant in Chile now if it did not already possess one.

The local competitive enhancements do not overcome the cost advantages associated with scale production in larger markets as long as Chile operates under open import conditions.

Although current circumstances would not lead GM to open a plant in Chile, the company may be equally reluctant to forgo its local presence and rely wholly on exports to the market. In addition to strategic location considerations, GM's decision is affected by vested interests and institutional loyalty to established operations. For example, the rotation of expatriate managers through the Chilean company has developed an internal network of ex-managers who feel a personal stake in the plant's continued operation. The subsidiary is small enough that a managing director must be involved in the full scope of its operations and thereby becomes familiar with many of the individual workers.

The replacement of expatriates with local managers is an explicit objective for many countries and companies for good and legitimate reasons. Additionally, persuasive market considerations will override personal experiences in corporate decision making when the case is clear. Nevertheless, it also may be true that smaller units within a large global corporation can sometimes benefit in marginal decisions, when hard market calculations are not overwhelming, from the existence of former managers who have direct knowledge and a personal understanding of the foreign subsidiary's operations.

The public policy valuation of GM's Chilean assembly operation is highly dependent on the objectives being weighed, as was evident in the debate over possible changes in the country's incentive program for the automotive sector. GM's role has been largely defined by the contours of the country's past policy decisions. Market realities dictate that automotive MNCs will not make significant capital investments to develop large production sites in Chile, so the relevant question for the firms with remaining establishments in the country is whether their operations can be maintained or perhaps expanded somewhat through export promotion efforts.

Chilean public authorities will ultimately decide the future of the country's two remaining assembly plants and related supply operations. In this sense the GM story is more linked to Chile's past than to the broad thrust of its recent economic and political changes. Still, the case is a useful comparative measure of the scope and pace of recent developments and an applied test of how the democratic government balances various objectives and the socioeconomic costs implicit in policy decisions in the automotive sector.

Adapting the Past to the Present—Goodyear

Goodyear's investment in Chile provides another bridge between past and present as foreign investors adapted to the changing political and economic environment. Goodyear entered Chile in 1978, after nearly two years of negotiations with the Pinochet government. The company took over a plant originally owned by General Tire, a long-time producer in the country that had continued to operate during the Allende years as the manager and minority partner in a joint venture (INSA) with the government.

Andean Pact arrangements had given Chile a leading role in tire production for the region's automobile industry, leading to construction of a larger manufacturing capacity than justified solely by the domestic market. This regional importance helped convince the Allende regime to retain foreign MNC involvement in the venture. Firestone also was interested in serving the regional market through a Chilean production base but declined to enter the General Tire/CORFO venture as an additional partner.[12]

These historical factors presented a particular dilemma for the Pinochet government following the overthrow of the Allende regime. The relatively significant size of established tire production facilities made them a prime candidate for early reactivation and enhancement since they could help boost the country's economic recovery. The government wanted private ownership for INSA, in part due to ideological beliefs but also because the facilities needed a new infusion of capital and management skills. Foreign firms were reluctant to reenter the country, however. Political uncertainties, combined with the Pinochet government's obvious reappraisal of Andean Pact participation, made potential investors hesitate to commit new capital to a Chilean tire production venture.

Goodyear agreed in 1978 to purchase INSA for over $20 million as part of a corporate international expansion strategy. The firm brought in new equipment and increased worker training. The INSA workforce had ballooned during the Allende government to around 2,500 workers although output was only approximately 500 tires a day. Goodyear agreed to retain initially about one-half the number of workers; this was still in excess of production requirements. By comparison, the Goodyear facility at the end of the 1980s produced over 4,000 tires daily with somewhat under 1,000 employees. Further progress was achieved through reinvested earnings, sometimes amounting to several million dollars annually.

The next key investment decision arrived in the mid-1980s as Chile struggled to recover from its recession. At that time the plant was operating at less than two-thirds capacity and was losing money. Goodyear either had to pursue an exit strategy or increase its investment in plant modernization and seek export market outlets. The firm decided on the latter course of action.

Rather than recycling older equipment, Goodyear sought to establish high quality manufacturing at its plants worldwide. The Chilean plant produces top line tires designed at the firm's European technology center. Goodyear's modern radial tire manufacturing process is not matched by its closest domestic competitor, Neumáticos de Chile (NECSA), a firm with a smaller production capacity that is linked through a licensing agreement to Firestone (which was bought by Japan's Bridgestone corporation). In addition, Goodyear helped to rationalize and improve its franchised retailing network, recently investing over a million dollars to emphasize the service center areas at retailing establishments to help develop an even more differentiated product.

Goodyear can meet most of its Chilean market demand through local production although some specialty tires are imported to fill out the product line. Truck tires are an important area of business due to the importance of truck transportation along Chile's extensive length. Expansion of nontraditional export industries, particularly forestry and agriculture, strongly boosted truck tire sales in the late 1980s. This sector presents some special problems since northern mining areas in high desert regions are suited to heavy radial tires while rough roads in southern forestry areas make the ride too rough on rigid radial products. One decision facing the firm is whether this differentiated demand is large enough to justify investing in local radial truck tire production to complement its radial automobile tire line.

A key achievement for Chile's Goodyear facility that expanded capacity usage and provided greater stability against domestic economic downturns was the development of an important export market. Goodyear and GM worked in tandem to accomplish this objective. GM's interest arose from a combination of Chile's export incentive program for the automotive sector and certain tire industry developments in the United States. GM uses some Chile-produced tires for its cars manufactured in Brazil, but the crucial export sales agreement involved using Goodyear facilities in Chile to manufacture spare tires for GM cars in the United States.

A visit from GM's purchasing manager convinced the U.S. headquarters that Goodyear could supply a top quality tire at a competitive price from its Chile plant. Spare tires are not a high-profit item for tire manufacturers. GM wanted to diversify its supplier base somewhat to assure that its needs would be met during expansionary times when the market is tight in the United States and tire manufacturers must make choices between the profitability of their various lines. For Goodyear in Chile, an export contract for spare tires also would not be its most profitable line of business, but the deal would be relatively more important to the operation for its stability and diversification value.

The transaction required some difficult planning and negotiation for all parties involved through their MNC networks. U.S. labor unions would be unhappy with losing any current production to an affiliated overseas company, so the deal had to be arranged as an add-on to normal GM purchases from Goodyear in the United States. GM's move to on-time inventory systems also presented potential problems when the parts supplier would be so distant geographically. Nevertheless, the various problems were overcome through intracorporate coordination and the firms reached agreement on the new export initiative in 1986. Nearly 10 percent of GM's U.S.-produced cars come equipped with spare tires produced in Chile and in mid-1990 Goodyear shipped its one millionth tire under this contract. Goodyear sells some additional Chilean output through its own chain of stores, raising total exports from Goodyear Chile to approximately 350,000 tires annually, or about 15 percent of the plant's output by value and more than that proportion by unit volume.

In addition to production technology and marketing improvements, Goodyear management in Chile instituted a number of worker policy changes to enhance productivity and increase worker benefits. Although a small union operates at the company, most changes were made during the Pinochet government when union powers were severely restricted by the state. The company provides free medical coverage, transportation to and from work, lunches and other meals during overtime hours, and pays better than the average wage rate as well as occasional bonuses in profitable times.

Worker pay changed from a piece-rate or an hourly system to a monthly salary. This approach usually draws skepticism among corporate management due to predictions that worker output and productivity will drop, but Goodyear's belief in the integrity and work ethic of its Chilean employees was rewarded when productivity levels were sustained. This labor relations approach was consistent with the company's emphasis on quality control, since a piece-rate system in particular can encourage output over assured product quality. Workers also were evaluated in two categories as single- or multi-skilled, with the latter employees paid more highly. The differential encouraged worker interest and involvement in receiving training on additional operating tasks, increasing their skill level and remuneration while giving the company added flexibility in moving workers among various tasks depending on production needs.

Tires represent the core business line for Goodyear in Chile, but like some other local MNC affiliates the company has developed several additional associated operations. In this case the firm's related industrial product lines included rubber tubing, wrappings for pipelines (with export sales to neighboring countries), and conveyor belts used especially in the local mining and forestry industries. The company also manufactures several vinyl products, such as the covering used on automobile dashboards.

Finally, the Chilean operation includes a battery plant, the only one Goodyear owns anywhere in the world, that was inherited as part of the old INSA complex. Battery casings are often made of rubber, although many are now produced from plastic materials instead. The company faced another decision on whether to invest in a modernization of the battery facility or get out of this line of business. Opting to keep the plant open but lacking relevant internal expertise, Goodyear arranged for a technological upgrade from Johnson Controls. The plant now supplies roughly three-fourths of the domestic market with the balance met mainly through imports from foreign facilities.

Goodyear's decision to acquire the Chilean production facility helped to retain and modernize an industrial plant that otherwise likely would have been closed. Chile does not enjoy large natural advantages in a field such as tire production. The internal market is not sufficiently large to generate a self-sustained national operation capable of top quality production without close links to a global producer, probably necessitating a strong equity position. Most inputs to tire production in Chile must be imported, notably costly petroleum-based components. The development of an MNC-linked export market helps offset some of the foreign exchange bill derived from the imported inputs. Chile does assist local production by maintaining a tariff surcharge on imported tires, but this policy does not appear to have played a large role in Goodyear's investment decisions and is probably less important to operational developments than the automotive sector's export incentive program.

CHEMICAL AND ELECTRICAL PRODUCTS

The Chemical Complex—Dow and Occidental

The history of two important investments by Dow and Occidental in a related chemical complex near Concepción illustrates the evolving role of foreign MNCs in Chile's chemical industry. The story runs from a government-induced creation, through the economic and political turmoil of the 1970s, to an adjusted market outlook in the mid-1980s. As in the Goodyear case, these investments originated from regional economic planning that sought to alter Chile's limited attractiveness based on market forces as a site for chemical manufacturing. Subsequent developments offer several insights into how MNC organizations and operations can influence alternative options and outcomes in a country's relationship with foreign investors.

Dow entered Chile in response to an open international bid let by the Frei government for investment partners to help build a petrochemical complex linked to regional trade and economic integration plans. The company took a 70 percent stake in constructing a plant (Petrodow) to produce low-density polyethylene and polyvinyl chloride. Dow's minority partner was the state oil company (ENAP), which developed a nearby ethylene plant and Petroquímica Chilena, a state-owned company formed to produce chlorine and soda as part of a design for an interrelated chemical complex.

By itself, Chile did not offer natural advantages in raw materials or a domestic market sufficient to attract a petrochemical investment in these fields. Regional market potential permitted construction of a plant with roughly double the capacity of Chile's domestic consumption and brought support for the project from international development agencies. Dow was expanding in Latin America at the time in line with its international corporate strategy, leading to its winning bid to develop one of the main plants for Chile's chemical complex.

Petrodow began operations in 1971, but shortly thereafter encountered labor and other problems common during those turbulent times. The Allende government considered the petrochemical complex a strategic national industry and on October 18, 1972 the government expropriated Dow operations in Chile and nationalized the facility. Dow was invited to return immediately after the military coup and regained its former properties in January 1974. The next several years presented difficult business problems due to the oil price rise and ENAP's desire to increase initially contracted prices for its critical raw material inputs to the Petrodow operation in order to cover its own higher costs. A similar situation arose in the 1980s after another round of oil price hikes.

Arbitration in these contract disputes rose to very high levels in the Chilean government, but business agreements were also honored and the two joint venture partners continued their strong working relationship. The Pinochet government discussed selling ENAP's 20 percent and CORFO's 10 percent share to Dow as part of the general privatization campaign, but the parties did not agree on a mutually acceptable price. When Dow's original twenty-year agreement expired in 1988, the company renewed its investment through a D.L. 600 contract.

Dow adjusted, expanded, and improved the Petrodow facility over the years to reflect changing economic conditions, including growth in Chile's domestic consumption during the late 1970s. The polyethylene plant's initial capacity of 25,000 metric tons annually, originally nearly double domestic consumption patterns, could barely supply the expanded Chilean market until an expansion raised capacity to 43,000 metric tons. By 1990, Petrodow was selling 30,000 metric tons locally to capture three-quarters of the domestic market while exporting around 6,000 metric tons annually, mainly to Perú, Colombia, and the United States. Projected Chilean market demand by the end of the decade may reach close to 70,000 metric tons, suggesting that another 10,000 metric ton increase in plant capacity will be necessary just to maintain Petrodow's current market share.

Within this picture of healthy market growth, the relationship between product demand and MNC investment decisions must be put in a broader perspective. Despite the relative national success of Petrodow, the operation still does not meet most market investment criteria in the global petrochemical industry. Economies of scale considerations under contemporary technological and world market conditions favor investment in a plant with a production capacity of at least 150,000 metric tons annually. Thus, even with good market growth, Chile cannot match the parallel changes occurring in other global factors and would still not be a location of choice, absent nonmarket factors, for investment in a new facility. However, Dow has an investment stake in Petrodow and incremental facility expansion is less costly than new "greenfield" investments, making retention and further improvement of its position in Chile a more attractive option.

Dow exports, and many of its imported inputs, come through the network of affiliated enterprises in other countries. Petrodow by contract maintains no direct staff for domestic and export marketing because Dow can supply needed services internally on a more cost-effective basis. All Petrodow exports are sold in foreign markets as Dow products, relieving the Chilean firm of the need to develop its own marketing channels, product recognition, pricing expertise, and other such essential elements to compete successfully in world markets. In a sense, the Dow intracompany network substitutes partially for the governmentally designed regional marketing arrangements originally projected to develop when the project was first put out for bids.

In addition to the periodic need for investments in expanded capacity, which typically in petrochemicals must come in lump-sum increments, Dow also invests nearly one million dollars annually on operational improvements involving updated technology, training, safety, and environmental protection. Dow's worldwide quality and safety standards apply to Petrodow. Inspectors from the United States or Europe visit the facility at least every year and a half to check operations and direct needed improvements. Petrodow can rely on Dow's international support in the plastics area and technical experts work with local users of Petrodow products to help manage application or service problems.

Dow also emphasizes employee training and follows a policy of rotating management personnel through different international operations to increase their exposure and improve communication within Dow's worldwide organization. The company is known as providing an exceptionally good training ground for international managers and several Chilean projects, most notably the Cape Horn Methanol facility, have benefitted from attracting experienced managers from the Dow system.

Dow's structure involves international reporting relationships organized by region, function, and lines of business. New investments are considered within the context of other competitive financing needs. Dow has several other business interests in Chile, including sales to the mining and agriculture industries, the latter through a new joint venture (DowElanco) with Eli Lilly. Nevertheless, Petrodow represents roughly three-fourths of Dow's business in Chile. The company did, however, close the chloride part of the plant in the early 1980s after concluding that its small size was too limiting to permit a profitable operation. Additionally, Dow considered becoming involved in one of the nearby related facilities when Petroquímica Chilena was sold to private investors in the late 1970s. While Dow decided against this transaction, in part due to safety and environmental concerns relating to the involvement of mercury in the plant's production process, other foreign investors took up the challenge. The plant eventually ended up under the ownership of Occidental Chemical.

Diamond Shamrock originally purchased the chlorine and soda production plant from the Pinochet government, quickly adding several million dollars in new technology and other improvements. The firm maintained the business until late 1987, when Diamond Shamrock sold all its chemical operations worldwide to Occidental Chemical. The Petroquímica Chilena plant was a very small component in this transaction. Although Occidental owns several chemical enterprises in Latin America, the facilities do not engage in closely integrated exchanges among themselves or with related firms in other regions. Petroquímica essentially operates on a stand-alone basis and procures nearly all of its inputs locally. The facility suffered from some price increases, most recently (in the late 1980s) a rapid run-up in the cost of electricity, which represents an important part of the plant's production process.

Plant outputs serve a variety of local industrial needs, including uses in the forestry sector's cellulose production, copper mining processes, and iron and steel manufacturing; treatments for potable water; and as disinfectants. The firm holds nearly an 80 percent market share in many of its product areas. Some local competition exists, for example from a "captive" CMPC plant that supplies the needs of its own related cellulose facilities, but Occidental probably could not seek further aggressive expansion of its business without encountering problems with Chile's anti-monopoly commission. Exports do not represent a current nor likely a future growth area, because of the absence of organized marketing channels and potential safety hazards in the transport of some products.

Safety and environmental controls were one of the major areas for an application of Occidental technology improvements. Pollution control standards were set significantly higher than required by local legal standards or prevailing business practices. A key challenge was met through the use of special filters and other improvements to increase the controls over mercury in the production process, addressing both worker and product safety concerns. Occidental invested several million dollars in these enhancements, registering the investment under D.L. 600.

Multinational Support for Local Initiative—GE/Electromat

General Electric (GE) initiated sales activity in Chile just before the beginning of the twentieth century, working through agents and representation by W.R. Grace & Company. Electromat originated separately, founded by local entrepreneurs as Fábrica Nacional de Artículos Eléctricos Rittig in 1939, to manufacture and sell wiring devices. That same year the German firm Osram established production in Chile to manufacture lamps and glass bulbs. The Chilean government seized Osram in July 1944 declaring it enemy property during World War II.

The Chilean government sold Osram's assets the following year to Electromat but retained a 30 percent interest in the firm through CORFO. The expanded company also linked itself to General Electric and the Grace subsidiary

Intermaco, with each firm acquiring nearly 21 percent of the shares while providing technical assistance that enabled Electromat to initiate production of glass bulbs and lamps. General Electric increased its stake in Electromat to 70 percent over the next two decades, acquiring shares from both Grace and CORFO. During this time the business shifted and expanded, discontinuing the manufacture of wiring devices but adding fluorescent lamp production and increasing the output of electric bulbs.

Electromat encountered some difficulties beginning in the 1960s from government import restrictions, devaluations, and price controls that disrupted normal business planning and practices. The Allende period proved even more difficult due to further supply disruptions and labor problems that eventually led to government intervention and seizure of the firm in November 1972. The subsequent military government restored the company to its owners in 1974, but the deteriorated facilities required extensive repair.

Although U.S. executives headed the firm prior to nationalization, local managers assumed the task of restarting Electromat's operations with GE financial support and technical assistance. The company faced a new competitive environment as Chile rapidly removed quota and tariff barriers protecting the domestic marketplace. Fortunately for Electromat, the firm's main product line involved several natural trade barriers that made the adjustment somewhat easier. Light bulbs are a high-volume, low-unit price product with breakage problems in transport. These characteristics normally give local manufacturers some natural advantages over importers except in higher-priced specialty lighting. Electromat's management team successfully guided the firm through the start-up and adjustment period, entering the 1980s ready to embark on a new growth phase that survived even through the decade's early economic turbulence and recession.

Two factors combined to shape the recent development pattern in Electromat's operations. GE's global structure and management system provided support and encouraged coordination among its decentralized subsidiaries without imposing undue central control over local management decisions. Electromat executives would meet several times a year with related GE managers from other national units to exchange information and discuss business opportunities. The approach favored interaffiliate transactions as long as the products supplied were of comparable quality and close in price to items available outside the corporate network. These interaffiliate relationships provided export as well as import channels for Electromat's products.

GE exercised policy direction primarily through financial controls. Potential investments involving a new infusion of parent company capital received careful scrutiny and competed with proposals from many other business units. By contrast, Electromat had broader discretion regarding business decisions involving the use of reinvested local earnings. The company's performance yielded enough profits, with the exception of one year in the midst of the recession, to fund expansion plans. GE generally left nearly one-third of its dividend portion plus depreciation funds in the country for reinvestment purposes.

The second key factor shaping Electromat's recent development was local management's initiative in seizing opportunities presented by the GE network to enhance operations in Chile and to explore new lines of business lying outside GE's traditional field of operation. While this decentralized flexibility poses some risks for GE as well as Electromat, the offsetting benefits offer a chance to experiment with new adaptations and build a more diversified business base able to withstand downturns in main product lines.

One example of local initiative came in the late 1970s from a recognition that light bulb production shares some similar technologies with the manufacture of other glass containers. Electromat decided to acquire assets from two local firms engaged in the production of pharmaceutical glass, forming a new line of business that initially concentrated on producing glass vials for the pharmaceutical industry. While GE could provide some relevant technical assistance, this move constituted a departure from the norm since no similar operations existed in the global GE network. Electromat pushed its initiative a step farther in 1980, when it signed a technical assistance agreement with Wheaton International to provide expertise involving the production of plastic containers, enabling Electromat to expand into this market the following year.

Another product line involving a business relationship with a firm outside the GE family developed from modifications Electromat made to some machinery it imported from GE. The company wanted to add motor control centers to some older machinery and required equipment in addition to GE-supplied switches. The French Telemecanique company supplied the necessary parts and developed an agreement enabling Electromat to produce and sell motor control centers for applications in other industries. Still another business line, that of GE-Fanuc programmable controllers, made it possible for Electromat to build a system CODELCO employs in its mining operations to send water control signals long distances over power lines.

The process of upgrading older GE machinery also yielded unexpected business, including exports to the United States, toward the end of the decade. Electromat management invested in developing a metal mechanic capability to refurbish and improve the imported equipment for application to local market needs and to produce spare parts that GE no longer stocked. GE gradually lost its own metal mechanic capability in this field in the United States as labor rates up to $40 per hour priced the function out of business.

Recognizing the quality of Electromat's work developed for local application, GE agreed to an arrangement beginning in 1988 whereby Electromat would produce spare parts for export to GE. This arrangement extended into the area of complete older machines, with GE essentially selling the equipment to Electromat for refurbishing with sales of the improved machinery back to GE or its affiliates in other countries. The sales price differential reflected roughly 75 percent value added by Electromat's improvements through skilled labor and technical capabilities GE had abandoned in its original operations. In one case Electromat's contribution proved so vital to GE that a piece of large refurbished equipment was shipped by air at great cost from Chile to the United States so that a production line could resume operations on schedule.

Sales within GE's worldwide network provide Electromat with important outlets for their products, with exports amounting to several million dollars. A company report listed sales to GE affiliates in Brazil, Venezuela, Uruguay, the Philippines, Turkey, and Canada. Electromat in turn maintains technical assistance and product representation arrangements with some of these firms as well as with Wheaton Industries and Telemecanique. The small size of Chile's domestic market cannot justify local production of many diversified GE products, so over the 1980s Electromat expanded its representation of items such as aircraft engines. In addition, Electromat opened a warehousing and small production facility in the Iquique free zone in northern Chile from which it initiated export sales to neighboring Perú and Bolivia.[13]

In retrospect, the GE/Electromat relationship developed almost more along the lines of a joint venture than a parent-subsidiary arrangement, with unanticipated benefits accruing to both parties. This approach appears possible in part due to GE's decentralized and flexible management structure. Equally important may be the relatively small size of the Chilean market and Electromat's ability to generate self-sustaining profits for reinvestment purposes, both of which gave the Chilean operation more freedom from headquarters scrutiny and control than may be true in countries with larger internal market potential, especially if parent funds are required to initiate new programs.

GE's main contributions are technology and interaffiliate global business channels. An independent local company could not obtain technology upgrades as quickly or as cheaply on the open market as they flow through the GE network. Training is an important related element for Electromat personnel with access to GE programs in the United States. Within the Chilean operations, some 40 percent of roughly 300 Electromat employees are involved in corporate-sponsored training programs. Electromat's local initiatives provide GE with a profitable and increasingly diversified operation that can return dividends while sustaining a steady reinvestment campaign. The developed capability to upgrade older machinery, experiment with adapted product lines, and coordinate technical assistance and product representation arrangements with other affiliates all enhance the value of Electromat's local market success. (In April 1991 Electromat's corporate name was changed to General Electric de Chile.)

FOODS, BEVERAGES AND CONSUMER PRODUCTS

Establishing a New Old Tradition—Williamson Balfour

The history of Williamson Balfour conforms to the tradition of old British trading companies that were the predecessors of modern MNCs, but boasts an uniquely Chilean origin. The enterprise began in 1851, when three young Scotsmen established a partnership, Balfour, Williamson and Company, to manage trade between Liverpool and South America. The following year the firm set up its first trading house in Valparaíso, using its own ships to import European products that it distributed through a network of offices in more than twenty cities running the length of Chile as well as in several surrounding countries. The ships returned with loads of nitrate and wool. By the middle of the twentieth century, business expanded into financing nitrate and railway projects, operating flour mills, and serving as an agent for shipping and insurance companies. Among the company's more unusual activities were administering Easter Island under a concession agreement from 1903 to 1946, and introducing rice farming into Chile in the region around Talca.[14]

After World War II the import business focused on important products not manufactured locally, including agricultural machinery, specialty steel, tin plate, tea, and coffee. The company also served as an agent to distribute some goods produced by local enterprises. The Bank of London and South America acquired the parent firm in the early 1960s, obtaining all its Chilean holdings. The bank sold the mills in 1965, and the Allende government nationalized many of the other activities at the beginning of the 1970s. These portions of the enterprise essentially disappeared, with just the insurance and hardware parts of the business remaining private and emerging in the post-Allende period. Royal International Insurance Holdings purchased the insurance firm (La República) in 1980, and the following year the British holding company Inchcape acquired the remaining assets. Not until 1989, however, did Inchcape establish its right to use the old Williamson Balfour name.

Inchcape's ownership represents a reestablishment of the trading company tradition. This firm's own origins trace to merchant partnerships involved in British trade with India, East Africa, the Middle East, and the Far East during the 1800s. The Scottish Mackay family, bearers of the title "Earl of Inchcape," drew together several of these businesses to form the Inchcape group in 1958. The notions of history and tradition deepened even further in 1974, when the group added the Assam Company, the world's oldest commercial tea company founded in 1839. Personal contacts had existed between the Mackay and Williamson families even prior to Inchcape's acquisition of the remaining former Williamson Balfour interests in South America, an area where Inchcape was weak, particularly along the west coast. Today the Inchcape group operates in over sixty countries, providing service and representation for many of the world's best known companies. The group focuses on three main areas: services includes shipping, insurance, buying, inspection, and testing; motors includes both distribution and retail businesses; and marketing handles consumer goods, industrial products, business machines, and wines and spirits.

Inchcape's 1981 purchase of the Williamson Balfour operations in Chile proved to be a good time to buy but a difficult time to rebuild operations. The company's condition was deteriorating, with losses of several hundred thousand dollars on sales of only roughly $1.5 million and a total employment of under fifty people. Losses continued in 1982, but business picked up the following year and corporate expansion added new opportunities and employment. By the end of the decade when the company reacquired the right to use the Williamson Balfour name, the enterprise had grown to nearly 1,000 employees with sales exceeding $50 million. The parent exercises control mainly through the financial side of the business, leaving the local subsidiary relatively free to conduct its own operations, even in most parts of the import business. The three main lines of business developed in Chile cover industrial products, agricultural equipment, and bottling activities.

The industrial division carries on the old trading tradition, representing over fifty international suppliers through sales offices throughout the country serving many industrial sectors as well as a chain of 1,200 hardware stores. Main import and distribution lines include tools, abrasives, sealants, specialty steel, wood-working equipment, and other related items. Although the Chilean market is too small to foster local manufacture of most such products, Williamson Balfour does produce and distribute some compression packings and flame-resistant safety clothing. While its export business is small, the firm is exploring possible opportunities to increase this activity, at least in part to establish a more balanced trading relationship as both a conscious MNC policy response to host country goals and as a hedge against the possibility of future import business restrictions. This orientation appears to stem from historical experiences with national political swings in the region and around the world.

The core of the agricultural business division grew from a 1983 agreement for Williamson Balfour to act as the exclusive representative of Ford Tractor in Chile. This activity expanded in 1986, when Ford acquired the New Holland agricultural equipment line from the Sperry Corporation, enabling Williamson Balfour to add harvesters and hay equipment to its sales of agricultural and industrial tractors, power plants, generators, and other Ford Tractor products. A 1988 agreement with British AE Auto Parts increased the firm's representation for the sale of replacement parts. The company uses a nationwide sales and service network of twenty-two dealers to manage this business. An overnight parts delivery system supports this operation as part of an effort to assure customers that dealers can get equipment up and running again as soon as possible, a critical factor for time-sensitive agricultural operations where many repairs must take place out in the fields.

The third line of business also began in 1983, when Williamson Balfour acquired three existing bottling plants and the accompanying franchise to produce and distribute Coca-Cola products from a local bottler whose debt load forced a partial sale of assets. This expansion occurred through a D.L. 600 investment, but the firm took advantage of the Chapter XIX debt conversion channel a couple of years later to buy another plant and territorial franchise area around Viña del Mar. In 1990, the company opened a new bottling facility in the southern city of Puerto Montt, built at a cost of $3 million and creating 160 new jobs. This addition gave Williamson Balfour five of the twelve Coca-Cola plants in Chile, generating an estimated direct and indirect employment of around 1,600 people. The company also bottles and sells several local drinks of Industrial Sud-Andina.

Old and New Investors in Consumer Goods

Beverage sales are typical of a consumer goods sector that reflects the involvement of both old and new foreign investors. If the British tea companies symbolize the historical roots of MNC organizations, then Coca-Cola's global operations represent one of the best-known contemporary embodiments of this tradition. Established in Chile since the mid-1900s, the Coca-Cola Export Corporation operates through a franchise system employed by the company worldwide, importing a few key ingredients to supply local bottlers who handle manufacture and distribution of the final product. The franchise arrangement possesses several advantages, limiting Coca-Cola's direct financial investment and adding local adaptation and marketing capabilities.

Coca-Cola's direct investment in Chile is registered under the D.L. 600 mechanism, although some bottling operations have used Chapter XIX financing, as illustrated in the Williamson Balfour case. The firm has four franchisees and has controlled around 60 percent of the market. Franchisees can receive technical assistance and financial support from the company, which additionally organizes most publicity for the products, although local bottlers can also arrange marketing campaigns. While incorporating changes in its product line and upgrading activities, the company has not diversified its Chilean investment. Nevertheless, the head of the regional division indicated in an interview at the end of 1989 that the company would likely consider making an investment or technological contribution in another industrial area as part of its concept of good corporate citizenship.[15]

Much of Coca-Cola's effort, of course, will be devoted to fighting the infamous "cola wars." The local battlefront was reopened at the beginning of 1986, when Pepsi-Cola announced its reentry to Chile. The Pepsi campaign was aided by Chapter XIX investments by American Express and Citibank, as discussed in the previous chapter. The third major competitor in this field is

Compañía de Cervecerías Unidas (CCU), controlled through a joint venture arrangement by the local Luksic group and the Paulaner group, one of the most important beer producers in Germany. Paulaner used the Chapter XIX mechanism to acquire a share of CCU at the end of 1986 when the Chilean enterprise still carried an enormous debt load stemming from its role in the Cruzat-Larraín group which broke apart during the recession.

CCU encompasses a mix of foreign and local brands, producing and distributing seven carbonated drinks along with several other beverages. Paulaner's interest lay primarily in CCU's beer operations. The company controls a near-total 98 percent of the Chilean market. The Paulaner connection led to a one-half million dollar investment in producing a new premium beer launched in mid-1990, aimed primarily at expanding the total market rather than shifting customers between CCU's various brands. This local-foreign partnership also initiated exports in 1987, with rapidly growing sales to nearly all Latin American countries as well as the United States and Europe.[16]

Nestlé qualifies as one of the older foreign investors in Chile's consumer goods market, initiating its activities in 1934, with a condensed milk plant operated as Sociedad Industrial Lechera Miraflores. The company experienced relatively steady growth, opening five factories since 1936, the last one in 1963,— a Maggi food product line. Three years later the firm acquired the company producing the Savory line of ice cream, expanding production after a couple of years to include frozen foods marketed under the Findus label. Nestlé maintained its operations despite a number of difficulties during the Allende government, suffering mainly from the high cost of imported machinery needed to improve its manufacturing facilities.[17]

In the mid-1980s, Nestlé added several more brands through a two-stage acquisition. A heavily indebted local group first sold Prolac, whose refrigerated products included the Yely label and Chamonix ice cream. With the firm still unable to recover and creditor banks assuming control, Nestlé then bought the well-established McKay and Hucke lines of cookies and chocolates. The purchase price of around $50 million was well above the next highest offer, in part reflecting its value to Nestlé but also as a step to avoid later potential criticism of the sale. This caution regarding actions that might harm the company's broader, long-term interests in the country also influenced Nestlé's decision not to seek Chapter XIX debt swap financing for this or other investments due to the general public controversy about the mechanism and in line with its general investment policies in the country.

The company's contribution as a foreign investor stems from the financing and technological applications it brings to its local operations, as well as the employment of some 2,900 people. Nestlé prefers full ownership of its ventures, mainly to assure the quality control essential to maintain its market image and identification. A regional laboratory works to assure the security and high quality of the company's food products. Although it exports a few milk-based products to surrounding countries and some dehydrated goods and cookies to the United States and Europe, the firm's local operations are essentially decentralized and self-contained with little trade occurring between the Nestlé subsidiaries. The company's products are based on the country's natural resources, essentially following an import substitution pattern wherever there are competing foreign-manufactured products.

For example, the company spent nearly $7 million to create production facilities and launch a corn flakes cereal in 1988, since there was no local production facility in the country and such products were available to Chilean consumers only through imports by another MNC's subsidiary in Brazil. The main exception to purchasing raw materials locally is coffee, which is not produced in Chile. Nestlé imports it from Brazil. Significantly, however, the firm imports coffee beans and does the value-added processing locally. (One reason the company may have the option of taking this step is that, despite its small population, Chile has one of the highest per capita consumption rates for soluble coffee in Latin America.) Most of the firm's product lines face significant competition from a combination of imported and locally produced goods, including the milk-related Soprole operations acquired in the mid-1980s by the New Zealand Dairy Board.

Nestlé does not favor backward integration to ownership of farms or plantations that provide the raw material inputs for its products. The firm does establish a service with veterinarians, agronomists, and other agricultural experts to assist its suppliers, many of whom are small and medium-size farmers. For example, nearly 70 percent of its milk supply comes from small and medium-size producers who receive technical assistance from Nestlé. The firm also contracts for the pick-up and delivery of milk from rural areas, leading to a common early-morning scene along rough Chilean backroads where small children help wheel a few milk cans from their family farm to the roadside for pick-up.

Lever is another foreign investor in the consumer products area whose approach resembles many characteristics of the Nestlé strategy. A subsidiary of the Anglo-Dutch Unilever enterprise, the company entered Chile in the late 1920s, expanding in mid-century through a joint venture with a local firm until moving to a favored full ownership mode in 1982. Lever supports a very diversified product line, essentially following the parent company's expertise in food, detergents, and personal care items. The company operated throughout the Allende period, determined to remain in the country with a long-term business commitment despite the uncertainty and economic problems.

Like Nestlé the Lever operation is decentralized in terms of decision-making and essentially self-supporting in producing locally the products that it sells in the Chilean market, with little interchange among Lever units in other countries. The company's operations support an employment of close to 1,800 workers. Lever strives to avoid lay-offs, even during recessionary downturns such as occurred in the early 1980s, and invests heavily to provide an extensive training program that in 1989 encompassed over three-fourths of the workforce. The firm mirrored Nestlé in a decision not to engage in any Chapter XIX financing, also in part to avoid possible fallout on the company's long-term business interests from public criticism of the debt conversion program.

Lever also faces significant competition. Different firms challenge various products along its diversified product line and the company has moved out of a couple of business areas. The firm's largest worldwide competitor is Procter and Gamble (P&G), which left Chile in 1963 as violence rose in a climate of increasing political and economic uncertainty. Ironically, P&G sold its plant to Lever and had some difficulty reentering the country in the early 1980s. Working first through distributors, in 1983 P&G decided to purchase an underfinanced firm, Laboratorio Geka, that needed modernization and expansion. P&G invested through both D.L. 600 and Chapter XIX to rebuild its business, progressively moving some products from imports to local production as their sales volume increased and employment rose to a few hundred workers. The firm was unable to overtake Lever as the market leader, however, causing a top P&G executive to lament publicly the company's earlier decision to leave Chile.[18]

Foreign investors that choose a strategy of producing locally rather than importing for national sales must attain a certain minimum market share to sustain an investment in manufacturing facilities. This fact of business life is particularly true in the consumer products field for low-value, low-cost items where volume production and sales are essential to profitability. In a country of 13 million people, not too many enterprises can sustain the minimum market share necessary to maintain production, leading to potential debates about concentration ratios. The critical offsetting factors in Chile are the competition available through the country's open import policy, although that option sacrifices some value-added benefits from local production, and the anti-monopoly regulatory mechanism that thus far has proven generally effective.

PHARMACEUTICALS

Pharmaceutical MNCs and Chile's Patent Law Revision

The activities of pharmaceutical MNCs in Chile revolve around the implementation and eventual revision of a 1931 patent law that excluded food and medicines from coverage. During the Frei administration in the late 1960s, Chile used a World Health Organization list of essential drugs to develop its own Formulario Nacional. Centralized hospital purchases of these key drugs were regulated to favor low-cost generic products. A state enterprise, Laboratorio Chile, focused on these drugs and received government funding to improve quality and assure the safety of its products. The generic system extended to purchases by many pharmacies, especially as the Allende administration increased exchange controls on foreign firms and broadened the government's reach into the economy.

The Pinochet government removed price controls while progressively phasing out requirements covering how many drugs on the Formulario Nacional a pharmaceutical company must produce in order to sell in the country. Laboratorio Chile was privatized and other local pharmaceutical companies were formed, often picking a dozen or so top generic drugs to produce and sell at very low prices. Hospital purchases were made on a price basis that favored generic products. Doctors who trained at these institutions became familiar with those products, making them more likely to prescribe their usage to private patients as well, building further the public's confidence in generic products.

The generic companies in Chile gained strength and credibility throughout the 1980s, increasing their market share from 58 percent in 1982 to nearly 70 percent by 1986. The number of local firms grew to almost forty, while fourteen European and seventeen U.S. pharmaceutical MNCs also participated in the market. The basic challenge posed by generic firms for the pharmaceutical MNCs was their ability to sell at very low cost since they did not conduct research on new medicines and therefore had no substantial research expenses to cover.[19]

Patent protection grants a firm a limited time of monopoly production and sales for its product. Without a protected period of initially high prices, the research pharmaceutical companies cannot recover invested costs and gain revenue to fund their next round of investigations. Discoveries in the pharmaceutical field typically consume ten years and nearly $100 million in testing and development before a new drug is approved for sale to customers. In Chile, firms could copy drug formulas, sometimes registering a generic product and marketing it quickly enough to establish a solid market share before the innovating firm even launched its own branded discovery.

The Chilean market was certainly not large enough by itself to determine a pharmaceutical MNC's success or failure, or even that of an individual drug discovery. However, the patent protection problem in Chile was part of a broader concern for the protection of intellectual property rights (IPRs) that became a major international trade issue in the 1980s. The United States adopted improved IPR protection as a priority objective, pushing forcefully for its inclusion in the Uruguay round of GATT trade negotiations. Congressional legislation supported this initiative as well as bilateral U.S. trade pressure on countries that did not provide adequate IPR protection. These moves tied a developing country's benefits under the U.S. Generalized System of Preferences (GSP) program to the IPR issue and authorized possible retaliation under Section 301 of the U.S Trade Act for cases where a lack of proper IPR protection was found to constitute an unfair trade practice that harmed U.S. enterprises.

Research pharmaceutical MNCs aggressively promoted efforts to raise the IPR issue in international forums and supported bilateral government actions to extend patent protection to markets where it did not already exist. Other industries joined in this international effort. Computer software firms raised some particular complaints about copying and unauthorized uses of their products in Chile. However, the growth of Chile's generic drug industry and the specific exclusion of medicines from the country's patent law focused the IPR debate primarily on pharmaceuticals. The issue became a central irritant in relations between Chile and the United States even though nearly as many pharmaceutical MNCs from Europe operated in the Chilean market as from the United States. In a broader context, the resolution of this dispute gained significance due to its possible precedential effect on international standard-setting negotiations as well as the pattern it might set for formulating patent protection laws throughout the Latin American region.

The Pinochet regime's free trade orientation and push into global export markets underscored the importance of maintaining good trade relations with major consuming countries, particularly the United States, which was the principal market for Chilean products. The incipient success of several nontraditional export industries hinged on this relationship, especially the sensitive agricultural sector that was depending heavily on developing a market in the United States for counter-seasonal fruit exports. When U.S. negotiators raised the patent protection issue with Chilean authorities, the government agreed to develop a proposal for a legal revision that would extend patent protection to pharmaceutical products. No evident action occurred over the next couple years, however, leading the Pharmaceutical Manufacturers Association (PMA) in the United States to file a Section 301 petition against Chile. As this case developed, the Chilean economics minister made a new commitment in April 1988 on behalf of the government to move ahead on a new law. Several days later the PMA withdrew its petition.[20]

This situation continued up to the national elections and into the transition to the Aylwin administration. The Pinochet government prepared a new law and appeared ready to enact it through the decree procedure since the reconstituted legislative branch had not yet resumed authority. In the end, however, the matter was handed over to the new democratic government's officials who then faced a debate about whether the proposed changes could become effective through decreed regulations or whether the newly elected legislators should consider the issue. After much dispute over legal technicalities and political requirements, the legislature did finally consider the issue and through vigorous debate passed a new law in late 1990, which established patent protection for pharmaceutical products.

The domestic debate on this issue highlighted the clash between local generic companies and the pharmaceutical MNCs. It was marked by nationalistic appeals and charges of exploitation by foreign MNCs backed by

U.S. government pressure. Local firms acted through the Asociación Industrial de Laboratorios Farmacéuticos Chilenos (Asilfa), whose president denounced the "pressures exerted by the transnational enterprises and by the ambassador of the United States in Chile." He called on Chilean legislators to act in the national interest and not allow external pressure to harm the health of Chilean citizens, arguing, "A long time ago Chile quit being a colony, transforming itself into a country with dignity and sovereignty."[21]

On the other side, some corporate and U.S. government representatives grew equally incensed about the Chilean government's repeated failure to deliver on assurances of remedial action and the local generic companies' continuing use of perceived unfair business practices. While workers from local pharmaceutical firms protested outside a Santiago hotel, the assistant U.S. trade representative for Latin America addressed a meeting of the American Chamber of Commerce (AmCham) in Chile, linking continued access to the U.S. market to progress on the IPR issue. "It just does not go over well in the United States that we provide access to the market to countries, to put it bluntly, that are stealing from us."[22]

Broader business interests worried about the possible consequences of this escalating controversy. The Amcham supported a patent law reform that would extend coverage to pharmaceutical products but opposed the use of U.S. trade sanctions as running counter to the organization's goal of promoting commerce between the two countries. Chilean exporter groups similarly urged action that would avoid penalties against their products in the U.S. market. In addition to guarding current sales, Chilean exporters stood to gain further if the United States renewed Chile's access to the GSP program. This decision appeared linked to a successful resolution of the IPR issue as well as passage of legislation to reestablish organized labor rights in Chile.

Although the patent law debate covered many arguments, the opposing camps staked out clear primary contentions. Supporters of the pharmaceutical MNCs' position argued that, until Chile extended adequate IPR protection to patentable drugs, it would not have a fully modern and responsible trade policy and therefore should not expect to benefit from greater trade or investment with countries accepting such obligations. Opponents contended that granting patent protection to pharmaceutical MNCs would result in exploitatively higher prices to the detriment of the local populace's health and welfare as well as the exclusion of national pharmaceutical companies. The practical struggle between these two positions came down to the formulation of specific legislative provisions, focusing primarily on how long patent protection should run, when it would start, and whether the government should use compulsory licensing or parallel importing to control cases where a patent-holder is judged to be abusing its monopoly power.

The Chilean Congress passed a patent law revision bill toward the end of 1990, and President Aylwin approved it after using presidential veto power to alter a couple of provisions regarding the effective length of patent protection and standards for judging the existence of an abuse of monopoly power. Neither side was fully satisfied. The local companies felt the administration had conceded far too much to U.S. pressure, and the MNCs complained that the law failed to grant adequate pipeline protection to cover products under development even though no local price increases would be felt for a decade or more.

Adjusting Local Operations in Pharmaceuticals

The pharmaceutical MNCs operating in Chile had to adjust their local business to the changing economic, political, and legal environment during the 1980s, taking best advantage of available opportunities while staying within organizational and policy constraints set by the overall firm's global strategy. The resulting actions belied a more heterogeneous composition among the pharmaceutical MNC community than was implied by the group's essentially united stand on patent reform issues. Thus, while the policy debate over patent law protection dominated public perception of the industry and influenced corporate decision making, the controversy does not fully reflect the nature of these firms' applied operations.

For example, Schering-Plough operates through a decentralized organization that gives the national unit in Chile operational flexibility and decision-making authority. Confronted by the generic companies' challenge, the firm responded by launching its own generic product line in 1988, using a common box without the company's name on it. This strategy derived from a contingency plan to recover volume quickly while the company registered other research compounds. The move helped rebuild volume, thereby supporting a base for other, more profitable operations. The firm does not maintain a generic line in other countries, where the main problem they face is usually governmental price controls rather than an expanding competitive challenge from local generic firms.

This local strategy was the clear exception among pharmaceutical MNCs and engendered some criticism from them. Most companies either did not consider the Chilean market significant enough to formulate a special approach to address its idiosyncrasies or else decided that introducing a generic line risked jeopardizing the firm's general pricing strategy and policies. Schering-Plough still supported the common MNCs' position regarding IPRs in general and patent law reform specifically in the case of Chile. The company imposed two requirements on its local line of generic products. The first mandate was that the drugs had to meet the same quality standards imposed on the firm's other production. Secondly, the company would respect all existing patents applicable outside Chile. This restricted the generic line to older, standard drugs no longer under patent protection, limiting production to only around 10 percent of the

Formulario Nacional list.

Ciba-Geigy also grants some adjustment flexibility to local operations under a philosophy of directed autonomy. The pharmaceutical division sets general strategies on a worldwide scale, letting the local organizations manage each national market. Headquarters requires that all units meet corporate standards for manufacturing and quality control processes, and to that effect audits of national operations are regularly conducted. Beyond that, the headquarters role varies with the level of a proposed project's financial commitment. Ciba-Geigy responded to Chile's changing pharmaceutical market by improving the efficiency of its operations and by increasing its involvement in self-medication products, thereby attempting to sustain the critical mass needed to maintain a pharmaceutical business in the country.

With Chile's open import policies, pharmaceutical MNCs could attempt to serve the market from production bases elsewhere. Part of Ciba-Geigy's calculation regarding an exit option, however, in addition to the interest in maintaining a direct contact and involvement in the country, was the potential cost of reintroducing an investment later if circumstances should change. For pharmaceutical firms, finding space in a previously abandoned market is often difficult, as is the task of recruiting good employees and rebuilding the company's local image and reputation among doctors and other health care professionals.

Ciba-Geigy's activity in Chile may also reflect the fact that the corporation's pharmaceutical division established a special operation (Servipharm) in 1977. Servipharm's specific purpose is to supply products on the essential drugs list as inexpensively as possible in developing countries. While the operation aims at being economically viable, the group does not have to meet the same type of return on investment standards imposed on corporate profit centers and operations in other parts of the world. In essence, this broader corporate effort addresses the generic drug issue, at least in relation to the essential drugs list, in the context of a corporate social responsibility program related to social and economic development objectives.[23]

In addition to pharmaceuticals, Ciba-Geigy's business in Chile includes agricultural chemicals, dye-stuffs and other chemicals, and a small plastics operation. The agrochemical division has expanded in line with the country's increased agricultural output, stimulated by the increase in nontraditional exports.

Pfizer also operates an agricultural/veterinarian division and a small chemical operation along with its pharmaceutical business in Chile. The agricultural operation increased to nearly 60 percent of the business in the late 1980s as the pharmaceutical sector was reduced to just over one-third. Premixed sales to Chile's booming salmon-growing operations accounted for much of the increased business. The pharmaceutical division had to scale back its sales force as volume dropped and focus on maintaining profitable market niches. Internationally, Pfizer was one of the most prominent corporate leaders in the campaign to gain better IPR protection through both bilateral and multilateral negotiations.

One advantage that local operations enjoy over import sales is the ability to vary product doses and delivery systems to better fit the local market. Pharmaceutical MNCs centralize basic research and development functions and export the active ingredients for drugs to their overseas subsidiaries. Local production facilities such as exist in Chile are therefore essentially mixing and packaging operations. The mixing process is essential, however, in controlling the drug's delivery capabilities by determining when and where the product will dissolve in order to get the medicine to the right place in the body at the right time. Careful product and process control at the mixing stage is thus essential to assure a drug's effectiveness even if firms use the same chemical formulas in the drug's manufacture.

The challenge for an MNC's local pharmaceutical division is to maintain sufficient volume and revenue not only to sustain operations but also to justify periodic upgrading of equipment and procedures to meet improved quality control standards adopted and imposed globally by the parent corporation. With a small national market, particularly one open to imports, these improvements may not always be deemed cost-effective. Local firms can often operate with good, albeit lower, quality standards that give them another competitive advantage to go with the absence of heavy cost burdens from basic research expenditures.

These calculations and comparisons with local generic operations lead to much of the controversy over pharmaceutical MNCs and their pricing and research policies. Roughly two-thirds of a subsidiary's expenses are for product cost, a substantial part of which represents purchases from the parent corporation of active ingredients needed to produce the drugs. Marketing, administration, and finance comprise the major remaining expenses. The parent firm's pricing policy is set to recover research and development expenses incurred in the product's discovery and testing stages and to help fund new investigations. By contrast, the generic firms are more self-contained, particularly if they obtain or produce the formula ingredients without paying the research cost portion of the expenses. The resulting differential can substantially reduce the unit volume of subsidiaries of research-based companies, leading to the charges of unfair competition. The ability to generate a cumulative revenue flow sufficient to fund the research operations of pharmaceutical MNCs is the critical element of a patent protection period recognized and respected in all markets.

This international pricing policy can appear exploitative from an individual nation's perspective, particularly from the vantage point of developing countries with small markets where serious health care needs are combined with severe income constraints. A corollary criticism results from the research concentration by pharmaceutical MNCs on seeking remedies for ailments prevalent in the richer developed nations. Their health problems do not reflect the current needs of the majority of developing country inhabitants, much less the threats posed by special tropical or other regionally located diseases that can plague populations in low-income countries. Some MNC critics in developing countries object to helping fund this next round of research rather than just helping recoup the past costs of current products, particularly when the research focuses on ailments associated with levels of economic development to which many nations can only aspire in the distant future.

This argument does not fit Chile as well as it fits other developing country regions. While faced with some serious income distribution problems and a need for further improvement in the health care delivery system, Chile does not face special disease or other medical problems significantly different from those in many industrialized countries. The broader controversy about pharmaceutical MNCs and developing countries nevertheless colored some of the discussion of their role in Chile during the debate over the patent law revision. The local consumer association in particular called for Chile to stand with other Third World countries in opposing the pharmaceutical MNCs' position on patent protection and intellectual property rights.[24]

Chile's pharmaceutical industry will continue changing well into the 1990s as corporate strategies adjust to passage of the patent law revision as well as to a global restructuring among major pharmaceutical firms. Several of Chile's larger generic companies had already extended their operations by experimenting with "branded generic" products to seek slightly higher prices, evaluating possible commercial alliances with research MNCs, and going multinational themselves in pursuing business in neighboring countries. A couple of pharmaceutical MNCs chose to leave the Chilean and some other Latin American markets, sometimes opting to serve it through a licensing arrangement with a local company. Many more changes will result from the wave of mergers sweeping through the global pharmaceutical industry as firms combine their resources to meet the ever-increasing costs of basic research and product development and testing.

INVESTMENT STRATEGIES IN GENERAL BUSINESS SECTORS

Many initial foreign investments in general business sectors occurred as a part of global MNC expansion in the two decades following World War II. During this period, Latin America experimented with regional market concepts that essentially required foreign firms to establish a local presence in order to participate in key industrial sectors. Although regional market hopes dimmed, most investors wanted to maintain their market presence once it was established. The operations fit the firms' worldwide strategy, and incremental expenditures to maintain an existing operation could avoid higher costs of reentering the market at a later time. From a current perspective, if these enterprises had entered the 1980s without ongoing ties to the area, free to allocate investment funds among all available world regions, the MNC presence throughout Latin America would be significantly weaker than it is today.

The sampling of important foreign industrial activities examined above reveals a range of strategic corporate responses to historical conditions and contemporary political and economic changes. Some investors operated profitably behind protectionist barriers through the 1960s, supplying essential technology or management skills, albeit at a higher-than-competitive market price. These firms had to adjust with the rest of Chilean business to the economic shock treatment of the mid-1970s. Sometimes the foreign unit built on its existing investment and shifted activities to reflect new market realities, drawing on the parent firm's global support network. The most successful cases of subsidiary adjustment relied heavily on local initiative and innovation as permitted in a decentralized or flexible MNC management structure.

Technology was the key ingredient and main value-added benefit in the foreign investment strategies examined in this chapter. When Chile adopted an open import policy, local subsidiaries could better use their global networks to draw in technological improvements. Open trade policies simultaneously created a competitive climate that motivated firms to undertake modernization efforts, increasing business efficiencies both directly and indirectly. For example, the local availability of technological advances in computer and telecommunications products enhanced the performance of other business sectors while linking Chile more closely to international trade and financial markets.

Financing proved an important second-level component in the investment strategies. Recent projects typically involved incremental funding installments over time as opposed to the large up-front financing packages required in mining or forestry natural resource complexes. The exception to this rule was the heavy financial commitment required to expand and improve Chile's telecommunications system. In this case foreign investor leverage proved crucial to raising the funds for extensive development programs and for arranging CTC's historic entry into the North American financial market. Foreign investors made sporadic use of debt-to-equity swaps, generally funding new or improved activities through reinvested earnings. The principal advantage of debt conversions, which appeared critical in several instances, related to their impact on internal corporate evaluations of competing project proposals. The lowered financial cost and implicit government support represented by the Chapter XIX program helped win project approvals in companies with strong regional or international corporate planning controls.

Most of these general industry investments did not generate significant export sales. A few companies utilized overseas channels to help offset lost regional market prospects or to diversify local market dependence and bring their own trade account into better balance. Lacking the clear national comparative advantages enjoyed by investors in mineral or other resource-based industries, these firms' operations related more to import substitution strategies than export promotion. The enterprises generally moved to greater local processing as their market share increased enough to justify such operations but continued to import products in other areas to offer customers a full product line.

Ownership strategies tended to favor full control over joint ventures in line with concern about assuring quality control and protecting the investor's brand image as well as the security of its technological innovations. Most firms appeared open to cooperative business arrangements with local enterprises, however, evaluating these undertakings on their applied merits within a specific timeframe and set of marketplace objectives. Total employment varied depending on the specific sector involved, but worker training and advancement potential constituted key elements within most firms' employee relations systems, perhaps reflecting the relatively high level of technology involved in a unit's operations.

Foreign investors also exist in other segments of the Chilean economy not specifically mentioned above. Both research and space limitations prevent a fully comprehensive analysis of all business fields. The primary areas not covered in this study relate to general service sectors, particularly fields such as construction, advertising and tourism. The first two business functions are largely connected to the operation of other industrial projects, many of which are discussed in the study. Tourism is also important for Chile and recently attracted some important new foreign investment from European firms interested in developing skiing and seaside resorts, as well as general hotel accommodations. Related foreign investment occurred in Chile's air transport sector, with both the privatized LAN Chile (35 percent to SAS) and competitor LADECO (Iberia and Ansett with 35 and 25 percent, respectively) taking on foreign partners.[25]

This analysis concludes the cross-sectoral portrait of the strategy, operations, and decision-making processes of key foreign investors in Chile. The next chapter assesses this activity in relation to the main strategic issues developed from past research on foreign investment in developing countries. The results show an evolved, more mature relationship between foreign investors and Chile. Useful policy landmarks point the way to maintain and enhance these improvements while suggesting how to shape similarly beneficial relationships in other host countries. At the same time, the comparison highlights the key elements of successful corporate investment strategies used to cope with the challenges of investing in a restructuring economy.

NOTES

Information in this chapter is drawn from interviews with corporate executives, government officials, and other knowledgeable experts in the field. The most comprehensive published materials used include the following: Rafael Aldunate, *El mundo en Chile: La inversión extranjera* (Santiago: Zig-Zag, 1990); Joaquín Lavín, *Chile Revolución Silenciosa* (Santiago: Zig-Zag, 1987); Chilean Investment Committee, *Industry*, 3rd ed. (Santiago: Comité de Inversiones Extranjeras (Chile), July 1988); and selected articles from two large newspapers: *El Mercurio* and *Estrategia*. Additional selected citations are provided in the text where necessary for specific references.

1. Salomon Brothers Inc. and International Finance Corporation, *Compañía de Teléfonos de Chile S.A. (Telephone Company of Chile)*, Prospectus, dated July 20, 1990; *CTC (Compañía de Teléfonos de Chile S.A.)*, Annual Report 1989; and "Chile: Into the 1990s," supplement, *Euromoney* (August 1989), 13–16, 40.

2. Andrés Benitez Pereira, "Actualidad: con la venta de Compañía de Teléfonos, el grupo australiano termina sus actividades en Chile," *El Mercurio*, March 21, 1990; and Salomon Brothers.

3. "Los nuevos dueños de CTC," *El Mercurio*, April 29, 1990.

4. "Looking South," *The Wall Street Journal*, September 20, 1991; "Más líneas y más inversión," *El Mercurio*, August 4, 1991; and "En 1992 CTC emitiría bonos en el exterior," *El Diario*, July 26, 1991.

5. "En el mercado secundario de acciones: US$ 233 millones buscan colocar en el exterior cinco empresas nacionales," *El Mercurio*, February 15, 1991.

6. "$31.700 millones ganó la CTC durante 1990," *El Mercurio*, February 15, 1991.

7. "Exportan cajas de cambio chilenas a renault de francia," *El Mercurio*, March 22, 1990; and "Por todo Octubre: Franco Chilena para producción de vehículos," *El Mercurio*, October 1, 1991.

8. "Afirmó gerente de General Motors: La industria automotriz ahorra divisas al país," *El Mercurio*, December 18, 1990.

9. "Según estudio de Nissan Cidef: Más de US$ 9 millones en subsidio recibió General Motors del fisco de Chile," *El Mercurio*, December 24, 1990; "Economistas de Ilades: Es innecesario modificar el estatuto automotriz," *El Mercurio*, December 11, 1990; and "Afirmó gerente de General Motors."

10. "Afirmó gerente de General Motors."

11. "Durante este año: Mil autos exportará filial chilena de General Motors," *El Mercurio*, September 9, 1991; and "Incentiva exportaciones de partes y piezas: Fué despachado proyecto sobre estatuto automotor," *El Mercurio*, October 2, 1991.

12. The Council of the Americas, *The Andean Pact: Definition, Design and Analysis* (New York: The Council of the Americas, 1973) sec. 3: 44–45.

13. *Electromat 1989*, Annual Report, Santiago, 1989.

14. Corporate Affairs, Inchcape plc., *Inchcape: The International Services and Marketing Group* (UK: Westdale Press); and *Williamson and Balfour Chile*, Williamson and Balfour, Santiago.

15. "El inconformismo de la Coca-Cola," *El Mercurio*, December 20, 1989; "Presidente de la Coca Cola: 'Seguirémos creciendo en Chile'," *El Mercurio*, January 21, 1990; and "Concesiones: La otra forma de crecer," *El Mercurio*, March 21, 1990.

16. "US$ 35 millones invierte CCU durante este año," *El Mercurio*, March 19, 1991; and "Paulaner: Parte producción de nueva cerveza," *El Mercurio*, June 7, 1990.

17. *Nestlé en Chile desde 1934*, Nestlé company pamphlet.

18. "Procter & Gamble Fixes Aim on Tough Market: The Latin Americans," *The Wall Street Journal*, June 15, 1990, A4.

19. "On Patents and Retaliation," *Journal of the Chilean-American Chamber of Commerce* (Santiago, July 1989), 6.

20. "Patentes farmacéuticas: Una ley aún sin remedio," *El Mercurio*, January 28, 1990; and United States Trade Representative, *GSP Country Reinstatement Hearings For Chile, Paraguay and Central Africa*, prepared by Neal R. Gross, Open Session, June 27, 1990.

21. "Asociación de farmacéuticas: Extrañeza por anuncios de aprobación de ley de patentes," *El Mercurio*, January 20, 1990. (translated from Spanish).

22. "Patentes farmacéuticas: Una ley aún sin remedio;" and "On Patents and Retaliation," 6.

23. "Ciba-Geigy and the Third World: Policy Facts and Examples," corporate pamphlet, prepared by Ciba-Geigy.

24. "Informó Carlos Ominami: Los fármacos no deberían subir en el mediano plazo," *El Mercurio*, February 2, 1990; and "Al presidente Aylwin: Achico solicitará revisión total en ley de patentes," *El Mercurio*, April 7, 1990.

25. "Going Global: Airlines of World Scramble for Routes and Lament Protectionism in an Industry Shakeout," *The Wall Street Journal*, July 23, 1991.

7

Assessing the Key Strategic Issues

A mixture of political, social, economic, and business elements define the key strategic investment issues for foreign corporations and host nations. This chapter measures a historical checklist of these issues as they developed from research in the 1960s and 1970s against the evolution of foreign investment operations in Chile, examining their application over time and across industries. The results show a maturing partnership between foreign investors and Chile that suggests the reformulation or eclipse of some traditional issues while pointing to other less-studied strategic elements that deserve greater attention.

OWNERSHIP AND CONTROL

Ownership ranked as the central issue in policy debates between foreign investors and developing countries through the 1970s. Chileanization and nationalization programs under presidents Frei and Allende embodied Chile's quest for greater local ownership, a drive mirroring the Andean Pact's minority foreign ownership requirements contained in Decision 24. The most emotional controversies typically revolved around foreign ownership of natural resources—primarily copper in the case of Chile. More generally, ownership issues stood as a political symbol and operational linchpin for asserting national government control over foreign investor activities.

The price of extending national control over foreign investors proved high in terms of compensation or retaliation in cases of forced expropriations. Host governments also gradually recognized that gaining ownership of in-place physical assets often did not capture the real value of corporate resources and assuredly did not guarantee access to essential product or process updates generated elsewhere in an MNC's global network. Both governments and foreign investors further learned that full or even majority ownership is not always required to exercise effective control over a business operation.

Chile's policy since the mid-1970s places very few ownership restrictions on foreign investments outside some social or security-sensitive areas and certain natural resource deposits that remain under state control. The key policy standard is nondiscriminatory national treatment, guaranteeing foreign and domestic investors the same ownership opportunities in the private sector. This approach leaves investors free to arrange a business structure of their own choosing, unbound in most areas by maximum foreign ownership restrictions or local participation requirements. In response, firms have chosen diverse investment strategies that display no simple pattern nor necessary preference for full ownership.

Foreign investors tended most to full ownership by a single firm when the business dealt with high technology products or where brand name identification and assurances of quality control were essential to the company's market success. A partial exception to these conditions is the use of franchising arrangements, such as in the soft drink industry, to cover processing and distribution functions. In these cases contractual restrictions enable the firm to retain tight control over product quality, advertising, and other elements essential to brand name image without requiring direct equity investments in all business functions.

Full ownership investments by a single enterprise were most prevalent in Chile's general manufacturing and high technology sectors, especially where a business could be established and expanded in staged increments. Service sector companies also often sought full ownership, a preference that became more pronounced among enterprises with significant local market experience. In a few cases, best exemplified by Exxon's interest in La Disputada, an investor pursued a go-it-alone strategy in major natural resource projects, but this approach was unusual. Projects involving such large initial capital outlays usually require joint venture arrangements among several firms to spread both cost and risk.

The proclivity for mixed-ownership arrangements in large natural resource projects showed up strongly in Chile's mining and forestry sectors. A few joint ventures included local partners, such as CMPC in Celpac and the Luksic group with the Pelambres and El Lince copper operations. More typically, however, several foreign companies joined forces to finance and develop these undertakings. Part of the tendency to form alliances between foreign investors rather than with local firms arose because only a small number of local enterprises in Chile possessed the size, resources, and experience to provide ideal joint venture partners. The number of large, financially healthy private enterprises declined dramatically with the recession of the early 1980s, just as foreign investor interest in minerals and forestry projects was accelerating.

Chile also lacked a statute directly authorizing joint ventures as a legal form of corporate organization. Although joint ventures could be approved by the proper authorities on a case-by-case basis, the Chilean business community had little practical experience operating under such arrangements. Most major firms were associated with family-based business groups rather than establishing working relationships with fully independent companies. In addition, the extensive network of state enterprises had, until recently, left little room for the development of a broad and diverse private industrial sector.

Ideal joint venture partners bring a full package of assets to a project, including money, technical expertise, relevant practical experience, stability, a compatible management philosophy, a good reputation, and knowledge of the local community. Once the few, highly attractive Chilean companies committed themselves to joint ventures with foreign partners, subsequent investors had to either join with other foreign enterprises or forge a Chilean partnership on a narrower asset base, such as a local firm's undeveloped natural resource claim or its established consumer recognition. Foreign banks became untraditional equity investors in some large projects through the Chapter XIX program, helping to fill the local financing gap.

Recession-induced financial problems led some local firms to seek mixed-ownership arrangements with foreign investors in order to sustain or expand business activities. Alliances formed on such a narrow interest base often evolved rather quickly, sometimes moving to full foreign ownership (such as Pacific Telecom's staged acquisition of CIDCOM) while in other instances the foreign investor phased out of the venture (for example, BANESTO's sale of its Banco O'Higgins holdings). Among the most important contributions of Chilean partners to mixed-ownership joint ventures were experienced management, a knowledge of local conditions, assistance in product or marketing adjustments, and the use of existing facilities or a known resource base. These assets eased a foreign investor's initial entry and sometimes permitted a staged investment and expansion strategy.

The foreign investors most likely to seek strong local joint venture partners were firms with limited investment experience in the region, such as Simpson Paper in the Celpac forestry project. Chilean firms were least likely to be selected for a joint venture arrangement under three circumstances: when a project required a heavy up-front financial commitment; the resulting product output was designed for export sales to developed country markets; or the foreign investor already possessed substantial direct business experience in Chile. In general, the joint ownership arrangements with the greatest chance of success over time appear to be ventures in which each partner contributes complementary operational expertise rather than only shared financial resources, and where the partners agree in advance on clearly defined roles.

Many start-up or large expansion projects evolved through an operational cycle that resulted in related ownership changes. For example, the Bond group helped arrange initial financing to energize the El Indio and CTC expansions, but subsequent owners of those two enterprises brought operational experience needed to build the business over the longer term. Such ownership changes come from matching evolving opportunities with relevant business expertise, a process adjudicated by market forces. An enterprise's development may thus involve a shift from joint venture to full ownership or acquisition by a third party firm as the business evolves. Local ownership requirements that restrict the pool of business expertise available to participate in an open bidding process will simultaneously reduce the chances for an enterprise's further development. One foundation for Chile's success in using foreign investment to promote economic growth has been its acceptance of open and flexible ownership arrangements.

These conclusions raise questions about the significance of the ownership issue as a national policy concern in the relationship between MNCs and developing countries, at least in the case of Chile. Historically the concept's importance derived from three interrelated elements. First, the nationality of corporate ownership carried symbolic and psychological importance for a country's political leadership. Foreign ownership of local resources represented more than just a foreign proprietor. In virtually all cases the investor came from a richer developed country, generally the United States, thereby associating foreign corporate ownership with politically charged debates about U.S. hemispheric hegemony. Direct investment also introduced an internal foreign presence that was more overt and intrusive than economic influence flowing through traditional trade channels. In this context, foreign ownership of a country's natural resources, or the acquisition of existing production facilities by foreign investors, was deemed particularly objectionable.

This first element of the ownership issue is superficial yet powerful. The same symbolism and much the same political message was carried in warnings about "The American Challenge" in Europe during the 1960s. A recent echo can be heard in the U.S. public outcry against a Japanese firm's purchase of New York's Rockefeller Center.[1] These protests strongly influenced the policy debate about foreign ownership of national assets in the developed countries, even though they lacked the history of colonial dependency that underlies much of the developing countries' uneasiness with foreign investors.

Despite this political impact, the symbolic and psychological component of the ownership issue represents only its most superficial importance. A second policy layer is uncovered when ownership is recognized and consciously used as a simple measure for the complex concept of control. The desire for control, in turn, derives not from some intrinsic importance, but rather from the influence it represents over the distribution of benefits arising from corporate operations. This third element, which focuses on outcome rather than process, is the real substantive core of the policy debate over foreign ownership issues.

Examination of foreign investments in Chile reveals how poorly direct ownership measures may reflect the actual control exercised by corporate management over related business operations. For example, Coca-Cola can maintain effective control over critical aspects of its bottlers' and distributors' operations through franchising agreements without acquiring an equity stake in that part of the business. Dole's Standard Trading sets quality standards and influences production techniques among Chile's independent fruit growers through purchasing and technical assistance practices without necessitating corporate ownership of farms and plantations. Bankers Trust was restricted to minority ownership of the Provida pension fund but exercises effective management control over its business activities. On the other hand, many foreign banks attained significant equity ownership in various industrial enterprises through Chapter XIX investments without exercising or even desiring managerial control over operational decision making.

As these examples illustrate, specific ownership measures bear a problematic relationship to real control over business activities. This linkage became more tenuous over the past two decades as enterprises attempted to offset foreign investment risk. Intercorporate alliances proliferated among MNCs based in different nations, with a marked growth in low and nonequity forms of MNC business arrangements. All nations, not just developing countries, are finding ownership a less than adequate measure of corporate control. As nations grow more economically interdependent and intercorporate alliances spread, an MNC's nationality becomes both less discernible and less necessarily indicative of how corporate benefits will be distributed geographically. A country cannot maintain tight national control over business activities in the modern global economy unless it is willing to pursue a policy of autarky and pay the concomitant price of slower economic development and reduced living standards.[2]

A necessary result of Chile's decision to follow an internationalization strategy must be a downgrading of the importance of MNC ownership measures and a refocusing of attention on investor performance in producing benefits for the economy and the nation. This results-oriented approach is more tedious and complicated than relying on a defined ownership standard to represent the presumed benefit distribution of corporate activity. Nevertheless, the true significance of ownership and control issues lies with performance, not perception, and performance judgments require an inductive evaluation process. This approach builds upward from an examination of individual case results, measured against appropriate expectation standards to a generalized conclusion that reflects the impact of foreign investment on a specific host country. In this sense the following discussion of more specific benefit issues suggests some components for such an evaluation that would assess how foreign investors operate in relation to topics that affect the national well-being of host countries.

INVESTMENT CAPITAL AND FINANCING METHODS

Capital ranks as the asset most closely associated with the strategy, power, and potential benefits of foreign investment. Multiple methods are available to raise capital for a particular project, however, and public policy implications often vary with the type of financing selected. Foreign investments in Chile over the past decade employed a range of financing mechanisms that reflected prevailing conditions in the country as well as differing proclivities toward financing methods among industries and specific companies. The power to arrange needed financial packages for large undertakings stands out as a prominent strategic advantage for many investments. Other elements evident in the Chilean experience are the use of innovative and flexible financing approaches, the ability to sustain investments over the longer term, and the important role of reinvested earnings for staged expansion and innovation.

Chile's D.L. 600 Foreign Investment Statute recognizes several forms of capital investment, including freely convertible foreign currency, tangible goods, technology susceptible to capitalization, credits, debt capitalization, and capitalized profits entitled to transfer abroad. This range gives prospective investors needed flexibility to structure the best financing package to suit the requirements of a particular project. The simple notion that a foreign investment involves the use of a parent corporation's funds to establish or expand a subsidiary operation in a developing country belies the diverse reality of how individual projects are financed.

Large, capital-intensive projects usually required the greatest diversity and creativity in financial arrangements, especially where the foreign investor was relatively inexperienced in the region or the joint venture included a significant local partner. Since the debt crisis shut Chile off from world financial markets, foreign commercial loans were not available to local companies and could be mobilized by foreign investors for individual projects only with some difficulty. In these cases, the foreign investors' direct capital contributions, and their essential role in mobilizing credit packages unavailable to local companies, permitted business activity that otherwise would not have occurred in Chile during the 1980s.

Creditors generally required the principal corporate sponsors to sink a substantial amount of their own equity capital into the project as both a demonstration of shared risk and a guarantee that the project would receive due management attention and priority. At least one-third of a project's capital usually had to come from the controlling owners before commercial lenders would contribute a similar amount. In addition, banks sometimes required the parent firm to guarantee the loan directly rather than accepting the local subsidiary's contractual obligation. La Coipa's financing agreement exemplifies this added condition. Prior investors had been unable to obtain adequate financing, lacking Placer's established credibility, reputation, and proven track record in this type of project. Even then, Placer still had to sign production timing agreements providing direct guarantees from the parent corporation in order to close the deal on needed bank financing.

The Chapter XIX program provided a related stimulus to large, capital-intensive projects. This mechanism permitted commercial banks holding Chilean debt to take untraditional equity positions in many projects, filling financing gaps that otherwise would have been difficult to bridge. Foreign banks, already heavily exposed in Latin America, were not willing to extend new credits to projects in those countries even if the ventures had foreign corporate involvement and backing. This restriction seriously limited the number of traditional financing institutions from whom foreign credits could be obtained and the debt conversion option partially offset this condition by increasing the pool of potential equity participants.

Principal industrial investors in long-term projects, especially the large mining ventures, seldom used the debt conversion mechanism themselves. This finding may result partly from the fact that other investment partners, such as the foreign banks, essentially used up the portion of the project that could be financed in this manner. In addition to potential government limits on the level of Chapter XIX financing in a particular project, debt conversion funds could only address the portion of the project's needs payable in local currency. On the other hand, even in ventures where bank-related investors did not preempt debt conversion financing potential, industrial companies often elected not to seek Chapter XIX funding for large, long-term start-up ventures. Many experienced corporate investors preferred the legal guarantees of D.L. 600 investments, expressing discomfort with the political controversy attached to debt swap transactions.

A very important financing component, often overlooked in policy discussions about foreign investment, is the use of supplier credits. This element plays a particularly crucial role in financing strategies for large, capital-intensive projects. Chile's general separation from international commercial lending enhanced this channel's importance for supplying the foreign currency requirements for purchases of imported equipment and other supplies. Foreign exporters helped secure financing assistance from their governments' trade promotion agencies, with the Chilean project benefitting from export competition among the industrialized countries. Subsidized financing packages were used to support exports to developing countries whose debt problems left them little hard currency to pay import bills.

Foreign investors with wide experience and established relationships with firms throughout the world possessed greater knowledge and easier access than local firms to potential equipment suppliers. This global span enabled investors to shop around for the best available financing package from government export assistance agencies, including the ability to shift sourcing locations for supplies obtained within an MNC's own intrafirm network. Supplier credits provided a major share of the hard currency financing needed for most large capital equipment purchases, thereby limiting the principal investor's own direct exposure. Repayment schedules could be structured to coincide with the start-up revenue flow from the project's earnings, especially when the venture generated foreign exchange through its own export sales.

The Celpac forestry complex offers a prominent example of a flexible and creative financing strategy. Celpac's principal investors made substantial direct equity contributions, thereby increasing their leverage in attracting the participation of financial institutions. Chapter XIX funding played an essential role in solidifying the participation of a relatively inexperienced foreign investor with needed production expertise (Simpson Paper) as well as the commercial bank partners. In addition to debt conversion, a creative bank participation arrangement involved shifting from active loans to an equity position linked with a profit-sharing agreement. Export credits provided by several supplier countries filled out the remaining financing requirements.

Celpac was one of several key ventures to include participation by the World Bank's International Finance Corporation (IFC). This agency played a valuable role in financing strategies, sometimes taking an equity stake in the venture as well as participating in a collective package of credits. IFC involvement often provided a stamp of approval for other potential creditors who lacked technical expertise to evaluate fully the merits of a particular project. Pursuing its development goals, the IFC also sought to translate a particular project's success into broader systemic progress, for example by selling its shares in Mantos Blancos to the public in a manner designed to help build Chile's local stock market.

The IFC also participated in the huge Escondida project, which offers another example of creative financing strategy. In this case the owners' equity stake amounted to over 40 percent of the required financing while the majority component came from advance sales contracts committing most of the mine's copper output to foreign refineries for as long as twelve years. A particularly unusual feature in this package was the participation of foreign government agencies in financing future imports rather than current exports. Foreign investor leadership, including credible project managers in Chile and foreign refiners who could lobby their governments for financing support, proved essential to the viability of this enormous undertaking.

In a few exceptional cases, a single corporation can self-finance a large investment, translating equity ownership into full control and (hopefully) eventual profit taking. Exxon's purchase, expansion, and modernization of La Disputada is the exception that proves this rule in Chile. The case also highlights the ability of a foreign investor to sustain an initially unprofitable project through periods of unexpected and costly difficulties. Cape Horn Methanol provides another demonstration of sustained investor commitment, although that project required a complex financing package involving several investors and innovative pricing agreements.

Smaller start-up investments and the expansion of existing industrial operations generally required a less complicated financing strategy, particularly for projects oriented to domestic sales rather than exports. Foreign investors new to Chile often met these capital requirements on their own. The Chapter XIX mechanism offered a possible but not a necessary option in most of these cases, with investors obtaining Chilean debt on secondary markets if conversion ratios were attractive. This approach was most evident where the primary foreign investor relied heavily on financial or trading expertise for its competitive advantage. Firms primarily oriented to production and marketing activities sometimes followed or joined these original lead investors who had identified the opportunity, bringing more operational expertise to sustain the business.

Investors were prone to use Chapter XIX financing as part of a strategy to expand or modernize existing operations in several types of circumstances. Banks or other financial investors that purchased an equity position in an established or privatized enterprise usually allocated some of that funding to undertake immediate improvements in the company's operations. Industrial subsidiaries presented a different scenario, especially in MNCs with a centralized organizational structure. In these cases, the use of debt conversion financing in a Chilean expansion project often provided enough of an unusual attraction and marginal benefit to gain an advantage over competing proposals during intra-MNC deliberations.

Established subsidiaries of decentralized investors were less likely to seek approval for Chapter XIX financing. With the exception of the 1982–83 recession period, these operations usually generated profits they could draw on for expansion and improvement projects. Individual corporations varied widely in their specific reinvestment policies, but most routinely devoted at least one-third on their profits to reinvestment activities in the country. Many MNCs accepted reduced profit repatriation for a time to finance major expansions or forays into a new line of business. Approval for these types of projects were far easier to obtain, with greater flexibility for local initiative, when the project was financed through reinvested earnings rather than requiring a new capital infusion from the headquarter's account.[3]

Some aspects of recent financing strategies in Chile are unlikely to continue, while the importance of other new elements could progressively expand. Debt conversion has fallen victim to its own success and will not play a major role in the coming years. This change signifies a reduced role for untraditional equity investments by banking institutions and other financial enterprises whose aggressive use of debt conversion opportunities sometimes drew in other mainline corporate investors. On the other hand, Chile's reentry to international capital markets will provide new voluntary lending opportunities that have been absent over the past decade. Foreign investors are likely to be among the first beneficiaries, but domestic companies should also gain greater access to this financing as long as Chile continues to show solid economic progress.

The gradual development of Chile's own capital markets and their progressive integration with global financial mechanisms offer long-term potential for raising new capital resources. The activity of foreign investment funds in Chile and CTC's pioneering listing on the New York Stock Exchange illustrate how linked market developments can create initially limited but important new financing options. Future growth in the number of publicly held companies and the use of capital markets for corporate expansion projects will create greater breadth and depth in strategic financing alternatives for Chilean investors. These developments will also blur further the ownership distinction between local and foreign companies based on the nationality of their capital funding.

An assessment of the capital and financing elements of foreign investment strategies in Chile, examined inductively from the beginning of the actual funding of individual projects over the 1980s, reveals a complex but more realistic picture of MNC/host country relations than arises from aggregate balance of payments analyses of foreign investment statistics. Certainly Chile gained additional investment capital that was a necessary if not entirely sufficient condition for achieving its economic growth objectives. At the end of the 1980s, Chile required an annual investment rate of 20 percent of GDP to reach an economic growth target of 5 percent; foreign investors were supplying one-fourth to one-third of the needed investment capital. A balance of payments view would warn that direct investment inflows in the 1980s will lead to capital and profit repatriation outflows in the 1990s and beyond, but the country reaps other benefits from associated business activity in the interim while corporate reinvestment policies suggest a willingness to temper profit taking as long as good local market opportunities exist.

Direct investors also assume commercial risk, meaning that capital outflows do not occur unless the business enterprise is successful. This situation is certainly preferable to basing development prospects on foreign loans to public sector entities that require repayment regardless of the related project's success. Public funds are also better invested in essential social welfare or economic infrastructure improvements than in substituting for private risk capital. Since Chile's domestic business community lacks sufficient size and depth to exploit the range of commercially promising prospects, foreign corporations broaden the pool of available investors, particularly for projects that carry heavy risk capital requirements such as exploring for natural resource deposits. Overall, Chile's recent history of foreign investment suggests a successful transition period for the country in terms of capital and financing methods, with a promising future linked to more developed and internationally integrated capital markets.

TECHNOLOGY TRANSFER, APPLICATION, AND ADAPTATION

Technology is probably the second element after capital most closely associated with foreign investment. Some technology can be capitalized although its value may be difficult to determine and is subject to dispute. Far more diverse than a "black box" concept, technology comes embodied within equipment and in the organization of a production process; explained on paper and written electronically in software programs; discovered in laboratories and accumulated over the years in the minds of experienced managers.

Foreign investments in Chile cover a wide range of technology transfer, application, and adaptation strategies. The country's small internal market argues against locating basic research facilities there, although Chile does host regional development laboratories for several corporations. In addition, Fundación Chile represents an unique form of MNC/host country cooperation in technology transfer, giving Chile special capabilities to exploit globally available technology and apply it to goals of national economic development.

Investment strategies reflect sectoral distinctions regarding the type of technology employed and the nature of its application and adaptation. Mining projects generally do not involve new technological breakthroughs but do rely heavily on experienced management know-how to combine state-of-the-art equipment and processes in large-scale projects. The value of managerial know-how should not be underestimated as a strategic technological advantage or contribution. Bringing together the numerous, interrelated components of a huge mining complex so that all parts function smoothly and efficiently is a major achievement in itself. To accomplish this task months ahead of schedule, as Escondida did, saves literally millions of dollars in financing costs while generating even more revenue through early output earnings.

Certain aspects of Chilean mining operations push at the borders of the known, for example in high-altitude mining techniques, but most simply employ the best technology available from an investor's global experience. Since foreign mining corporations reentered Chile slowly following the country's nationalization and expropriation actions, the technologies associated with their mining investments benefit from recent improvements and constitute a significant advance over methods incorporated in most older, existing operations. Nowhere is this difference more apparent than in the areas of safety and environmental protection. Virtually every major foreign investor incorporates technological processes that insure that new operations meet the policy standard set by the MNC for its facilities worldwide, yielding results far better than required by Chilean regulations. Local facilities, including state-owned and operated mines, did not devote significant time or financial resources to improving their performance on these concerns until very recently and therefore lag seriously behind the performance of new foreign investors.

The most important technologies associated with foreign investment strategies in nontraditional export sectors relate to quality improvement and control measures. To compete effectively in international markets, Chilean products must meet high quality standards on an assured and consistent basis. World-class technology is transferred through MNC channels more quickly and with greater assurance of periodic upgrading than technology sold to unrelated firms on the open market. Foreign investors have played a significant role in raising production standards in Chile's nontraditional export sectors, introducing modern process technology and quality control programs that improved the competitiveness of Chilean exports on world markets.

Improved forestry management techniques employed by foreign investors from New Zealand illustrate the valuable know-how that is spreading from these operations to locally owned plantations, improving the quality and yield from Chilean forests. Upgraded technology incorporated in the growing number of new, high-quality cellulose plants exemplifies another forestry-sector contribution. The country's leading local firm, CMPC, turned to Simpson Paper to bring in new process technology for the Celpac complex. This joint venture strategy promised to provide better technology, with upgrade potential, than CMPC had derived from an older technical assistance agreement with another foreign paper products company.

In fishing, Japanese and other foreign boats with advanced capabilities opened new offshore Chilean fisheries, especially in turbulent southern waters, while foreign-supplied technology helped establish cultivated salmon and other fresh fish exports as well as raising the quality of fish meal production. Foreign investment strategies in agriculture also involved technologies that increased quality standards. Foreign investors sometimes engaged directly in growing activities, for example through their participation in a few vineyards. More commonly, investors concentrated on processing and marketing strategies, providing technical assistance and enforcing quality control measures on independent growers through tough purchasing standards. In effect, the investors gathered and transmitted information on market requirements in different parts of the world, and then led the improvement in local standards necessary for Chilean products to gain entree in new foreign markets.

Service sector investments registered perhaps the most dramatic jump in the strategic use of technological capabilities. Both Chile's open trade policy and the vigorous competition in its internal market spur investors to offer new products and services soon after their introduction in developed countries and ahead of other, even larger, hemispheric markets. The participation of multiple foreign investors, free to import and sell or utilize the latest available computer and communications technologies, thrust Chile into the forefront among Latin American nations in such fields as banking and insurance services, mobile phones, telecommunications networks, and local software development and data processing capability. Improvements in these types of business services enhance the performance of other industrial sectors while employing Chile's human capital advantages in well-educated personnel.

Local initiative in applying and adapting these capabilities can also lead to new competitive niches for Chilean operations, such as Electromat's success in refurbishing and improving old GE machinery. Kodak's finished furniture enterprise is a more elaborate attempt to create local capability, reaching out to bring into Chile experienced managers and advanced machinery. Fundación Chile pursues an even broader technology strategy, giving Chile a special tool to develop pioneering ventures based on foreign technology transfers aimed primarily at stimulating follow-on private sector investments in new business activities with export potential. This quasi-public, nonprofit institution offers an ideal mechanism for promoting national development, but its unique history makes it difficult for other nations to replicate the same cooperative format or generate the sustained financial commitment necessary to underwrite such an approach.

Recent experience with technology transfer, application, and adaptation in Chile highlights the diversity of the technology role in foreign investment strategies. Technology does not exist in the abstract; it is determined in form, content, and utility within a specific business plan and public policy context. Over the past decade, Chile provided an environment conducive to technology transfer as part of foreign investment strategies framed by free market forces. The technological component proved most important in business services infrastructure, quality control processes, and project management and innovation. Thus technology is an essential element in Chile's economic progress, but it must be assessed within the context of an investor's overall business strategy.

EXPORT PROMOTION AND IMPORT SUBSTITUTION

Import substitution strategies dominated many national economic development programs until the mid-1970s when the success of newly industrializing countries in Asia called attention to export-led growth. Chile turned from an emphasis on import substitution to export promotion as part of its internationalization strategy, opening Chilean markets to competition from imported products while seeking to expand nontraditional exports to overseas markets.

Foreign investors emerge as more important partners for Chile in this new development strategy than they were in the old approach. These firms provide international market access through their global experience and established trade channels, with their success aiding the acceptance of other Chilean products as well as their own. Import substitution goals are still pursued to some degree, but they are difficult to implement efficiently and are less relevant to typical investor strategies in a country with a small internal market. Under these circumstances, success in import substitution may require higher market concentration ratios, involving possible trade-offs with a country's competition policy.

Creating a viable nontraditional export industry requires more than discerning a country's areas of potential competitive advantage. Producers must surmount scale, quality, and recognition barriers that confront new entrants, particularly in developed country markets. A foreign investor's established reputation and name recognition can help overcome initial reluctance among distributors, retailers, and consumers regarding an otherwise unknown product. Kodak's willingness to back its export venture in finished furniture exemplifies this advantage, in this case extending even to products with which the corporation is not normally associated. Unifrutti's pathway for Chilean fruit exports into Middle Eastern countries is another example, although in this case the closely held nature of those markets offers less potential transference to other Chilean exporters.

Scale considerations also influence investment strategies, especially for sales in high consumption markets where new producers must be willing and able to guarantee sufficient output in order to even gain the attention of mass merchandisers. This element ties into the recognition factor for identifiable consumer products because advertising and other promotional devices that facilitate a new seller's entry are not cost-effective without a substantial sales base. Producers of nontraditional exports take a large risk in building or expanding production facilities based on new market expectations. Foreign investors can use their global market position and experience to assess and bear this risk more easily than smaller domestic enterprises.

Product quality has become the sine qua non of success in the contemporary international marketplace. In many restructuring economies, domestic firms long protected by import barriers from the discipline of free consumer choice face a formidable adjustment challenge. Foreign investors that might be tempted to relax their production standards a bit for sales restricted to a protected domestic market cannot risk their reputation and position in markets worldwide by exporting goods from one country's facilities that do not match the company's quality standards at other locations. Hence these investors have both the motivation and, through technology transfer, the methodology to incorporate top quality control standards in an investment strategy designed to export from a new production site.

Dependability of supply and, where relevant, availability of local servicing are two additional considerations importers must weigh in deciding whether to purchase goods from a new nontraditional exporter. Chile's geographic distance from most major developed country markets increases the perception of risk from a disruption of supplies. Exporters with their own transportation system, and perhaps even multiple production locations that could substitute for supply problems in one area, help offset this risk factor. A foreign investment strategy can often take advantage of in-place infrastructure to accommodate another, even nontraditional export item, making the production decision easier and quicker than for firms that must piece together a new supply and marketing network.

The clearest illustration in Chile of this strategic investment advantage lies in agricultural products with pull-through export effects from the transport, sales, and distribution infrastructure of a company such as Dole's Standard Trading subsidiary. The importance of supply dependability is also evident in Cape Horn Methanol's decision to purchase its own delivery vessels in order to reassure potential customers regarding the reliability of its shipping schedules.

Intra-MNC trade sometimes provides a convenient and profitable export channel for both the company and the country, encompassing most links needed to establish a nontraditional export chain. Electromat applied its metal-mechanic capabilities to improving older machinery, finding a ready export market in GE's affiliated enterprises around the world. In developing a joint venture to support its own software needs in Chile, Kodak also provided a first-step export channel for this company to other subsidiaries in neighboring countries. Unisys's marketing of Chilean software products offers a similar illustration that reaches beyond the intracorporate network to broader export sales.

Many investors derive their competitive advantages by internalizing the full export chain from local production through final overseas sales and service. A wide variety of arrangements are possible and profitable in today's integrated world economy, however, including options that incorporate efficient local producers of high quality products. These firms can enter into long-term sales contracts or other types of agreements with a foreign enterprise that may involve little or no equity stake by the foreign firm in the producing country. In a sense, the Delaware River Port Authority in the United States forged such a relationship with Chilean fruit exporters, providing the basic management and physical infrastructure needed to handle efficiently the increased volume passing through the main entry port in Philadelphia.

In addition to direct business advantages, foreign tie-ins also create potential political allies inside developed country markets who can help resist rising protectionist pressures that could close or limit market access. In some cases the result may be a muting of protectionist outcries by dividing corporate interests, at times within the same investor, such as between home and host country copper production sites, or the slightly overlapping seasons for fresh fruit harvests in Chile and California. Retailing firms may eventually add to this alliance, but few have strong enough ties to Chilean producers at this time to constitute a potent political force without the involvement of direct foreign investors. Thus far investor political support has been most evident in actions that stressed the maintenance and improvement of bilateral trade relations rather than a weighing in on product-specific cases. Included in this category are support for restoring Chile to the U.S. Generalized System of Preference (GSP) tariff program, negotiating a bilateral free trade agreement, and opposing U.S.

trade retaliation, even when called for by the pharmaceutical MNCs over the patent reform issue.

The import substitution part of Chile's trade policy goals relates less clearly and directly to foreign investment strategies. Investors could move from importer to local producer, but in an open, free market economy this step must be carefully weighed against the option of serving the market through imports from existing facilities elsewhere. Chile's small internal market mitigates against local production in many product areas that are unconnected to export potential. The main exceptions are certain consumer goods such as food and beverages where sufficient market size exists and transportation, taste, or other relevant factors confer clear advantages on local production.

Only a few corporations will be able to gain sufficient market share in a small country to justify a move from importer to local producer. In the process, that sector's market concentration ratio is likely to increase. This outcome arises particularly when foreign firms enter the country by acquiring existing local producers rather than through grassroots construction that adds a new market presence. In Chile's case, most acquisitions occurred following the financial crisis brought on by the 1982–83 recession. At that time, many acquired firms faced closure, so concentration ratios may have increased as much or more without the foreign investment. Government regulation against abuses of market power and remaining or potential competition from alternative import sources can work in tandem to control possible negative consequences from increased market concentration. This effort links an effective competition policy to import substitution objectives.

In general, recent Chilean policy has focused more on export promotion than import substitution. Imports sometimes served to introduce greater competitive discipline to raise local producers' standards to world quality levels. Foreign investment strategies proved more advantageous for the export effort than in import substitution. In a few cases, investor policies led to specific attempts to enhance the company's trade balance effect, such as Kodak's nontraditional export venture in finished furniture and Nestlé's locally produced corn flakes challenge to imported products. While it is clear that Chile does not possess the market advantages to attract local manufacture in many product categories, foreign investors in the country do appear to operate in ways supportive of the country's stated trade policy goals.

EMPLOYMENT AND LABOR RELATIONS

Employment ranks among the top development issues for many countries where finding a solution to problems of unemployment and underemployment is both morally and politically imperative. The basic economic theory of comparative advantage suggests that foreign investors will be attracted to developing countries to exploit excess labor as a factor of production, creating many new jobs through investments in labor-intensive industries. This view is reinforced by organized labor's charges in developed countries that foreign investment involves "runaway plants" that export jobs from the investor's home country.

Economic changes carried out by the Pinochet regime imposed serious penalties on the workforce as real wages declined sharply and unemployment in the late 1970s more than doubled historical averages. Even during the economic boom of 1980–81, unemployment remained above 15 percent if one includes people covered by the government's emergency employment programs. Emergency efforts employed over half a million people during the recession in 1983. In recent years Chile's unemployment picture has improved dramatically. By 1988, real wages were recovering and unemployment dipped below 6 percent. Spot shortages appeared in certain middle-level job categories, such as foremen in expanding export industries. Significant levels of underemployment remain along with troublesome areas of structural unemployment. These problems especially affect a large group of unemployed young people drawn from a generation that slipped through the system untrained during societal upheavals in the 1970s.

Foreign investments in Chile vary greatly in their job-creating content but are generally not of the type that directly produce a large number of new permanent jobs relative to the total workforce (nor do they show evidence of a shift in employment from the home countries). Indirect job creation and other multiplier effects from economic growth stimulated by foreign investment offer more significant employment benefits. Investor practices provide collateral advantages in labor relations, training programs, and the possibility of gaining management experience in international business operations.

The largest number of jobs created by individual foreign investments arise from huge mining projects such as El Indio, La Coipa and La Escondida. These additions come in impressive, lump-sum increments ranging from 500 up to 1,500 permanent employees. Large cellulose projects such as Celpac and Santa Fe involve similar although smaller job gains, amounting to 300-400 employees. Only a limited number of projects with this magnitude exist, however, and the job figures are comparatively small if measured in relation to the amount of capital invested. The larger the mining project, the more capital-intensive is its operation. Despite mining's critical role in the Chilean economy, the sector as a whole employs only slightly more than 2 percent of the nation's labor force.

Indirect job creation and the rural location of these large natural resource projects generate a number of employment-related benefits. Temporary construction jobs are significant, averaging approximately three times the projected number of permanent employee positions. The effects of local payroll spending by the operation's permanent workforce and the facility's continual need for supplies generate additional indirect employment on a two- or three-to-one ratio. In less developed areas, many of these employment opportunities go to people who otherwise might migrate to overpopulated areas in Chile's central metropolitan region. The investments also help redistribute income and improve living standards in poorer areas. Some projects build new housing for their workers and aid them to become owners, helping relieve some pressures from Chile's general housing shortage.   Companies also make infrastructure improvements connected with project construction, including building or modernizing roads, port facilities, and communications links that are usually accessible to other local interests, thereby assisting regional economic development.

General industry investments in manufacturing facilities involve fewer jobs individually. Outside mining and nontraditional exports, plant size is geared to domestic market potential. The use of modern production processes requires fewer but more highly skilled workers. The skill factor, linked to both quality control requirements and general employee policies, enhances the importance of training programs in industrial investments. Efforts such as those of Lever Chile can involve a large proportion of the firm's workforce in programs organized locally, as well as providing training at an investor's foreign locations.

Internationally trained Chilean managers constitute a great asset for Chile in its drive to develop globally competitive industries. Chilean managers with overseas experience head operations throughout the economy, including both foreign and locally owned enterprises. Most individuals retain a strong attachment to Chile, and their desire to live and work in the country leads many to accept initially lower positions in order to return. Virtually all foreign executives interviewed also valued their Chilean assignments. In one case, a foreign manager asked to return to Chile, leaving a much higher headquarters position with global business responsibilities.[4]

Consumer goods companies and some service sector firms also provide substantial employment. Acquisitions are more frequent in these cases, making job creation assessments difficult compared to the start-up of new greenfield projects. Nevertheless, many acquisitions appeared to save jobs in companies whose impending failure would have meant greater unemployment. Follow-on investments in expansion projects usually generated an additional increment of new jobs in the reorganized enterprise.

Foreign investments in processing and marketing food products provide indirect employment in agriculture. The tremendous expansion of fresh fruit and other agricultural exports, aided substantially by the transport, marketing, and quality control experience of foreign investors, requires labor-intensive harvesting and packing operations.   The fruit industry alone provides employment for almost one-tenth of the nation's workforce, about one-half in temporary seasonal jobs, many held by women in poor rural areas.   Most foreign investors do not integrate backwards into farm or plantation ownership, so their direct employment is concentrated at processing and shipping stages.

Similar indirect employment arises from food processing operations that focus on the domestic market. Nestlé's policy of buying milk from independent suppliers, seventy percent of them small and medium-size producers, helps sustain labor-intensive, family farm operations in rural areas. Most of this employment is not new, and some may be transferred through acquisition of locally owned firms. However, foreign investment in this sector also helps expand the market and its employment base by the introduction of new products that increase the demand for agricultural inputs. Other, more distant employment benefits result from multiplier effects that play out through general economic expansion, including activities supported by the foreign investment funds and other forms of noncontrolling investments.

The fishing industry presents a special case of employment policy related to foreign investment. Investors played an important role in developing new fisheries and expanding export markets for Chilean fish products. Resource limitations are now capping further growth in traditional fishing activities, although aquaculture projects and deep-sea fishing may still increase. More foreign investors introducing capital-intensive and technologically sophisticated operations could raise the efficiency of the catch, but likely at the expense of traditional, labor-intensive artisanal fishing fleets. Under these circumstances, the Chilean government opted through its fishing law revision to maintain artisanal employment interests, even though that meant introducing discriminatory provisions against future foreign ownership, noting that similar sectoral restrictions exist in most other countries.

Foreign investments in Chile do not provide substantiation for the concern of organized labor in home countries that investors transfer jobs through runaway plants that move abroad to exploit low-cost labor. Chilean labor costs are lower than in developed nations but do not constitute the primary determinant for most foreign investments. Labor savings are welcome in minerals and forestry operations but are overshadowed by ore grade and growing time considerations. Most other export industries also share this basic raw material determinant. Copper and fresh fruit shipments from Chile may flow through international business channels to compete with U.S.-sourced alternatives, and Chile's natural advantages in lithium production may eventually result in some output shifts away from U.S. deposit sites, but these cases do not fit the typical labor-based scenarios for runaway plants.

Chile's small domestic market also does not attract the type of major manufacturing operations that substitute host country employment for significant numbers of home country export-related jobs. The closest example found in this study of direct job transfers due to labor cost considerations was Electromat's metal mechanic work in improving older GE machinery. This worker skill capability became priced out of the U.S. market, but interestingly, no centrally planned transfer of this function to Chile occurred on the basis of lower labor costs. Electromat's own local initiative developed that capability separately.

The company needed to adapt older machines to its own use, adding innovations and fashioning spare parts no longer easily available through the GE network. This local initiative built a skill level that GE discovered and exploited as its own needs arose and Electromat was able to offer the best product at the best price.

Goodyear and GM's deal was another case for possible runaway plant evidence, shifting spare tire purchases from Goodyear's U.S. plants to its Chilean facility. In fact, however, the parties carefully structured the transaction as an add-on to normal sales from Goodyear's U.S. facilities, in part in deference to maintaining good labor relations. This move moderated if not eliminated competitive changes in sourcing patterns for low-profit spares versus higher-value, full-performance tires.

Some part of the growing Chilean textile trade with the United States may involve a shift in export platforms from other developing countries where quota limits have been reached, but this impact appears small and determined more by government-structured trade controls than by foreign investment factors. The potential also exists for increased labor-intensive work (such as data-processing) that might be conducted through Chile's technologically sophisticated communications links. Thus far these opportunities are being explored more by local firms than by foreign investors looking to shift work from the developed nations.

With regard to local labor-management relations, foreign investors operated clearly within the prevailing legal framework during the Pinochet regime and did not seriously challenge or initiate efforts to change the tight constraints placed by the military government on union activities. Most investors are nevertheless used to negotiating with labor unions in many different countries and appeared more open to dealing with Chilean labor groups than most traditional and conservative local businesses. Foreign firms are more likely than Chilean enterprises to use professional personnel officers who are responsible for organizing and managing the company's labor relations structure. These executives bring experience from other global operations and often introduce innovative proposals to improve work conditions in the Chilean environment.

The flexible work system introduced in the harsh labor conditions at La Coipa and the negotiated work rule changes at La Disputada are relevant examples of such policies. Wage rates at foreign firms generally rank a little above the local average, but usually not so much higher as to seriously skew the job market and capture all the best workers away from local employers. Foreign investors also invest more heavily in workplace safety in line with their worldwide standards, and offer more extensive training programs including opportunities for overseas technical education and managerial experience.

The leader of Chile's most important labor organization, Central Unica de Trabajadores (CUT), acknowledged the generally good relations between foreign companies and their local employees in an interview published in September

1990. He stated, "As far as the multinational sector is concerned, workers themselves have expressed satisfaction with salaries, training programs and benefits."[5] The head of Chile's national business association, the Confederación de la Producción y del Comercio, echoed this finding, reporting that: "According to our polls, the Chilean worker holds the multinational enterprise in high esteem—more than its local counterpart."[6] Overall, foreign investors in Chile provide new direct and even more numerous indirect job opportunities while engaging in good labor practices, often above local business standards, including the introduction of work system innovations that benefit both labor and management.

INVESTMENT RULES AND REVENUE

The content and stability of a host nation's rules governing foreign investment shape the viability of particular investment strategies. Evaluating these factors in countries with restructuring economies is especially difficult as new laws are formulated and political fortunes change. Chile's relationship with foreign investors evolved over the years in line with changes in its investment regulations and the political support that determined their implementation and longevity. Examining this experience helps identify the importance of specific regulatory features and the nature of foreign investor responses to an improved investment climate.

Historical experiences in Chile made guarantees against expropriations and the stability of a fair tax regime the most evident concerns of foreign investors after the early 1970s. Statutory provisions on these subjects, along with a nondiscriminatory national treatment standard, became the cornerstone of the new foreign investment law devised by the Pinochet government. Chile's D.L 600 statute represented a significant break with the past compared both to the country's recent actions against foreign investors and the general hostility MNCs still encountered in most developing countries in the mid-1970s. Providing for one of the strongest contractual guarantees with the state available in any country, its national treatment standard was equally sweeping, covering entry, expansion, and general operations. Taxation provisions offered a guaranteed tax rate for at least a decade and permitted one change to the prevailing national tax standard at the investor's option. These commitments were important substantively and as a strong signal that foreign investors were welcome in the country.

Developing countries seeking foreign investment must first break onto corporate lists of potential investment sites to be investigated. This challenge is difficult for nations that acquire a reputation of hostility to foreign investors. The Allende government's actions removed Chile from even the long lists of desirable investment locations, imprinting a highly negative image of the country on the minds of corporate executives. The dramatic events connected with the military coup temporarily drew attention back to Chile, but more as another world event rather than as an action that immediately implied a more stable and conducive environment for business investment. Indeed, the continuing violence and repression that followed reinforced the hesitation in corporate boardrooms to reconsider Chile's status as an investment site, especially among firms headquartered in nations led by socialist-leaning governments.

This historical and political context helps explain why foreign investors did not immediately respond en masse to the very positive policies adopted in D.L. 600. Deeds speak louder than words in reassuring foreign investors regarding professed changes in a country's investment climate, and it remained for Chile to negotiate several early demonstration cases to turn policy into practice before corporate attention refocused on the nation's investment potential. Some former investors returned to reclaim their properties but generally assumed a cautious approach toward further expansion and exposure. The greatest impact came from a couple of cases of new investment, particularly in the El Indio gold project. Mining sector firms had incurred the highest losses from past Chilean actions but a follow-the-leader spirit prevails in the never-ending search for promising new mineral deposits. El Indio helped refocus investor attention on Chile's resource potential.

The Chilean government was willing to refine its investment rules during these early negotiations to satisfy the remaining concerns of potential investors. In retrospect, these actions proved sufficient in terms of the legal framework. Actual investment decisions then turned more on economic and business factors that gradually improved in Chile, especially after the government settled on the right package of macroeconomic policies in the mid-1980s.

Despite the overt importance given by MNC spokesmen to international law standards and bilateral investment treaties, foreign investors did not avoid Chile because it lacked bilateral investment treaties or failed to disavow the Calvo doctrine regarding the primacy of local law. Chile did leave the Andean Pact with its restrictive foreign investment conditions, but the country did not otherwise move to change its formal relationship to the debate about international law standards on foreign investment. The strong national guarantees, coupled with the government's willingness to permit practical mechanisms such as offshore accounts for projects with significant export earnings and sometimes a negotiated deference to foreign legal standards, ultimately proved sufficient for most investors.

Interestingly, the Aylwin government began negotiations on bilateral investment treaties with European governments in 1991. This new approach appeared to stem from several factors, including: a desire to formalize improved economic relations with a number of countries following Chile's democratic transition; a response to increased competition for foreign investment as more countries equalled or surpassed Chile's liberal investment statute; and a concern that smaller and medium-size investors that lacked the leverage, global experience, and large legal staffs of major enterprises, might be more attracted to Chile within the framework of formal international legal guarantees.

Chile has not offered a bevy of financial or other special treatment bonuses to lure new foreign investors, choosing to balance its few disincentives to investment with equally minor incentives and rely essentially on free market decision making. While providing some assistance for export promotion efforts, the government avoids attaching special performance requirements to new investment approvals. An important financial provision of D.L. 600 permits immediate remittance of profits and early repatriation of capital, with access to the formal foreign exchange market. The foreign investment statute also offers the option of a guaranteed tax rate. Considered extremely liberal at the time of their adoption, these two provisions have declined in their attractiveness relative to some newer investment codes being introduced in other countries. The same fate befell Chile's Chapter XIX regulations, particularly the longer capital repatriation restriction, but the swift decline in Chilean debt available for conversion tempers concern about this program's competitiveness.

Taxation policy deserves special attention because it weighs heavily in cost-benefit evaluations of the relationship between foreign investors and host countries. Chile had used tax increases on foreign copper companies to claim additional benefits for the state, with rates up to 60 percent. The idea of a guaranteed tax rate, even one as high as the initial 49.5 percent, was therefore conceived as attractive to foreign investment. Many investors did, in fact, view the provision favorably, particularly for large mining projects that qualified for the twenty-year term guarantee. The rate itself was not especially attractive, but investors valued the government's willingness to commit itself to a specified taxation level for long enough to provide a stable planning horizon for major corporate projects that often were not profitable until many years after the initial investment.

In practice, most investors are exercising their option to be taxed under the prevailing national rate, which has been substantially lower than the guaranteed rate. These firms cannot switch back to the guaranteed rate in the future, so this action is a vote of confidence in Chilean government policy. While the current tax rate may increase somewhat, companies are betting that the government recognizes that highly exploitative rates would inhibit needed private investment, both domestic and foreign. On the government side, public coffers still gain significant added revenue from the supplemental tax on profits that leave the country. Whenever profits are remitted abroad, the business income is subject to the additional tax of nearly one-third, on top of the normal income tax paid by both local and foreign firms.

Policy questions arise regarding the appropriate level of taxation on foreign investment. In reality, a host country's choices cannot be made in isolation and must reflect both tax policies in potentially competing investment locations and the tax policy of home countries. Regarding the latter consideration, key factors are whether the parent firm is taxed on foreign source income, whether it receives credit for taxes already paid on that income in the host country, and how the relative tax rates compare. For example, the prevailing Chilean tax on foreign investors is roughly comparable to the taxes due when income is remitted to U.S. parent corporations. These firms can take a full credit for income taxes paid in Chile up to the amount of U.S. taxes due on that income. If the Chilean rate were below the U.S. rate, the investor could end up paying the remaining amount to the U.S. Treasury rather than to the Chilean government. On the other hand, if the Chilean rate exceeded the U.S. rate, investors essentially would find their total tax bill that much higher, which would act as a disincentive to conduct or expand operations in Chile.

Tax revenue is the most direct and easily measurable benefit host governments continually extract from foreign investors. Almost regardless of the prevailing level, the temptation always exists to increase the rate just a bit more in order to retain more of the profit within the country and place it at the disposal of state spending decisions. This approach can yield incremental increases in the short term as companies take time to adjust operations and weigh future investment decisions. The approach will reach a point of diminishing returns, however, as it surpasses the limits defined by offsetting home country tax policies and raises concerns among prospective foreign investors regarding the stability of the host nation's policy framework.

Chile recognized how the international context can influence the effectiveness of its own taxation policies. In 1991, the Aylwin government began negotiations to establish bilateral tax treaties with some important home countries that would set mutually defined parameters for tax issues affecting foreign investments, thereby providing governments and corporations alike with a more stable and predictable business environment. If successful, these agreements will mark another new step in the maturing relationship between Chile and the international investment community.

Several other public policy areas that are neither a direct part of Chile's investment rules nor of its tax revenue system also affect the investment strategies and operational decisions of foreign investors. The country is moving gradually to improve and update a number of policy standards, balancing the dual needs of modernization and general stability. Labor reform was addressed early by the new democratic government, restoring many organized labor rights and establishing a framework for direct and free labor-management negotiations. Foreign investors had recognized the need for reform and appeared somewhat more ready than many traditional local businesses to bargain with a revitalized labor movement, fearing only that radical labor activists might return to methods of politically inspired work disruptions.

Environmental and transportation policy are two other areas often cited by foreign investors as in need of modernizing legal changes. Existing Chilean environmental standards are largely outdated and scattered haphazardly among numerous sectoral laws and regulations. Estimates hold that as many as 3,000 separate provisions can be interpreted as dealing with environmental regulation, but together they do not comprise a coherent environmental policy.[7] Most foreign investors follow international corporate standards that surpass Chilean requirements. To the extent that these investors compete with local enterprises in environmentally sensitive sectors, the foreign firms may face a competitive disadvantage regarding spending on environmental controls, a difference that could be narrowed through the formulation and enforcement of improved environmental regulations. This condition applies most dramatically to the mining sector but appears in other natural resource and manufacturing industries as well.

Transportation policy affecting roads, railways, and port facilities also requires change to handle the tremendous expansion of Chile's export industries. The transportation link is vital to many foreign investors and equally important to continued growth in the Chilean economy, including its decentralized regional development. As Chile entered the 1990s, road and port facilities loomed as potential bottlenecks to moving fruit, forestry, agricultural, and mineral exports to overseas markets. The largely state-run railway system was ready to collapse, starved for investment capital and inefficient in its staffing and operations. The Pinochet government had begun changes in the port sector, introducing more competitive private sector management. The Aylwin administration proposed further changes to attract private investment to improve the railway system and undertake certain high-priority improvements in road projects susceptible to private sector involvement. These legal changes could also lead to assistance from multilateral lending institutions for the projects' implementation.

A final policy area important to foreign investment strategies is antitrust or competition policy. Chile's standards and procedures have been generally appropriate and well-administered, but the country's recent rapid economic development raises new challenges that demand further modernization of regulations to ensure vigorous competition in key business sectors. Communications and transportation stand out as areas needing special attention due to their critical infrastructure role in serving many other sectors of the economy.

Foreign investors are often accused of engaging in restrictive business practices, abusing monopolistic powers derived from their size and global span. Chile had often protested the cartel-like leverage exerted by oligopolistic copper companies when Kennecott and Anaconda dominated the country's mining industry. More recently, the general proliferation of foreign investors from many countries in various industries has multiplied the number of alternative investors, increasing competition for potential projects. Still, while the number of bidders may be up, only a handful of major investors will actually be able to operate in business sectors dependent on a small internal market, meaning that government rules and regulators must maintain adequate competition criteria for those operations.

Competition is probably the single most important element of a dynamic business environment that will lead investors to employ their resources efficiently, generating a distribution of economic benefits for the host society. If a government determines that certain types of benefits are more essential than others at a particular time, it may choose to alter policy regulations to favor job creation, export promotion, or other specific goals and objectives. Nevertheless, the maintenance of a competitive business environment must be a priority task for a host government. Chile has sustained one of the most competitive environments in the developing world and benefitted accordingly from the resources mobilized by business investors to battle their rivals, both foreign and domestic.

A companion requirement to appropriate public policy is competent administration. Chile has built a reputation among foreign managers as a country with highly professional government regulators, essentially untainted by occurrences of corruption that are far too common in many developing countries. The foreign investment rules are transparent and the regulatory approval process is administered in a timely and straight forward fashion. The Chapter XIX program involved a more cumbersome and lengthy application and follow-up procedure, resulting in some rules infractions, both purposeful and unintended. The procedure also sparked complaints that supporters and former members of the Pinochet government may have received favorable treatment, but no charges of serious legal violations had yet emerged well over a year into an investigation launched by the Aylwin administration.

Chile's economic and political restructuring in the mid-1970s shifted the nation from being a leading critic of MNCs to actively encouraging new foreign investment. The country's subsequent experience demonstrates that a welcoming political attitude, even when coupled with reasonable investment rules, is not necessarily enough to stimulate a substantial infusion of new foreign capital. Although Chile negotiated some successful demonstration cases in the late 1970s, most foreign investors waited and watched until the mid-1980s. By then, Chile's financial policy reforms had created a more solid basis for sustained economic growth, and political improvements were underway, even though full democratization was not yet assured. A major inflow of foreign investment occurred at the end of the decade as the democratic transition took hold and the new government's support for existing basic economic principles was affirmed. These results reinforce the view that foreign investment strategies and specific investment decisions depend on many aspects of a restructuring economy's climate in addition to the critical rules and revenue regulations that directly govern foreign investment issues.

BUSINESS AND SOCIETAL IMPACT

Foreign investors operating within a host country necessarily interact with and influence their surrounding society. Critics have charged that investors sometimes impose inappropriate cultural values on the host society, interfere in the nation's political process, and ally themselves with conservative local business groups to preserve the existing distribution of economic power and privileges. Such criticisms may influence the development of political attitudes toward foreign investment in restructuring economies. Chile's experience provides a relevant contemporary test for the validity of these charges.

The major human costs of societal transformation in Chile emerged during the military government's enforced shift from a statist to a free market economy, coming on top of the economic and social disruption suffered during the Allende years. This changeover predated most significant foreign investment, which responded to the altered economic circumstances in a lagged fashion rather than serving as causal agents of the change. Foreign investor influence is more evident in the internationalization process that developed a decade later and with new products and process applications that have altered specific aspects of Chilean life.

The most obvious foreign influence comes from products and systems introduced from developed country economies. Some innovations provide unquestioned aid, such as satellite communications and mobile telephones that link remote mine locations with metropolitan areas, or the personal computers that speed records processing and enhance customer service among Chile's highly competitive commercial banks. Other more-debated impacts emerge at the mass retailing level. Opinions differ over the home video rental franchises, gas station convenience stores, do-it-yourself lumber yards, automatic cash machines, and shopping mall complexes that have caught on rapidly, particularly around metropolitan Santiago.

Advertising is increasingly patterned after techniques and actual campaigns employed in more developed countries. Some critics question whether Chile's welfare really improved because of the foreign investment that marked Pepsi-Cola's reentry to the country, extending the battlefield for the cola wars to the far tip of South America. The regional head for Pepsi-Cola's Andean division boasted that a principal effect of Pepsi's return to Chile was an increase in per capita consumption of soft drinks from 32 liters in 1987 to 60 liters in 1990, second only to Mexico in the Latin American area. He also pointed to the success of marketing campaigns that included bringing musicians such as Rod Stewart, Bon Jovi, and Cindy Lauper to Chile for the first time.[8] A second example of debated impact arose when Avon introduced direct selling into the streets of Santiago neighborhoods. This action created thousands of new part-time jobs with flexible hours for lower- to middle-class homemakers but in the process engendered questions about promoting greater expenditures in poorer neighborhoods on personal care products and jewelry.

These types of concerns do not arise as uniquely from foreign investment as in the past, however. Ideas are transmitted quickly around the world today, flowing more rapidly than products and certainly faster than the process of direct investment. This reality means that the cultural impact of many foreign ideas and innovations will arrive, for better or worse, in advance of the foreign investors.

For example, McDonalds did not open its first store in Chile until 1990 (just in time to demonstrate its powerful symbolic identification with foreign influence by attracting terrorist bomb threats protesting U.S. President George Bush's visit to the country). In terms of cultural impact, the company arrived relatively late, trailing the establishment of various local fast-food burger outlets that were already mounting a challenge to traditional alternative foods such as the *lomito* and *churasco*. The idea traveled much faster than the foreign investment in this case. Chilean entrepreneurs also capture retailing ideas and reexport them through their own MNC mechanisms, as with the establishment of Chilean-owned Jumbo supermarkets in neighboring countries.[9] To debate the limitation of foreign product influences in Chile or in other restructuring economies is an exercise in futility unless the countries attempt to isolate themselves from the global economy.

Specific societal impacts from foreign investment may stem less from products than from processes, however. Operating within a domestic business environment, foreign subsidiaries and joint venture arrangements can introduce new production attitudes and methods that alter the society as surely as, and perhaps more fundamentally than, more obvious consumption-based changes. These effects involve the relationship between foreign investors and the local business community, including how such investment influences traditional business structures.

The historical alliance of interests in Chile between conservative local businesses and foreign investors broke apart as early as the Alessandri administration. A relatively small number of powerful family groups controlled major interconnected parts of the Chilean business community and had relatively few tie-ins to foreign corporations. The 1982–83 recession destroyed several business groups and set the stage for acquisitions of financially weakened enterprises, leading to a greater foreign investor presence in activities traditionally dominated by local groups. In a few cases investors forged joint ventures with remaining large domestic companies, but more often the foreign firms operated on their own or negotiated arrangements with relatively new entrepreneurs in the Chilean business community.

The impact of increased foreign investment on the Chilean business community is evident in both new applied processes and gradual system adjustments. Advanced financial analysis techniques migrated from foreign enterprises to local institutions, as did the companion use of computer and data processing operations. Similar changes are occurring in labor relations. Foreign mining projects pioneered new work rule structures and the increasing use of professional personnel managers will eventually alter labor relations practices in large industrial enterprises throughout the country.

Even more far-reaching changes will likely result from the steady revolution taking place in Chile's capital markets. Building on the impact from the country's privatized pension system, foreign investors are helping to make Chile's stocks and bonds markets an increasingly attractive option for corporate financing needs. The cases where Bankers Trust and the IFC helped take corporations public illustrate this role in expanding the size and quality of corporate shares available to private investors, both domestic and foreign. Traditional banks represented around 70 percent of Chile's financial system in 1987, but this role declined to under 50 percent in 1990, as corporate bond issues began to replace bank credits as a device for financing business expansion.[10]

These developments have several important implications. In placing issues on a public exchange, firms must disclose more information than is traditional in a business community dominated by closely controlled family groups. Increased public shareholdings will also give more of the general public an opportunity to gain a real stake in private business, either directly or through intermediary pension and insurance fund investments. Entrepreneurs with new ideas will also gain better access to financing on the exchanges or through commercial banks that are not tied so tightly to existing industrial groups.

True venture capital funds for small businesspeople will take longer to develop, probably requiring further assistance from multilateral development institutions. However, these changes will contribute to broadening the base of the Chilean business community, altering the manner in which private investment decisions are made. Rather than forming an exclusive alliance with a small number of existing business elites to maintain the status quo, foreign investors have introduced a new dynamism into the local business structure, helping to open financial opportunities for a wider segment of the population.

The lack of democratic accountability through the 1980s makes it difficult to assess Chile's public policy process, but there is no substantial evidence that foreign investors exerted undue or even significant influence on the government. Several companies played a role in refining the foreign investment rules during preliminary discussions and then through formal negotiations with government authorities. However, one could equally well infer from the privatization process that domestic business interests were favored over foreign investors. The first round of state enterprise sales in the late 1970s was dominated by domestic buyers. Foreign investors were essentially brought in only after the recession had claimed many local companies, including some recent purchasers of privatized assets. Foreign banks pressed their interests aggressively with the government in official debt restructuring, but this process was settled amicably in negotiations among the Chilean government, the creditor banks, and the International Monetary Fund (which also pressured the banks to negotiate a satisfactory arrangement).

Foreign investors are sometimes portrayed as staunch allies of repressive regimes that offer a stable and conservative pro-business climate. Contrary to this portrait, most foreign investors in Chile appeared to maintain a legally correct but politically uncommitted stance toward the military regime. In this sense, the corporations did what they are urged to do by many diplomatic officials in United Nations bodies who call on MNCs to practice noninterference in the political affairs of host nations. Without established channels for democratically approved types of participation, the companies essentially restricted their actions to project-specific negotiations. The strained relations existing between the Pinochet regime and many home country governments, as well as protests stemming from certain institutional investor groups in some developed countries, undoubtedly contributed to the investors' desire to maintain a low political profile in their dealings with the Chilean government.

The two most controversial recent examples of foreign investor lobbying are connected with revision of the fishing and patent laws. These issues began during the Pinochet government and carried over into the Aylwin administration. This transition led to a change from narrowly directed representations to the relevant government ministers to a broader lobbying campaign that included political parties and members of the newly elected Congress. Fishing and pharmaceutical firms worked both individually and through their sectoral associations. Other foreign investors expressed support for the principles of national treatment and effective intellectual property rights protection, but took no active part in the lobbying process.

The transition to democracy may increase investor involvement in the public policy process. After nearly seventeen years without public interplay among private interest groups in a representative legislature, a whole generation of public and private sector leaders needs to be trained in the rules of the democratic game. One response by the Chilean-American Chamber of Commerce to the democratic transition was to sponsor a seminar on the lobbying process. The discussion focused on the appropriate objectives, procedures, and role of private lobbying in the legislative process. Providing useful and timely information to elected officials can aid their deliberations on public policy issues. This form of political participation is generally accepted as a legitimate activity for foreign investors as well as domestic enterprises and, when properly construed and carried out, does not constitute interference in a nation's internal affairs.

Finally, U.S. investors in Chile have also given strong support to the Enterprise for the Americas Initiative and to Chilean-U.S. economic relations, including Chile's call for discussion of a Free Trade Agreement with the United States.[11] In mid-1991, a cooperation agreement was announced between the

Chilean-American Chamber of Commerce and the Confederación de la Producción y del Comercio, the two most important business organizations in this bilateral relationship. The groups formed a joint office to represent private sector interests in the anticipated free trade negotiations. These investors and importers in the United States constitute two important U.S. political constituencies with a self-interest in maintaining and promoting good Chilean-U.S. relations.

Chile's recent experience with foreign investment thus offers little support for concerns over past criticisms about foreign investor actions. Little evidence exists of undue involvement in domestic politics and available indicators suggest that foreign investment may serve to diminish rather than increase the influence of traditionally dominant business groups. Foreign investment does appear to speed social and cultural change, but judgements on appropriateness or the potential for avoiding altered values depend on subjective interpretations that are not easily generalizable. More broadly, challenges to traditional societal values will inevitably arise from the increasingly interdependent ties between nations. These ties, only partly due to business activities, are not dependent on foreign direct investment for their transmission. Restructuring economies already experiencing major societal changes need not view foreign investment as uniquely threatening to national values.

GLOBAL CORPORATIONS AND LOCAL OPERATIONS

Over the quarter century since MNCs burst onto the world stage as a recognized phenomenon, their organizational structures have evolved while their numbers multiplied. The simple image of a parent company directing wholly owned foreign subsidiaries gave way to a panoply of arrangements among enterprises and over time within the same corporation. These evolving corporate networks result in both opportunities and costs for the investor and the host country alike. Investment strategies must consider how local operations can fit best within constantly evolving global priorities, especially where a venture represents a relatively small investment for the parent enterprise.

Global corporate structures influenced the strategies pursued by subsidiary operations in Chile, whose small size and sometimes ancillary role within the company made these investments incidental to decisions on broad business strategy. This secondary or even marginal role can become an asset for both the parent and subsidiary if administrative structures permit decentralized experiments and adaptation. Some investors used Chile as a valuable testing ground for business innovations. The economy is small enough to provide quick and visible feedback from a controlled initiative, yet dynamic and competitive enough to permit a good test of a new product or marketing concept.

The investors taking best advantage of this opportunity for local innovation exhibited a relatively decentralized organizational structure with locally experienced managers in charge of Chilean operations. The critical element of centralized direction was how financial control was exercised over local decision-making. Smaller subsidiaries whose revenue flow was not critical to parent income had greater flexibility. Established units generating sufficient local profit to fund a new project gained approval for their proposals more easily than subsidiaries requiring a new capital infusion from headquarters.

Most innovations emerged from a recognition of opportunity by local executives rather than as a consciously directed strategy of corporate headquarters. Chilean managers with a good understanding of the product line and strong credibility with regional or headquarters management were most likely to discern and pursue new opportunities. Expatriate managers on standard rotation through an overseas subsidiary usually lacked the experience, perception, and perhaps motivation to engage in a somewhat risky experiment in a foreign environment. This weakness was sometimes overcome by foreign executives who had an extended assignment in Chile or returned for a second tour.

Electromat's innovations enhanced local operations and proved unexpectedly valuable to its GE parent as well as to subsidiary units elsewhere. Cemento Melón used a combination of British and local executive experience to explore lines of business (such as ready-mix concrete) not pursued by parent Blue Circle in the United Kingdom as well as to extend into complementary wood products where Chile has a comparative advantage. In both cases the reinvestment of local profits from ongoing operations was critical to the new project's success.

Bankers Trust's experimental venture in pension fund management showed similar characteristics. Debt conversion gave the enterprise a ready base of local investment capital while the unprecedented financial crisis increased the bank's willingness to consider novel undertakings. This innovation is paying off handsomely for the bank in Chile while providing experience for a potentially important new line of business in other countries. Citibank's citicenter model and the insurance joint venture between Santander and Kemper reflect more conscious decisions to use the Chilean economy as a testing ground for new products and relationships. Avon's local unit is similarly experimenting with a new marketing concept, utilizing separate sales forces for their cosmetics and jewelry product lines.

Some subsidiaries have been unusually successful in arguing their case for local flexibility, gaining approval for projects that could affect broader corporate interests. Schering-Plough's local unit opened a generic line of unpatented drugs that was not permitted to subsidiaries in other countries. Kodak's Chilean unit convinced headquarters management to lend corporate backing to its finished furniture venture, even though the undertaking lay far outside past corporate experience and carried some risk to the company's valuable reputation. Although these two cases appear at the extreme of organizational flexibility and responsiveness, their existence demonstrates the diversity in international investor administrative controls and the potential latitude for local investment strategies.

Chile's recent experience also yields numerous examples of important structural changes and reorganizations of investments that result from global strategy adjustments by the parent corporation. Neither local personnel nor Chilean authorities could affect most decisions to reduce or sell subsidiary investments, often learning about them after the fact. By maintaining general policy stability, however, the government encouraged new corporations to replace the original investors. This process did not always work quickly and easily, but in most cases the results proved satisfactory and often actually improved the investment's prospects for success.

For example, the Bond Group's withdrawal from Chile was dictated by overriding financial pressures on the parent enterprise. The excellent prospects for the group's Chilean investments attracted other potential investors, making those assets prime candidates for early sale. Both CTC and El Indio appear to be at least as well off, if not better positioned for sustained future growth, under their new owners. Another case of altered corporate strategy arises from AMAX's decision to seek a buyer for its majority stake in the Minsal project. This change stemmed from a strategic corporate decision to concentrate resources in fewer industrial sectors, primarily to finance an expansion in aluminum production.

Mergers and acquisitions among international firms also affect investments in Chile that are not a significant part of the main transaction. In the financial community, Midland's acquisition of Crocker Bank brought an accompanying heavy debt portfolio that drew Midland deeply into Chilean operations long after it had resold the major Crocker assets. Hongkong Bank similarly gained Chilean debt interests from its takeover of Marine Midland. Recent mergers between Bank of America and Security Pacific, and Chemical Bank and Manufacturers Hanover, will bring a restructuring and consolidation of those banks' presence in the Chilean economy.

Occidental gained the Petroquímica Chilena plant when it acquired Diamond Shamrock's worldwide chemical interests. In this case Occidental essentially continued the operation as a stand-alone enterprise without important changes.[12] The merger between Allied and Signal did not affect the Cape Horn Methanol project which ultimately shifted with its executive sponsors to the spinoff Henley Group. While the commitment of first Signal and then The Henley Group was instrumental in getting this project launched, Cape Horn Methanol may have found a better long-term home following its purchase by Fletcher Challenge. The Chilean investment has become more central to the new parent firm's business, expanding its capabilities and making it a major force in the world methanol market.

These examples illustrate that local operations always face potential changes, at times quite unexpected, from the foreign investor's evolving priorities, including restructuring that occurs among global firms in a given business sector.   Decisions may be quite unrelated to the profitability or other performance measures of a particular subsidiary, especially smaller operations considered less central to an investor's main line of business. These facts of global business life lie essentially beyond the power of host governments to affect without taking exceptional steps that may jeopardize the stability of a general investment regime.   Despite this apparent constraint on effective sovereign power, early evidence from recent reshufflings among the foreign investment community does not suggest any necessary detriment to the restructuring of Chile's economy.   Within a stable investment framework, transfers in investor ownership under the direction of market forces can reallocate productive resources, often to the ultimate benefit of the local project and the host economy.

A final added twist to Chile's relationship with foreign investment structures is the transition of some Chilean enterprises to foreign operations. CTC's direct entry onto the New York Stock Exchange raises policy issues qualitatively different from those raised by the dispersed holdings of foreign investment funds on Santiago's own stock market. ENAP, SONDA, CMPC, and others are extending their operations and investments into neighboring economies, looking to garner new resources and expand markets to complement strong positions at home. The overseas CODELCO/MADECO joint ventures in copper product manufacture presage likely developments by more companies in search of enhanced experience, technology, and market knowledge available only through a direct business presence in other countries.

NOTES

1. For a treatment of the European reaction to U.S. foreign direct investment in the 1960s, see Jean-Jacques Servan-Schreiber, *The American Challenge* (New York: Atheneum, 1968). A discussion of the U.S. government reaction to Mitsubishi's purchase of a controlling interest in Rockefeller Center may be found in "Buy America While Stocks Last," *Economist* (December 16, 1989).

2. United Nations Centre on Transnational Corporations (UNCTC), *The New Code Environment*, series A, no. 16 (New York: United Nations, April 1990); UNCTC, *Transnational Corporations in World Development: Trends and Prospects*, New York: United Nations, 1988; and John Kline, "Trade Competitiveness and Corporate Nationality," *The Columbia Journal of World Business*, vol. 24, no. 3 (Fall 1989).

3. These findings are consistent but extend somewhat the conclusions reached by Louis Goodman in *Small Nations, Giant Firms* (New York: Holmes and Meier, 1987). His work emphasized the importance of minimizing the time headquarters senior management would spend on proposed projects in a marginal developing country. He

also pointed to the use of MNC financial approvals as the primary channel to exercise centralized control. This study found that a decentralized management structure minimizes headquarters attention to marginal operations, and projects that involved reinvested earnings from existing enterprises passed through MNC financial control channels more easily than the requests for new capital transfers or further debt obligations usually needed to establish a subsidiary in a host country.

4. A conversation with Louis Goodman revealed that this nearly universal attraction to Chile's work and living conditions stood in sharp contrast to attitudes expressed by foreign executives he interviewed in the 1973–74 period. The differing results are probably attributable to the calmer social and political environment in Chile in 1990, including a more positive attitude toward private business and foreign investment as well as the business sector's dynamism, which created opportunities for experimentation and growth.

5. "Manuel Bustos, CUT President: 'We're not Against any Company, Just the Labor Legislation Currently in Effect'," *Journal of the Chilean-American Chamber of Commerce* (September 1990), 9.

6. "Manuel Feliú, President of Confederación de la Producción y del Comercio: 'Conditions in Large Companies Are Better than Those of Smaller Ones'," *Journal of the Chilean-American Chamber of Commerce* (September 1990), 8, 10.

7. Carlos Castilho, "Los negocios se ponen verdes," *América Economía* (July 1991), 51.

8. "En América Latina: Chile, Segundo Consumidor Per Capita de Gaseosas," *El Mercurio*, August 27, 1990.

9. Various examples of this development are contained in Joaquín Lavín and Luis Larraín, *Chile: Sociedad Emergente* (Santiago: Zig-Zag, 1989); and Joaquín Lavín, *Chile: Revolución Silenciosa* (Santiago: Zig-Zag, 1987).

10. "Los bancos: ¿Los buenos, los malos, los feos?" *El Mercurio*, September 8, 1991.

11. "Enterprise for the Americas Initiative: Chile Should be a Foundation Member," *Journal of the Chilean-American Chamber of Commerce* (October 1990); "Fast Track on Track—What Next?" *Journal of the Chilean-American Chamber of Commerce* (June 1991), 5; and "Chamber President Ed Tillman: 'Free Trade Requires a Lot More Than the Removal of Tariffs'," *Journal of the Chilean-American Chamber of Commerce* (June 1991), 6-9.

12. A major corporate restructuring of Occidental itself may yet bring changes in the wake of the December 1990 death of the corporation's longtime head, Armand Hammer.

8

Conclusion

Chile has undergone a dramatic economic and political restructuring since the 1970s. While not a determinative factor, foreign investment played an important role in this process, expanding local production and linking the country to foreign markets and economic resources. This chapter will first consider near-term projections for investor relations with Chile, at least through the turn of the century. A few broad conclusions are then offered summarizing how Chile's experience can be instructive for developing foreign investment strategies in other nations undergoing a similar restructuring process. Finally, research results are used to suggest several modifications to concepts and theories regarding foreign investment in host developing countries.

THE FOREIGN INVESTMENT OUTLOOK IN CHILE

Gauging the outlook for foreign investors in Chile requires assessing recent developments in their historical context as well as in relation to the specific challenges confronting Chile in the 1990s. Foreign direct investment is an ongoing process. An initial investment decision simply opens the door to a series of business choices and operational actions that determine an investor's role in the host economy. Similarly, Chile's attractiveness as an investment site will continue to evolve, both in its internal environment and in comparison to possible alternative investment locations. Physical, economic, and public policy barriers still exist that could retard current investor expansion and slow new interest unless corrective action is taken.

Chile's advantage going into the 1990s is the partnership it has developed with the foreign investment community. Past visions of national hostility and instability have all but faded from investors' minds, replaced by a confidence built on the experience of working through general policy and investment-specific issues in a mutually satisfactory and beneficial manner. This working partnership should be able to address remaining problems and foreseeable new issues in a similar fashion as long as general policy stability is maintained and foreign investors engage in responsive and responsible competition within that policy framework.

Chile's solid reputation among international investors was reflected in a report card on country investment risk published in *The Wall Street Journal* on September 20, 1991. Drawing on ratings from the Economist Intelligence Unit (EIU) and the International Country Risk Guide (ICRG), the article concluded that "Chile is rated one of Latin America's least-risky bets." The ICRG ranked Chile just slightly behind Venezuela and Mexico on a composite score including judgments on political, financial, and economic risk. The EIU placed Chile near the top of its B rated category and the article reports that Chile "may soon be the only Latin country in the A, or least-risk, group."[1]

Discussions of risk measures highlight potential negative aspects of investing abroad. An editorial in the *Journal of the Chilean-American Chamber of Commerce* in August 1991 expressed similar conclusions regarding investment in Chile but phrased them in a more positive fashion in its lead paragraph.

> Any doubts that might have existed at the inception of the Aylwin administration in connection with the political will of maintaining Chile as an attractive place for foreign investment should by this time be totally dispelled. Chile continues to be a leading country in the world to attract foreign investment due to its political stability, high quality of the relevant governmental authorities, absence of corruption, non-discrimination against foreigners and a growing consensus as to the maintenance of an open-market economy.[2]

The editorial went on to endorse the fundamental stability of the D.L. 600 foreign investment statute while noting several positive modifications that allowed offshore escrow accounts and jurisdictional coverage of certain loan agreements by non-Chilean courts.

The immediate stimulus for this Amcham editorial was the Central Bank's response to strong foreign investor criticism of a new reserve requirement, leading to creation of a mechanism to purchase and resell Central Bank notes in ways that helped minimize negative effects on large investment projects. The reserve requirement was instituted largely to discourage the inflow of speculative foreign capital, attracted by Chile's economic success, which was causing an appreciation of the peso. The government did not want to discourage long-term investors or harm the country's reputation for investment policy stability, but along with lowering the uniform tariff rate from 15 percent to 11 percent, the reserve requirement was needed to help restrain inflationary pressures.

The Amcham opposed the reserve requirement but, with the Central Bank's modification in hand, expressed confidence that it would be lifted as soon as possible. As in the earlier controversy over the revised fishing law and national treatment guarantees, the government and the foreign investment community recognized mutual long-term interests and resolved the issue in a manner that maintained past commitments while addressing immediate needs.

Chilean authorities still confront a series of policy questions that will help affect foreign investor reactions during the current decade. As the worldwide battle for scarce investment capital heats up, many countries in Latin America and elsewhere are adopting measures to attract foreign investment that surpass Chile's early precedent-setting law. Further modifications in Chilean regulations have been urged to maintain the country's competitive position vis-à-vis other investment sites. In January 1992 the government announced a proposal to reduce the time restriction on capital repatriation from three years to one and lower the guaranteed 49.5 percent tax rate to 42 percent.

These two changes might marginally improve the attractiveness of Chile's investment climate but are probably less important than maintenance of the statute's overall stability and the government's demonstrated willingness to work with the foreign investment community to address practical implementation problems that arise from new policy measures or particular project needs. Large investments, especially in mining and forestry, operate with expected long periods of return that will be relatively unaffected by a reduction in repatriation restrictions on invested capital. The shorter time horizon could be more attractive to certain smaller manufacturing or service projects, but a partially offsetting danger is that the inflow of speculative capital might also be increased, a problem that Chile already confronted in 1991.

Lowering the guaranteed tax rate could improve Chile's comparative attractiveness for long-term investment, but the immediate importance of this measure is questionable. The tax rate guarantee appears most effective when investor confidence in a country's political and economic stability falls in a middle range. In a highly uncertain climate, investors may doubt that even a state-guaranteed tax rate will be respected under possible scenarios of political change. On the other hand, during a period of general investor confidence in a nation, the value of a guaranteed rate at any level much higher than the prevailing norm is going to be minimal, as demonstrated by the dominant choice among investors to opt out of Chile's rate guarantee plan as soon as their operations turned profitable.

The D.L. 600 tax provision was certainly more influential in investment decisions during the late 1970s than it is in the 1990s. As long as other conditions remain favorable, reducing the guaranteed rate is unlikely to produce significant results unless the reduction nearly eliminates the spread between the prevailing and the guaranteed rate, essentially offering a cheap tax insurance policy. The 42 percent rate would roughly halve the difference. Ironically, if

Chile's investment climate were to turn more threatening (but not too much), the tax rate guarantee would again become a more influential factor. Under current conditions, successful negotiation of bilateral tax treaties with major investor countries may be a more important priority for Chile. In addition, future decisions on a whole range of normal business taxes that affect both foreign and domestic firms will probably have a greater impact on how investors view Chile's general business climate than the foreign investment-specific effects of changing the guaranteed tax rate.

The reduction of Chile's restructurable foreign commercial debt has essentially removed the Chapter XIX debt conversion program from the list of issues that frame the country's foreign investment climate. The program's demise is convincing proof of its success although continued follow-up monitoring of approvals already granted is essential to assure that agreed investment conditions are met. Developments in labor relations are less directly connected to foreign investment policy but will nonetheless affect foreign investor decisions. Chile's new democratic government enacted essential labor reforms that were carefully balanced in their economic and political impact. Long denied fundamental workers' rights, Chile's organized labor movement reacted responsibly to its regained powers, seeking needed wage improvements without pressing excessive demands or resorting to disruptive activities that might undermine the economy's growth. Continued real wage improvements are needed but must be combined with productivity gains in order not to damage the competitiveness of Chilean business in an open economy. While wage increases are the clearest indicator of labor gains, other benefits should also be fully recognized and valued, including improvements in safety and training opportunities.

Foreign investor wage rates will remain somewhat above the national average and should not be pushed so far ahead of the local norm as to distort the labor market by preemptively drawing all the best workers. Safety and training programs implemented by most foreign investors carry less distortionary potential and can help foster further improvements among local businesses. The pattern for business-labor interaction will be set more by domestic social and political elements than by the actions or decisions of foreign investors. All involved parties must help maintain appropriate bargaining relationships, recognizing legitimate organized labor rights and tactics while avoiding the violence and politicization associated with past eras. This challenge will be one of the most difficult for Chile to sustain in the coming years, resting largely on a new generation of tripartite leaders in the labor, business, and political communities.

Environmental and competition policy are two other areas where foreign investors seek clarifications and predictability. Chilean economic progress overtook past regulatory standards and confronted the society with new choices among competing priorities. The need for a modernization of environmental laws is most evident. The absence of clear standards delayed significant investments involving native forests while insufficient standards and enforcement procedures in mining and related processing activities have already caused a deterioration of air, land, and water quality in several areas of the country.

Most large foreign investment projects follow environmental practices clearly above local regulations, despite increased cost requirements, consistent with global corporate policy. These firms anticipate a modernization of environmental policy that would bring Chilean practices more in line with advanced international standards. The Aylwin administration is moving ahead with an environmental commission on legal reforms. Progress will be easiest with areas such as the native forests that set prospective standards as opposed to mining regulations that imply significant corrective and rehabilitative expenditures that may fall most heavily on state-run enterprises.

Competition policy has been relatively successful in the past but is also under pressure from Chile's rapid economic modernization. The size of many foreign investments and the market share needed to sustain certain operations make competition policy a key element in shaping future investor relations. Permissible market shares may have to be quite large in some sectors to achieve necessary economies of scale in a relatively small economy. Open import and investment policies help sustain competitive discipline, but effective regulatory monitoring and enforcement will remain essential. Periodic review and revision of sector-specific competition standards and goals is advisable. The communications and transportation sectors have already been identified as requiring early attention due to the impact of recent technological change and evolving societal needs.

Physical as well as policy bottlenecks threaten future growth in certain economic sectors, particularly those associated with the expansion of nontraditional exports. Transportation links are vital. Roads, railways and port facilities are already strained in some locales and face still increasing demands from projected output growth, especially in forestry. Electrical energy and water and sewerage facilities also require further expansion and modernization to avoid infrastructure bottlenecks to future development. Policy reforms are underway to open some of these areas to increased participation by private investors, both foreign and domestic.

A critical policy issue for Chile and for other restructuring economies is how the nation's leadership manages the objective of seeking greater value added from foreign investment activities. This goal is becoming an ever more popular theme in the Chilean political community. To the extent that the objective is pursued through voluntary studies and limited local assistance programs, investor relations will not be negatively affected. If pressures rise on foreign investors to meet specific pre-selected and government-determined measures of increasing value added, market forces will lose their ability to direct and enhance Chile's competitiveness on international markets.

An important tenet of Chile's foreign investment strategy was to encourage local value added without becoming too specific or directive regarding particular projects. For example, the Celpac and Santa Fe ventures helped introduce short-fibre cellulose technology based on eucalyptus wood resources, opening up a new field of forestry development for Chile. Foreign investors contributed capital, technology, management, and marketing assistance to these projects. Chilean authorities did not attempt to force local production of paper as well, which occurs closer to consuming markets that can sustain economies of scale across a full product line. More sensibly, ProChile and Fundación Chile are providing some technological and marketing assistance for forestry activities such as furniture manufacture for export and housing construction for the domestic market.

A similar situation arises in minerals processing, specifically with regard to the proposal to build a new copper refinery complex. Escondida endured strong criticism during its development stage for selling future output through forward contracts to overseas refineries. If Chilean policy had forced Escondida to use existing Chilean refineries or help build a new one, financing for the entire project would have collapsed. The political attractiveness of more local value-added processing from Chile's growing mineral output is undeniable, but the economic feasibility is not always so apparent.

Outside the natural resource area, if Chile had attempted to force local production of computers through performance requirements or protection guarantees, it would have failed. By allowing easy importation of advanced computer equipment produced elsewhere, the Chilean economy has discovered new competitive advantages in software development, data processing, and enhanced financial services that would never have developed locally without access to state-of-the-art foreign computers. The basic argument is that Chile and other restructuring economies should encourage, but not strictly specify, greater value-added activities as part of their foreign investment strategy.

Local joint ventures can increase the capability and competence of national enterprises while limiting the foreign investor's capital and other resource commitments to a given project. This concept should include the reverse notion of joint ventures outside the country where Chilean enterprises can learn new approaches and foreign market responses that can enhance production and marketing activities back home. One policy improvement for Chile would be a specific law governing the incorporation of joint ventures, both to regularize this increasingly frequent form of corporate activity and to stimulate broader local familiarity with such working relationships.

Developments in Chile's capital markets will also shape future foreign investment trends while influencing the structure and activities of the local business community. Chile's privatization program and foreign investment policy were important stimulants to the dynamic growth and increasing sophistication of its capital markets. Privatized pension funds and other institutional investors (including nine foreign investment funds) have given the nation's stock market a breadth, depth, and longer-term perspective that differs radically from the small and speculatively volatile stock exchange that previously existed. One source ranked Chile as the most attractive location for stock investments over the past fifteen years, yielding a combined annual return of approximately 30 percent.[3] A number of Chile's family groups have already chosen to sell stock in various related enterprises, undertaking the accompanying changes and commitments implied by financial and other information disclosure requirements necessary for publicly listed corporations. These actions will alter many historical notions regarding ownership, control, asset concentration, and other tenets of Chile's traditional private business sector.[4]

This process is far from complete in either the stock market, which is increasingly tied to foreign stock exchanges, or in other elements of Chile's financial markets. Venture capital funds are lacking to assist new local entrepreneurs and many medium-size businesses do not yet have sufficient access to longer-term capital. Key national banks remain heavily indebted to the Central Bank which carries their bad debt portfolios at a significant public cost. The banking sector will likely undergo a restructuring and probably a downsizing. Regulations on various financial sector participants will require periodic revision, including an adjustment of restrictions on pension fund investments and the redefinition of appropriate activities for pension fund managers, insurance companies, and banking institutions. Despite this seemingly full agenda of needed changes, the reality is that most of them stem directly from the very dynamism of Chile's capital markets—a result of the significant achievements already attained.

Chile's general internationalization policy helps attract foreign investors and leads them to employ their resources most efficiently. The GATT declared Chile one of the most open economies in the world. Its uniform tariff is down to 11 percent. Further staged reductions with selected countries are set to occur through mechanisms such as the recent trade accord with Mexico. Few nontariff measures or incentive programs exist to distort trade and investment flows. Chile thus stands as a near-model for a free and open market economy. The country's total trade in goods and services now amounts to nearly three-quarters of national output, a figure superior to Japan's and roughly comparable to South Korea's.[5]

The key challenges to maintaining Chile's open international access over the current decade will likely come in the negotiation and balancing of bilateral, regional, and multilateral accords. Bilateral trade agreements with hemispheric neighbors and the United States, as well as investment and taxation treaties with principal investor countries, will be important stepping stones to solidifying market access for Chile's vital export sectors and establishing clear framework rules to facilitate new investment flows. Regional agreements are perhaps more politically than economically desirable at this time given the continuing disparity and volatility of economic reforms in many hemispheric nations. Chile will also be challenged in multilateral forums such as the GATT to assume a more prominent role befitting its economic success and stake in the international trading system. As more of Chile's own companies increase their foreign ties, including through equity investments and joint ventures, the nation will need to broaden further its own global vision.

Finally, lest this projection suggest too far-flung a policy agenda, the most basic challenge of all will still be at home—to consolidate the country's democratic transition and move forward with its social progress in meeting pressing human needs. The achievement of both these objectives will be a critical ingredient to continuing Chile's recent success story in attracting investment. Foreign investors can assist in attaining these goals through their contribution to national economic growth and competitiveness. Nevertheless, the hard work of political accommodation and social progress will depend fundamentally on the Chilean people who must use their regained liberties in a manner that binds social divisions and lifts the poorer segments of the population. Stability is highly valued by foreign investors, but this does not mean a static or highly conservative society. Real stability requires progress in order to open new economic and social opportunities that sow hope and raise aspirations for improvement throughout the society. This is Chile's challenge through the turn of the century, and the nation is poised to realize its ambitions, both internally and externally.

COUNTRIES IN ECONOMIC AND POLITICAL TRANSITION

Having ventured a projection on continued foreign investment in Chile, the next task is to consider the degree to which Chile can serve as a model for other countries facing economic and political transition. The tremendous number of inherent variables among different country situations makes any discussion of models suspect except at a very general level. Nevertheless, Chile's experience does contain useful insights on foreign investment strategies that could be adjusted to address other unique national circumstances. The previous chapter assessed key strategic elements of corporate and government policies and outlined how government policies affect decisions by potential investors and what types of operations and impacts will likely result from foreign direct investment. This section offers a few conclusions broad enough to be generalizable to most countries facing economic and political transitions with challenges similar to the ones Chile has overcome.

The first obvious conclusion is that foreign investment policies cannot be viewed in isolation. Potential investors look not only at the pertinent foreign investment statute but also at the full policy context within which the corporation must operate. The country's complete package of external economic policies is relevant because MNC operations integrate trade and monetary elements as well as investment in structuring business dealings. One key to Chile's success is that its recent external macroeconomic policies coherently embrace an open economy approach which allows foreign investors to make the most efficient use of advantages deriving from their global reach and organization. Similarly, this external strategy was linked to a domestic shift in Chile from a statist philosophy to free market policies that increased the role of private business, corrected public deficits, and constrained chronic inflation.

The political context is also important to an investor's evaluation of a potential host location. Beyond political and social stability factors common to country risk assessments, the Chilean experience appears to show that democracy makes a difference. Despite attractive economic policies and growth prospects, foreign investors from some countries avoided Chile entirely or entered the country slowly only after democratic processes were reemerging. This behavior was most evident with investors from socialist-oriented European countries. In most cases legal prohibitions were not used to control the companies' actions. Investors appeared influenced by the lack of facilitative government programs and a sensitivity to political and societal attitudes in their home countries.

Obviously other investors did enter Chile during the military junta's rule. Democracy's difference is therefore not between foreign investment and no foreign investment, but rather in the level and diversity of potential foreign investors. The vast majority of foreign private investment is controlled by corporations headquartered in democratic nations. A functioning democratic process in a potential host country will facilitate a diplomatic context that encourages the broadest involvement and greatest competition among foreign investors for participation in a host country's economic opportunities.

Research conducted for this book cannot determine whether Chile's successful economic transition could have taken place without the dictatorial powers available to the military regime during the suspension of democratic procedures. The fundamental disruption to entrenched economic, political, and social patterns which occurred during the 1970s facilitated the wholesale reorientation in policies and attitudes that occurred, but whether or not similar changes could have been carried out by a democratic government is a topic for hypothetical speculation. (The author's personal opinion is that the deep disruption of societal patterns was a necessary precondition, but the repression and longevity of military rule were not essential.) The most persuasive arguments in this debate may develop from the outcome of experiments now underway in other countries attempting a similar radical reorientation under democratic rules. For these countries, this book's research offers no clear reason to cast doubt on their likely success.

Chile's experience does provide some clues regarding the relative importance of specific foreign investment policies. Among the elements showing the greatest positive influence on potential foreign investors were Chile's strong contractual guarantees from the state, a broad national treatment standard, few restricted areas for investment, immediate profit remission and relatively quick capital repatriation with effective access to foreign exchange, and possible offshore accounts for export earnings from major projects. The taxation rate guarantee was influential early in light of historical circumstances but has declined in importance. The decision to avoid using special investment incentives has not inhibited the nation's attractiveness for foreign investors and has aided the market-directed allocation of economic opportunities.

Generally beneficial effects from the Chapter XIX debt-swap program commend it for careful consideration in other countries, especially if combined with privatization actions that can help contain the program's inflationary potential. In addition to relieving some of the nation's debt repayment burden, the conversion process stimulated greater economic activity and drew in new nonbank foreign investors. Chile's conditional approval of debt-swap transactions required regulatory monitoring of investor implementation, revealing cases of both apparently inadvertent noncompliance and outright fraud. Opportunities for improper actions will occur under conditions of dynamic change in a restructuring economy, but Chile's experience suggests that these instances need not be numerous if appropriate caution is exercised. Competent regulatory supervision acts as both a deterrent and a remedy for such violations. High quality professionalism among regulatory officials throughout a host country's public structure is a key ingredient in devising a successful formula for economic development, including implementation of a foreign investment strategy.

Joint ventures arrangements traditionally favored by developing host countries seek to balance the benefits of foreign investment with a desire for local participation and control. In this area, Chile's experience points to the need for flexibility in terms of both corporate organization and the process of selecting potential partners. Most host developing countries with restructuring economies will share Chile's circumstances in having a limited number of experienced and attractive local enterprises available as potential joint venture partners, particularly if the economy is in the midst of a transition away from a statist regime and undergoing a broad privatization campaign. A clear legal and regulatory framework can facilitate joint venture formation within the host economy and in endeavors that reach outside its borders. However, national policy should give both local and foreign businesses room to adapt organizationally to the demands of an economy in transition. Joint venture arrangements are generally not permanent marriages and may require evolutionary or even revolutionary adjustments to accommodate the changing needs of the partners and of the project.

Finally, Chilean experience highlights the lagged response of business investment plans to fundamental changes in a nation's investment policy and climate. Some corporations are more entrepreneurial than others in their willingness to assume risk and break new ground in hope of reaping a greater reward. The broad international investment community appears more fundamentally conservative, however, preferring to watch how the pioneering investors fare in their negotiations and operations. This conclusion means that early demonstration cases will be important. A careful balance must be struck between the need for responsive refinements to initial policy in order to meet legitimate business concerns and the general requirement to maintain essential policy stability. Evidence of consistent implementation as well as good policy formulation is necessary to establish a solid reputation for a host country that lacks a proven track record among international investors—or worse, one that has earned the image of being an unreliable partner.

The good news from the Chilean experience is that even a very unfavorable past image can be overcome by good policy choices, consistent implementation, and time. Foreign direct investment is not a quick-fix salvation for countries with restructuring economies. But the development of a working partnership with foreign investors can produce significant, mutually beneficial results over a medium to longer-term period of perhaps three to eight years. This is the conclusion that makes the lessons worth learning.

REASSESSING FOREIGN INVESTMENT THEORIES

The research conducted for this book found limited relevance to many theories developed during the 1960s and 1970s regarding foreign investment in developing countries. Some of Chile's idiosyncrasies as an investment location may account for part of this result, although the country's prominent role in historical investment patterns indicates that it can serve as a valid referent point for theoretical applications. More likely is the hypothesis that Chile's recent experience lies at the forefront of several changes underway in the relationship between foreign investors and host developing countries that may lead to modifications in theoretical assumptions and applications.[6]

The book departs from many past analyses of development strategies and bargaining approaches between investors and host countries, including their implicit assumptions of continuing private property disputes and heavy statist intervention in the economy. In this respect, recent Chilean experience is not directly comparable to past research environments from which prevailing theory was drawn. However, the economic and political transformations now taking place in many developing countries may shape investor/host country relationships over the coming decade, bringing them closer to the pattern established in Chile.

The various iterations of *dependencia* theory find little support in current research results. Gone is the era when the MNC behemoths of Kennecott,

Anaconda, and ITT dominated the Chilean landscape. The number and diversity of foreign investors operating in Chile expanded markedly in the 1980s, bringing greater competition and choice to economic transactions. The United States is still clearly the major home country for foreign investment in Chile, but investors from many nations are now represented in a diversification amplified by improved diplomatic relations resulting from the democratic transition.

Dependency theorists predict few local benefits from foreign investment, a condition that does not apply in Chile. Foreign capital contributed between one-quarter to one-third of the investment that fueled Chile's economic growth and investor contributions to nontraditional export expansion helped build the nation's sustained trade surplus. Competition has been vigorous, stimulated partly by the country's open economy policies. With investor diversity and domestic economic growth have come opportunities for domestic enterprises to enter cooperative ventures with foreign firms, including arrangements that reach into the investor's home market or third country locations where the Chilean partner can gain valuable overseas experience. A number of important Chilean firms, several initially developed from MNC-related business activities, are themselves now becoming foreign investors.

So-called bargaining school theories also found scant support in this study, primarily because they rely heavily on assumptions of negotiations and renegotiations between a statist political system and a centrally directed MNC.[7] Chile no longer meets the traditional statist model and does not engage in project-specific bargaining except at the margins of a particular proposed investment. Most key investment rules are already clearly specified in the foreign investment statute, including special provisions that may be invoked for large mining or export-oriented projects. After negotiation of the first several demonstration cases that helped refine the regulations, the investment application process and approval procedure has been standardized and transparent. Investors with particular problems can raise them with the Foreign Investment Committee and seek clarifications or modifications to the regulations, but bargaining as envisaged in traditional theory does not occur except on relatively minor contract provisions.

Chile's policy decision not to offer special incentives to attract investment, and to maintain minimal disincentives or restrictions on investors, gives government authorities little to offer in a bargaining process that is not already generally available. Similarly, the theoretical concept of renegotiations does not match recent Chilean experience. Contract terms under the D.L. 600 foreign investment statute are guaranteed by the state of Chile and have been fully respected for the specified life of the contract. Renewed investment contracts are signed, and approval for expanded or diversified investments by established investors is given, through essentially the same review process used by a newly entering investor. The Chapter XIX debt-swap program did assume more the character of a bargaining process, especially toward its latter stages when the government tightened the qualifying criteria. Nevertheless, the process never reached the discretionary dimensions suggested in bargaining school literature and has now essentially ended as a significant channel for new investment.

Evidence on the investor side of the bargaining process is somewhat mixed regarding the basic assumptions of centrally directed corporate negotiations. This concept appears valid in cases of new entrants, but the behavior of existing subsidiaries shows greater variation regarding the extent of active headquarters direction in expansion or diversification projects. Main variables involve the management structure of the global organization; whether the subsidiary is managed by local nationals or experienced, long-term expatriates; and the extent to which local earnings can be used to finance new proposals. These observations suggest factors that merit further research regarding their effect on behavioral model assumptions.

Centrally directed or not, the foreign investor essentially lacked a governmental partner with which to bargain over investment terms and conditions. The hypothesized bargaining process in Chile was more likely to take place between potential joint venture partners. Occasionally the foreign investor's prospective partner might be a state agency, such as in the negotiation of special petroleum operating contracts (SPOCs), but the extensive privatization program reduced both the number and scope of such public enterprises. In most cases joint venture bargaining occurred with local private firms or with other foreign investors, thereby placing it outside the normal context of bargaining school theory. This experience suggests that application of this traditional theory may be limited in countries where the government adopts broadly liberal, standardized, and transparent investment regulations and implements a privatization program that severely reduces the size and scope of statist intervention in the economy.

If traditional dependency and bargaining school theories do not fit well with contemporary Chilean experience, an alternative approach is to examine extended firm behavior within the context of the country's new development policy. Chile's open market economic strategy essentially sets broad framework principles and rules, leaving the central role in most applied investment decisions up to the individual investors to determine in line with their evaluation of international competitive forces. An important aspect of this approach is the evolution of a well-coordinated macroeconomic policy that integrates investment, trade, and monetary concerns.

Chile's success in attracting foreign investment is not attributable solely to its investment regulations, but also to the liberal trade regime that allows investors to use efficiently their globally coordinated competitive advantages. Monetary policy must also be right. The major inflow of long-term productive investment did not materialize until after Chile established a realistic "crawling peg" exchange rate policy following the early 1980s recession and formulated a responsible debt management strategy that included the Chapter XIX debt conversion program. Chile combined this external macroeconomic policy package with continued internal reforms that turned away from statist solutions, shrinking the public sector and controlling governmental expenditures. The final piece of this policy puzzle was added toward the end of the 1980s with the political democratization process. Theoretical or comparative studies assessing Chile's experience should consider this full policy framework within which individual investment decisions are made.

The companion element of behavioral firm analysis must also examine the role of global corporate organization and strategy decisions. Chile's internationalization policy leaves its economy relatively open to external influences, including the effects of foreign investor decisions. As a smaller economy, Chile does not command the central attention of most parent company decision-makers, even for many foreign investments of seemingly major size and importance. Hence, changes in an investor's global corporate condition or business strategy can cause significant changes in Chile, as occurred with St. Joe Minerals, the Bond Group, Diamond Shamrock, AMAX, and several merged banks. Follow-up research must evaluate the future disposition of some of these cases to justify final conclusions, but early developments suggest that Chile's open economy policy allows efficient and effective evolution of project ownership, mediated by market forces, that mitigates the impact of temporary disruptions from strategic changes that may, in fact, aid longer-run project development.

The book's research also touched on several other theoretical concepts. Interview questions probed for evidence of a learning curve effect on the business strategies chosen by experienced versus new investors in Chile. The only significant distinction were more frequent references by the former group to historical swings in relations with the host country, implying greater caution regarding the long-term continuation of Chile's current policy positions. These expressions generally arose in connection with local subsidiary initiatives that sought to deepen ties with the national economy. Among the actions undertaken by experienced investors were steps to broaden local ownership in the enterprise and to seek export opportunities to balance the company's imports.

Several case examples also suggest a possible extension of the investment "hostage" concept developed primarily in the bargaining school literature. This notion holds that once large, up-front capital costs are sunk into a project such as a new mine, the investment becomes more vulnerable to host government decisions, creating an "obsolescing bargain" that increases the leverage of local authorities. A modified hostage effect may apply to cases such as Citibank and AIG investments in Chile, where the impact is not on the government's bargaining leverage, but rather on motivating self-imposed investor constraints. These firms' investments are integrally connected to the corporations' image and reputation, whereby damage suffered in one area of business can harm other activities.

Service sector operations typically do not face the physical vulnerability to seizure posed by large mining investments, but their assets based on reputation, trust, and confidence are similarly exposed to potential public damage. (Hence, Citibank adopted a cautious strategy regarding investing in privatized enterprises or using Chapter XIX debt conversion financing.) This type of asset vulnerability appears to increase proportionately with the size and scope of the firm's investments and its commitment to a long-term presence in the country. In these instances, the modified hostage effect can moderate the presumed power of a large capital investment. These investors face behavior constraints that allow less discretion and flexibility than small investors have regarding strategies that may be inconsistent with host country norms and objectives.[8]

Research in Chile also indicates a possible reshuffling of traditional strategic investment issues. The elements clearly gaining in strategic importance are technology, export marketing, capital mobilization, and MNC organizational structures. Technology was not so important in the location of basic research and development facilities, but rather for its application to (1) improved quality control standards, (2) managerial skills needed to develop and coordinate complex business activities, (3) technological processes to enhance plant safety and environmental protection, and (4) advanced computer and communications services to support other business activities. International marketing assumed increased importance from Chile's emphasis on export promotion where a foreign investor's reputation, credibility, and efficient delivery system assisted new market entry and export diversification objectives. Traditional issues appearing less significant in this study are employment, import substitution, host/home country conflicts, and concerns over the impact of foreign investment on the host society's values.

Two important issues showed somewhat untraditional applications in contemporary Chile. Investment rules and regulations were central concerns to both sides in the investor/host country relationship. However, after initial formulation and refinement of the basic rules, their continued stability, including strong national treatment guarantees, shifted the focus to normal regulatory implementation. Foreign investor concerns came to differ little from most local business issues, with distinctions arising more from contrasting perspectives and planning horizons than from government policy issues.

Ownership emerged as an increasingly complex and multidimensional issue that is changing globally as corporations form transnational alliances and world stock exchanges spread public shareholdings. In Chile, distinctions between the functional roles among equity owners appeared more significant than their nationality, particularly due to bank participation through debt conversions. The increasing role of institutional investors and joint venture arrangements also helped alter traditional notions of parent/subsidiary relations, highlighting the differences between ownership and control.

Results from research in one country certainly do not invalidate established theories, although they can demonstrate limitations or areas of inapplicability to situations in the country studied. Perhaps more importantly, to the extent that Chile is indeed at the forefront of some critical policy changes that shape relations between host developing countries and foreign investors, this research may point to useful theory modifications or new areas for further study as the trends evolve further and are examined in other national settings.

TOWARD A NEW CENTURY

Chile has moved forward economically despite its small market and other limitations. The nation lacks the inherent resources to match the attractiveness of Brazil, Argentina, or many other developing countries. Nonetheless, Chile is succeeding at translating its economic potential into reality, including some unrecognized competitiveness in employing advanced technological processes. A central element in this success is the nation's turn to an outward-looking development strategy that links its fortunes with the global economy, sharing in the benefits and accommodating the disciplines of an open system. Foreign investment is a vital component of this outward extension, forming a bridge for the flow of resources and skills that have spurred Chile's economic growth.

The research and company cases contained in this book are a summary of developments up through 1990, in most instances updated into late 1991. Specific circumstances will continue to evolve as both the country and its invested companies respond to a dynamic economic environment. The period covered by the main analysis, however, constitutes the critical transition time when key decisions by the host government and the international investment community reshaped mutual perceptions and positions into a more mature partnership. The full story of Chile's growth and progress is yet to be told, but this initial transition period is fast drawing to a close. A solid foundation is laid and mutual bonds forged that should sustain the partnership into the foreseeable future.

Chile's overall saga will continue with many other transition challenges still to be met, some of which naturally will also affect foreign investment prospects. The political transition must be further consolidated as the society relearns and reproves the functions of democratic institutions. Relations between the civilian government and the professional military must reestablish the historical pattern of mutual confidence in the support of constitutional government. Cases of human rights violations and disappeared persons must be resolved openly to the society's satisfaction so that deep emotional scars from these incidents can inform rather than inhibit the learning and healing process already underway.

Continued economic stability with sustained growth is essential for Chile to meet individual advancement and social service requirements among its poorer citizens. The economic gap does not appear so wide nor the problems so intractable as in many other developing countries. This recognition simply increases the imperative on capable segments of the society to take the measures necessary to achieve further improvements, particularly in the sectors of health, housing, and education that the Aylwin administration has chosen as its priorities. The economic system must produce the resources needed to address these challenges, so stable economic regulations and productive labor-management negotiations will be essential ingredients for this success. Overall, these various tasks pose formidable but certainly not insurmountable challenges for Chilean society, and the nation has already made great progress toward their attainment.

Developments in Chile form one of the most interesting of the many powerful stories in the contemporary world concerning economic and political change. Chile's tale extends over a quarter century of pendulum-like swings, but current policies appear well-rooted in a broad political and social consensus. The nation's prospects are among the brightest for developing countries and its evolved attitude and position on foreign investment are a central component of this assessment. Chile and its foreign investors have forged a more mature, productive, and mutually beneficial partnership as the country moves toward a new century.

NOTES

1. "Report Card: Rating Risk in the Hot Countries," *The Wall Street Journal*, September 20, 1991.

2. "Chile's Foreign Investment Climate," *Journal of the Chilean-American Chamber of Commerce* (August 1991), 5.

3. Jane Bryant Quinn, "For Money, Look South," *Newsweek*, July 1, 1991, 46.

4. "Abrete, sésamo," *El Mercurio*, June 30, 1991.

5. "What Chile Will Gain," *Journal of the Chilean-American Chamber of Commerce* (August 1991), 11.

6. This book will not attempt a literature review of the various theories regarding foreign investment in developing countries. Readers unfamiliar with the literature will find a brief review essay in Stephen Haggard, "The Political Economy of Foreign Direct Investment in Latin America," *Latin American Research Review*, vol. 24, no. 1 (1989).

7. The basis of the "bargaining school" approach is provided by Raymond Vernon, *Sovereignty at Bay: The Multinational Spread of U.S. Enterprises* (New York: Basic Books, 1971).

8. This "modified hostage" effect challenges the presumption of many *dependencia* writers who equate MNC size and diversity with a type of corporate power that threatens the host country. For example, the authors of *Mapa de la Extrema Riqueza* construct tables of MNC share-holding in Chilean enterprises, many acquired from privatization actions or takeovers of recession-weakened domestic firms. Share-holdings are then

translated into assumed control in order to draw a picture of huge corporate networks, implying that size equals unchecked power which will result in abuse. Neither the managerial control link nor the projected harm is well documented. By contrast, this book's research shows a different picture of ownership-control linkages as well as the actual results from specific corporate operations. The "modified hostage" effect casts further doubt on the assumption that size and diversity necessarily mean unchecked abusive power.

Appendix: Research Methodology

Research for this book included interviews with over seventy foreign investors operating in Chile. Discussions with local businesspeople, other private experts, and government officials provided additional information and acted as a cross-check on the interviews. A literature search provided the policy context for issues involving foreign investment in developing countries. Historical detail is excerpted from studies examining particular periods or political events in Chile and from comparative analyses of foreign investment in the Latin American region.

Four criteria influenced the selection of target firms for interviews: corporate nationality, history in Chile, form of ownership, and cross-sectoral coverage. U.S.-based investors constituted the largest component, reflecting their dominant position in Chile's foreign investment community. Enterprises from other nations were also included, incorporating especially regions of increasing investor interest such as Canada, Japan, New Zealand, and a number of European nations. The nationality factor overlaps somewhat with the history criteria since both experienced, long-term investors and newer entrants to Chile were selected.

The ownership factor was designed to incorporate investments that were wholly owned by a single firm, joint ventures involving several foreign companies or a foreign investor and a local partner, and operations that had evolved from one structure to another. Sectoral choices were determined from a review of Chile's economic development strategy and key policy decisions. The three core sectors selected are: mining activities, which lie at the heart of Chile's traditional and continuing economic strength; nontraditional export industries built primarily around Chile's forestry, agriculture, and fishing resources; and financial service industries that link the management of external debt problems with the mobilization of needed investment capital. A fourth sector of general industrial firms was included to provide potentially contrasting information and to explore issue-specific analyses, such as the evolution of historical foreign investments in chemicals and automobiles and the contemporary policy controversy over pharmaceutical patent protection.

In the sectors selected, most but not all important foreign investors were contacted. Corporations surveyed are weighted toward those with large investment projects due to their economic impact and significant link to public policy developments and reactions. A special attempt was made to investigate investment projects that bore a known relationship to the formulation or early implementation of public policy decisions regarding foreign investment. The research design centered on investigating foreign investment strategies (including both the investment and subsequent operational decisions), so results present an assessment as developed from the investor outward, examining how these enterprises react to their external competitive and public policy environment.

In nearly all cases, the principal interviewee was the general manager or equivalently titled executive in the MNC's local affiliate or joint venture operation. These individuals generally combined operational responsibility for the local enterprise with direct reporting ties to the next highest level in the MNC's management network. The managers were roughly equally divided between Chilean and foreign citizens, although this factor was not an initial control element in the firms' selection. Many times the manager would call other executives to join the session or provide additional information afterward if the conversation raised questions beyond the manager's direct experience, particularly where decisions or events preceded the manager's tenure.

Preliminary data and public commentary on the corporation were gathered and examined independently in advance of each interview, permitting the preparation of specific lines of inquiry and the use of some internal cross-checks on information accuracy. All interviews sought information on a basic core of items, to include the history of the investor's experience in Chile, a qualitative discussion and ranking of factors that had influenced corporate investment decisions, specific examples of perceived benefits from the investment, an assessment of the competitive climate in the industry, a description of business linkages in the country, an identification of international trade ties, and information on intra-MNC relationships, both operational and managerial. These areas were covered using a general discussion, open-answer format rather than a set checklist of questions in order to maintain a conversational approach that would encourage self-initiated reflections by the executive.

The interviews, conducted in Spanish or English at the executive's initiative, typically lasted around one and one-half hours. A few sessions ended in less than an hour; more than a dozen ran several hours. Interviews were not taped to avoid establishing an atmosphere of excessive formality and caution. Brief notes taken during the interview were used to develop an extensive written record of the discussion immediately afterward. Additional corporate documentation was gathered when available and relevant. The basic interviews were conducted in 1990. In cases where a lengthy description of an investor's operations appears in the text of this book, the executive was given an opportunity to review the relevant draft and invited to comment on its accuracy and offer up-dated information. No similar review occurred in sections of the book containing the author's specific analysis or assessment of investor actions in Chile.

The companies listed below comprise the core research group where the author directly interviewed corporate executives in the Chilean operations. In some cases the principal foreign investor(s) are not immediately identifiable from the given corporate name. Varying degrees of ownership among multiple investors in many of these enterprises make a complete identification list confusing and impractical in this type of format, but such information is presented in the textural descriptions of each firm and its activities.

Administradora de Fondos de Pensiones
  Santa María S.A.
AMAX de Chile, Inc.
American Express Bank
Andueza y Compañía (Corredores de
  Seguros S.A.)
Armco Chile S.A.
Banco BICE
Banco O'Higgins
Banco Santander
Bank of America
Bank of Boston
Bank of Tokyo, Ltd.
Bankers Trust Company
C. Itoh & Company (Chile) Ltda.
Cape Horn Methanol Ltd.
Cargill Chile Ltda.
Carter Holt Harvey International Ltd.
Caterpillar Americas Company
CDE Chilean Mining Corporation
Celulosa del Pacífico S.A.
Cemento Melón S.A.
Chase Manhattan Bank N.A.
Chevron Minera Corporation of Chile
Chicago Continental Bank
Chile Hunt Oil Company
Ciba-Geigy
CIDCOM S.A.
Cigna Compañía de Seguros (Chile)
Citibank N.A.
Coca-Cola Export Corporation
Compañía de Teléfonos de Chile
Compañía Minera Disputada de
  Las Condes
Compañía Minera Mantos de Oro
Compañía Minera San José Ltda.
Cosméticos Avon S.A.

Dow Química Chilena S.A.
Empresa de Desarrollo Pesquero
  de Chile
Empresas CCT, S.A.
Esso Chile Petrolera Limitada
Fletcher Challenge Limited
Forestal e Industrial Santa Fe S.A.
Fundación Chile
General Electric Company
General Motors Chile S.A.
Goodyear de Chile S.A.I.C.
Hongkong & Shanghai Banking
  Corporation
IBM de Chile S.A.C.
Inversiones Interamericana S.A.
Inversiones Pathfinder Chile S.A.
Kodak Chilena S.A.F.
Lever Chile S.A.
Manufacturers Hanover Bank Chile
Marine Midland Bank N.A.
Midland Bank plc
Minera Escondida Limitada
Mitsubishi Chile Ltda.
Mitsui Chilena Comercial Ltda.
NCR de Chile S.A.
NMB Bank Chile
Nestlé Chile S.A.
Occidental Chemical—Chile S.A.I.
Pfizer de Chile
Procter & Gamble Chile S.A.
Schering-Plough Cía. Ltda
Security Pacific Chile S.A.
Shell Chile
Simpson Company
Socimer Austral Ltda.
Standard Trading Company S.A.
Sumitomo Corporation

3M Chile S.A.   Williamson Balfour S.A.
Unisys (Chile) Corporation   Xerox de Chile S.A.

Selected Bibliography

Aldunate, Rafael. *El mundo en Chile: La inversión extranjera*. Santiago: Zig-Zag, 1990.

Baklanoff, Eric N. *Expropriation of U.S. Investments in Cuba, Mexico, and Chile*. Praeger Special Studies in International Economics and Development. New York: Praeger Publishers, 1975.

Bergsman, Joel, and Wayne Edisis. "Debt-Equity Swaps and Foreign Direct Investment in Latin America." International Finance Corporation Discussion Paper No. 2. Washington, D.C.: The World Bank and International Finance Corporation, 1988.

Bitar, Sergio. *Chile para todos*. Santiago: Editorial Planeta Chilena, 1988.

Bohan, Merwin L. and Morton Pomeranz. *Investment in Chile: Basic Information for United States Businessmen*. Prepared for the U.S. Department of Commerce. Bureau of Foreign Commerce. Washington, D.C.: GPO, 1960.

Cáceres, Carlos F., Felipe Larraín B. and Gregory C. Nicolaidis, eds. *Exportar un gran desafío para Chile*. Santiago: Editorial Universitaria, March 1988.

The Chilean-American Chamber of Commerce, Journal of. Various Issues.

Cohen, Benjamin J. "High Finance, High Politics." in *Uncertain Futures: Commercial Banks and the Third World*. ed. Richard E. Feinberg and Valeriana Kallab. U.S. Third World Policy Perspectives. no. 2. Overseas Development Council. New Brunswick, N.J.: Transaction Books, 1984.

Comité de Inversiones Extranjeras (Chile). Santiago:

    —*Chile for Investors*. Designed by Altamira Comunicaciones. Santiago: Impresora Cabo de Hornos, 1988.

    —*Fishery: Chile*. 3rd ed. July 1988.

    —*Foreign Investment Report: Chile: Informe sobre inversión extranjera*. Various Issues.

    —*Forestry: Chile*. 3rd ed. July 1988.

    —*Industry: Chile*. 3rd ed. July 1988.

    —*Legal Framework: Chile*. 3rd ed. July 1988.

    —*Mining: Chile*. 3rd ed. July 1988.

    —*Textile: Chile*. 3rd ed. July 1988.

Corbo, Vittorio, and Jaime de Melo, eds. *Scrambling for Survival: How Firms Adjusted to the Recent Reforms in Argentina, Chile and Uruguay*. World Bank Staff Working Papers. no. 764. Washington, D.C.: The World Bank, 1985.

Council of the Americas. *The Andean Pact: Definition, Design and Analysis*. New York: Council of the Americas, 1973.

Council of the Americas. *Coping with Crisis: U.S. Investment and Latin America's Continuing Economic Problems*. A Council of the Americas Survey of Company Operations, Policy Reforms, and Investment Prospects in Twelve Latin American Countries. New York: Council of the Americas, January 1987.

Dealing with the Debt Crisis: World Bank Symposium. ed. Ishrat Husain and Ishac Diwan. World Bank Publications, 1989.

Economic Commission of the Concertación por la Democracia. *Chile's Economic Challenge 1990-1994*. Prepared for Patricio Aylwin's presidential campaign. 1989.

Economist Intelligence Unit. *Chile: Country Profile 1989-1990*. London: The Economist Intelligence Unit Limited, 1989.

Embassy of the United States. Economic Section. Santiago:

    —*Chile: Economic Trends*. Prepared by Tom Kelly. June 1991.

    —*Chile: Economic Trends Report*. November 1990.

    —*Chile: Industrial Outlook Report*:

        "Chilean Fisheries Sector: Growth: A Marketing Challenge for Maturing Fisheries." November 1989.

        "Chilean Forestry Sector: An Emerging Giant." September 1989.

        "Minerals." March 1989.

    —*Chile: Minerals Benchmark Report*. May 1990.

    —*Chile: Sectoral Outlook Report*. "Chilean Agriculture: Integrating into World Markets." Prepared by Mark D. Roberts and Carlos F. Capurro. May 1990.

"La Escondida: Proyecto que se convierte en realidad." *Minería Chilena*. no. 93. Santiago. January-February 1989.

Estrategia. Various Issues. See especially:

    —No. 582. March 19-25, 1990.

    —No. 594. June 11-17, 1990.

Euromoney. supplement:

    —"Chile: Building On Success." September 1990.

    —"Chile: Into the 1990s." August 1989.

    —"Debt Management: Latin America Sets the Pace." September 1988.

    —"Global Debt: The Equity Solution." January 1988.

Fajnyzller, Fernando, et. al. *Corporaciones Multinacionales en América Latina*. Buenos Aires: Ediciones Periferia S.R.L., 1973.

Falcoff, Mark, Arturo Valenzuela, and Susan Kaufman Purcell. *Chile: Prospects for Democracy*. New York: Council on Foreign Relations, 1988.

Feinberg, Richard E., and Ricardo Ffrench-Davis, ed. *Development and External Debt in Latin America: Bases for a New Consensus.* Notre Dame, Ind.: University of Notre Dame Press, 1988.

Feinberg, Richard E., and Valeriana Kallab, ed. *Adjustment Crisis in the Third World.* U.S. Third World Policy Perspectives. no. 1. Overseas Development Council. New Brunswick, N.J.: Transaction Books, 1984.

Ffrench-Davis, Ricardo. *Estados Unidos, América Latina y la economía internacional: Algunos aspectos centrales en los años ochenta.* Notas técnicas no. 77. CIEPLAN. Santiago. September 1985.

Ffrench-Davis, Ricardo. *Orígen y destino de las exportaciones Chilenas: 1965-80.* Notas técnicas no. 31. CIEPLAN. Santiago. May 1981.

Financial Sector Reform: Its Role in Growth and Development. Washington, D.C.: The Institute of International Finance, Inc. February 1990.

Fontaine Aldunate, Arturo. *Los economistas y el presidente Pinochet.* Santiago: Zig-Zag, 1988.

Fostering Foreign Direct Investment in Latin America. Washington, D.C.: The Institute of International Finance, Inc. 1990.

Foxley, Alejandro. *Latin American Experiments in Neoconservative Economics.* Berkeley: University of California Press, 1983.

Foxley, Alejandro, et. al. *Reconstrucción económica para la democracia.* CIEPLAN. Santiago: Editorial Aconcagua, 1983.

Goodman, Louis. *Small Nations, Giant Firms.* New York: Holmes and Meier, 1987.

Gutiérrez A., Alejandro. *Inversión extranjera en la minería del cobre en Chile 1974-84.* Notas técnicas no. 72. CIEPLAN. Santiago. June 1985.

Gunnerman, John P., ed. *The Nation-State and Transnational Corporations in Conflict: With Special Reference to Latin America.* Praeger Special Studies in International Economics and Development. New York: Praeger Publishers, 1975.

Haggard, Stephen. "The Political Economy of Foreign Direct Investment in Latin America. *Latin American Research Review.* vol. 24. no.1. 1989.

Ibáñez, Fernán. "Venture Capital and Entrepreneurial Development." Background Paper for the 1989 World Development Report. The World Bank. Washington, D.C. August 1989.

Kahler, Miles, ed. *The Politics of International Debt.* Ithaca, N.Y.: Cornell University Press, 1986.

Kirsch, Henry. *Industrial Development in a Traditional Society: The Conflict of Entrepreneurship and Modernization in Chile.* Gainesville: The University Presses of Florida, 1977.

Kline, John. "Trade Competitiveness and Corporate Nationality." *The Columbia Journal of World Business.* vol. 24. no. 3. Fall 1989.

Lahera, Eugenio. *Quince años de la decisión 24. Evaluación y Perspectivas.* Notas técnicas no. 82. CIEPLAN. Santiago. June 1986.

Langton Clarke. *Investing in Chile.* 1990-1991 ed. Santiago: Langton Clarke, a member firm of Coopers & Lybrand International, June 30, 1990.

Larraín, Felipe, and Andrés Velasco. *Can Swaps Solve the Debt Crisis? Lessons from the Chilean Experience*. Princeton Studies in International Finance. no. 69. Princeton, N.J.: Princeton University, November 1990.

Lavín, Joaquín. *Chile Revolución Silenciosa*. Santiago: Zig-Zag, 1987.

Lavín, Joaquín, and Luis Larraín. *Chile: Sociedad emergente*. Santiago: Zig-Zag, 1989.

Mabon, Thomas S. "An Analysis of the Industrial Sector: The Chilean Case, 1964-1971." Master's thesis, Georgetown University, Washington, D.C., September 1973.

Meissner, Frank. *Technology Transfer in the Developing World: The Case of the Chile Foundation*. New York: Praeger Publishers, 1988.

Meller, Patricio. *Las empresas transnacionales y los países en desarrollo: Aspectos económicos*. Apuntes CIEPLAN no. 23. March 1980.

Memoria Período 1974-1989. Ministerio de Minería. República de Chile.

Molina Silva, Sergio. *El proceso de cambio en Chile: La experiencia 1965-1970*. Santiago: Editorial Universitaria, 1972.

Moran, Theodore H. *Multinational Corporations and the Politics of Dependence: Copper in Chile*. Princeton, N.J.: Princeton University Press, 1974.

Moran, Theodore H. "Transnational Strategies of Protection and Defense by MNCs," *International Organization*. vol. 27. no. 2. (Spring 1973).

Muñoz, Oscar. *Chile y su industrialización: pasado, crisis y opciones*. Santiago: CIEPLAN, 1986.

Muñoz, Oscar. *El estado y los empresarios: Experiencias comparadas y sus implicaciones para Chile*. Colección estudios CIEPLAN no. 25. Santiago. December 1988.

Muñoz, O., and H. Ortega. *La agricultura y la política económica chilena (1974-86)*. Separata no. 2. vol. 3 (1). Madrid: Ministerio de Agricultura Pesca y Alimentación, Instituto Nacional de Investigaciones Agrarias, June 1988.

Neoestructuralismo, neomonetarismo y procesos de ajuste en América Latina. Colección estudios CIEPLAN. Número especial 23. Santiago: La Corporación de Investigaciones Económicas para Latinoamérica (CIEPLAN), March 1988.

Un nuevo socialismo democrático en Chile. Colección estudios CIEPLAN. Número 24. Santiago: Corporación de Investigaciones Económicas para Latinoamérica (CIEPLAN), June 1988.

Ominami, Carlos, and Roberto Madrid. *La inserción de Chile en los mercados internacionales: Elementos para la evaluación del desarrollo exportador y propuesta de políticas*. Santiago: Dos Mundos Sociedad de Profesionales, 1989.

"Oportunidades de Inversión en Chile." Seminar. Santiago. May 15-16, 1990:

   —Bass, Jonathan. "Inversión extranjera en la agroindustria chilena: 'La experiencia de Standard Trading Co. S.A.'" Speech. Photocopy.

   —Botín, D. Emilio. Speech. Photocopy.

   —Dreyfus, Edward M. "Citicorp/Citibank: Inversiones en Chile vía conversión en deuda externa." Speech. Photocopy.

   —Guiloff I., Hernán. Speech. Photocopy.

—Hickman, Robert. Speech. Photocopy.

—Martín López-Quesada, Francisco. Speech. Photocopy.

—Tillman, Edward. Speech. Photocopy.

Prebisch, Raúl. "Commercial Policy in the Underdeveloped Countries." *American Economic Review*. vol. 49. no. 2 (May 1959).

Prebisch, Raúl. *The Economic Development of Latin America and Its Principal Problems*. Economic Commission for Latin America. Lake Success, N.Y.: United Nations, Department of Economic Affairs, 1950.

Prebisch, Raúl, et. al. *CEPAL Review*. United Nations Economic Commission for Latin America and the Caribbean. no. 25. Santiago, Chile. April 1985.

Remmer, Karen. *Military Rule in Latin America*. Boston: Unwin Hyman, 1989.

"Robert Hickman: Minera Escondida inicia operaciones en marzo de 1991." *Minería Chilena*. no. 101. Santiago, October 1989.

Rozas, Patricio and Gustavo Marín. *1988: "El Mapa de la Extrema Riqueza" 10 años después*. Santiago: Impresiones Goméz Ltda. 1989.

Schneider Vega, Roberto. *Captación de inversión extranjera significativa en Chile: Un análisis de lo que busca el inversionista potencial*. Memoria de Prueba para optar al Grado de Licenciado en Ciencias Económicas y al Título de Ingeniero Comercial. Universidad de Chile. Santiago, 1974.

Servan-Schreiber, Jean-Jacques. *The American Challenge*. New York: Atheneum, 1968.

Select Committee to Study Governmental Operations with Respect to Intelligence Activities. *Covert Action in Chile 1963-1973*. Staff report prepared for the United States Senate. 94 Cong. 1 Sess. (1975).

Senate Committee on Foreign Relations, Subcommittee on Multinational Corporations. *Multinational Corporations and United States Foreign Policy*. Part 1. Hearings. 93 Cong. (1973).

South Pacific Mail. Santiago. Various issues: "Mining Survey 1990." supplement. June 1990.

Stallings, Barbara. *Class Conflict and Economic Development in Chile, 1958-1973*. Stanford, Calif.: Stanford University Press, 1978.

Stoever, William A. "Renegotiations: The Cutting Edge of Relations Between MNCs and LDCs." *Columbia Journal of World Business*. Spring 1979.

Sunkel, Osvaldo. "Big Business and 'Dependencia': A Latin American Point of View." *Foreign Affairs* (April 1972).

Tomic Errázuriz, Esteban. *El retiro de Chile del Pacto Andino*. Apuntes CIEPLAN no. 58. Santiago: Corporación de Investigaciones Económicas para Latinoamérica, November 1985.

Trabajo de asesoría económica al congreso nacional (TASC). Various Issues.

Treverton, Gregory F. *Case Study in Ethics and International Affairs: Covert Intervention in Chile, 1970-1973*. no. 3. New York: Carnegie Council on International Affairs, 1990.

Tybout, James, Jaime de Melo, and Vittorio Corbo. *The Effects of Trade Reforms on Scale and Technical Efficiency*. Policy, Research, and External Affairs Working

Papers. Country Economics Department. Washington, D.C. The World Bank, August 1990.

United Nations Centre on Transnational Corporations (UNCTC). *The New Code Environment*. series A. no. 16. New York: United Nations, April 1990.

United Nations Centre on Transnational Corporations (UNCTC). *Transnational Corporations in World Development: Trends and Prospects*. New York: United Nations, 1988.

United States Trade Representative. *GSP Country Reinstatement Hearings for Chile, Paraguay and Central Africa*. Prepared by Neal R. Gross. Open Session. June 27, 1990.

Valenzuela, Arturo. *The Breakdown of Democratic Regimes: Chile*. Baltimore: The Johns Hopkins University Press, 1976.

Valenzuela, Arturo. *Political Brokers in Chile: Local Government in a Centralized Polity*. Durham, N.C.: Duke University Press, 1977.

Valenzuela, Arturo, and J. Samuel Valenzuela. *Chile: Politics and Society*. New Brunswick, N.J.: Transaction Books, 1976.

Vernon, Raymond. *Sovereignty at Bay: The Multinational Spread of U.S. Enterprises*. New York: Basic Books, 1971.

Vignolo, Carlos, et. al. *La industria chilena: 4 visiones sectoriales*. Santiago: Centro de Estudios del Desarrollo, 1986.

Villemain, Aylette. "Public Policy and Private Investment in Chile: The Life and Hard Times of the Corporación de Fomento de la Producción (CORFO) 1939-1980." Master's Thesis, Georgetown University, Washington, D.C., May 1983.

Whelan, James R. *Out of the Ashes: Life, Death and Transfiguration of Democracy in Chile, 1833-1988*. Washington, D.C.: Regnery Gateway, 1989.

Williamson, John. *The Progress of Policy Reform in Latin America*. Policy Analysis in International Economics. no. 28. Washington, D.C.: Institute for International Economics, January 1990.

World Bank. *Chile: An Economy in Transition*. Washington, D.C.: Latin America and the Caribbean Regional Office of the World Bank, 1979.

Zabala H., Ricardo. *Inversión Extranjera Directa en Chile: 1954-1986*. Documento de Trabajo no. 90. Santiago: Centro de Estudios Públicos, October 1987.

Zeitlin, Maurice, and Richard Earl Ratcliff. *Landlords and Capitalists: The Dominant Class of Chile*. Princeton, N.J.: Princeton University Press, 1988.

Index

About the Author

JOHN M. KLINE is Deputy Director of the Landegger Program in International Business Diplomacy at the Georgetown University School of Foreign Service. Formerly Director of International Economic Policy at the National Association of Manufacturers, Dr. Kline is the author of *International Codes and Multinational Business* (Quorum, 1985) and *State Government Influence in U.S. International Economic Policy*, as well as numerous scholarly articles. He has conducted studies for the UN Centre on Transnational Corporations and the Inter-American Development Bank and is a member of the U.S. State Department's Advisory Committee on International Investment.